MADE E-Z
G U I D E S

Financing Your Business

Harold R. Lacy

Made E-Z

NOTICE:

THIS PRODUCT IS NOT INTENDED TO PROVIDE LEGAL ADVICE. IT CONTAINS
GENERAL INFORMATION FOR EDUCATIONAL PURPOSES ONLY. PLEASE CONSULT
AN ATTORNEY IN ALL LEGAL MATTERS. THIS PRODUCT WAS NOT NECESSARILY
PREPARED BY A PERSON LICENSED TO PRACTICE LAW IN YOUR STATE.

Financing Your Business Made E-Z™
© Copyright 2001 Made E-Z Products, Inc.
Printed in the United States of America

MADE E-Z
PRODUCTS

384 South Military Trail
Deerfield Beach, FL 33442
Tel. 954-480-8933
Fax 954-480-8906

http://www.MadeE-Z.com
All rights reserved.

3 4 5 6 7 8 9 10

This publication is designed to provide accurate and authoritative information in
regard to subject matter covered. It is sold with the understanding that neither the
publisher nor author is engaged in rendering legal, accounting, or other professional
services. If legal advice or other expert assistance is required, the services of a
competent professional should be sought. From: *A Declaration of Principles jointly
adopted by a Committee of the American Bar Association and a Committee of
Publishers.*

Financing Your Business Made E-Z™
Harold R. Lacy

Library of Congress Control Number: 2001126804

Limited warranty and disclaimer

This self-help product is intended to be used by the consumer for his/her own benefit. It may not be reproduced in whole or in part, resold or used for commercial purposes without written permission from the publisher. In addition to copyright violations, the unauthorized reproduction and use of this product to benefit a second party may be considered the unauthorized practice of law.

This product is designed to provide authoritative and accurate information in regard to the subject matter covered. However, the accuracy of the information is not guaranteed, as laws and regulations may change or be subject to differing interpretations. Consequently, you may be responsible for following alternative procedures, or using material or forms different from those supplied with this product. It is strongly advised that you examine the laws of your state before acting upon any of the material contained in this product.

As with any matter, common sense should determine whether you need the assistance of an attorney. We urge you to consult with an attorney, qualified estate planner, or tax professional, or to seek any other relevant expert advice whenever substantial sums of money are involved, you doubt the suitability of the product you have purchased, or if there is anything about the product that you do not understand including its adequacy to protect you. Even if you are completely satisfied with this product, we encourage you to have your attorney review it.

Neither the author, publisher, distributor nor retailer are engaged in rendering legal, accounting or other professional services. Accordingly, the publisher, author, distributor and retailer shall have neither liability nor responsibility to any party for any loss or damage caused or alleged to be caused by the use of this product.

Copyright Notice

The purchaser of this guide is hereby authorized to reproduce in any form or by any means, electronic or mechanical, including photocopying, all forms and documents contained in this guide, provided it is for non-profit, educational or private use. Such reproduction requires no further permission from the publisher and/or payment of any permission fee.

The reproduction of any form or document in any other publication intended for sale is prohibited without the written permission of the publisher. Publication for nonprofit use should provide proper attribution to Made E-Z Products™.

Table of contents

Introduction to Financing Your Business Made E-Z™

Persistence will give you power to prevail over all problems.

I recommend that one should read chapters 1-6 in order. This gives you an overall view of the many financial sources available. This is very important since most entrepreneurs make the mistake of focusing on only ONE source for their financing.

After you complete chapters 1-6, I recommend the following plan of action to get started on pursuing your financing sources:

Chapter 6 . . . . Business Plan
Chapter 3 . . . . Banks and Bankers
Chapter 1 . . . . Formal and Informal Investors
Chapter 2 . . . . SBA Programs
Chapter 4 . . . . Non-Bank Alternatives
Chapter 5 . . . . Buying a Business-Financing Sources

You may ask, "Why weren't the chapters arranged to follow the action plan?" I learned from my seminars that most people are aware of the importance of the business plan. What they are REALLY interested in learning are WHERE to find money and HOW to approach and deal with the different money sources. Eighty-five percent of start-up businesses are funded by "angels." That is why "angels" are discussed in Chapter 1.

You may also ask, "Then why is the chapter on banks and bankers listed before angels, which is discussed in the chapter on formal and informal investors?" There are several important reasons for meeting with the bankers prior to meeting with angels and other sources of financing.

1) It is a tremendous learning process to discover the criteria that the financing/investor world is looking for in a company. The money world is "uncharted territory" for most people seeking funding for their business.

2) The banker will provide a critique of your business plan and its feasibility.

3) The feedback and criticism from the banker should be used to polish your business plan to overcome objections from other lenders/investors.

4) The banker will lay out the issues that prevent the bank from committing to your request. Issues such as inadequate cash flow, weak managerial experience, inadequate secondary financial support, etc. Now that you have been turned down, go back and review the banker's criticism(s). Assess the criticisms to see if they can be overcome. For example, offering of a limited guarantor to

The fastest and most efficient method of obtaining funding is to utilize the "piggyback" approach.

overcome the lack of secondary financial support; obtain additional written commitments from potential customers that will allow you to revise your cash flow statement to meet the banker's requirements.

5) Even if you are not able to obtain some of your initial financing from the banker, you will have obtained an invaluable lesson in dealing with other money sources such as "angels." You usually only have one chance with an "angel," so you want to make the very best presentation possible.

6) Last, but not least, the banker can be a tremendous resource for directing you to a financing source that meets your needs. The banker has a tremendous network of alternative lenders and investors. Don't be afraid to ask the banker for referrals to his sources that would be a good match for your type of funding request.

DEFINITION

Piggyback financing utilizes a combination of financing sources together to obtain the total amount of funding needed for the business.

An example of "Piggyback" financing is when you need $50,000. It is much easier to combine several financing sources that will be discussed in Chapters 1-6.

For example:

"Angel" investor	15,000
Bank loan	15,000
Lease financing	10,000
Accounts Receivable financing	5,000
Your funds	5,000
TOTAL	$50,000

You might ask yourself, "Wouldn't it be a lot easier and save time just to have one financing source for the entire $50,000?" Yes, it would. The challenge is that there are fewer people who have $50,000 available for investing as compared to the vast number of people who have $5,000-$20,000 available. Most investors like the comfort level of knowing that there are other investors sharing the risk.

> *note*
>
> Piggyback financing is very successful since there is a feeling among lenders/investors that if someone else is in the "deal," there is a greater comfort level.

In this book, we share with you the full spectrum of financing sources available to new and growing businesses. We explore such areas as organizing your needs, planning your approach, and writing your business plan. We investigate formal and informal venture capital, delve into government funding, outline how to develop a winning relationship with your banker, explain leasing and reveal alternative funding strategies.

We hope to achieve three objectives:

- identify the various sources of financing available to you

- learn about the advantages and disadvantages of each type of financing source

- help match your financing needs with the right financing source

Why you need this book now

In the past few years, there have been many changes in the business world and job markets. These changes are driving a record number of people out of the roller-coaster corporate world and into something that they have some control over: being their own boss by owning their own business. This can mean buying a business or franchise, or starting a business from scratch.

As recently as seven to ten years ago, most people thought of a job as something you stepped into once you graduated from high school or college and stayed with for a long time. Many people would remain with the same company for their entire working lives, then get the gold watch and the nice retirement plan. Anyone who started or purchased a business was not envied. Why? With your own business, you had no job security. You worked lots of extra hours for no prestige and no company benefits.

My, how quickly times have changed. The cover story in the February 26, 1996, issue of *Newsweek* was titled "Corporate Killers." It featured pictures of CEOs of a dozen major corporations such as AT&T, IBM, Scott Paper, Delta Airlines, Chemical Bank, Boeing, Sears Roebuck, General Motors and others. Below each picture appeared the number of jobs the CEO had eliminated during the previous 12 months. IBM: 60,000 jobs. AT&T: 40,000. Boeing: 28,000. Sears: 50,000. General Motors: 74,000. And on, and on, and on, for a total of 374,000 jobs at 12 companies in just one year.

These companies are not fly-by-night operations; they have been an integral component of our economy and way of life for years. This is not a temporary situation of downsizing, rightsizing, corporate lay-offs, cast-offs, whatever you call them. It is a profound shift in the way our economy works.

A recent report by the Department of Labor indicated that people in the 35-50 age group can expect three to five career changes by the time they reach retirement. That's three to five career changes, not job changes. This is going to be pretty traumatic for most people, having the boss say to them, "We don't need you anymore, Fred, not because of the job you were doing, but because we have to improve our bottom line. We have to improve our return to the stockholders." Wall Street loves layoffs!

Buying yourself a job

Many people—you might be one of them—have had just about enough of constantly being in fear of losing their jobs because of a corporate decision.

> note
> With any large-ticket item—a car, a house, a boat—financing is the key. Very few of us are able to write that check right out of our checkbook.

There is a new term for those who are opting to get out of the rat race. We say they are "buying themselves a job."

When people buy a business or franchise or start a new business, they are really buying themselves a job. And whenever you buy something, you have to pay for it somehow.

It is the same for buying a business. Financing is the key to opening the door to that American dream of being your own boss. What is financing after all but using other people's money to achieve your goals? The challenge of financing is not that there aren't enough funds available. The challenge today is finding the right source of funding that meets the needs of you, the borrower, in terms of the interest rate, terms of repayment, collateral, guarantee of the spouse, the application process and the turnaround time it takes to obtain these funds.

How it works

Let me share with you my personal experience with using other people's money to finance one of my dreams. In 1991 I was contacted by two members of a local athletic club that had been taken over by a bank when the developer defaulted on another real estate project.

Although the club was successful in the past, the bank had to close it when the developer came in during the middle of the night and removed all of the athletic equipment, weights, desk, inventory, telephones; you name it, it was gone.

After six months of bureaucratic procrastination, the bank finally decided it would bite the bullet and reopen the club, which meant spending close to $450,000 dollars in the purchase of new equipment and working capital to get the business going again. The only smart thing the bank did was hire an experienced manager to start rebuilding the club and its membership.

When I was contacted by the two members, we reviewed the current situation of the club:

1)   The new manager had been able to rebuild the membership from zero to 1100 members in less than a year; the club would reach the break-even point within two to four months.

2)   The bank was under tremendous pressure from the board of directors and examiners to get rid of the loan: sell the club and get the loan off the books.

Just to test the waters, we made a ridiculously low offer of $225,000. To our great surprise, the bank accepted it.

Then came the fun part of putting together a loan package. We finally came up with a bank loan of $125,000 secured with equipment and accounts receivable, and a $100,000 investor loan for a 5 percent share of the club. This combination of bank loan and investor financing allowed us to finance 100 percent of the purchase price with not one dime of our own money.

That was 1991. Today the membership of the Lakewood Athletic Club has grown from 1100 members to over 2500. The original bank loan was paid off in 18 months with the increased cash flow from new memberships. The club is doing extremely well, is rated in the top clubs in the nation, and I'm in the process of selling out to my partners for a sizable profit. Of course $1 would have been a profit when you remember we had none of our own money invested.

While someone is busy telling me it cannot be done, others are busy doing it.

Henry Fosdick

Remember the basics

Why would anyone want to sell when the business is doing so well? Just remember four basic words of investing: Buy low, sell high.

Sounds simple, but it's much harder to put into practice. Just talk to a few stock market investors who waited just a little too long to get out and took a big hit.

Communicating effectively means having a winning business plan, one that communicates in the language of lenders—both traditional and nontraditional—and investors. They are looking for written documentation of what you and your product or service are all about, something they can read and analyze.

> **E-Z TIP**
>
> Timing is the key. Don't be greedy. There is plenty of money available out there, if you can communicate effectively to the right source of funds.

Before you sit down to write your business plan, it is critical to determine your attitude toward commitment and change. Do you possess the necessary traits found in successful entrepreneurs who look upon change as opportunity? Whenever there is change, there are winners and losers. The losers are the ones who did not have their business antennas up, picking up how the needs of the market were changing.

Show me someone who has done something worthwhile, and I'll show you someone who has overcome adversity.

Lou Holtz

Funding sources: formal and informal

1

Chapter 1

Funding sources: formal and informal

What you'll find in this chapter:

⯈ Formal and informal venture capital investors

⯈ What to look for in an ideal investor

⯈ Do's and don'ts to approaching an investor

⯈ How to interview prospective investors

⯈ Why funding requests may be rejected

There is only one success—to be able to spend your life in your own way.

Christopher Morley

In this first chapter, we discuss formal and informal venture capital investors—there is a major difference. We talk about the things you should look for in the ideal investors, and itemize the do's and don'ts of approaching them. We outline the five-step process for interviewing and screening prospective investors and, finally, we share the top six reasons why funding requests are rejected by investors and lenders.

Internal and external sources

When looking for capital, first decide whether it should come from internal or external sources.

Internal sources are your own assets and liquidity. Self-financing is composed of actual cash investments or equities held in real estate or partnerships. These can be used as capital in the business or used as collateral on a loan to inject capital into the business.

External sources can be banks, suppliers, finance companies, leasing companies, etc.

Even if you can't generate all the capital requirements internally, it will be very attractive to an outside investor to demonstrate that you have enough confidence in the business

> *note*
>
> By utilizing self-financing, you maintain total control over the business.

that you were able, through your resources, to generate some of the capital needed. It is very rare, indeed, to see an outside investor fund 100 percent of a business when the owner has not demonstrated his or her ability or creative ingenuity to come up with a share of the capital.

> *E-Z TIP* It is important to understand that in most cases of external financing, lenders are looking for some amount of internal financing that has already been put in place. They are looking for the owner's commitment or "blood equity" backed up with some dollar amount.

An excellent way of combining the internal with external funding sources is to inject your own funds into the business and use the guarantee of the co-signer for the balance. For example, after completing a cash flow forecast (this is covered in more detail in Chapter 6 on business plans), it is determined that you need $50,000 and that you have only $20,000 in liquid assets and equities to inject into the company.

Angels and venture capitalists

Let's compare informal and formal funding sources.

♦ **Venture Capitalists.** This is probably one of the most misunderstood and overused terms in today's list of financing sources for small businesses. You may even have heard someone say to a budding business person who was turned down for a loan, "Go talk to a venture capitalist. They finance high-risk companies."

> **note** It is much easier to obtain outside investors who will co-sign or guarantee a loan for $30,000 once they see that you already injected your own funds into the business.

The actual number of start-up businesses funded through venture capital sources in 1995 was 270. That is less than .001 of 1 percent of the businesses launched that year. You can see why we're not going to spend much time on formal venture capitalists as a source of funding for most small businesses.

♦ **Angels.** The more viable source of funding for the start-up or existing business is the informal venture capitalist, or angel.

The term originated during the 1800s in New York City, in the early days of Broadway. Since the production of Broadway plays was—and still is—a high-risk venture, banks would not even listen to loan proposals from producers. But the show must go on, so the producers approached a group

> **note** Angels provide more than 85 percent of the funding for start-up businesses.

of prominent, successful businessmen for the financing. Because of the glamour of being associated with the theater, this group took the risk and provided the capital on very fair terms without stringent requirements and equity control. For their magnanimity, the investors were called angels.

DEFINITION

The term *angel* now refers to any outside investor who provides the initial capital for new or risky business, is very fair about repayment and other loan requirements and does not take advantage of the business owner's situation.

Identifying angels

> *note* Angels are a key source of funding for the business that does not have a track record and is seeking that initial funding. And they are all around us.

First, let's prepare a list of potential angels you may already know: Your doctor, or any doctor you are acquainted with. Likewise your dentist, lawyers, accountants, financial planners, insurance agents, fellow entrepreneurs, business owners, associates of yours in professional and social organizations, relatives, friends, former employers, former employees, potential suppliers, customer clients and financial consultants.

> **E-Z TIP** You must look upon these contacts as the springboard to their network of contacts. That's where you will find your angels.

You may be thinking, "I bought this book just for the inside information that I should contact my rich brother-in-law for funding my business? How do I get my money back?" Just hold that thought. What you have done is assume that this list of contacts is the ultimate list of angels. Wrong. They are just the bridge to a much bigger pool of potential investors and lenders.

Review your list to make sure that the people on it have the critical common denominator: They associate or work with clients or friends that have excess capital to invest. For example, your insurance agent. She might not necessarily have the excess capital to invest, but works with and associates with hundreds of clients and friends who probably fit your investor profile.

If you win a man to your cause, you will first have to convince him that you are his sincere friend.

Abraham Lincoln

Now do the same for your doctor, attorney, friends, relatives, and so on. You can see the potential network pool of investors gets very large very quickly. Again, think of these contacts as the bridge to other people they know who have access to money and are looking for some type of investment.

A recent study showed that the average person is surrounded by about 250 friends and relatives. Now take your list. Let's just say you have 6 people listed as potential contacts. By multiplying each one of these possible contacts by 250, you could come up with 1,500 potential sources for the funding of your business.

If you focus just on the initial list, you are short-changing yourself over 99 percent of the potential networking contacts that these people have developed over the years.

You can also add to your potential angel pool by looking through your local newspaper. There's generally a section in the business or classified ad section called "Business Opportunities" or "Capital Available." These ads usually say something like: I have $20,000 to invest in an on-going business, or, I have $15,000 to invest in a start-up, early stage development company.

With nothing to lose except the time you spend with that person, you can't afford not to follow up. Otherwise, you'll never know if that could have been the perfect match for you, if that could have been your angel.

Understanding angels

How do you know if you are in the presence of a possible angel? He most likely was in the business arena for a number of years, was successful and has recently sold the business or taken early retirement. Angels generally have excess capital and financial security, but are missing the substance that motivated them for all of those years: the drive of playing the business game, of dealing with the daily challenges of business and developing solutions to these challenges.

note At this stage of life, they're not too anxious to re-enter that arena of daily battles, but they are looking for a chance to use their experience and expertise in a growing company that will allow them to reestablish their identity and contacts. When they're meeting with their buddies at the golf club or at a social occasion, the first question that always seems to come up is, "What are you doing now that you sold your business or retired?" The typical response of "Well, playing lots of golf, or traveling" will quickly end most conversations.

Think of your many contacts as a means to an end— money for your business.

But, if they can say that they just became an investor in a small growing company that provides supplies and equipment to the snow-board industry, which, as we know, is growing very rapidly, it gets other people's attention.

note The angel gets the satisfaction of being able to share with friends and associates new information and that makes the angel feel good about himself, gives him something to look forward to and provides an identity at the same time.

Another common trait of angels is that often they have become bored with their own careers or jobs and are looking for something that will provide excitement to their lives. The excitement of sharing new and different experiences, like being an investor in a small growing company, appeals to those driven by the excitement of risk/reward situations.

When you help others to grow, you grow yourself.

There's even the somewhat benevolent notion of an older angel assisting a young entrepreneur.

The best exercise on earth is to reach down and pull a person up.

In Robert J. Gaston's book, *Finding Private Venture Capital for Your Firm,* he provides the profile of a typical informal investor or angel:

- Occupation: Close to 70 percent are business owners or managers.

- Age: Angels are generally 20 years older than the entrepreneurs they are financing.

- Gender and Race: Close to 84 percent are white males.

- Education: Over 70 percent have a college degree.

- Income: The average annual income is $90,000.

- Wealth: The average net worth is $750,000.

- Deal Acceptance Rate: 20 percent. This rate is not bad when you compare it to less than .001 percent for formal venture capital firms.

- Co-Investors: Only 1 of 12 angels is a sole investor.

Five characteristics of the ideal investor

There are five characteristics that you should look for in the ideal investor. Your investor might have only a few of these traits. That's fine, but the more traits that they have, the greater benefit to you. It will be the icing on the cake made out of money.

1) **Experience.** Not necessarily limited to the area of your particular business, but successful experience with business or businesses, preferably with a new growing company or one that has successfully overcome previous business challenges.

2) **Understanding of the risks involved in the business.** You want someone who is emotionally stable to deal with the sometimes roller-coaster growth cycles of a business.

3) **Ability to inject additional funds into the business if the business starts growing faster than expected.** Additional capital is a necessity and a paradox when a business starts growing rapidly. Most people think that more and faster growth will solve cash flow problems, but actually it creates a greater demand for capital.

4) **Mutual agreement on when and what type of exit will take place for the company.** In other words, how and when is the investor going to be repaid? Is it going to be through a long-term payment program that will start within the next couple of years? Or, will it come from the sale of the business? Or, will it be from refinancing from other sources such as the bank? This needs to be discussed and agreed upon prior to obtaining and investing the funds in the business.

> *note* Having an investor who can provide or have access to additional funds for this growth is important.

> ⚠ **CAUTION** Once the money is invested, it is very difficult, and sometimes impossible, to come to agreement as to how the investor is going to get the money back and when.

5) **Emergency backup.** You should have available to you not only the investor's advice and counsel when needed, but also meaningful assistance if an emergency comes up, such as rapid growth or illness.

The indirect approach: the key to finding money

Now that you know what angels look like and where to find them, how do you use your contact list to reach them? For starters, here's what not to do:

Have you ever had a good friend or relative verbally share his or her idea of how he or she is going to make you rich, if you just part with a little bit of your money, like maybe $25,000? They really hate coming to you for the money, but all their liquidity is temporarily tied up in that new surround-sound TV with the mini-dish, the boat, the snowmobiles, the new RV. Sound familiar?

The Indirect Approach. This is the technique that is utilized by professional fund-raisers and money people—IT WORKS!

How interested would the people on your contact list or potential angels be in investing in your business if you approached them that way? We have all been victims of the direct approach. It is not much fun and doesn't get results.

It is important that you have a clear understanding of how the "indirect approach" works and can be utilized in your search for funding. Reread this section, if necessary. It is that important.

When you contact the people on your list *do not solicit them for the money*. What you want to say is that you respect them for their success and position in the business community and they are the type of person you are looking for as an investor in your company. But—and this is critical—

The key to success when approaching your winning contact list is to use the "indirect approach."

you need to say that you do not want to infringe on your relationship by approaching them to invest in your business. However, you would be very appreciative if they would pass your business plan on to some of their friends or associates who might be in a position and have the interest to invest in a growing company.

You need to tell them that the investment money is not as important to you as putting together the right team, one that works together and is on the same page as far as objectives and management goals. Because you are acting in a professional, businesslike manner, one of two things will happen when you approach your contacts this way.

1) They will start reading the business plan as soon as you leave. You created a great amount of curiosity about your business. Within a couple of days they will contact you and say, "I have just a few questions I'd like to go over about your business plan." They contacted you because you have not placed any pressure on them by asking them for their money. You used the indirect approach, which gets winning results. Your contact has now become your angel.

2) If your contact is not in a position to invest in the business, they will direct your business plan to one or several of their many contacts who will become your ultimate angel. So you can see, you win either way.

The last one in

Another effective strategy when meeting with angels is the "last-one-in" approach.

Remember when you were a kid and went swimming with your friends at a new lake? You looked around, no one's in the water. How deep is the water? How cold is it? Are there any creatures in there? Any hidden rocks, tree limbs, or broken glass?

Secret: The "Last One In" technique removes any mistrust in dealing with financial matters.

You knew your friends were probably asking themselves the very same questions. But it seems like there's always someone who jumps in first and hollers to the rest of us, "Hey, the water's fine, come on in." Then you see the magic of "the herd" go into action and everybody jumps in.

There is comfort and security knowing that other people are going to be investing in the deal. You can use this bit of human nature to your advantage by telling potential investors that their commitment is contingent upon you raising the balance of the investment from other sources.

note Most people don't want to be the "first in the water" or in unfamiliar situations such as investing in a new business venture.

Say, for example, that you're trying to raise $25,000. You ask your angel if, once you have obtained commitments for the other $20,000, he would come in at that point with $5,000? Most people will make that commitment, once they see that their participation is contingent upon you raising the balance from other sources. Now go out and contact some more angels and use the same approach. Get the commitment from everyone before they actually have to put the money into the business.

Talking to angels

One of the most often asked questions I hear at my seminars is, "Where do I find these financial "angels'?" Attempts to develop a formal "angel" directory has had very limited success. The reason? "Angels" are usually interested in becoming involved in ONE company at a time. They are usually private people and don't want to see their names on a nationally-distributed "list."

note There is a 5-step checklist to follow when interviewing investors. It covers the essential points upon which any business relationship between the two of you will be built.

1) **Have a partnership agreement that is mutually agreed upon.**
This is vital to spell out the duties and responsibilities of each

investor. You need to make sure that it is crystal clear that they have access to the books and information about the business, but they will not be allowed to participate in the day-to-day operations of the business unless you specifically request it.

CAUTION

You are the person in control, the captain of the ship. This needs to be spelled out very carefully and agreed upon.

2) **Be positive.** The angel is going to read your reactions and confidence about the business. This will be a very important aspect in the decision-making process, and confidence needs to be tempered and sincere. It is important to be upbeat and positive when discussing the potential for the business and where you think it's going, but the so-called "cheerleader" type of confidence is often detrimental.

3) **Deal with the investor directly, not through intermediaries or brokers or on the telephone.** You need to be face-to-face with the investor or the lender. There are a lot of unscrupulous individuals out there trying to get information about different opportunities.

CAUTION

You don't want to be in a position of talking to a possible future competitor, so have a potential investor or lender sign a one-page confidentiality agreement before discussions progress very far.

4) **Listen to the potential investor.** Be open to suggestions. You don't necessarily have to follow any or all of these suggestions, but at least be open to listen, and to take suggestions and ideas under advisement. You can learn the most enlightening things about business from other entrepreneurs or investors.

5) **Look beyond the cash.** In addition to funds, quite a number of investors have strong financial statements and strong banking ties. They can use their signature as a way of obtaining funds for your business. Sometimes the bank will even use the collateral or equity of the investor as a way of making a loan to the company. This would be a substitute for the cash injection, and definitely a subject to explore.

The biggest step you can take is the one you take when
you meet the other person halfway.

Why "deals" are rejected by money people

You'll notice that all our approaches to investors include delivering a

Learning from other people's mistakes leads to success faster.

written business plan, one that describes how the money is going to be used, the cash flow projections, the background and descriptions of any unique skills of management, the strength and weakness of the competition, and a detailed marketing plan. These are just a few of the key items that investors need to know before investing in any type of business.

We'll talk more about this when we discuss the elements of the winning business plan in Chapter 6. Keep in mind even informal investors need a formal proposal to evaluate before they hand over any money.

The importance of a well-prepared business plan can't be overstated. Just look at what investors say are the most frequent reasons they reject deals:

- **The business plan was not written from the perspective of the investor or lender:** It did not list the benefits and answer some of the questions and concerns that affect the investor or lender. Often the business plan is written entirely from the perspective of the borrower and doesn't identify the true needs and benefits to the person providing the risk capital. This is covered in more detail in Chapter 6.

- **Inadequate growth potential.** If the business plan shows a limited future, or a growth potential of less than 25 percent over the next five years, investors will not feel that the return is adequate for their risk capital.

- **Investors' lack of knowledge of the industry and management personnel of the company.** The information presented in the business plan does not answer all their questions or leaves them feeling less than confident.

- **Management's lack of experience or talent in the position of handling the responsibilities of running the business on a day-to-day basis.** The entrepreneur may be good at marketing, but can he or she manage money, hire the "right" personnel, retain the good employees?

- **Lack of "blood equity" in the business.** The investor has to see proof that the business owner has invested time, energy and funds to get the business to this stage. The investor is looking for the personal investment and commitment of the owner of the business, so there is a sharing of the risk in case the business runs into stormy economic conditions.

- **The lack of a proprietary interest,** that is, a patent, copyright, or exclusive territory. How difficult would it be for potential competition to enter the marketplace?

Alternative sources

Another method of alternative financing for start-up businesses is utilizing your credit cards.

The key thing to consider, if this is the last option, is to make sure that your profit margins are great enough to cover the 18 percent interest that is usually charged on credit card balances.

It makes a lot of sense to start asking six months to a year ahead of time for an increase in your existing credit card limits in order to get the maximum amounts available. You can take advantage of the new credit card solicitations that we receive almost

> *note* Although plastic is not a recommended primary source for most businesses, you would be surprised how many businesses were started through lines of credit on cards.

on a daily basis. A person could obtain, over a year, five credit cards with a limit of $5,000 each, thus creating a $25,000 capital injection, which should be able to fund the majority of start-up businesses.

To give you an idea of the full potential of credit cards as a source of funding for your business, an article in the *Rocky Mountain News*, July 22, 1996 stated: During a six-month period, a newspaper reporter collected the credit card company solicitations she had received, for a total of more than $295,000 in credit. Although many of these offers were for credit limits of $1000 to $3000, there were some as high as $10,000, and in one case, the offer extended a line of credit for $25,000.

This should be looked upon as only a short-term financing source which will eventually be replaced by bank financing, investor financing or other sources that will have a lower interest rate. But, at that point, you'll be classified as an existing business.

One of the best kept secrets for locating capital is by placing a well-written ad in the *Wall Street Journal* (1-800-975-8609). There have been large sums of money raised through sources looking at investing in small companies. *Investor Magazine* is also a good source for investors in private companies. The magazine has regional issues for every area of the United States, so that your article can reach investors in your area.

International Investor Magazine's phone number is 1-212-224-3300. Call if you have an item of interest that might qualify your company for an article.

Funding sources: government

Chapter 2

Funding sources: government

What you'll find in this chapter:

- Introduction to the SBA
- How SCORE might help you
- What you get from the SBDCs
- State, county, and city funds
- New programs for funding small business

In this chapter we explore the Small Business Administration or SBA. We discuss the Service Corps of Retired Executives (SCORE): and Small Business Development Centers (SBDCs). Both are funded by the federal government and are provided as a free service to small businesses. We also look at how states, counties and cities have stepped up their funding of small businesses with exciting and creative new programs.

Don't overlook local government financial assistance

State and local governments are increasingly eager to help small businesses for two reasons:

1) Cities were duped in their efforts to attract the glamour names of the Fortune 500 companies. These companies have become skilled

in playing one city against another to obtain generous concessions in the form of property tax and income tax abatements, low-cost industrial revenue bonds to build their plants, and so on. In fact, most of the corporations that took advantage of these financial incentives in the past decade are also at the top of the list of companies downsizing and laying off employees in this country. Thus, the promised job growth hasn't materialized.

> **note** Local governments are realizing they can get a better return on dollars invested in programs designed to assist small businesses.

2) Numbers from the Department of Labor show very clearly that the new growth in jobs is in small businesses.

One of the major misconceptions about government sources of financing, whether it be from the federal, state or local level, is that these agencies are in the same category as welfare or food stamps.

Many small business owners look upon government loan programs as entitlement programs with no stipulations on the types of qualifying businesses, collateral, or repayment. The truth of the matter is that these agencies, although they arc operated by the government, now use lending techniques and analyses similar to commercial banks.

Some of these programs are discussed in more detail at the end of this chapter. See the Resource Guide at the back of this book for more information.

The SBA

Don't overlook some of the new programs that are being developed to provide better financial assistance to the small business.

Secret: Forget the old "horror stories" about dealing with the SBA. The SBA has become "user friendly" over the past 5 years.

The Small Business Administration, or SBA, operates a number of programs to identify specific needs that commercial banks have not adequately fulfilled.

> **note** It is important to understand that the SBA does not make direct loans as an agency. Rather, it assists businesses by making loan guarantees through participating banks and other institutions.

A bank would use the guarantee of the SBA when a loan request does not meet all the bank's requirements for collateral, cash flow, management ability, and the risk of the industry. The bank would like to make the loan but there is a discomfort level with the borrower not meeting all of the bank's credit requirements.

note SBA-guaranteed loans do not utilize government funds, but use the money that is on deposit at banks and other institutions. The guarantee is made by the SBA for up to 90 percent of the face value of the loan.

Although the focus of the SBA loan program is to emphasize the repayment ability of a company, the agency still looks at collateral and personal guarantees as a way of "shoring up" a loan request.

SBA programs

Some of the more popular SBA loan programs are:

- The 7A Guaranteed Loan Program
- The LODOC Loan Program
- The 504 Debenture Loan Program
- Micro-Loan Program
- 8A Program
- Greenline Program

- Small Business Investment Corporation
- Small Business Development Companies
- Economic Opportunity Loans

The 7A Guaranteed Loan Program

These are loans made for working capital, equipment, acquisitions, purchase and/or remodeling of property, and inventory. The maximum loan amount is $500,000, which the SBA will guarantee up to 75 percent. Some of the collateral the SBA will consider includes:

- publicly traded stocks and bonds
- certificates of deposit
- savings accounts
- . cash value of life insurance policies
- . real estate
- accounts receivable
- machinery
- land and buildings.

The major advantages of a 7A loan are the relatively low down payment requirements and the longer term for repayment, seven to ten years rather than two to five years for banks. In addition to lower interest rates and higher advance rates, the loan can be paid off at any time without a prepayment penalty. This is very important to a business that will need further refinancing down the road due to rapid growth.

LODOC Program

This is an acronym for LOW DOCumentation. This program, adopted by the SBA in 1992, simplifies the application process to about 3 days, thus reducing the time and bureaucracy that has been associated with traditional SBA loans. For loan requests under $50,000 there is only a single-page application. For loans of $50,000 to $100,000, the applicant needs to furnish income tax returns for the

> **note**
> The LODOC program is the most successful program in SBA's history; loan volume tripled in just the last two years.

past 3 years and a personal financial statement, in addition to the single-page application.

504 Debenture Loan Program

.Although this is not primarily for start-up businesses, it is for those businesses that are growing and want to acquire commercial property or equipment. This program was initiated through the help of certified development companies, which fund 40 percent of the loan through a Second Mortgage Debenture. The remaining balance—60 percent of the loan—is made up of a first mortgage on the property, provided by the participating bank. The borrower only has to provide 10 percent of the bank's down payment portion. Loan terms run between 10 and 20 years, and the rate is fixed. As with the 7A program, the 504 program takes into consideration the number of jobs to be created with the new funds and how it will help the community.

> **note**
> To find out more about the Micro-Loan Program in your area, contact the regional SBA office to obtain the name of the participating nonprofit organization.

Micro-Loan Program

The purpose of this program, which was started in 1993, is to provide start-up capital in relatively small amounts of $25,000 or less to those small businesses considered too small by the commercial banks. Proceeds of the loan can be used for working capital, equipment purchases, or as a revolving line of credit. The loan is guaranteed by the SBA and operated by nonprofit organizations that work with small businesses in securing alternative funding. It is currently operating in 46 states; the average loan size is approximately $10,000 to $12,000. Over half of these loan funds have gone to women-owned businesses with another 30 percent going to minority-owned businesses.

SA Program

This provides specialized management and technical assistance to minorities starting or expanding their businesses. It also provides assistance with government procurement opportunities.

Greenline Program

This program has been started on a test basis in several states to assist small businesses with working capital lines of credit. Although the loan is administered through commercial lenders and the loan amounts are based upon the business's level of accounts receivable and inventory, which is usually controlled by an outside resource.

Small Business Investment Corporation

This type of vendor operates in conjunction with the federal government and provides loans to business start-ups. Every dollar that is invested in the business by the SBIC is matched with $3 to $4 of SBA-guaranteed loans. The advantage to the small business owner is the amount of leverage that is available to a company utilizing the SBIC.

Small Business Development Companies

The main difference between this financing source and the Small Business Investment Corporation is that the funds come exclusively from private corporations and private businesses. The main focus of the SBDC is for long-term financing as opposed to short-term working capital. In addition,

SBDCs provide counseling and assistance in various aspects of running a small business: technical assistance, training, finance, human resources, marketing and manufacturing. See the Resource Guide at the back of this book for names of Small Business Investment Corporations and Small Business Development Companies in your area.

Economic Opportunity Loans

These are funds that are made available to small businesses owned by persons with low incomes. To be eligible, the business must be owned at least 50 percent by someone classified as low income who was denied financing from banks and other financial institutions because of economic or social challenges. Repayment on these loans is very flexible and very generous in providing a long-term payout, with most loans having to be repaid within 10 years and real estate loans in 25 years.

More SBA help

In addition to these programs, the SBA also operates the Women's Loan Program, the Vietnam Veterans Loan Program, the Handicapped Assistance Loan Program and other minority assistance. Moreover, the SBA made special provisions to help small businesses that were negatively affected by federal pollution regulations and occupational and safety health requirements.

Another special program offers guarantees for loans to small general contractors to finance the construction or renovation of residential and/or commercial buildings for ultimate sale. Loans may be used for the acquisition of properties, immediate construction,

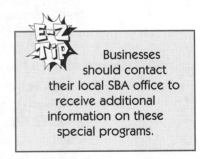

Businesses should contact their local SBA office to receive additional information on these special programs.

significant rehabilitation, and the acquisition of vacant land. The applicant must show a satisfactory ability in constructing and renovating projects and have less than $750,000 outstanding on any SBA loan. Loans are guaranteed up to 90 percent for loans up to $155,000, 85 percent when the loans go up to $750,000. Maturities cannot exceed 36 months, plus a reasonable time for construction or renovation. Principal payment is required in a single payment at the time of sale, with interest payments required semiannually; interest must be paid by the applicant's own resources and not from the loan.

SBA lenders: there is a difference

It is important to be aware that all SBA lenders are not the same. The three major categories are:

1) *Preferred lenders* are both bank and non-bank institutions that have a reliable history of making good credit-judgment on loans. Working with preferred lenders reduces the processing time since they can make the final decision on a loan approval without going to the SBA. This is important.

CAUTION Not all SBA lenders are created equal. Pay close attention to the subtle, but major, difference between preferred and certified SBA lenders. It could make the difference between success and failure in obtaining your funding.

2) *Certified lenders* are banks and non-banks that participate in the SBA loan program on a regular basis and are involved with the SBA training and certification. A longer processing time can be experienced with certified lenders since the loan must still be reviewed and approved by the SBA, although the turnaround time was reduced to 3 to 5 days.

3) *Participant lenders* make SBA loans on an infrequent basis. The disadvantage of this type of lender—and this category includes the majority of banks and non-bank lenders—is that after the loan is approved by the lender, it still must be reviewed and approved by the SBA. This not only takes longer, but also opens the door for further scrutiny by the SBA loan analyst who has not had any personal contact with you, the borrower.

SBA loan documentation

Any SBA lender will require the following information when considering a loan request. For new businesses:

- the SBA Application Form, which describes the loan amount and purpose of the loan
- the background and roles of key managers and the owners
- personal financial statements and income tax returns for two years
- projection of profit and loss and cash flow statements for two years
- the list of any available collateral
- the business plan

For existing businesses:

- income tax returns for the last three years
- income statements for the last three years
- personal financial statements of the owners
- a list of the collateral available
- the business plan

Advantages and disadvantages of SBA loans

The "advantages" far outweigh the "disadvantages." When considering SBA loans, be aware of the advantages and disadvantages. Some of the advantages are:

- **Longer maturity.** Through the SBA loan program, a business can obtain a working capital loan for up to 7 years, equipment loans for up to 10 years and real estate loans for LIP to 25 years. These repayment programs are much more liberal than a conventional bank loan.

> **E-Z TIP**
> Another advantage of SBA loans is that the real estate loans only require a 10 percent down payment, as compared to the 20-25 percent down payment usually required.

- **Competitive interest rates.** SBA loan rates are usually lower than conventional loan rates because of the reduction in risk to the banks based on the SBA's guarantee.

- **Capital leverage**. Most banks are limited to making loans to companies that have a debt-to-worth ratio of 2:1, while the SBA can go up to a 4:1 ratio.

- **No prepayment penalty.** If your company is growing rapidly and you can either pay the loan off or need to finance for a larger amount, no additional payment will be assessed.

- **Eligibility.** SBA loans emphasize the cash flow of the borrower and the company, and put less emphasis on collateral. Collateral is obtained and required, but it becomes a secondary source.

- **Collateral.** Because of the SBA guarantees, a wider range of collateral can be used to secure a loan, such as jewelry, antiques, paintings and rare coins. Banks don't accept this type of collateral, which is referred to as pawn shop collateral.

The disadvantages of SBA loans include:

- ◆ **Collateral.** Applicants are often surprised when the lender requires that the loan be secured in addition to the SBA guarantee.

- ◆ **Paperwork.** Although the red tape and bureaucracy were reduced substantially, there is more SBA paperwork required than for a regular bank loan.

- ◆ **Negative covenants.** In exchange for the SBA guaranteeing your business loan, the agency might put limits on how much you spend for salaries and certain capital improvements without getting prior approval.

note The SBA believes that the primary reason for most small business failures is poor management.

- ◆ **Longer process.** If you do not have USC a preferred lender, you have to go through the qualification process twice, since the bank will have to submit the loan to the SBA again after it is approved internally.

Free management assistance programs

Because of this, the agency has set up management training programs to assist small businesses in the areas of finance, marketing, human resources and other key areas of running a small business. These programs are presented through colleges, chambers of commerce and different business associations in the form of individual counseling, SBA-sponsored courses, conferences, workshops and publications.

Business assistance is provided primarily through the Service Corps of Retired Executives, or SCORE, through Small Business Institutes, known as SBIs, and Small Business Development Centers, known as SBDCs and other associations. SCORE

note The SBDC and SCORE are probably the best resources available to small businesses from start-ups to growing businesses. Their assistance is FREE!

is staffed by more than 14,000 retired executives who provide management consulting to small businesses; SBA matches the background of the SCORE volunteer with the individual needs of the business owner. The advantage of SCORE counseling is that it is a free service from seasoned and experienced entrepreneurs. The disadvantage is that a great majority of the former and retired executives are not up-to-date on current technological advances and assistance that can help the small business owner.

The SBI is a cooperative program with the SBA and more than 600 colleges and universities around the country. SBI sites provide senior and graduate students who work with small businesses under the guidance of their faculty advisors. The small business owner benefits from this free consulting while the students benefit from the real-life experience of working in a business.

note SBDCs also use the resources of colleges and universities in conjunction with local, state and federal programs to provide one-on-one management training and technical assistance to small businesses from experts in their respective fields. This service is also free.

See the Resource Guide at the back of this book for the location and phone number for the nearest SBDC office.

Assistance for women-owned businesses

In addition to the SBA programs, the following organizations assist women in their businesses:

- **The Association of Enterprise Opportunities** provides a list of micro-lenders in your region. Contact AEO at 320 North Michigan Avenue, Suite 804, Chicago, IL 60601.

- **The National Association of Women Business Owners** provides initiative and supports women business owners. Contact the Ohio Department of Development, 77 South High Street, Columbus, OH 43255.

- **The Office of Women Business Ownership** provides the latest information on federal loans and other programs for women. Contact the Business Women's Ownership, SBA Central Office, 409 3rd Street, Washington, DC 20416.

- **Compass Rose** offers training and financial support programs for female entrepreneurs. Contact the Compass Rose Corporation at 20 Moore's Road, Frazer, PA 19355. See the Resource Guide at the back of this book for more programs and information.

Local and state programs

There are numerous state, county and municipal programs being developed to meet the needs of those businesses that do not qualify for traditional bank financing or federal assistance.

DEFINITION

♦ **Community Development Corporations,** also known as *CDCs,* receive grants from both state and federal government sources to finance businesses in economically depressed areas where unemployment is running high. CDCs specialize in start-up businesses and those that will create the largest number of jobs per investment dollar. CDCs have a great deal of flexibility in structuring the loan and collateral requirements. Loans can run up to $500,000, repayable over 10 years.

In addition to loans, CDC Services will also provide assistance in analyzing and preparing your financial projections and gathering and interpreting data about your target market. They will also assist in finding and developing plant sites and providing generalized business counseling.

♦ **The Economic Development Agency** of your county and city can help you locate information on programs set up to assist start-ups and small businesses. These loan programs, referred to as GAP loans and micro-loan programs (for loans of less than $10,000), are run in conjunction with local banks, where the loan initially originates. If the applicant is deficient in the

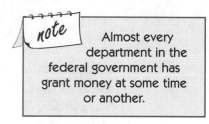
note Almost every department in the federal government has grant money at some time or another.

areas of collateral, repayment, cash flow, etc., but the bank is willing to make the loan because of a strong interest in this type of business, the lender will approach the local municipal or county economic development to fund the remaining balance of the loan.

For the nearest Community Development Corporation in your area, see the Resource Guide in the back of this book. To locate the offices in your particular area for state loan programs and grants, contact the Economic Development Agency at the state level.

Another resource for local and state financial programs is the World Wide Web. Check each state's Web site—addresses are listed in the Resource Guide at the back of this book—for the programs available and links to cities you are interested in.

Government grants

In addition to making loans, the federal government and the SBA are involved with making grants, which do not have to be paid back. The most successful grant program is called the Small Business Innovation Research Program, designed to support advances in research in the scientific and engineering areas and to encourage conversion of research and development from government and military uses into commercial applications. These grants range from $50,000 to $500,000.

Far better it is to dare mighty things, to win glorious triumphs, even though checkered by failure, than to take rank with those poor spirits who neither enjoy much nor suffer much, because they live in the gray twilight that knows not victory nor defeat.

Theodore Roosevelt

Banks and bankers

Chapter 3

Banks and bankers

What you'll find in this chapter:

➠ What you need to know about bankers

➠ Insider tips to nurture your bank ties

➠ Four types of commercial loans

➠ Key elements to get your loan approved

➠ "5Cs" test used by bankers to analyze loans

Banks are where you get the money only after you have proven that you don't need it.

Bob Hope

In this chapter we look at the expectations of the decision-makers who will act on your application for financing. We talk about dealing with banks and bankers and share some inside tips on how to nurture that important banking relationship. We discuss the four types of commercial loans and how to determine which is best for your company's needs, and the six key elements that need to be addressed in order to get a loan request approved. We also outline the famous "5C's" test used by bankers to analyze your loan request and the questions most often asked by bankers during the loan interview.

> **note**
> Very few companies have grown successfully without a solid banking relationship.

Banks don't make loans

It's important to realize that banks don't make loans; bankers do. There is a difference. Banks are large institutions with bureaucratic red tape. Bankers are individuals like you and me who are subject to the same likes and dislikes.

One of the key components to finding a lender who understands your business is to deal with a loan officer who is at least a vice president or above. Previous experience is a key factor in a banker's willingness to take risks. A junior loan officer is more concerned about making a bad loan—and a bad impression on the higher-ups—than a seasoned loan officer.

Bankers, junior and senior, are sometimes guilty of using the baby-with-the-bathwater analysis when looking at loan requests. For example, if the banker or the bank has recently sustained a serious loss on a business in the health-care field, it will be very difficult to overcome this negative experience if your business is also in the health-care field. Although it has nothing to do with you, your business might get a better reception at another institution.

Money talks but it never debates.

Getting to know your banker

Given all that, where does one begin in nurturing the banker, and what are some of the things that work and what are some of the things that should be avoided in developing that relationship? Before we discuss that, ask yourself a few questions to see if you are a candidate for improving and nurturing your banking relationship.

- Do you know where your banker grew up, his home town, where he went to school, what he majored in? Do you know anything about his family, brothers, sisters, spouse, children? What are the banker's favorite sports? What interests is he involved in outside the bank?

- Have you gone out socially with your banker during the last 12 months? Did you invite your banker to the company Christmas party or picnic? Much better is a gift, such as a book about the banker's hobby or interest, that shows that you thought about the banker as a

 Did you give your banker a small Christmas gift last year, something under $25 and preferably non-alcoholic? With most bankers, the traditional bottle of "Christmas cheer" has a negative effect.

person during the holiday season. The banker does not look upon such a gift as bribery or trying to buy influence; it's taken as an expression of a personal thought.

- Have you taken your banker on a tour of your facility to point out improvements in the plant and equipment during the last six months? Have you referred, or better yet, introduced another customer to your banker in the last 12 months? Does your banker know your attorney and accountant by name?

- Do you know the name of your banker's boss? And, more importantly, do you know the banker's lending limit—and the banker's boss' lending limit—before you have to go to the loan committee?

What do these types of questions have to do with getting a loan? Everything. When you can answer these questions "yes," what you are doing is establishing that important relationship with the banker. You have to have that relationship established with the banker before he or she feels comfortable with the loan.

It's much more difficult to turn down a request from someone we enjoy and have respect for. It's also much easier to turn down a request from someone you really don't know and haven't established a relationship with, and who only comes to you when they need something.

You have to remember, bankers are people, too, and they want to be liked, they really do. They've got a job to do and they've got lots of regulations to deal with. But, if you keep that in mind, you'll see how critical establishing that relationship is to the overall lending process.

Even if you're not a banker, you can probably understand that it is a lot easier to deal with and to honor requests from people we enjoy and relate to.

Start a relationship before you are strapped for cash

It sounds odd, but the key to nurturing or establishing a banking relationship is showing the banker that you do not need the money today. The best time to approach the banker is when you do not need a loan.

It's much more effective for you, the borrower, to start out by saying, "I don't need a loan today, but if the business continues to grow as my accountant or my financial planner is projecting, we're going to be needing some capital down the road to fund this additional growth." Bankers love that.

A common denominator of poor decisions is "snap judgments." Bankers are trained to take their time in analyzing a loan request in order to obtain more and more information.

The worst time to be establishing a banking relationship is when you do need the loan today. It takes your negotiating power completely off the table and puts the banker on the defensive.

The absolutely worst type of loan requests come on Friday at 3 p.m.— and they do come in. The bank has a $150,000 loan out to a company; the owner calls and says, "Harold, I need to have $10,000 put in our checking account immediately to cover payroll. If not we're going to have to shut down and you'll just have to come in and take over the plant and the equipment on Monday." These are phone calls that can wreck any relationship that might have existed between the business owner and the banker before the phone call. Even if you get your funding from an outside source, it is critical to have a banking relationship established for future needs. If nothing else, your commercial checking account can be used as a reference in obtaining credit from suppliers. It is much more effective to give suppliers an actual person to talk to, as in, "Call Mr. Jones at First National Bank," when they ask for the name of your banker.

Have a back-up banker

In today's ever-changing financial world with bank mergers and acquisitions, it is becoming imperative to establish a secondary or backup

Don't put all of your financial "eggs" in one basket.

banking relationship, one that can be implemented immediately, if necessary. Some of the following suggestions apply not only to existing businesses, but also to start-up businesses that are going to need to nurture or establish a primary banking relationship.

When establishing a secondary or backup banking relationship, let the banker know that you're pleased with your present banking relationship, but that your accountant, financial planner or your advisory board has suggested that you establish a backup banking relationship as a prudent business practice. These are very, very positive statements to the banker, letting him or her know that you're planning ahead and that you don't need the money today. It's not a last minute, fill-in-the-gap situation.

Ask for referrals

One of the necessary first steps in establishing or nurturing that banking relationship is to talk to your friends, your associates, social contacts, other businesses that you deal with. Ask them for the name of a banker they have enjoyed working with and to whom they could refer you. This serves two purposes:

1) It serves as a screening device to locate an aggressive banker because the people you're asking are going to be friends or people who know you on a personal basis. They're not going to be referring you to someone who has been unfair or hard to deal with.

2) When you call the banker for the appointment, you are going to use that person's name as a referral. It helps tremendously in getting your foot in the door by using the customer's name. After you've obtained the names of several bankers, try to get a mix of several from the large chain banks and a couple from the local independent banks. Four seems to be an ideal number.

Set the appointment

Don't call for the banker directly. Call for the secretary. The secretary controls this banker's life and screens everything.

You then call the respective banks and ask for the secretary to the banker you are calling. It's very important that you get to know the secretary and be as friendly as you can. Let the secretary know early in the conversation that the bank's customer,

"John Jones," recommended that you talk to this banker to discuss your business and that you want to make an appointment. That will get you in the door without a problem because bankers are very sensitive to bad publicity, and if someone referred you to them, that carries a lot of weight.

Dress appropriately

When you meet with the banker, dress appropriately, that is, appropriate for your profession. If you're a carpenter or a contractor, don't wear a three-piece suit, silk shirt and silk tie. That's not the look the banker expects from someone who is supposedly out in the field doing work.

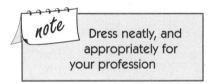
note Dress neatly, and appropriately for your profession

Take control

note One has to realize early that negotiating with the banker is NOT played on a "level playing field." Think about the last time you visited the bank. The atmosphere is intimidating: you walk past an armed security guard, who seems to be scrutinizing you; video cameras are everywhere; huge steel doors and bars are in the vault area; the banker's oversized desk keeps distance between you and the banker; and the overstuffed chair that faces the banker makes you feel like the banker is looking "down" at you.

When you introduce yourself to the banker, share two things right off the bat:

1) **You are interviewing several banks in the area** to establish your account or a secondary banking relationship, and this bank was recommended by a customer, John Jones. Put the banker in a position where he or she is going to have to sell the bank to you because you're looking at several competitors. You have the added

bonus of being referred by a customer, someone who knows the bank. This is a very effective door-opener and is the beginning of leveling the playing field with the banker.

2) **You're not here today to seek a loan,** but you're meeting with different bankers to find a mutually beneficial banking relationship.

You're looking for a bank that can handle your present needs and also be able to handle your future needs if you continue to grow according to your projections for present sales levels. Very positive things for you to be communicating to the banker.

> ⚠ **CAUTION** You don't want your business plan to be reviewed while you are trying to sell yourself and your company. You want the banker's undivided attention.

Let the banker know that you are aware that the schedule is tight, but you do have a couple of questions before leaving a business plan for him or her to read at his or her convenience. At this point, you have endeared yourself to the banker by recognizing that he or she is short on time.

It also gives you a good reason not to present the business plan at the outset. If you do, the banker will pick it up and start reading it while you're talking. This is a very critical time of establishing that banking relationship. So save the business plan for the end of the meeting and you'll stay in control of the situation.

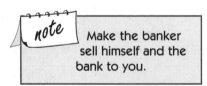

note Make the banker sell himself and the bank to you.

Ask questions

Some of the questions you might want to ask the banker:

- What is the banker's or bank's experience and feelings about businesses in your particular industry or service? Is it something they have had good or bad loan experience with? Or, is this one area where they haven't had any experience at all? You want to hear about how interested and knowledgeable they are about your business.

DEFINITION

- How long has the loan officer been with the bank? What is the bank's "*CAMEL*" rating? This is an acronym for a system used by federal and state regulatory agencies in recent years to rate the bank's performance, much like Moody's rating for the bond market.

The CAMEL covers five separate categories:

- capital

- assets

- management

- earnings

- liquidity

These five separate categories are rated from 1 to 5: 1 being excellent, 5 representing a serious problem. A composite of scores in the five areas gives the bank an overall rating between 1 and 5. This is public information, and asking for it is a good, effective way of letting the banker know that you are not only interested in obtaining a loan, but you're interested in doing business with someone who is going to be around tomorrow.

> **E-Z TIP** You can obtain a credit rating report on a bank by calling either VeriBank, 1-800-442-2657 or Sheshunoff Information Services, 800-456-2340. The cost for the reports is $10 for the first bank and $5 for each additional bank requested.

If the banker hesitates about giving you this information, you can bet the bank's rating must be in the 4 to 5 range. If it's in the 1 or 2 category, they are going to be very proud of sharing that information with you. In the 3 category, they might hem and haw a little bit, but this is important information, because you want to deal with a bank that is on sound footing.

- What are the bank's procedures for any loan requests in the future? You need to know if you are going to be working with this loan officer or if your request is something that has to go to the loan committee. This is a very tactful way of finding out what the loan officer's lending limit is and if you're going to need to nurture the loan officer's boss, too, since you want the largest number of people on your side in that loan committee.

If you can avoid having your loan go before the dreaded loan committee, all the better, because to the people you've not established a relationship with on the loan committee, you're just a piece of paper. It is very easy to turn down those loan requests.

- What additional information will the bank need in addition to your business plan? What do they want from you in addition to income tax returns? Do they want projections for three to five years, or do they want to see an accounts receivable aging? What is the normal turnaround time once these items are submitted before you get a decision?

At the end of the meeting, hand the loan officer your business plan, and ask when you can get back in touch to answer any questions. The banker will always have questions on the business plan, if only to show you he has read it and how smart he is. They love to impress you and try to test your knowledge about the business in the business plan.

When we pray for rain, we must be willing to put up with some mud.

Visiting the new accounts department

Now you will start "tilting" the banker's "playing field" in your favor. This is where the fun begins!

Before you leave the loan officer's desk, ask for directions to the new accounts department. This sends a positive message to the banker that you're interested or you would not be asking for information on new accounts. Most of the time, the banker will take you over personally to the new accounts department and introduce you. Establishing a depository account is a very sensitive and important part of a banking relationship. The depository accounts are the source of funding for new loans, the new inventory that enables the bank to make a profit.

You won't spend very much time in the new accounts area, just long enough to describe the type of business that you have and ask for recommendations on the type of account and services to meet your needs. Before you leave, you want to get a copy of the brochure that describes the services along with the cost, so you can study them at a later time.

It is very important to the banker that the bank get not only the loan, but also the depository relationship.

The other thing you want to ask for—and this is an absolute must—is any free item they are giving to customers, such as pens, matches, calendars, mugs inscribed with "I had coffee with the president of ABC Bank," anything that has the bank's name on it. Don't be shy; they love to give this stuff away.

Now that you have this "stuff," take it back to the office and put it away. You'll need it later.

Call the bankers back

note There is nothing wrong with saying "I don't know the answer, but let me get with my accountant, or my sales marketing people to get you a more definite answer."

After you interviewed four banks, you should be able to select the two that seem to show the most interest and that you feel the most comfortable with. Contact the bankers you spoke to and ask if they have any questions about your business plan. Answer the bankers' questions directly and confidently. If you don't know the answer, don't guess. Let the bankers know that you would like to research that question and get back to them, because you want to make sure that you are accurate.

Bankers respect hearing that as opposed to someone who tries to "shoot from the hip." It gives them a very uncomfortable feeling when someone doesn't take the time to get the right information.

You also want to tell the bankers that you are going to keep them posted of the progress of your business by dropping off monthly profit and loss statements so they can keep updated on your progress.

Bring the bankers home

You now want to invite each banker to your facility for a tour of the business. Remember the "stuff" from all of the banks that you visited? Take out the items you picked up from a competing bank and place them in appropriate, strategic positions around your office. For example, put a wall

E-Z TIP It is important to get the banker on your "turf." It is very difficult to develop the relationship with the banker on the banker's "turf."

calendar off to one side behind your desk. Put the matches off to another side of the desk; pens in a naturally visible area; fill the mug with coffee.

DEFINITION

This is where you will have fun watching the eyes of the banker as you're talking about your business. As you look down, just look up very quickly. The banker's eyes will be on that calendar or those matches or those pens, getting the message, "Oh, no! Our competitor has been out here trying to hustle this account, too. This must be a highly sought-after business. Just look at all the stuff around here." Psychologically, when more than one person is after something, there is competition. This is another way of leveling that banking playing field so that when you are ready to ask for a loan, the lender is ready to listen.

Types of loans

There are four types of commercial loans.

1. **Single payment loan.** It is usually for one year or less and used for a particular purpose, such as to get a large discount by making an early payment for a large purchase, or to fund cash flow on a temporary basis when there is excess inventory.

2. **Installment loan.** This is offered with monthly payments For a set period of time and is usually secured with machinery, equipment, automobiles, trucks, computers and other types of depreciating assets.

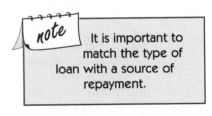

note It is important to match the type of loan with a source of repayment.

3. **Term loan.** This is for a multi-year period and payable on a monthly or quarterly basis from cash flow. It is used to fund long-term expansion programs.

4. **Revolving line of credit.** This is a type of loan that provides a source of funds set at a certain amount on which you, the borrower, can draw down when the cash flow is running low and pay back at your convenience when the cash flow improves. These types of lines of credit are usually set up for seasonal purposes, or to even out monthly cash flow.

If the payment is going to be coming from a single, identifiable source, it should be a short-term loan. If the funds to repay the loan are to be coming out of profits or cash flow over a period of time, the loan should be a long-term loan. Most companies have a combination of two or more commercial loans to match the funding source with the needs.

What bankers look at

When evaluating your loan request, bankers generally look at six different areas:

1) Quality of management

Quality of management is determined by previous experience dealing with challenging situations as a manager or owner of a business. It is not absolutely necessary to have experience in a particular industry. It is more important to demonstrate the ability to deal with challenges and successfully turn a problem situation into a positive one. An example would be to show that as a manager of a department of your previous employer or company you improved the profit margin from 10 percent to 30 percent, or reduced employee turnover from 10

> ⚠️ **CAUTION** Bankers are not comfortable with someone who hopes that a problem will go away. They are looking more for a person who takes the bull by the horns and deals with the situation immediately.

percent down to 1 percent. What the banker is trying to determine is your ability to deal with the continuing challenges that face the small business.

2) The accounting system

Specifically, does it provide accurate information? If the pro-formas or the financial statements are not presented using standard accounting format, the

> **note** No matter how good the management is, if the market trends are negative, the banker feels, it's very much like swimming upstream.

banker feels very uncomfortable with the quality and credibility of the numbers. An example of this would be a company's balance sheet which does not depreciate for fixed assets.

3) Market trends for the product or service that the small business is providing

Bankers feel more comfortable with growth trends that are supported with outside independent research and articles showing that this is a growth industry for the next five to seven years, not a buggy-whip industry that is either obsolete or in a state of decline.

4) Structure of management and ownership

Bankers realize it is very difficult for the owner to be a specialist in all aspects of operating a business: finance, marketing and human resources. Bankers feel very comfortable with people who acknowledge and realize that there are certain areas they are stronger in than others. What steps is the owner taking to bring in assistance or to outsource those functions in which he or she is not strong?

Bankers like to see owners who are self-confident, but also realistic in the areas where they need assistance. Bankers also love to see companies set up advisory boards that meet twice a year or more.

5) Profitability

Bankers have moved away from looking at collateral as a main source of repaying loans and are looking more at the cash flow and cash flow projections of the company. Banks' previous experience selling collateral and realizing only five to ten cents on the dollar has forced them to abandon their traditional priorities.

6) The company's pro-forma profit and loss statements and the cash flow statements and projections

The banker is especially interested in the assumptions that provide support for a sudden increase in sales or a sudden decrease in operating expenses.

The "5C's" test

Although banking has become more sophisticated in the past few years, the"5C's Test" is still the foundation of lending decisions. Small business owners often hear of the famous "5C's" that bankers use in testing the company:

Character

Character comes first on the list, because bankers feel very uncomfortable if this element is missing. They are able to assess the character issue through referrals and determining the honesty of the individual in previous situations and business dealings with other clients.

They are also able to ascertain the character of an individual by taking a look at the personal financial statement and determining if the owner is conservative by keeping a percentage of assets in liquidity.

A banker feels uncomfortable seeing a non-liquid statement, especially if the assets are "toys" such as boats, recreational vehicles, mountain property, speculative investments, etc.

The banker also gets a feel for the character of the person through conversations in which the customer reveals priorities for the business. The customer who brags to the banker about avoiding taxes by understating income leaves the banker wondering what else the person is doing that might be misleading.

Capacity

DEFINITION

Capacity is how you dealt with problems and challenges in the past. Bankers have found that poor business judgment can be a major cause of failure. Bankers like to know that the borrower understands how cash moves through the company and how poor credit policies and poor collection policies can adversely affect the cash flow and the integrity of the company. The banker understands, and expects the business owner to comprehend, that sales are not the paramount answer to a successful company.

The banker also expects the borrower to understand the factors necessary to be successful. The banker wants to ensure that the borrower has a clear focus on why his product or service is better than that of competitors. The banker looks for the borrower to acknowledge and understand the risks associated with his particular business, and any contingency plans that the company might need to put in place if the economy faces a downturn, or if a new competitor enters the market.

Conditions

DEFINITION

Conditions are the external factors facing the company, such as the present economy of the local area and also the national market if the product or service is sold outside the local area.

Collateral

Collateral has moved behind cash flow in importance, but is still taken as supplemental support for the loan. The borrower can play a key role in educating the banker as to the true market value of specialized equipment and collateral by providing appraisals

note The value placed on the collateral is what the banker feels it can be sold for in a distressed situation, and the business owner should not be taken aback by such a low figure.

and letters from buyers and suppliers of this type of merchandise.

Capital

DEFINITION

Capital is the "blood equity" invested by the owner in the business. Banks are very conservative lenders and will not make a 100 percent capital loan to start a business. One of the key criteria in the loan decision is how much the owner would stand to lose if the business were to fail. The greater amount of investment or blood equity on the part of the owner, the greater the chances that the loan will be approved.

What bankers ask

Bankers love to ask questions. "He who holds the gold, makes the rules." The questions are intended not only to obtain needed information about you and your company, but also to judge your management style, i.e., do you acknowledge when you don't have the answer to a question or are you one who always "shoots from the hip?" It is very important to acknowledge when you don't know the answer to their question, that you research it and get back with them in the next few days. This wins points with bankers.

Although each banker has different requirements, there are several questions that most bankers will always ask. You, the borrower, must be completely straightforward with your answers.

There are two "schools" of thought on how much to seek from the bank. I recommend requesting a smaller amount in order to get your "foot" in the door of the bank.

♦ **How much money do you want?** This might seem like a very basic question but it is important, since there are two schools of thought on the amount of loan to request. One says to obtain the largest loan you can possibly get. The other says to go for the minimum loan that will get you through the first six to nine months of operation while you build your relationship and track record with the banker.

It is much easier to obtain the second loan from the banker if you can demonstrate a successful track record in meeting or exceeding your projections. You are also cutting down your chances for rejection since it is much easier to get a loan for $50,000 than one for $100,000. The higher the loan amount, the greater the chance of the bank taking a loss. This is just part of the banker's personality, so with a lower loan amount there's also a lower threshold of potential loss in the banker's mind.

It is much easier and acceptable to the banking institution to come in six to nine months later with an additional loan request to support a growing business. It is much more difficult to try to get that commitment prior to establishing that important relationship with the banker and a track record to support the larger loan amount.

◆ **What you are going to do with the money?** Again, this sounds very basic, but often a borrower is evasive and fails to identify the benefits of the loan to the business. Be specific in identifying that the loan is going to be used to purchase a temporary increase in inventory that you were able to pick up at a low price which will be repaid from the turnover of receivables, or to purchase a machine which would increase productivity and thus reduce your operating costs by 15 to 20 percent.

Don't make the mistake of trying to repay a capital loan with short-term working capital proceeds.

◆ **What are the benefits to your company** of borrowing additional funds and taking the additional risk? The benefits need to be clearly spelled out in terms of profit, market penetration, additional product lines or stabilization of customer base.

◆ **When will the loan be repaid?** This is very important, because there are several types of loans and it is important that you be in control of the type that will be ultimately undertaken. Don't rely on the bankers to make this decision for you. The bank would like to have your loan paid back yesterday.

The key determining factor is the source of repayment. If it's going to come within a short time, within one year, it can be a single payment loan. If it's going to require payment from cash flow, it should be a term loan spread out over several years.

◆ **How is the loan going to be repaid?** Are we talking about cash flow, which would repay a long term capital loan? Or, about the turnover of inventory and receivables and a leveling off of inventory, which will allow excess cash to reduce the loan? Or, are we talking about refinancing from another financing source.? Or, about initial investors injecting money into the company to repay the loan?

◆ **What are your contingency plans** in case something happens so the loan cannot be repaid on schedule? What steps are you as a business owner going to take, such as reducing inventory, reducing operating costs, reducing overhead? What is it going to take to generate the funds necessary to repay the bank loan?

Follow-up

This seemingly small gesture elevates you from the rest of the banker's commercial clients. It is extremely effective in developing the important relationship with the banker.

Once you negotiate a loan with the banker, don't forget to send a personal thank-you note. And, one to the banker's boss, letting the boss know how professional the loan officer was in dealing with your loan request, and that you will recommend the bank to your business associates. This might seem like a small and subtle thing to do, but bankers really do cherish these rare acknowledgments of appreciation.

You can get anything in life you want, if you help enough people get what they want.

Zig Ziglar

Funding sources: non-bank alternatives

4

Chapter 4

Funding sources:
non-bank
alternatives

Persistence will give you power to prevail over all problems.

In this chapter, we talk about the use of non-bank sources such as accounts receivable, factoring, inventory financing, lease financing and real estate financing. We also look at how to choose alternative financing for your business.

Accounts receivable financing

This is one of the fastest growing areas of money sources for most businesses. It has gotten very competitive and costs have dropped in recent years. Don't overlook this growing source of funding.

DEFINITION

Accounts receivable means the money owed to your company for the sale of merchandise or services to your customers. and it can be an excellent source of financing if your customers are creditworthy. The nice thing about accounts receivable financing is that the lender is basing the decision not so much on the strength of you, the borrower, but upon the credit strength and financial strength of your customers.

Your first choice for obtaining accounts receivable financing should be a commercial bank, because the costs are the lowest.

You need to contact the larger commercial banks in your area to see if they are set up to handle accounts receivable financing; some specialize in this area.

The procedures for obtaining such financing are similar to those for other types of loans, except for some additional reporting to keep the lender informed of the status of the collection of the accounts. You are usually required to send a lender a weekly report based upon the payments you received and any new receivables that have been created from new sales.

As the payments are collected they are applied to the loan on the same percentage basis that the bank is advancing on the receivables, usually 70 to 80 percent. The remaining amount collected from your customers then goes into your account.

Factoring advantages and disadvantages

Factoring is another way of utilizing accounts receivable to raise cash. The cost of having a non-bank company that specializes only in collection of accounts receivable is more expensive, but the paperwork and time-frame to obtain approval is much shorter than a commercial bank.

There are certain advantages and disadvantages to factoring.

Advantages

- **You receive immediate cash** once you receive the purchase invoice of a customer.

- **Reduced cost of collecting the receivables.** The factoring company is responsible for collecting all moneys from the customer. This eliminates the need to have a staff person in your company doing the bookkeeping, credit collection and follow-up work on these accounts.

- **The accounting and collection knowledge of the factor** is very strong. Since the factor will be keeping the accounting records on a daily basis, you will have access to instant verification and status reports of your customers' accounts.

Disadvantages

DEFINITION

- **The factor may make the accounts receivable commitment on a *recourse basis,*** depending on the creditworthiness of your customers. This means that if the factor is unable to collect the full amount from the customer for any reason, the factor will look to you, the borrower, to reimburse him for the difference.

- **Notifying your customers to send payments to a post office box** instead of directly to your company. This is the factor's way of controlling the receivables and having immediate collection and notification of any potential problems. Some businesses are sensitive to having their customers notified that they are using a factor for their financing. However, as the banking and financial industry has changed and factoring has become more popular over the last five to seven years, this disadvantage is rapidly disappearing.

CAUTION

◆ **The cost of using a factor is higher than a commercial bank.**
It can run between 5 percent and 15 percent discount based upon
the quality, dollar amount and number of invoices being processed.
(That means that when you receive payment from your customers,
the factor will keep 5 to 15 percent of the payment and deposit the
balance in your account.) The larger the dollar amount, the fewer
the invoices and the higher
the quality of the customer,
the lower the cost of
factoring. Factors look at not
only the financial strength of
the customer, but also that
of the borrower and the
type of industry that the
customer is in.

You can locate
factors in your area
by looking in the
Yellow Pages under
"Factors."

It is important to take a look at the total picture and balance both the
costs and benefits of factoring, since some companies have experienced a
large savings in the collection on accounts receivable by using factors.

Inventory financing

Although inventory financing is somewhat limited since lenders also
want accounts receivables that accompany the inventory's collateral, there are
certain companies that specialize in making loans secured by inventory.

There are two types of inventory financing:

DEFINITION

1) *Floor planning* is usually done by the dealer selling the inventory,
   such as an automobile dealer.

2) *Warehouse financing* is usually done by an outside company that
   monitors the inventory by bonding one of your own employees to
   keep track of what is sold and new merchandise that arrives. This
   way, the warehouse control company knows how much collateral is
   present on the premises on any given day.

This form of financing can be expensive, depending upon the nature of the collateral. If the collateral is specialized or a seasonal type of merchandise, the risk that the lender will not be able to sell it to get the amount of the loan back is higher, and therefore the costs are higher. If the merchandise is universally used and not seasonal, the costs of inventory financing are reduced substantially.

Lease financing

Both the processing time and paperwork are much less than the bank's requirements. The three main sources of lease financing are:

DEFINITION

1) **General equipment** leasing companies are not limited to one particular type of equipment on which they provide financing. These companies handle both new and used equipment.

DEFINITION

2) **Specialized equipment** lenders deal with high-dollar types of equipment; they developed a reputation for being able to sell the specialized equipment to a secondary market in case of repossession or sale at the end of the lease term. Companies in this area usually deal with aircraft, medical equipment, construction equipment, large computer systems and dry cleaning equipment.

DEFINITION

3) **Vendor financing** is when the seller of the equipment has a captive leasing company or an arrangement with a leasing company to facilitate the

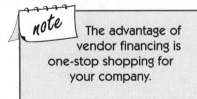

note The advantage of vendor financing is one-stop shopping for your company.

financing on the equipment. There are usually side agreements with the seller of the equipment that any equipment will be resold by the dealer if it is repossessed or turned in at the end of the lease term. The vendors have a better access to a secondary market of buyers for this used equipment than would other lenders, such as banks.

Providing lease financing on-site greatly increases sales if customers do not have to go out and find their own financing. It is definitely a sales enhancer.

Advantages and requirements of leasing

note

There are also tax benefits to leasing equipment which should be discussed with your accountant.

This area of financing has become very creative in the past five years. Always remember to acquire appreciating assets and lease depreciating assets. Advantages of leasing include:

- No capital investment or down payment on the equipment. This is very important for new or growing companies that can better utilize their funds in purchasing inventory which turns over much quicker and produces a greater profit.

- You can get out of a leasing agreement when the equipment is technologically out-of-date or of no use to you and your business at the end of the lease.

- You can also have a maintenance contract incorporated in the lease payments, so that someone else is responsible for the maintenance and upkeep of the leased equipment.

- Leasing can also turn equipment that is already owned by your company into instant cash. This can be created with a sale/lease-back arrangement, in which you temporarily sell your equipment for immediate cash, then lease the equipment back for two to five years.

There are several general requirements for leasing:

- Some type of business plan that provides the information the leasing company will need to access the market and the type of customers you will deal with.

- The cash flow projections and cash flow statements of the business. Like a bank, leasing companies are interested in the ability of the company to generate enough cash flow to make the payments, rather than to liquidate the assets for cash.

- The obsolescence factor. How quickly is equipment being replaced by new technology and improved performance? Computers are a good example of the rapid obsolescence factor incorporated in the cost of leasing. On the other hand, the leasing of a commercial oven or forklift has very low obsolescence and therefore the costs are reduced.

- If the lease is a sale/lease-back arrangement, how the proceeds will be used in the company and how leasing helps the company. The leasing company will want to know specifically if the proceeds will be used to purchase such things as additional inventory, or to make improvements in the plant and equipment which would result in higher productivity.

- What type of maintenance procedures or policies are in place. The leasing company wants to insure that the equipment will not be subject to excessive wear during the course of the lease.

- The credit history of the company. The leasing company is concerned how the money is going to be repaid, and a previous credit history that demonstrates current payment is highly sought after and preferred.

Real estate financing

An ideal source of financing for a start-up business is the use of real estate financing. You can use your own real estate as collateral, or the real estate of another person.

There are a number of sources for commercial real estate financing.

- **Mortgage brokers and mortgage bankers** are firms that represent a number of different types of lenders specializing in different types of commercial real estate properties. They have a wide choice with regard to terms and rates based upon that particular lender's experience with that type of real estate.

note The rule of thumb is that the lender will advance you 75 percent to 90 percent of the net equity of the property. Some aggressive lenders offer loans up to 100 percent of net equity.

- **Savings and loans** specialize in real estate lending more so than the commercial banks. They have well-established secondary markets on to which they can sell the loans. However, the recent problems in the savings and loan industry have resulted in the consolidation of many institutions, leaving fewer in the marketplace.

- **Banks** make real estate commercial loans, but only if you are an established customer and if they have access to selling the loan off into a secondary market. Banks will often put a balloon payment on the loan within five to seven years since they are not specializing in long-term fixed rates.

- **Life insurance companies** are also very active in commercial real estate. Their markets are usually the larger dollar properties of $1 million and above. It is the same with pension funds, although their loan floor limit is in the $250,000 range.

- **Commercial finance companies** also make real estate loans on commercial buildings, but their limit is usually $300,000 or less. Rates are slightly higher than other types of real estate lenders.

- **"Money to loan."** As a last resort, you can always obtain financing on commercial real estate properties by reviewing the Business Opportunity section in the newspaper under "Money to Loan." Of course, this source of money is very expensive, and should be used only as a last resort.

Shopping for alternative financing

It is important when shopping for non-bank sources of financing to interview a number of different sources. Each seems to have its own unique policies and niches in the marketplace which also correlate to the cost.

When interviewing alternative funding sources, be prepared to discuss the following topics:

note Financially strong customers have more appeal than relatively new companies that have not established a credit history

- ◆ Information to show that the business is fairly stable and not subject to volatile changes.

- ◆ The credit-worthiness of your customers.

- ◆ Factors also like to see a large customer base rather than just a few large customers, although they will make advances on single, large accounts receivable purchases based upon the credit- worthiness of the customer.

◆ The average size of your receivables. Obviously, 100 accounts at $1,000 each are more attractive than 500 at $20 each.

◆ The type of industry that you are in will be used to assess any particular problems you may face. For example, some industries such as construction and health care are notorious for slow pay, while restaurants are known for their instability. With commercial real estate, you will have to shop the loan with several mortgage brokers to find the highest advance rating, best terms of repayment and lowest interest rates. Mortgage brokers will do all the leg work in locating the best lender to match your type of real estate and the terms and conditions you are seeking.

I would never have amounted to anything were it not for adversity.
I was forced to come up the hard way.

J.C. Penney

Buying an existing business or franchise

5

Chapter 5

Buying an existing business or franchise

What you'll find in this chapter:

- ➡ Advantages and disadvantages of a franchise
- ➡ How to blend product lines
- ➡ Sources of funding to buy a franchise
- ➡ How to analyze the franchise's prospect
- ➡ Key tips to starting your franchise hunt

The creation of something new is not accomplished by the intellect but by the play instinct acting from inner necessity. The creative mind plays with objects it loves.

Carl G. Jung

In this chapter we discuss the advantages and disadvantages of purchasing an existing business or franchise operation. You will see how you can blend your new, improved product or service with an existing business that handles similar products or services. We also reveal the number one source of over 85 percent of the funding for the purchase of an existing business, and discuss some key items to look for in different franchises.

Why buy a business?

Before you go full speed ahead with starting your own business, give some serious consideration to acquiring an existing business. The existing business should be one that is in the same industry as your new concept, but will allow you to add your product or service to an established market/clientele. It is easier than you think and the financing options are tremendous.

By purchasing an existing business to add to your product or service as opposed to starting a business from scratch you will greatly minimize the risk. You will also have available money sources start-ups could not tap.

Buying a business can be advantageous to two different groups of people:

1) Those who identified a particular market for a product or service. By purchasing an existing business they will now be able to operate with very little change to the business in the future.

2) Those who identified a particular business or industry that they feel very comfortable with. Through the introduction of additional product or services that complement and expand the existing product or service line to the same market, they can grow more rapidly.

Seller financing

note Seller financing is probably the least expensive and easiest financing available to acquire a business.

The main advantage for either one of these groups is that the seller will usually finance most of the purchase; in some cases up to 80 to 90 percent. In other words, the seller becomes the banker. This is a major stress reliever for a potential buyer, since dealing with the seller for the financing is much easier, faster and results in less brain damage than dealing with commercial banks or other traditional lenders.

But why wouldn't a seller want to sell the business only for cash and get on with his or her life?

Advantages to the seller

- **There are very few potential buyers who can raise or borrow the full amount of the purchase price.** This cuts down tremendously on the market and affects the selling price, which will be reinforced by the business broker or agent listing the business for sale (who, by the way, is getting a commission based upon the selling price).

- **Long-term capital gains tax,** which will allow the tax liability to be spread out over a number of years, in anticipation of lower capital-gains tax rates in the future.

- **If the seller obtained all cash for the business, he'd be faced with the prospect of finding another investment.** It must have returns comparable to the rate of return on the seller carry-back note, with the same degree of risk. Not an easy thing to find these days.

Advantages to the buyer

- **The willingness of the seller to carry a note back on the sale of the business creates a great value in the eyes of the buyer.** It makes the buyer feel comfortable that the seller is not selling blue sky or a business likely to fail in the next several years because of market conditions, competition, or information known only to the seller.

♦ **In the seller, you have a long-term expert** who can be called upon in case there are any challenges or problems with the business.

♦ **In order to assure the payback of the note, the seller will be very cooperative in working with you** in dealing with unforeseen problems, and is much easier to deal with than a commercial bank or outside lenders. Sellers have often renegotiated the term, the interest rate and the amount of the carry-back note when the buyer has run into problems with the business, in order to protect the integrity of the note.

> *note*
>
> Seller financing lets you use the profits of a company to buy yourself a job.

♦ **Often, the interest rate is below commercial bank rates,** with terms up to ten years.

♦ **Collateral is not an issue** with the seller since you are using the assets of the business as collateral for the loan. Only on rare occasions do sellers take personal collateral to secure the carry-back note, and this is usually associated with a lack of proven managerial experience on the part of the buyer.

6. **The mathematics of purchasing a business with seller financing are extremely attractive.** On the purchase of a $500,000 business it is much easier to accumulate personal funds and to utilize informal venture capitalists to come up with a $100,000 down payment, instead of $500,000 for the outright purchase of the business. It is much easier to convince other investors and lenders to advance the funds for the $100,000 down payment, even though you have little or no money invested in the company, when the seller is willing to carry back 80 percent of the purchase price of an existing business with a proven cash flow.

Buying a franchise

Purchasing a franchise can also be an ideal way of buying yourself a job with minimal personal cash investment. The successful nature of franchising provides a formal training program based upon what has worked for previous franchises. Minimizing the possibility of repeating mistakes minimizes the chance for failure. The success rate with the majority of franchises runs in the 80 to 90 percent rate, which is very attractive to most investors.

Advantages of financing a franchise

- **Most franchise companies have established banking relationships.** This helps facilitate establishing your own relationship with the bank when the franchiser has already opened the door for you.

- **The lease financing of equipment** is made available through previously arranged contacts with leasing companies by the franchiser at preferential rates.

- **It is much easier to get angels and other investors** in a well-known franchise name. There is comfort and security in knowing the success rate of other franchisees and being familiar with the name of the franchise.

When looking for the "right" franchise, many people overlook the basic rule of working, i.e., do something that you enjoy. When you are doing something that you enjoy, you are never working!

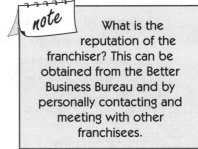

- **It is much easier to sell a well-known name franchise than an individual company.** With any business, ultimately you are going to probably want to sell it. Name recognition does count, and a premium is paid by the future buyer just as you paid a franchise fee.

- **There is a full support team of technical and managerial systems** to secure your success, along with the camaraderie of other franchisees who can be called upon for their advice with any problems that might come up. This is a tremendous support system which is not available to the individual small business owner.

- **A number of successful franchises do not require nor do they seek out previous experience in that particular industry.** They feel by not having preconceived ideas and habits, the franchise owner will more quickly learn and fit into the methods and philosophies of the franchiser.

> *note* What is the reputation of the franchiser? This can be obtained from the Better Business Bureau and by personally contacting and meeting with other franchisees.

Locating the "right" franchise

Some key areas in evaluating the different franchises are:

- How many years has a franchise been in business and how many units have been sold? How many have been taken back?

- Have the figures the franchise company shows for an average perspective franchise been certified based upon existing performances of other franchises?

◆ What kind of assistance will be provided to the franchisee? This includes the formal management training and continuing education seminars on upgrading management skills, promotion and financing assistance.

◆ What assistance will the franchiser provide in seeking a possible location? What information is there to document why a certain site fits into the success profile of the franchiser?

◆ How rigid is the company in allowing you, the franchisee, to make changes for your market, which might be different from other franchises?

One of the drawbacks of purchasing a franchise is that although you own the business you are subject to some very strict conveyance rules and regulations about how you actually operate the business. In the overall theory of franchising, this has many pluses, but for some individuals who are independent-minded and are looking to run the show, franchising might not be the most attractive means of going into business.

Patience is a virtue that carries a lot of wait.

The winning business plan

6

Chapter 6

The winning business plan

What you'll find in this chapter:

➡ Why you need a business plan

➡ How to write a winning business plan

➡ Making your business plan look great

➡ What key items you should cover in the plan

➡ The best way to present data in your plan

The meeting of preparation with opportunity generates the offspring called luck.

Anthony Robbins

A winning business plan means the difference between an accepted financing application and rejection. In this chapter, we'll uncover the secrets that turn a business plan into a "winner."

Love it or hate it, you need it

The business plan causes a love-it or hate-it reaction in most small business owners. For those who are preparing a business plan for the first time, it is an exercise that is unfamiliar, tedious and foreign to their natural skills and what they do on a daily basis. It can be a process looked upon with great hesitation.

On the other hand, there are those who look upon the business plan for what it is: a tremendous marketing tool to communicate to bankers, investors and others.

Professional managers, entrepreneurs and lenders are trained to analyze businesses by reviewing business plans. Verbal requests are forbidden. Investors prefer the written business plan because they want the supporting data that they need to make their decision in front of them in black-and-white. That doesn't mean you can't use the business plan to tell the world what is so great about your business. In fact, you can even brag about yourself by writing in the third person what would be offensive if you were using the word "I."

For example, if you were to say, "I was able to reduce the overhead by 10 percent and I was also able to increase sales by 15 percent," it would sound pretty arrogant. The same information presented in the third person seems much more impressive: "Overhead was reduced by 10 percent and sales increased by 15 percent through the efforts of John Jones. A new cost savings program that shares part of the savings with the employees has been the key to these improvements in the company."

E-Z TIP The business plan should be thought of as a bridge to the land of capital. Without the business plan, there is no way to cross over the challenges and obstacles between you and your business dreams.

Do it yourself

As a former banker, I'm a strong advocate of the owner or owners being involved in the preparation of the business plan. Hiring a ghostwriter who specializes in business plans is a waste of thousands of dollars and is a sure way of turning off investors and lenders.

The business plans prepared by professionals are beautiful documents to look at and read, no question. Unfortunately, they're usually written from the perspective of someone who has no financial risk at stake—and in most cases, no experience in your particular industry—trying to sell the investor or lender on an idea. If you aren't involved in the preparation of the plan, you could find yourself in the very embarrassing position of not being able to answer questions from the banker or investor about items the writer included in the plan to make the company look like something it's not.

note New business plan software has taken the "brain damage" out of preparing a professional-looking business plan in a relatively short period of time.

The good news is that inexpensive user-friendly software greatly facilitates the process of preparing a business plan. Two excellent programs— *Bizplan Builder* and Tim Berry's *Business Plan Tool Kit*—are question-driven and have templates for projecting profit and loss and cash flow statements. These templates contain the formulas and perform the mathematical calculations; all you do is plug in your projected numbers. It's that simple and takes the "brain damage" out of preparing a business plan in a relatively short period of time.

Plan on the worst, hope for the best.

Rules for winning business plans

There are certain rules that should be followed when preparing a business plan.

- **The initial appearance of the business plan is very important.** It should be typed on a typewriter or printed on a laser printer on white paper. Wrinkles, smudge marks and stains on any of the pages will reflect negatively on the business plan and your business.

- **The business plan should be well written and grammatically correct.** You don't have to be an English major to write the business plan, just have someone skilled in sentence structure review the plan for you. Even a local high school, college, graduate student or teacher can do this very reasonably.

- **Be realistic and positive in tone.** It is important not to lie or mislead the reader by using false data or false projections. Don't be afraid to discuss some of the negative aspects that you, the business owner, are facing. But do use the business plan as a sales tool by showing your contingency plans to deal with any adverse situations.

- **The business plan should be written at the level of the reader.** It is a major mistake to load the business plan with reams of technical jargon that distract the reader's attention. The reader is not so much interested in the technical

Don't tell investors how to make a watch. Tell them how the watch is going to make their lives better by giving them the time of day.

specs of your product as in the problems that will be solved by the product.

- **Don't write a thesis, just a business plan.** Another mistake is to oversell the company with a business plan that runs 40 to 60 pages. Can you imagine the first impression a lender or investor would have if you handed him or her a business plan that looked like the telephone directory of a small town? For most non-technical types of businesses, a good business plan can be written in 10 to 20 pages.

What the winning business plan needs

The following items should always be contained in the business plan to make it effective.

◆ **A separate cover letter.** This letter should be personally addressed to the recipient, by name, title, company (if any), address and current date. Putting the date on the business plan itself can be looked upon negatively if it isn't current. The reader wants to feel that the information is right off the press, not shopped around for a couple of months before it got to his or her desk.

The cover letter should also incorporate a summary of the loan request (see Chapter 3 for various types of loans and other details). It allows the reader to quickly review the overall request and help set the stage for how thoroughly they need to read the business plan. A loan request for $2 million will be read with greater scrutiny than a request for $50,000.

> *note* A one-page loan proposal can be a very effective tool in giving you the upper hand in negotiations with your banker or investor.

Although it may be uncomfortable to prepare a loan proposal, you must understand that you are giving the key elements that the investor or lender needs up front to make the lending decision.

Some of the items that should be included in a loan proposal are:

✦ **The important date the funds are needed.** It's helpful and impressive if you can give as much lead time as possible—weeks, preferably months—before you need the funds. This gives a positive impression of your managerial skills.

◆ **The sort of entity that will receive the funds.** Is the loan going to a corporation, partnership, or sole proprietorship? It is also helpful to add in this section that the owner or owners will also be guaranteeing the loan request. This demonstrates to the lender the borrower's confidence and willingness to stand behind the company in the request for these funds.

◆ **The amount of the loan request and the terms of repayment.** You should refer to a specific type of loan, whether it be short-term or long-term.

◆ **All collateral that is being offered.** This should include not only the collateral of the company in the form of accounts receivable, inventory and equipment, but also any personal assets, such as real estate, stocks and bonds, you are willing to pledge in order to secure the loan.

Do not be overly generous in offering personal assets unless the loan is weak and needs additional support. Let the lender or investor make that decision.

◆ **Table of Contents.** This is especially important to the reader under tremendous time constraints or who is interested in a particular section of the business plan. It allows the reader to go directly to that section, and it presents the business plan as being well organized.

◆ **Executive Summary.** This is usually a one- to two-page summary presented at the beginning of the business plan, but written at the very end of preparing the business plan itself. It contains highlights that will allow the reader to get a feel for the key elements covered in the remaining pages of the business plan.

◆ **Concept.** This should be very brief and tightly focused to address how the proposed business's products or services will save customers and clients time, money, energy and make their lives better and happier. What problems will it solve? How will it reduce the stress in people's lives? Some of the key elements that should be covered in the concept are:

  ✦ Who is the target market for the product or service of the business?

  ✦ What aspects of the product or service make it different from the competition?

  ✦ Are there patents filed or pending?

  ✦ What feature does your product or service have that the competition doesn't have? Match those features with the benefits provided and the problems that would be solved.

> *note* Emphasis should be placed upon previous successes in solving problems and turning around problem situations.

◆ **Company management and history.** For start-ups there will be no history to discuss in this section, but it will allow you to emphasize the background skills that management is bringing to the company A good example is if you were able to turn around your previous employer's manufacturing area in reducing costs by 10 percent and increasing productivity by 15 percent. Those are measurable accomplishments of turnaround situations that investors and lenders are looking for.

This section should also cover the personnel in management responsible for the three key areas: finance, marketing and human resources. Unfortunately in a start-up company or very small business, the owner is saddled with all three responsibilities.

It is imperative to demonstrate how you will be able to obtain help in those areas. Do you have an accountant, a human resource specialist, or a marketing expert you can call upon to obtain the necessary information and help for your business?

Another idea that is popular and cost-effective is to have an advisory board made up of key people that complement the strengths of management. In exchange for the cost of a lunch, you are able to tap into the experience of experts in finance, marketing, human resources and computers.

♦ **Description of the product or service.** This is probably one of the more challenging sections of the business plan to write, since the business owner seems to get carried away with how great the product or service is and goes into unnecessary detail. Lenders and investors want to know more about what makes this product or service sought after by the customer or client, and what makes it better than existing products or services on the market.

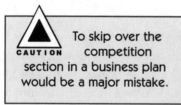

To skip over the competition section in a business plan would be a major mistake.

♦ **Competition.** This section of the business plan allows the reader to gain confidence in your knowledge of the market and how well you have researched and checked out the competition and the potential for change.

But, this is probably the section that most business owners hesitate including, because they lack the confidence of listing the names of their competitors, especially if the names are very familiar to the lender or investor. They are afraid the reader will ask, "Why would you be trying to compete with Wal-Mart or Kmart?"

Lenders and investors realize that there is competition out there. They want to know what you're going to do differently that will make you unique and perceived as being more desirable by the marketplace. They also want to know if you're aware of the strengths and weaknesses of the competition.

This is one section that most entrepreneurs want to leave out of the business plan. Why? They feel that the investor/banker will be "turned off" when they see in your business plan that you will be competing with the "Big Names," i.e., Wal-Mart, Pizza Hut, IBM, etc. Don't make the fatal mistake of leaving the competition out of your business plan.

This is an area where you can really make a company or idea stand out. It's a chance to turn lemons into lemonade. This is done very easily by constructing a grid at the beginning of the competition section. Set up the grid by putting the names of all of the competitors with your name at the top of the list on the left hand side of the grid. On the top horizontal section of the grid list some of the key features the marketplace is seeking: for example, 24-hour technical assistance, extended waranty options, user-friendly instructions, cost, financing, the availability of different models. This grid, when all the important features are graphically checked off, will make your company stand out from the competition as possessing most, if not all, of the qualities preferred by the marketplace.

♦ **Marketing plan.** Here is where you must document the benefits your customer gets from buying your product or service. It is important to be able to give statistics and cite studies that demonstrate the size of the market and any potential markets that can be looked upon for future expansion. In this section it must be made very clear why the market would want your product or service compared to others that is provided by your competitors.

note

Marketing to a target or niche is crucial to the success of any business venture, since very few products or services have universal appeal to all people

Some of the items that need to be covered in the marketing plan are:

note

✦ **A crystal clear description of the potential market.** The demographics must support and be described in terms of a typical customer or client, such as age, sex, education, income level, geographical location and any other factors that would help segment the market.

✦ **Advantages and benefits of your products.** Compare the cost of your competitor's product, the quality, the user-friendliness, and how users of your product will be able to save time or money, or in some cases both. You should also include testimonials of people who used your product or service that can further enhance its image.

✦ **Size of the market and its potential.** This is where you use data obtained from the library or local college as source documentation that lends credibility to the size of the

note

It is helpful to refer to a particular report that supports your ideas and include the full report in the Appendix.

marketplace. Also document what motivates the customer or clients through the use of outside resources and studies. This is also a good area to cite experts who project future trends and how these trends show that your market is growing and is expected to continue growing.

♦ **Plan of attack.** The investor or lender is very interested in the method you are going to use to sell your product and advertise to the ultimate target market you described earlier. The reader is looking for a detailed description of the process, for example, of going from manufacturing and distribution to the ultimate sales market. The type and medium of advertising and promotion to be used to reach the target market will be scrutinized closely to make sure that the business owner is using the rifle approach, rather than a shotgun approach. For

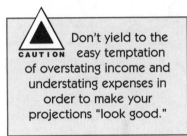

Don't yield to the easy temptation of overstating income and understating expenses in order to make your projections "look good."

example, if you have described the target market as 35-50 years old, female, college educated, with one or two children, living in the suburbs, the investor or lender would probably question your advertising program if you're placing ads in such magazines as *Guns and Ammo.*

♦ **Financial data.** This includes the previous year's financial statements. if available, or for start-ups, projections. The financial projections should include a projected balance sheet for the next two years and profit and loss and cash flow statements for the next two years.

The first year needs to be done month by month to show any seasonal or other changes that the company anticipates. The second year can be done on a quarterly basis, since the lender and investor will have less confidence in what will happen in Year 2 and beyond.

For an existing business, the projections will be used in conjunction with the previous year's performance to create a credible forecast.

It has often been said that lenders and investors are never presented with bad projections. All projections are looked upon as being optimistic, aggressive, and in some cases, unrealistic. There are several ways to overcome this built-in cynicism and prejudice. You can use the *Robert Morris Association ratio analysis* which gives key percentages and ratios for different business classifications. This is the textbook used by bankers and lenders in their own analysis; it is looked upon favorably if these numbers have already been incorporated into your projections. You can find the Robert Morris Association ratios at your local library.

If you provide only one set of projections, the reader might discount the figures so greatly it would make the numbers unacceptable for granting the loan.

Since the investors and lenders are looking at projections with a skeptical eye, the small business owner should prepare two sets of projections: one based upon what you hope the company will do with regards to sales and profits, and a second that is more tempered and conservative. With two sets of projections, the reader will come up with a compromise between the two that will be the real figures used in the final analysis.

A very important aspect of projections is the key assumptions upon which you are basing your numbers: for example, sales, cost of goods sold, salaries, overhead. The assumptions need to provide details on how you're figuring on a 30 percent increase in sales for Year 2, or why salaries went down 12 percent when sales have increased 20 percent.

♦ **Appendix.** The last section of the business plan should be put under a separate cover and not included with the plan itself. The Appendix is an area where you will include the resumes of the owner and key management people. The resumes should have such information as employment background, education, experience, skills, any special awards and areas of expertise.

If the business is established, a brief history should be included to give the reader an idea of how and when the business started, and any major changes that took place in the direction or operation of the business since its inception and why those changes were necessary.

> *note* The Appendix can be very bulky. It is really supplementary reading to the main ideas contained in the business plan, which is why it should be under separate cover.

You will also include in the Appendix studies and articles written about the industry supporting some of the conclusions in the marketing plan. You will also want to include collateral information about the technical aspects of the product, along with pictures and diagrams.

Get feedback on your plan

It is strongly advised after you have completed the business plan package that you submit it to several professionals with experience in reading and analyzing business plans. Listen to what they have to say and be prepared to make changes if they have suggestions to strengthen your presentation.

You can also get advice, for free, through the Small Business Development Corporation Center. See the Resource Guide in the back of this book for the location of the SBDC office nearest you, or call 800-689-1912.

Often people attempt to live their lives backwards; they try to have more things, or more money, in order to do more of what they want so that they will be happier. The way it actually works is the reverse. You must be who you really are, then, do what you need to do, in order to have what you want.

Margaret Young

Resources

●●● Online Resources ●●●

◆ **AltaVista Small Business**

   http://altavista.looksmart.com/eus1/eus65300

   *   /eus65319/r?l&izf&*

◆ **AOL.COM Business & Careers**

   http://www.aol.com/webcenters/workplace/home.adp

◆ **Association of Small Business Development Centers**

   http://www.asbdc-us.org

◆ **Council of Better Business Bureaus, Inc.**

   http://www.bbb.org

◆ **Education Index, Business Resources**
   http://www.educationindex.com/bus

◆ **Electric Library(r) Business Edition**
   http://www.business.elibrary.com

◆ **Institutional Investor Magazine**
   http://www.iimagazine.com

◆ **International Finance & Commodities Institute**
   http://finance.wat.ch/IFCI

◆ **LNET-LLC-The Limited Liability Companies and Partnerships Conference**
   http://www.stcl.edu/lnet-llc/lnet-llc.html

◆ **Limited Liability Company Website**
   http://www.llcweb.com

◆ **Minority Business Development Agency—U.S. Department of Commerce**
   http://www.mbda.gov

◆ **National Association of Women Business Owners (NAWBO)**
   http://www.nawbo.org/nawbo/nawbostart.nsf

◆ **National Small Business Development Center (SBDC) Research Network**

   http://www.smallbiz.suny.edu

◆ **Sheshunoff Information Services, Inc.**

   http://www.sheshunoff.com

◆ **U.S. Small Business Administration**

   http://www.sbaonline.sba.gov/starting

◆ **SBA-Office of Women's Business Ownership**

   http://www.sbaonline.sba.gov/womeninbusiness /index.html

◆ **Small Business Primer**

   http://www.ces.ncsu.edu/depts/fcs/business /welcome.html

◆ **U.S. Business Advisor**

   http://www.business.gov

◆ **Small Business Innovation Research (SBIR) Program**

   http://www.sba.gov/expanding/sbir.html

◆ **Wall Street Journal**

   http://advertising.wsj.com/mspubs/rep/p212.html

••• Related Sites •••

◆ **BizMove.com**
   http://www.bizmove.com

◆ **Biztalk.com Small Business Community**
   http://www.biztalk.com

◆ **Bplans.com!**
   http://www.bplans.com

◆ **BusinessTown.Com**
   http://www.businesstown.com

◆ **Council of Better Business Bureaus, Inc.**
   http://www.bbb.org

◆ **Education Index, Business Resources**
   http://www.educationindex.com/bus

◆ **Electric Library Business Edition**
   http://www.business.elibrary.com

◆ **Federal Trade Commission-Franchise and Business Opportunities**
   http://www.ftc.gov/bcp/menu-fran.htm

- **HotBot Directory/Small Business**

  http://directory.hotbot.com/Business/Small_Business

- **Inc. Online**

  http://www.inc.com

- **Infoseek: Small Business**

  http://infoseek.go.com/Center/Business/Small_business

- **Internal Revenue Service**

  http://www.irs.ustreas.gov/prod/cover.html

- **International Finance & Commodities Institute**

  http://finance.wat.ch/IFCI

- **Lycos Directory: Small Business**

  http://dir.lycos.com/Business/Small_Business

- **Netscape Women in Business**

  http://women.netscape.com/smallbusiness

- **National Foundation for Women Business Owners (NFWBO)**

  http://www.nfwbo.org

◆ **National Small Business Development Center (SBDC) Research Network**

   URL: http://www.smallbiz.suny.edu

◆ **National Small Business Network Resource Directory**

   http://businessknowhow.net/Directory/bkhDindex.asp

◆ **National Small Business United**

   http://www.nsbu.org

◆ **North American Securities Administrators Association (NASAA)**

   http://www.nasaa.org

◆ **North American Securities Administrators Association (NASAA)—Help For Small Business**

   http://www.nasaa.org/helpsmallbusiness

◆ **Service Core of Retired Executives**

   http://www.score.org

◆ **Small Business Advisor**

   http://www.isquare.com

◆ **Small Business Primer**

   URL: http://www.ces.ncsu.edu/depts/fcs/business/welcome.html

◆ **Small Business Resource**

  http://www.irl.co.uk/sbr

◆ **Small Business Taxes & Management**

  http://www.smbiz.com

◆ **Smalloffice.com**

  http://www.smalloffice.com

◆ **Tax and Accounting Sites Directory**

  http://www.taxsites.com

◆ **U.S. Business Advisor**

  URL: http://www.business.gov

◆ **U.S. Government Printing Office-Small Business**

  http://www.access.gpo.gov/su_docs/sale/sb-307.html

◆ **U.S. Small Business Administration**

  URL: http://www.sbaonline.sba.gov

◆ **U.S. Treasury Department-Business Services**

  http://www.ustreas.gov/busserv.html

◆ **Webcrawler: Small Business**

  http://quicken.webcrawler.com/small_business

◆ **Yahoo! Business and Economy: Marketing**

http://dir.yahoo.com/Business_and_Economy/Marketing

◆ **Yahoo! Small Business**

http://smallbusiness.yahoo.com

··· Legal Search Engines ···

◆ **All Law**

http://www.alllaw.com

◆ **American Law Sources On Line**

http://www.lawsource.com/also/searchfm.htm

◆ **Catalaw**

http://www.catalaw.com

◆ **FindLaw**

URL: http://www.findlaw.com

◆ **Hieros Gamos**

http://www.hg.org/hg.html

◆ **InternetOracle**

http://www.internetoracle.com/legal.htm

◆ **LawAid**

http://www.lawaid.com/search.html

◆ **LawCrawler**

http://www.lawcrawler.com

◆ **LawEngine, The**

   http://www.fastsearch.com/law

◆ **LawRunner**

   http://www.lawrunner.com

◆ **'Lectric Law Library**™

   http://www.lectlaw.com

◆ **Legal Search Engines**

   http://www.dreamscape.com/frankvad/search.legal.html

◆ **LEXIS/NEXIS Communications Center**

   http://www.lexis-nexis.com/lncc/general/search.html

◆ **Meta-Index for U.S. Legal Research**

   http://gsulaw.gsu.edu/metaindex

◆ **Seamless Website, The**

   http://seamless.com

◆ **USALaw**

   http://www.usalaw.com/linksrch.cfm

◆ **WestLaw**

   http://westdoc.com (Registered users only. Fee paid service.)

••• State Bar Associations •••

ALABAMA

Alabama State Bar
415 Dexter Avenue
Montgomery, AL 36104
mailing address:
PO Box 671
Montgomery, AL 36101
(334) 269-1515
http://www.alabar.org

ALASKA

Alaska Bar Association
510 L Street No. 602
Anchorage, AK 99501
mailing address:
PO Box 100279
Anchorage, AK 99510
http://www.alaskabar.org

ARIZONA

State Bar of Arizona
111 West Monroe
Phoenix, AZ 85003-1742
(602) 252-4804
http://www.azbar.org

ARKANSAS

Arkansas Bar Association
400 West Markham
Little Rock, AR 72201
(501) 375-4605
http://www.arkbar.org

CALIFORNIA

State Bar of California
555 Franklin Street
San Francisco, CA 94102
(415) 561-8200
http://www.calbar.org
Alameda County Bar
Association
http://www.acbanet.org

COLORADO

Colorado Bar Association
No. 950, 1900 Grant Street
Denver, CO 80203
(303) 860-1115
http://www.cobar.org

CONNECTICUT

Connecticut Bar Association
101 Corporate Place
Rocky Hill, CT 06067-1894
(203) 721-0025
http://www.ctbar.org

DELAWARE

Delaware State Bar Association
1225 King Street, 10th floor
Wilmington, DE 19801
(302) 658-5279
(302) 658-5278 (lawyer referral
service)
http://www.dsba.org

DISTRICT OF COLUMBIA

District of Columbia Bar
1250 H Street, NW, 6th Floor
Washington, DC 20005
(202) 737-4700

Bar Association of the District
of Columbia
1819 H Street, NW, 12th floor
Washington, DC 20006-3690
(202) 223-6600
http://www.badc.org

FLORIDA

The Florida Bar
The Florida Bar Center
650 Apalachee Parkway
Tallahassee, FL 32399-2300
(850) 561-5600
http://www.flabar.org

GEORGIA

State Bar of Georgia
800 The Hurt Building
50 Hurt Plaza
Atlanta, GA 30303
(404) 527-8700
http://www.gabar.org

HAWAII

Hawaii State Bar Association
1136 Union Mall
Penthouse 1
Honolulu, HI 96813
(808) 537-1868
http://www.hsba.org

IDAHO

Idaho State Bar
PO Box 895
Boise, ID 83701
(208) 334-4500
http://www2.state.id.us/isb

ILLINOIS

Illinois State Bar Association
424 South Second Street
Springfield, IL 62701
(217) 525-1760
http://www.illinoisbar.org

INDIANA

Indiana State Bar Association
230 East Ohio Street
Indianapolis, IN 46204
(317) 639-5465
http://www.ai.org/isba

IOWA

Iowa State Bar Association
521 East Locust
Des Moines, IA 50309
(515) 243-3179
http://www.iowabar.org

KANSAS

Kansas Bar Association
1200 Harrison Street
Topeka, KS 66612-1806
(785) 234-5696
http://www.ksbar.org

KENTUCKY

Kentucky Bar Association
514 West Main Street
Frankfort, KY 40601-1883
(502) 564-3795
http://www.kybar.org

LOUISIANA

Louisiana State Bar Association
601 St. Charles Avenue
New Orleans, LA 70130
(504) 566-1600
http://www.lsba.org

MAINE

Maine State Bar Association
124 State Street
PO Box 788
Augusta, ME 04330
(207) 622-7523
http://www.mainebar.org

MARYLAND

Maryland State Bar Association
520 West Fayette Street
Baltimore, MD 21201
(301) 685-7878
http://www.msba.org/msba

MASSACHUSETTS

Massachusetts Bar Association
20 West Street
Boston, MA 02111
(617) 542-3602
(617) 542-9103 (lawyer referral
service)
http://www.massbar.org

MICHIGAN

State Bar of Michigan
306 Townsend Street
Lansing, MI 48933-2083
(517) 372-9030
http://www.michbar.org

MINNESOTA

Minnesota State Bar Association
514 Nicollet Mall
Minneapolis, MN 55402
(612) 333-1183
http://www.mnbar.org

MISSISSIPPI

The Mississippi Bar
643 No. State Street
Jackson, Mississippi 39202
(601) 948-4471
http://www.msbar.org

MISSOURI

The Missouri Bar
P.O. Box 119, 326 Monroe
Jefferson City, Missouri 65102
(314) 635-4128
http://www.mobar.org

MONTANA

State Bar of Montana
46 North Main
PO Box 577
Helena, MT 59624
(406) 442-7660
http://www.montanabar.org

NEBRASKA

Nebraska State Bar Association
635 South 14th Street, 2nd floor
Lincoln, NE 68508
(402) 475-7091
http://www.nebar.com

NEVADA

State Bar of Nevada
201 Las Vegas Blvd.
Las Vegas, NV 89101
(702) 382-2200
http://www.nvbar.org

NEW HAMPSHIRE

New Hampshire Bar
Association
112 Pleasant Street
Concord, NH 03301
(603) 224-6942
http://www.nhbar.org

NEW JERSEY

New Jersey State Bar
Association
One Constitution Square
New Brunswick, NJ 08901-1500
(908) 249-5000

NEW MEXICO

State Bar of New Mexico
5121 Masthead N.E.
Albuquerque, NM 87125
mailing address:
PO Box 25883
Albuquerque, NM 87125
(505) 843-6132
http://www.nmbar.org

NEW YORK

New York State Bar Association
One Elk Street
Albany, NY 12207
(518) 463-3200
http://www.nysba.org

NORTH CAROLINA

North Carolina State Bar
208 Fayetteville Street Mall
Raleigh, NC 27601
mailing address:
PO Box 25908
Raleigh, NC 27611
(919) 828-4620
North Carolina Bar Association
1312 Annapolis Drive
Raleigh, NC 27608
mailing address:
PO Box 3688
Cary, NC 27519-3688
(919) 677-0561
http://www.ncbar.org

NORTH DAKOTA

State Bar Association of North
Dakota
515 1/2 East Broadway, suite 101
Bismarck, ND 58501
mailing address:
PO Box 2136
Bismarck, ND 58502
(701) 255-1404

OHIO

Ohio State Bar Association
1700 Lake Shore Drive
Columbus, OH 43204
mailing address:
PO Box 16562
Columbus, OH 43216-6562
(614) 487-2050
http://www.ohiobar.org

OKLAHOMA

Oklahoma Bar Association
1901 North Lincoln
Oklahoma City, OK 73105
(405) 524-2365
http://www.okbar.org

OREGON

Oregon State Bar
5200 S.W. Meadows Road
PO Box 1689
Lake Oswego, OR 97035-0889
(503) 620-0222
http://www.osbar.org

PENNSYLVANIA

Pennsylvania Bar Association
100 South Street
PO Box 186
Harrisburg, PA 17108
(717) 238-6715
http://www.pabar.org

Pennsylvania Bar Institute
http://www.pbi.org

PUERTO RICO

Puerto Rico Bar Association
PO Box 1900
San Juan, Puerto Rico 00903
(787) 721-3358

RHODE ISLAND

Rhode Island Bar Association
115 Cedar Street
Providence, RI 02903
(401) 421-5740
http://www.ribar.org

SOUTH CAROLINA

South Carolina Bar
950 Taylor Street
PO Box 608
Columbia, SC 29202
(803) 799-6653
http://www.scbar.org

SOUTH DAKOTA

State Bar of South Dakota
222 East Capitol
Pierre, SD 57501
(605) 224-7554
http://www.sdbar.org

TENNESSEE

Tennessee Bar Assn
3622 West End Avenue
Nashville, TN 37205
(615) 383-7421
http://www.tba.org

TEXAS

State Bar of Texas
1414 Colorado
PO Box 12487
Austin, TX 78711
(512) 463-1463
http://www.texasbar.com/start.htm

UTAH

Utah State Bar
645 South 200 East, Suite 310
Salt Lake City, UT 84111
(801) 531-9077
http://www.utahbar.org

VERMONT

Vermont Bar Association
PO Box 100
Montpelier, VT 05601
(802) 223-2020
http://www.vtbar.org

VIRGINIA

Virginia State Bar
707 East Main Street, suite 1500
Richmond, VA 23219-0501
(804) 775-0500

Virginia Bar Association
701 East Franklin St., Suite 1120
Richmond, VA 23219
(804) 644-0041
http://www.vbar.org

VIRGIN ISLANDS

Virgin Islands Bar Association
P.O. Box 4108
Christiansted, Virgin Islands
00822
(340) 778-7497

WASHINGTON

Washington State Bar
Association
500 Westin Street
2001 Sixth Avenue
Seattle, WA 98121-2599
(206) 727-8200
http://www.wsba.org

WEST VIRGINIA

West Virginia State Bar
2006 Kanawha Blvd. East
Charleston, WV 25311
(304) 558-2456
http://www.wvbar.org

West Virginia Bar Association
904 Security Building
100 Capitol Street
Charleston, WV 25301
(304) 342-1474

WISCONSIN

State Bar of Wisconsin
402 West Wilson Street
Madison, WI 53703
(608) 257-3838
http://www.wisbar.org/home.htm

WYOMING

Wyoming State Bar
500 Randall Avenue
Cheyenne, WY 82001
PO Box 109
Cheyenne, WY 82003
(307) 632-9061
http://www.wyomingbar.org

Appendix

Financial Resource Guide

ALABAMA	
Statewide Financing Information and Resources:	www.state.al.us

Alabama Development Office   (800) 248-0033
401 Adams Ave., Montgomery, AL 36130-4106

Economic Development
- Alabama Small Business Development   (205) 934-7260

Financial Assistance
- Economic Development Administration   (334) 223-7008
- Rural Development Administration   (334) 242-0400
- The TVA Economic Loan Fund   (800) 248-0033
- Revolving Loan Fund   (334) 652-3665

Minority/Women
- Office of Minority Business Enterprise   (334) 242-2220
- Appalachian Regional Grants   (334) 242-0400

Business Council of Alabama   (334) 834-6000
2 North Jackson Street, P.O. Box 76, Montgomery, AL 36101

SBA District Office   (205) 731-1344
2121 Eighth Ave, North, Suite 200, Birmingham, AL 35203-2398

Alabama Small Business Development Centers
University of Alabama at Birmingham   (205) 934-7260
1717 11th Ave., South, Suite 419, Birmingham, AL 35294

Auburn	(334) 844-4220	Mobile	(334) 460-6004
Birmingham (U. of AL.)	(205) 934-7260	Montgomery	(334) 229-4138
Florence	(205) 760-4624	Troy	(334) 670-3771
Huntsville	(205) 535-2061	Tuscaloosa	(205) 348-7011
Jacksonville	(205) 782-5271	(U. of AL)	
Livingston	(334) 652-3665		

Alabama Small Business Investment Companies
Birmingham-Alabama Small Business Investment Co.   (205) 324-5231
Birmingham-Javelin Capital   (205) 943-6662
Huntsville-Hickory Venture Capital Corporation   (205) 539-1931
Huntsville-FJC Growth Capital Corporation   (205) 922-2918
Mobile-Alabama Capital Corporation   (334) 476-0700
Mobile-First SBIC Alabama   (334) 476-0700

Alabama Certified Development Companies
Birmingham-Birmingham Citywide Local Devel. Corp.   (205) 254-2799
Mobile-Greater Mobile Development Corporation   (334) 434-7591
Montgomery-Southern Development Council   (334) 244-1801
Mountain Brook-Alabama Community Development Corp.   (205) 870-3360

Micro Loans
Wetumpka-Elmore Community Action   (334) 567-4361

ALASKA

Statewide Financing Information and Resources: www.state.ak.us

Department of Commerce and Economic Development   (907) 465-2510
State Office Building, Ninth Floor   (800) 478-LOAN
333 Willoughby Ave., P.O. Box 110800
Juneau, AK 99811-0800

Economic Development
• Division of Trade and Development
  Business Development Information Network   (907) 465-3961
• Economic Development, Fairbanks
  Native Association, Inc.   (907) 452-1648
Financial Assistance
• Division of Trade and Development   (907) 465-2017

- Division of Investments   (907) 465-2510
  Commercial Fishing Loan Program
  Small Business Economics Development Revolving Loan Fund
- Alaska Industrial Development   (907) 269-3000
  Loan Participation Program
  Development Finance Program
- Small Business Economic Development
  Revolving Loan Fund   (800) 478-LOAN

Minority/Women
- Alaska Business Development Center   (800) 478-3474
- Minority Business Development Center   (907) 274-5400

Rural Development
- Division of Community and Rural Development
  Rural Development Assistance   (907) 465-5539

Alaska State Chamber of Commerce   (907) 586-2323
217 Second Street, Suite 201, Juneau, AK 99801

SBA District Office   (907) 271-4022
222 W. Eighth Ave., Rm. A-36, P.O. Box 67, Ankorage, AK 99513-7559

Alaska Small Business Development Centers
University of Alaska at Anchorage   (907) 274-7232
430 West Seventh Avenue, Suite 110, Anchorage, AK 99501

Fairbanks	(907) 474-6400	Kenai	(907) 283-3335
Fairbanks	(907) 456-1701	Wasilla	(907) 373-7232
Juneau	(907) 463-3789		

Micro Loans
Juneau-Southeast Alaska Small Business Development Center   (907) 463-3789

ARIZONA

Statewide Financing Information and Resources: www.state.az.us

Business Development Finance Corporation   (520) 722-5626
186 East Broadway Boulevard, Tucson, AX 85701

Economic Development
- Arizona Department of Commerce   (520) 628-6850
- Arizona Small Business Development Center Network   (602) 731-8720

- Arizona Business Connection   (520) 628-6690
- Commerce and Economic Development Commission   (602) 280-1341
- Business Hotline   (520) 791-2519

Financial Assistance
- Business Development Finance Corporation   (800) 264-3377
- Small Business Financing Programs   (602) 280-1341
- Minority - Women   (800) 542-5684

Arizona Chamber of Commerce   (602) 248-9172
1221 East Osborn Road, Suite 100, Phoenix, AZ 85014

SBA District Office
2828 North Central Avenue, Suite 800, Phoenix, AZ 85004-1093

Arizona SBDC Network   (602) 731-8720
2411 West 14th Street, Room 132, Tempe, AZ 85281

Coolidge	(520) 426-4341	Prescott	(520) 757-0894
Flagstaff	(520) 526-5072	Show Low	(800) 266-7232
Holbrook	(520) 537-2976	Kingman	(520) 757-0894
Sierra Vista	(520) 515-5478	Nogales	(520) 287-2569
Thatcher	(520) 428-8590	Payson	(520) 474-8821
Tucson	(520) 748-4906	Phoenix	(602) 392-5223
Yuma	(520) 341-1650		

Arizona Small Business Investment Companies
Phoenix - Sundance Venture Partners, LP   (602) 252-5373
Tucson - First Commerce & Loan, LP   (602) 298-2500

Arizona Certified Development Companies
Phoenix - Southwest Business Finance Corporation   (602) 495-6495
Tucson - Business Development Finance Corporation   (602) 623-3377

Micro Loans
Phoenix - Chicanos Por La Causa   (602) 257-0700
Tucson - PPEP Housing Development   (602) 622-3553
(Greater Maricopa County)

ARKANSAS

Statewide Financing Information and Resources: www.state.ar.us

Arkansas Industrial Development Commission   (501) 682-1121
One State Capitol Mall, Little Rock, AR 72201

Economic Development
- Advocacy   (501) 682-7325
- Corporate Extension Service   (501) 671-2000
- The Arkansas Science and Technology Authority   (501) 324-9006
- General Business Assistance (SCORE)   (501) 324-5893
- Genesis Technology Business Incubator   (501) 575-7227
- Industrial Development   (501) 682-7675
- Small Business Programs   (501) 682-7782

Financial Assistance
- Arkansas Capital Corporation   (501) 374-9247
- Bond Guaranty Program   (501) 682-7682

Minority/Women
- Minority Business Development Program   (501) 682-1060

Arkansas State Chamber of Commerce   (501) 374-9225
410 Cross Street, P.O. Box 3645, Little Rock, AR 77203

SBA District   (501) 324-5871
2120 Riverfront Dr., Suite 100, Little Rock, AR 72202-1747

Arkansas Small Business Development Centers
University of Arkansas at Little Rock   (501) 324-9043
100 South Main Street, Suite 401, Little Rock, AR 72201

Arkadelphia	(501) 230-5224	West Memphis	(501) 733-6767
Fayetteville	(501) 575-5148	Magnolia	(501) 234-4030
Fort Smith	(501) 785-1376	Pine Bluff	(501) 536-0654
Harrison	(501) 741-8009	St. University	(501) 972-3517
Hot Springs	(501) 624-5448	Stuttgart	(501) 673-8707

Arkansas Small Business Investment Company
Little Rock-Small Business Investment Capital, Inc.   (501) 455-6599

Arkansas Certified Development Companies
Batsville-White River Planning & Development District, Inc.   (501) 793-5233
Fort Smith-Western Arkansas Planning & Devel. District, Inc.   (501) 785-2651
Harrison-Northwest Arkansas Development Company   (501) 741-8009
Hot Springs-W. Central Ark. Planning & Devel. District, Inc.   (501) 624-1036
Jonesboro-East Arkansas Planning & Development District   (501) 932-3957
Little Rock-Arkansas Certified Development Corporation   (501) 374-9247
Magnolia-Southwest Arkansas Regional Development Corp.   (501) 234-4039

Micro Loans
Arkadelphia-Arkansas Enterprises Group   (501) 246-9739
Forest City-Delta Community Development   (501) 633-9113
Batesville-White River Development   (501) 793-5233

CALIFORNIA	

Statewide Financing Information and Resources:	www.state.ca.us

California Office of Small Business   (916) 324-1295
California Trade and Commerce Agency
801 K Street, Suite 1700, Sacramento, CA 95814

Economic Development
- Small Business Development Center   (916) 324-5068
- Office of Business Development   (916) 322-3520
- Office of Economic Research   (916) 324-5853
- Office of Small Business   (916) 324-1295
- Small Business Helpline   (916) 327-4257

Financial Assistance
- Small Business Loan Guarantee Program   (916) 324-1295

International Trade
- California Office of Export Finance   (714) 562-5519

Minority/Women
- Office of Small and Minority Business   (916) 322-5060

California Chamber of Commerce   (916) 444-6670
1201 K Street, 12th Floor, P.O. Box 1736, Sacramento, CA 95812-1736

SBA District Offices - Fresno   (209)-487-5789
2719 North Air Fresno Drive, Suite 107, Fresno, CA 93727-1547
Glendale   (818) 552-3210
    330 North Brand Blvd., Suite 1200, Glendale, CA 91203-2304
Sacramento   (916) 498-6410
    660 J Street, Suite 215, Sacramento, CA 95814-2413
Santa Ana   (714) 550-5440
    200 West Santa Ana Blvd., Suite 700, Santa Ana, CA 92701
San Diego   (619) 557-5440
    550 West C Street, Suite 550, San Diego, CA 92101
San Francisco   (415) 744-6820
    211 Main Street, Fourth Floor, San Francisco, CA 94105-1988

California Small Business Development Centers
California Trade and Commerce Agency   (916) 324-5068
801 K Street, Suite 1700, Sacramento, CA 95814-3520

Aptos	(408) 479-6136	Napa	(707) 253-3210
Auburn	(916) 885-5488	Oakland	(510) 893-4114
Bakersfield	(805) 322-5881	Chico	(916) 895-9017
Palm Springs	(619) 864-1311	Chula Vista	(916) 482-6391
Clearlake	(707) 995-3440	Pomona	(909) 629-2247
Concord	(510) 646-5377	Crescent City	(707) 464-2168
Riverside	(909) 781-2345	El Centro	(619) 312-9800
Eureka	(707) 446-9720	Sacramento	(916) 563-3210
Fairfield	(707) 864-3382	Fresno	(209) 275-1223
Santa Ana	(714) 647-1172	Gilroy	(408) 847-0373
Santa Monica	(310) 398-8883	Irvine	(714) 509-2990
Santa Rosa	(707) 524-1770	La Jolla	(619) 453-9388
Stockton	(209) 474-5089	Los Angeles	(213) 846-1710
Torrance	(310) 787-6466	Markleville	(916) 694-2475
Merced	(209) 725-3800	Visalia	(209) 625-3051
Modesto	(209) 521-6177	San Francisco	(415) 561-1890

California Small Business Investment Companies

Alhambra-Calsafe Capital Corporation	(818) 289-3400
Beverly Hills-Ally Finance Corporation	(310) 550-8100
Cupertino-Novus Ventures, LP	(408) 252-3900
Cupertino-Sundance Venture Partners, LP	(408) 257-8100
Foundation Valley-First American Capital Funding, Inc.	(714) 965-7190
Fremont-Opportunity Capital Corporation	(510) 795-7000
Fremont-Opportunity Capital Partners II, L.P.	(510) 795-7000
Fresno-San Joaquin Investment Group, Inc.	(209) 233-3580
Glendale-Magna Pacific Investments (818) 547-0809	
Hayward-Asian American Capital Corporation	(510) 887-6888
Inglewood-Imperial Ventures, Inc.	(310) 417-5600
Laguna Hills-Hall Capital Management	(714) 707-5096
Los Altos-Aspen Venture West II, LP (415) 917-5670	
Los Altos-VI Capital, LP	(415) 949-9862
Los Angeles-Best Finance	(213) 937-1636
Los Angeles-Charterway Investment Corporation	(213) 689-9107
Los Angels-Union Venture Corporation	(213) 236-4092
Newport Beach-Marwit Capital Corporation	(714) 640-6234
Redwood City-Draper Fisher Associates, LP	(415) 599-9000
San Diego-Sorrento Growth Partners I, LP	(619) 452-3100
San Francisco-Bentley Capital	(415) 362-2868
San Francisco-Jupiter Partners	(415) 421-9990
San Francisco-Positive Enterprises, Inc.	(415) 885-6600
San Francisco-VK Capital Company	(415) 391-5600
Sherman Oaks-Western General Capital Corporation	(818) 986-5038

California Certified Development Companies

Arcata-Arcata Economic Development Corporation	(707) 822-4616
Arvin-Arvin Development Corporation	(805) 861-2041
Bakersfield-Mid State Development Corporation	(805) 322-4241
Citrus Heights-Econ. Devel. Foundation of Sacramento, Inc.	(916) 962-3669
Davis-California Statewide Certified Development	(916) 756-9310
Fresno-Fresno Certified Development Corporation	(209) 485-5735
Jackson-Amador Economic Development Corporation	(209) 223-0351
La Habra-La Habra Local Development Company, Inc.	(310) 690-6400
Lompoc-Central Coast Development Corporation	(805) 736-1445
Long Beach-Long Beach Area Certified Development Corp.	(310) 983-7450
Modesto-Stanislaus County Economic development Corp.	(209) 521-9333
Monterey Park-Business Finance Center	(213) 890-7049
Ontario-Enterprise Funding Corporation	(909) 981-2744
Pittsburgh-Los Medanos Fund, A Local Devel. Company	(510) 439-1056
Redding-\economic Development Corp. of Shasta County	(916) 225-5300
Sacramento-Greater Sacramento Certified Devel. Corp.	(916) 339-1096
San Diego-CD Small Business Finance Corporation	(619) 291-3594
San Francisco-Bay Area Business Development Company	(415) 541-0694
Santa Ana-Santa Ana Economic Development Corporation	(714) 647-1143
Stockton-Tracy/San Joaquin County CDC	(209) 468-2266
Tulare-Tulare County Economic Development Corporation	(209) 688-6666
Walnut Creek-Bay Area Employment Development	(510) 926-1020

COLORADO

Statewide Financing Information and Resources:	www.state.co.us
Office of Business Development	(303) 892-3840
1625 Broadway, Suite 1710, Denver, CO 80202	

Economic Development
• Office of Business Development	(303) 892-3840
• Colorado FIRST Customized Training Program	(303) 892-3840
• Business Assistance	(303) 592-5920

Financial Assistance
• Colorado Housing And Fiance Authority	(303) 297-2432
• Office of Business Development Finance Division	(303) 892-3840

Minority/Women
• Minority Business Office	(303) 892-3840
• Women's Business Office	(303) 892-3840
• MiCasa Resource Center	(303) 573-1302

Colorado Association of Commerce & Industry			(303) 831-7411
1776 Lincoln Street, Suite 1200, Denver, CO 80203			

SBA District Office (303) 844-3984
721 19th Street, Suite 426, Denver, CO80202-2599

Colorado Small Business Development Centers
Office of Business Development (303) 892-3809
Colorado Small Business Development Center
1625 Broadway, Suite 1710, Denver, CO 80202

Alamosa	(719) 589-7372		
Glenwood Springs	(800) 621-1647	Aurora	(303) 341-4849
Grand Junction	(970) 243-5242	Boulder	(303) 442-1475
Greeley (CoC)	(970) 352-3661		
Colorado Springs	(719) 592-1894	Lakewood	(303) 987-0710
Craig	(970) 824-7078	Lamar	(719) 336-8141
Delta	(970) 874-8772		
Littleton (CoC)	(303) 795-0142	Denver (CC)	(303) 620-8076
Pueblo	(719) 549-3224	Durango	(970) 247-7009
Stratton	(719) 348-5596	Fort Collins	(970) 226-0881
Trinidad	(719) 846-5645	Fort Morgan	(970) 267-3351
Westminster	(303) 460-1032		

Colorado Small Business Investment Company
Denver-Hanifen Imhoff Mezzanine Fund, LP (303) 291-5209

Colorado Certified Development Companies
Denver-Denver Urban Economic Development Corporation (303) 296-5570
Denver-Small Business Finance Corporation (303) 893-8989
Denver-Front Range Regional Economic Development (303) 657-0010
Colorado Spring-Pikes Peak Regional
Development Corporation (719) 471-2044
Pueblo-CEDD Development Company (719) 545-8680

Micro Loans
Denver-Denver Capital Corp. (303) 534-6161
Denver-Greater Denver Local Development Corp. (303) 860-0242

CONNECTICUT

Statewide Financing Information and Resources: www.state.ct.us

Office of Small Business Services (860) 258-4200

Department of Economic and Community Development
865 Brook Street, Rocky Hill, CT 06067-34056

Economic Development
- One-Stop Business Registry   (800) 392-2122
- Connecticut Innovations   (800) 392-2122
  -R&D, technology transfer, manufacturing applications
- Office of Business Ombudsman   (860) 258-4200
- Connecticut State Technology Extension Program   (800) 392-2122

Financial Assistance
- Connecticut Development Authority   (800) 392-2122
- Manufacturing Assistance   (800) 392-2122
  -tax credits, loan guarantees, investment and direct loans
- Connecticut Works Fund   (800) 392-2122
- Connecticut Works Funds   (800) 392-2122
  -loan guarantees, direct loans
- Connecticut Innovations, Inc.   (800) 392-2122
  -early state financing for high-tech companies

Minority/Women
- Urban lending   (800) 392-2122
  -targeted to women and minorities in distressed cities

Connecticut Business & Industry Association   (860) 244-1900
370 Asylum Street, Hartford, CT 06103

SBA District Office   (860) 240-4700
330 Main Street, Second Floor, Hartford, CT 06106

Connecticut Small Business Development Centers
University of Connecticut   (860) 486-4135
School of Business Admin., 2 Bourn Place, U-94, Storrs. CT 06269-5094

Bridgeport	(203) 330-4813	Groton	(860) 405-9002
Danbury	(203) 743-5565	Middletown	(203) 344-2158
Danielson	(203) 774-1133	New Haven	(203) 782-4390
Stamford	(203) 359-3220 x 302		
Willimantic	(860) 465-5349	Waterbury	(203) 757-8937
W. Hartford	(860) 570-9109		

Connecticut Small Business Investment Companies
Cheshire - AB SBIC, Inc.   (203) 272-0203
Farmington - Capitol Resource Company   (860) 677-1113
New Canaan - RFE Capital Partners, LP   (203) 966-2800
New Canaan - RFE Investment Partners V, LP   (203) 966-2800
New Haven - All State Venture Capital Corporation   (203) 787-5028

Hartford - First New England Capital, LP   (860) 293-3333
Rowayton - Canaan SBIC, LP   (203) 855-0400
Stamford - TSG Ventures, Inc.   (203) 406-1500
West Hartford - Capital Resource Co, of Connecticut   (203) 236-4336
Westport - Marcon Capital Corp.   (203) 221-8402

Connecticut Certified Development Companies
Danbury - Housatonic Industrial Development Corporation   (203) 743-0306
Hartford - Greater Hartford Business Development Center, Inc.   (860) 527-1301
Rocky Hill - Connecticut Business Development Corporation   (860) 258-7855

Micro Loans
New Haven - New Haven Community Investment Corp.   (203) 776-6172

DELAWARE

Statewide Financing Information and Resources: www.state.de.us
Delaware Economic Development Office   (302) 739-4271
99 Kings Highway, P.O. Box 1401, Dover, DE 19902

Economic Development/Procurement Assistance
• Business Development   (302) 739-4271
• Business Research   (302) 739-4221
• Education, Training and Recruitment   (302) 739-4271
• Small Business Advocate   (302) 739-4271

Financial Assistance
• Business Finance   (302) 739-4271
• Delaware Economic Development Authority   (302) 739-4271

Delaware State Chamber of Commerce   (302) 655-7221
1201 North Orange St., Suite 200, P.O. Box 671, Wilmington, DE 19899

SBA Branch Office   (302) 573-6294
824 North Market Street, Suite 610, Wilmington, DE 19801-3011

Delaware Small Business Development Centers
University of Delaware   (302) 831-1555
-Purnell Hall, Suite 005, Newark, DE 19716-2711
Dover   (302) 678-1555
Georgetown   (302) 856-1555

Delaware Small Investment Companies
Wilmington - Blue Rock Capital   (302) 426-0981
Wilmington - PNC Capital   (303) 427-5895

Delaware Certified Development Companies
Dover - Delaware Development Corporation   (302) 739-4271
Wilmington - Wilmington Economic Development Corp.   (302) 571-9088

Micro Loans
Wilmington - Wilmington Economic Development   (302) 571-9088

DISTRICT OF COLUMBIA

Statewide Financing Information and Resources: www.state.dc.us

Office of Economic Development   (202) 727-6600
717 14th Street, NW, Twelfth Floor, Washington, DC 20005

Economic Development
• Business Center   (202) 727-7100
• Department of Consumer and Regulatory Affairs   (202) 727-7000
• Incorporation/Corporate Division(202) 727-7278

Financial Assistance
• Economic Development Finance Corporation   (202) 775-8815
• Industrial Revenue Bond Program(202) 727-6600
• Loan Guarantee Program   (202) 535-1942

Minority Women
• Department of Human Rights and Minority
  Business Development   (302) 724-1385
• Washington, D.C. Minority Business
  Development Center   (202) 785-2886

District of Columbia Chamber of Commerce   (202) 638-3222

SBA District Office   (202) 606-4000
110 Vermont Avenue, NW, Suite 900, Washington, DC 20043-4500
District of Columbia Small Business Development Centers
Howard University   (202) 806-1550
Metropolitan Washington SBDC
2600 Sixth St., NW, Room 125, Washington, DC 20059
Development Corporation of Columbia Heights   (202) 483-4986
East of the River Community Development Corporation   (202) 561-4975
SBA Business Information Center   (202) 606-4000 x279
George Washington University Small Business Clinic   (202) 994-7463
Marshall Heights Community Development Organization   (202) 396-1200
Ward Five Community Development(202) 396-1200
Washington District Office   (202) 606-4000

District of Columbia Small Business Investment Companies
Washington, DC - Allied Investment Corporation   (202) 331-1112
Washington, DC - Allied Investment Corporation   (202) 331-1112
Washington, DC - Broadcast Investment Corp.   (202) 496-9250
Washington, DC - Capital Health Partners   (202) 965-2338

District of Columbia Certified Development Company
Washington, DC - Community First, Inc.   (202) 338-8993

Micro Loans
Washington, DC - Arch Development Corp.   (202) 889-5023
Washington, DC - J Street Development   (202) 544-8353

FLORIDA

Statewide Financing Information and Resources: www.state.fl.us

Enterprise Florida   (305) 377-8766
Suntrust Center
200 So. Orange Ave., Suite 1200, Orlando, FL 32801

Economic Development
• Technology Division   (407) 425-5313
• Tourism, Trade and Economic Development   (904) 487-2568
• Manufacturing Technology Division   (954) 941-0115

Financial Assistance
• Capital Division   (407) 425-5313
• Grant Division   (904) 488-6300

Minority/Women
• Enterprise Florida   (305) 377-8766
Florida Chamber of Commerce   (904) 425-1200
136 S. Bronough St., Tallahassee, FL 32302

SBA District Offices
Coral Gables   (305) 536-5521
1320 So. Dixie Hwy., Suite 301, Coral Gables, FL 33146-29211
Jacksonville   (904) 443-1900
7825 Baymeadows Way, Ste. 100, Jacksonville, FL 32256-7504

Florida Small Business Development Centers
University of West Florida   (904) 444-2060
19 West Garden Street, Suite 300, Pensacola, FL 32501

Bartow	(941) 534-4370	Boca Raton	(561) 362-5620
Miami, FL	(305) 919-5790	Dania	(954) 987-0100
Daytona Beach	(904) 947-5463	Ocala	(352) 629-8051
Fort Lauderdale	(954) 771-6520	Orlando	(407) 823-5554
Fort Myers	(941) 590-7316		
Pensacola (U. of W. FL)	(904) 474-2908	Fort Pierce	(561) 462-4756
Pensacola (Tech)	(904) 444-2066		
Fort Walton Beach	(904) 863-6543	Sanford	(407) 328-4722
Gainesville (CDC)	(377) 377-5621	St. Petersburg	(813) 341-4456
Jacksonville	(904) 646-2476	Tallahassee	(904) 599-3407
Lynn Haven	(904) 271-1108	Tampa	(813) 974-4371
Melbourne	(407) 632-1111 x 33201		

Florida Small Business Investment Companies
Miami - BAC Investment Corporation(305) 693-5919
Tampa - Market Capital Corporation (813) 248-5781
N. Miami Beach - PMC Corporation   (933) 933-5858

Florida Certified Development Companies

Gainesville - North Cent. Florida Areawide Devel. Co., Inc.	(352) 955-2199
Jacksonville - Business Devel. Corp. of Northeast Florida, Inc.	(904) 363-6350
Jacksonville - Jacksonville Economic Development Company	(904) 630-1906
Lake Worth - Florida Business Development Corporation	(561) 433-0233
St. Petersburg - St. Petersburg CDC, Inc.	(813) 895-2504
Tallahassee - Florida First Capital Finance Corporation, Inc.	(904) 487-0466
Tampa - Tampa Bay Economic Development Corporation	(813) 242-5442

Micro Loans

Pensacola - Community Equity Investments	(904) 444-2234
Gainesville - United Gainesville Community Development	(904) 376-8891

GEORGIA

Statewide Financing Information and Resources:	www.state.ga.us
Georgia Department of Industry, Trade, and Tourism P.O. Box 1776, Atlanta, GA30301	(404) 656-3545

Economic Development
* Small Business Revitalization Program   (404) 656-3872
* Business Development Corporation of Georgia   (404) 656-3556

Financial Assistance
* Department of Industry, Trade and Tourism   (404) 656-3556
* Business Loan Program

-Business and Industrial Loan Program
-Business Loan Guarantee Program
-Capital Network
-Intermediary Relending Program
-Regional Revolving Loan Funds

Minority/Women
• Office of Small and Minority Affairs   (404) 656-6315

Georgia Chamber of Commerce   (404) 223-2264
233 Peachtree St., Suite 200, Atlanta, GA 30303

SBA District Office   (404) 347-2441
1720 Peachtree Road, NW, Suite 600, Atlanta, GA 30309

Georgia Small Business Development Centers
University of Georgia   (706) 542-6762
Business Outreach Services
Chicopee Complex 1180 E. Broad St., Athens, GA 30602-5412

Albany	(912) 430-4303	Lawrenceville	(770) 806-2124
Athens (NE GA Dist.)	(706) 542-7436	Macon	(912) 751-6592
Athens (NW GA Dist.)	(770) 542-6756	Narietta	(770) 423-6450
Atlanta	(404) 651-3550	Morrow	(770) 961-3440
Augusta	(706) 737-1790	Savannah	(912) 356-2755
Brunswick	(912) 264-7343	Statesboro	(912) 681-5194
Columbus	(706) 649-7433	Valdosta	(912) 245-3738
Decatur	(404) 373-6930	Warner Robbins	(912) 953-9356
Gainesville	(770) 531-5681	Kennesaw	(770) 423-6450
LaGrange	(706) 812-7353		

Georgia Small Business Investment Companies
Atlanta-Cordova Capital Partners, LP-Enhanced Appreciation   (770) 951-1542
Atlanta-Renaissance Capital Corporation   (404) 658-9061
Atlanta-EGI/Nat West Ventures   (770) 399-5633

Georgia Certified Development Companies
Americus-Middle Flint Area Development Corporation   (912) 931-2909
Athens-Certified Development Company   (706) 369-5650
Atlanta-Atlanta Local Development Company   (404) 658-7000
Atlanta-Business Growth Corporation of Georgia   (770) 434-0273
Atlanta-Economic Development Corp. of Fulton Co.   (404) 730-8078
Augusta-CSRA Local Development Corporation   (706) 737-1823
Brunswick-Coastal Area District Development Authority   (912) 261-2500
Camilla-Sowega Economic Development Corporation   (912) 336-5617
Columbus-Uptown Columbus, Inc.   (706) 596-0111

Dalton-North Georgia Certified Development Company	(706) 226-1110
Eastman-Heart of Georgia Area Development Corporation	(912) 374-4773
Gainesville-Georgia Mountain Regional EDC	(770) 536-7839
LaGrange-Troup County Local Development Corporation	(706) 884-8671
Macon-Development Corporation of Middle Georgia	(912) 751-6160
Savannah-Small Business Assistance Corp. of Savannah	(912) 232-4700
Valdosta-South Georgia Regional Development Corporation	(912) 333-5277
Waycross-Financial Services Corp. of Southeast Georgia	(912) 285-6097

Micro Loans
Atlanta-Fulton County Development	(404) 659-5955
Savannah-Small Business Assistance	(912) 232-4700

HAWAII

Statewide Financing Information and Resources:	www.state.hi.us

Department of Business, Economic Development and Tourism (808) 586-2591
250 South Hotel Street, 5th Floor, Honolulu, HI 96813

Economic Development
• Business Action Center	(808) 586-2545
• Pacific Business Center	(808) 956-6286
• Business Information and Counseling Center	(808) 522-8131

Financial Assistance
• Financial Assistance Branch	(808) 586-2576
• Agricultural Loan Division	(808) 973-9460

Minority/Women
• Women in Business Committee	(808) 541-3024

The Chamber of Commerce of Hawaii	(808) 545-4300

1132 Bishop Street, Suite 200, Honolulu, HI

SBA District Office	(808) 541-2990

300 Ala Moana Blvd., Room 2213, Honolulu, Hi 96850-4981

Hawaii Small Business Development Centers
Hilo (University of Hawaii at Hilo)	(808) 933-3515

200 West Kawili Street, Hilo, HI 96720-4091
Honolulu	(808) 522-8131
Lihue	(808) 246-1748
Kihel	(808) 875-2402

Small Business Investment Centers
Honolulu-Bancorp Hawaii   (808) 537-8613

Hawaii Certified Development Company
Honolulu-HEDCO Local Development Corporation   (808) 521-6502

Micro Lenders
Honolulu-The Immigrant Center   (808) 845-3918

IDAHO

Statewide Financing Information and Resources: www.state.id.us

Department of Commerce   (208) 334-2470
700 West State Street, P.O. Box 83720, Boise, ID 83720-2700

Economic Development
• Division of Economic Development   (208) 334-2470
• Idaho Business Network   (808) 334-2470

Financial Assistance
• Pan Handle Area Council
  Business Center for Innovation and Development   (208) 772-0584
• Idaho Innovation Center   (208) 523-1026

Minority/Women
• Associated General Contractors of America   (208) 344-2531
Idaho Association of Commerce & Industry   (208) 343-1849
802 West Bannock St., Suite 308, P.O. Box 389, Boise, ID 83701

SBA District Office   (208) 334-1696
1020 Main Street, Suite 290, Boise, ID 83702-5745

Idaho Small Business Development Centers
Boise State University   (208) 385-1640
College of Business, 1910 University Drive, Boise, ID 83725

Boise	(208) 385-3875	Pocatello	(208) 232-4921
Idaho Falls	(208) 523-1087	Post Falls	(208) 769-3296
Lewiston	(208) 799-2465	Twin Falls	(208) 733-9554 x2450

Idaho Certified Development Companies
Boise-Capital Matrix, Inc.   (208) 322-7033
Hayden-Panhandle Area Council, Inc.   (208) 772-0584

Pocatello-Eastern Idaho Development Corporation	(208) 234-7541
Rexburg-East Central Idaho Planning & Development Co.	(208) 356-4525
Twin Falls-Region IV Development Corporation, Inc.	(208) 736-3064

Micro Loans
Hayden-Panhandle Area Council	(208) 772-0584

ILLINOIS

Statewide Financing Information and Resources:	www.state.il.us

Small Business Development Center (217) 524-5856
Department of commerce and Community Affairs
620 East Adams Street, Third Floor, Springfield, IL 62701

Economic Development
• Illinois First Stop Program-Toll-free in Illinois	(800) 252-2923
• Illinois Business Hotline-Toll-free in Illinois	(800) 252-2923
• Illinois SBDC Network-Toll-free in Illinois	(800) 252-2923

Financial Assistance
• Loan Administration Division-Springfield	(217) 782-3891
Chicago	(312) 814-2308

Minority/Women
• Office of Minority Business Development	(312) 814-3540
• Office of Women's Business Development	(312) 814-7176

The Illinois State Chamber of Commerce	(312) 983-7100

311 South Wacker Drive, Suite 1500, Chicago, IL 60606-6619

SBA District Offices-Chicago	(312) 353-4528

500 West Madison St., room 1250, Chicago, IL 60661-2511
Springfield (Branch Office)	(217) 492-4416

511 West Capitol Avenue, Suite 302, Springfield, IL 62704

Illinois Small Business Development Centers
Department of Commerce & Community Affairs	(217) 524-5856

620 East Adams Street, 3rd Floor, Springfield, IL62701
Chicago
Asian American Alliance	(312) 202-0600
Back of the Yards Neighborhood Council	(312) 523-4419
DCAA State of Illinois Center	(312) 814-6111
18th Street Development Corporation	(312) 733-2287
Greater N. Pulaski Economic Development Council	(312) 384-2262
Industrial Council	(312) 421-3941
Latin/American Chamber of Commerce	(312) 252-5211

Midwest Chicago Business Association			(773) 826-4055
North Business & Industrial Council			(312) 588-5855
University at Illinois at Chicago			(773) 996-4057
Women's Business Development			(312) 853-3477
Aurora	(630) 801-7900	Ina	(618) 437-5321 x335
Carbondale	(618) 536-2424	Joliet	(815) 727-6544
Centralia	(618) 532-2049	Kankakee	(815) 933-0376
Crystal Lake	(815) 455-6098	Macomb	(309) 298-2211
Danville	(217) 442-7232	Monmouth	(309) 734-4664
Decatur	(217) 875-8284	Oglesby	(815) 223-1740
Dixon	(815) 288-5605	Olney	(618) 395-3011
East Moline	(309) 755-2200	Palos Hills	(707) 974-5468
East St. Louis	(618) 583-2270	Peoria	(309) 677-2992
Edwardsville	(618) 692-2929	Quincy (Proc.)	(217) 228-5511
Elgin	(847) 888-7675		
River Grove	(708) 456-0300 x3593		
Evanston	(847) 866-1817	Rockford	(815) 968-4087
Glen Ellyn	(630) 942-2771	Springfield	(217) 789-1017
Godfrey	(618) 466-3411	Ullin	(618) 634-9618
Grayslake	(847) 223-3633	University Park	(708) 534-4929
Harrisburg	(618) 252-5001		

Illinois Small Business Investment Companies
Chicago-ABN AMRO Capital (312) 904-6445
Chicago-Nesbitt Burns Equity (312) 461-2021
Chicago-Shorebank Capital Corporation (312) 371-7030

Illinois Certified Development Companies
Chicago-CANDO City-Wide Development Corporation (312) 939-7171
Chicago-Greater North-Pulaski Local Development Corp. (312) 384-7074
Chicago-Somercor 504, Inc. (312) 360-3163
Collinsville-Small Business Finance Alliance (618) 344-4080
Northbrook-Greater Metropolitan Chicago Development (708) 251-2756
Peoria-Illinois Business Financial Servies (815) 987-8127
Salem-South Central IL. Regional Planning & Devel. Comm. (618) 548-4234
Springfield-Illinois Small Business Growth corporation (217) 522-2772
University Park-South towns Business Growth Corporation (708) 534-4924
Waukegan-Lake County Economic Development Corp. (847) 360-6350

Micro Loans
Chicago-Illinois Development Finance Authority (312) 793-5586
Peoria-Economic Dev. Council (309) 676-7500

INDIANA

Statewide Financing Information and Resources: www.state.in.us

State Information Center (317) 233-0800
402 West Washington Street, Room W160, Indianapolis, IN 46204

Economic Development
• Indiana Department of Commerce (317) 232-8800
  Administrative Service Division (317) 232-8782
  Business Development Division (317) 232-8888
• Indiana Small Business Development Corp. (ISBD Corp.) (317) 264-2820
• Indiana Small Business Development Centers (317) 264-6871

Financial Assistance
• Indiana Development Finance Authority (317) 233-4332
Minority/Women
• Women and Minority Business Assistance Program (317) 264-2820
• Minority Business Development Divisions (317) 232-3061

Indiana State Chamber of Commerce, Inc. (317) 264-3110
One North Capitol St., Suite 200, Indianapolis, In 46204-2248

SBA District Office
429 North Pennsylvania, Suite 100, Indianapolis, IN 46204-1873

Indiana Small Business Development Centers
Indiana Small Business Development Center (317) 261-3030
One North Capital, Suite 420, Indianapolis, IN 46204-2248

Bloomington	(812) 339-8937	Lafayette	(317) 742-2394
Columbus	(812) 372-6480	Madison	(812) 265-3127
Evansville	(812) 425-7232	Muncie	(317) 284-8144
Fort Wayne	(219) 426-0040	Portage	(219) 762-1696
Jeffersonville	(812) 288-6451	Richmond	(317) 962-2887
Kokomo	(317) 454-7922	Terre Haute	(812) 237-7676

Indiana Small Business Investment Companies
Indianapolis-Cambridge Ventures, LP (317) 469-9704
South Bend-1st Source Capital Corporation (219) 235-2180

Indiana Certified Development Companies
Evansville-Metro Small Business Assistance Corporation (812) 426-5857
Fort Wayne-Community Development Corp. of Fort Wayne (219) 427-1127
Hammond-Hammond Development Corporation (219) 853-6399

Indianapolis-Indiana Statewide Certified Development Corp.	(317) 469-6166
Indianapolis-Mid City Pioneer Corporation	(317) 974-0504
Portage-Northwest Indiana Regional Development Corp.	(219) 763-6303
South Bend-Business Development Corp. of South Bend	(219) 235-9278
Micro Loans	
Evansville-Metro Small Business Assistance	(812) 426-5857
Indianapolis-Eastside Community Investment	(317) 637-7300

IOWA

Statewide Financing Information and Resources:	www.state.ia.us
Department of Economic Development	(515) 242-4700
200 East Grand Avenue, Des Moines, IA 50309	
Economic Development	
• Center for Industrial Research and Service	(515) 294-3420
• Marketing and Business Expansion Bureau	(515) 242-4735
• Office of Ombudsman	(515) 281-3592
• Small Business Bureau	(515) 242-4750
• Small Business Helpline	(515) 532-1216
• Small Business Workforce Development	(515) 281-9013
Financial Assistance	
• Economic Development Set-Aside	(515) 242-4831
• Iowa Seed Capital Corporation	(515) 242-4860
Minority/Women	
• Linked Investments for Tomorrow Program	(515) 281-3287
• Targeted Small Business Financial Assistance Program	(515) 242-4813
• Targeted Small Business Program	(515) 242-4721
• Entrepreneurs with Disabilities Program	(515) 242-4948
• Self-Employment Loan Program	(515) 242-4793
Iowa Association of Business & Industry	(515) 244-6149
904 Walnut Street, Suite 100, Des Moines, IA 50309-3503	
SBA District Office	
Cedar Rapids	(319) 362-6405
215 Fourth Avenue, SE, Suite 200, Cedar Rapids, IA 52401-1806	
Des Moines	(515) 284-4422
210 Walnut Street, Room 749, Des Moines, IA 50309-2186	

Iowa Small Business Development Centers

Iowa State University			(515) 292-6351
College of Business Administration			
137 Lynn Avenue, Ames, IA 50014-7126			
Ames			(515) 296-7828
Fort Dodge	(800) 362-2793	Audubon	(712) 563-2623

Iowa City	(319) 335-3742	Cedar Falls	(319) 273-2696
Marion	(319) 377-8256	Council Bluffs	(712) 325-3260
Mason City	(315) 422-4342	Creston	(515) 782-4161
Ottumwa	(515) 683-5127	Davenport	(319) 322-4499
Sioux City	(712) 274-6418	Des Moines	(515) 271-2655
Spencer	(712) 262-4213	Dubuque	(319) 588-3350
West Burlington	(319) 752-2731		

Iowa Small Business Investment Companies

Cedar Rapids-MorAmerica Capital Corporation	(319) 363-8249

Iowa Certified Development Companies

Des Moines-Corp. for Economic Development in Des Moines	(515) 283-4004
Dubuque-ECIA Business Growth, Inc.	(515) 556-4166
Sioux City-Siouxland Economic Development Corporation	(712) 279-6286
Waterloo-Black Hawk County Econ. Devel. Committee, Inc.	(319) 235-2960
West Des Moines-Iowa Business Growth Company	(515) 223-4511

Micro Loans

Sioux City-Siouxland Economic Development	(712) 279-6286

KANSAS

Statewide Financing Information and Resources:	www.state.ks.us

Department of Commerce	(913) 296-3481
700 SW Harrison Street, Suite 1300, Topeka, KS 66603-3712	

Economic Development

• Administration Division	(913) 296-3481
• Kansas Technology Enterprise Corporation	(913) 296-5272

Financial Assistance

• Certified Development Companies	(316) 683-4422
• Power Certified Development Companies	(316) 267-3036
• Kansas Development Finance Authority	(913) 296-6747
• Kansas Venture Capital, Inc.	(913) 262-7117

Minority/Women
• Office of Minority

Kansas Chamber of Commerce & Industry	(913) 357-6321
835 SW Topeka Blvd., Topeka, KS 66612-1671	

SBA District Office	(316) 269-6616
100 East English Street, Suite 510, Wichita, KS 67202	

Kansas Small Business Development Centers
Wichita State University   (316) 978-3193
1845 Fairmount, Wichita, KS 67260-0148

Chanute	(316) 431-2820	Liberal	(316) 624-1951
Coffeyville	(316) 251-7700	Manhattan	(316) 532-5529
Dodge City	(316) 227-9247	Overland Park	(913) 469-3878
Fort Scott	(316) 223-2700	Parsons	(316) 421-6700
Garden City	(316) 276-9632	Pittsburg	(316) 235-4920
Hays	(913) 628-5340	Pratt	(316) 672-5641
Hutchinson	(316) 665-4950	Salina	(913) 826-2616
Independence	(316) 332-1420	Topeka	(913) 231-1010

Kansas Small Business Investment Company
Overland Park-Kansas Venture Capital   (913) 262-7117

Kansas Certified Development Companies
Dodge City-Great Plains Development, Inc.   (316) 227-6406
Emporia-Eastern Kansas Economic Development Group, Inc.   (316) 342-7041
Hill City-Pioneer Country Development, Inc.   (913) 674-3488
Kansas City-Avenue Area Incorporated   (913) 371-0065
Kansas City-Citywide Development Corporation   (913) 573-5733
Lawrence-Wakarusa Valley Development, Inc.   (913) 865-4425
Overland Park-Johnson County Development Co.   (913) 599-1717
Pittsburg-Mid-America. Inc.   (316) 235-4920
Topeka-Topeka/Shawnee County Development Corporation   (913) 368-3711
Wichita-South Central Kansas Economic Devel. District, Inc.   (316) 683-4422

Micro Loans
Kansas City-Center for Business Innovation   (816) 561-8567
Wichita-South Central Kansas EDC   (316) 683-4422

KENTUCKY

Statewide Financing Information and Resources: www.state.ky.us

Kentucky Cabinet for Economic Development   (502) 564-7140
2300 Capital Plaza Tower, Frankfort, KY 40601

Economic Development
* Business Information Clearinghouse   (502) 564-4252
* Office of Business and Technology   (502) 564-4252
* University of Kentucky's Management Center   (606) 257-8746

Financial Assistance
* Commonwealth Small Business Development Corporation   (502) 564-4320

151

- Kentucky Department of Financial Incentives   (502) 564-4554
- Kentucky Investment Capital Network   (502) 564-7140

Minority/Women
- Small and Minority Business Division   (502) 564-2064

Kentucky Chamber of Commerce   (502) 695-4700
464 Chenault Road, P.O. Box 817, Frankfort, KY 40602

SBA District Office
600 Dr., M.I. King Jr. Place, Room 188, Louisville, KY 40202

Kentucky Small Business Development Centers
    University of Kentucky   (606) 257-7668
    Center for Business Development
    225 Business and Economics Building, Lexington, KY 40506-0034

Ashland	(606) 329-8011	Bowling Green	(502) 745-1905
Middlesboro	(606) 242-2145	Elizabethtown	(502) 765-6737
Morehead	(606) 783-2895		
Highland Heights	(606) 572-2856	Murray	(502) 762-2856
Hopkinsville	(502) 886-8666	Owensboro	(502) 926-8085
Lexington	(606) 257-7666	Pikeville	(606) 432-5848
Louisville	(502) 574-4770	Somerset	(606) 677-6120

Kentucky Small Business Investment Companies
London-Mountain Ventures, Inc.   (606) 878-6635
Louisville-Equal Opportunity Finance, Inc.   (502) 423-1943

Kentucky Certified Development Companies
Ashland-Boyd Greenup Economic Development Corp.   (606) 324-5113
Bowling Green-Barren River Development Council   (502) 781-2381
Florence-Northern Kentucky Area Development District, Inc.   (606) 283-1885
Frankfort-Commonwealth Small Business Devel. Corp.   (502) 564-4554
Hopkinsville-Pennyrile Area Development District, Inc.   (502) 886-9484
Lexington-Urban County community Development Corp.   (606) 258-3131
Louisville-Metropolitan Capital Access Corporation   (502) 574-3051
Mayfield-Purchase Area Development District   (502) 247-7171

Micro Loans
Louisville-Louisville Central Development   (502) 583-8821
Lexington-Community Ventures   (606) 231-0054

LOUISIANA

Statewide Financing Information and Resources:	www.state.la.us

Department of Economic Development   (504) 342-3000
P.O. Box 94185, Baton Rouge, LA 70804

Economic Development
* Office of Commerce and Industry   (504) 342-5893
  Division of Business Services

Financial Assistance
* Office of Commerce and Industry, Financial Incentives   (504) 342-5398
* Louisiana Economic Development Corporation   (504) 342-5675

Minority/Women
* Division of Minority and Women's Business Enterprise   (504) 342-5373

Louisiana Association of Business & Industry   (504) 928-5388
P.O. Box 80258, Baton Rouge, LA 70898-0258

SBA District Office   (504) 589-2354
365 Canal Street, Suite 2250, New Orleans, LA 70130

Louisiana Small Business Development Centers
Northeast Louisiana University   (318) 342-5506
College of Business Administration, Room 2-57, Monroe, LA 71209-6435

Alexandria	(318) 484-2123		
New Orleans (UNO)	(504) 539-9292		
Baton Rouge	(504) 922-0998	(Loyola U.)	(504) 863-3474
Hammond	(504) 549-3831	(So. U.)	(504) 286-5308
Lafayette	(318) 262-5344	Ruston	(318) 257-3537
Lake Charles	(318) 475-5520	Shreveport	(318) 797-5144
Monroe	(318) 342-1224	Thibodaux	(504) 448-4242
Natchitoches	(318) 357-5611		

Louisiana Small Business Investment Company
Baton Rouge-Premier Venture Capital Corporation   (504) 332-4421
New Orleans-First Commerce Capital   (504) 623-1600

Louisiana Certified Development Companies
Alexandria-Kisatchie-Delta Regional Planning and Devel.   (318) 487-5454
Lafayette-Louisiana Capital Certified Development Co., Inc.   (318) 234-2977
Metairie-JEDCO Development Corporation   (504) 830-4860

Monroe-Northeast Louisiana Industries, Inc.	(318) 323-0878
New Orleans-Regional Business Development Loan Corp.	(504) 524-6172
Shreveport-Ark-La-Tex Investment & Development Corp.	(318) 632-2022

Micro Loans
Jennings-Greater Jennings Chamber of Commerce   (318) 824-0933

MAINE

Statewide Financing Information and Resources:	www.state.me.us

Department of Economic and Community Development   (207) 287-2656
State House Station #59
Augusta, ME, 04333-0949

Economic Development
- Office of Business Development   (207) 287-3153
- Business Answers   (207) 287-3153
  Toll-Free in Maine   (800) 872-3838
  Toll-free out of state   (800) 541-5872

Financial Assistance
- Finance Authority of Maine   (207) 623-3263
- Linked Investment Program   (207) 623-3263

Maine Chamber of Commerce & Industry   (207) 623-4568
7 Community Drive, Augusta, ME 04330-9412

SBA District Office   (207) 622-8378
40 Western Avenue, Room 512, Augusta, ME 04330

Maine Small Business Development Centers
University of Southern Maine   (207) 780-4420
93 Falmouth Street, P.O. Box 9300, Portland, ME 04104-9300

Auburn	(207) 783-9186	Portland	(207) 780-4949
Augusta	(207- 621-0243	Bangor	(207) 942-6389
Sanford	(207) 324-0316	Brunswick	(207) 882-4340
Caribou	(207) 498-8736	Wiscasset	(207) 882-4340
Machias	(207) 255-0983		

Maine Small Business Investment Company
Portland-North Atlantic Venture Fund II   (207) 772-1001

Maine Certified Development Companies
Auburn-Androscoggin Valley Council of Governments   (207) 783-9186
Bangor-Eastern Maine Development Corporation   (207) 942-6389
Wiscasset-Coastal Enterprises, Inc.   (207) 882-7552

Micro Loans
Caribou-Northern Maine Development   (207) 498-8736
Wiscasset-Coastal Enterprises   (207) 882-7552

MARYLAND

Statewide Financing Information and Resources: www.state.md.us

Department of Economic and Business Development   (410) 767-6300
Redwood Tower, 217 East Redwood St., Baltimore, MD21202

Economic Development
- Office of Regional Response   (410) 767-0523
- At-Risk Business   (410) 767-6517
- SBDC Network   (410) 767-6552

Financial Assistance
- Maryland Small Business Development Financing Authority (410) 767-6539

Minority/Women
- Office of Minority Affairs   (410) 767-8232
- Procurement Office   (410) 767-7215

Maryland Chamber of Commerce   (410) 269-0642
60 West Street, Suite 100, Annapolis, MD 21401

SBA District Office   (410) 962-4392
10 South Howard Street, Room 6220, Baltimore, MD 21202

Maryland Small Business Development Centers
University of Maryland, College Park   (301) 403-8300

Annapolis	(410) 224-4205	Landover	(301) 883-6491
Baltimore	(410) 659-1930	McHenry	(301) 387-3080
Bel Air	(410) 893-3837	Owings Mills	(410) 356-2888
Columbia	(410) 313-6550	Rockville	(301) 217-2345
Cumberland	(301) 724-6716	Salisbury	(410) 546-4325
Elkton	(410) 392-0597	Towson	(410) 832-5866

Frederick	(301) 846-2683	Waldorf	(301) 934-7583
Great Mills	(301) 863-6679	Westminster	(410) 857-8166
Hagerstown	(301) 797-0327	Wye Mills	(410) 827-5286

Maryland Small Business Investment Companies
Baltimore-Anthem Capital, LP   (410) 625-1510
Bethesda-Security Financial and Investment Corporation   (301) 951-4288
Silver Spring-Syncom Capital Corporation   (301) 608-3207

Maryland Certified Development Companies
Baltimore-Mid-Atlantic Business Finance Corporation   (410) 539-2449
Largo-Prince George's County Financial Services Corp.   (301) 386-5600

Micro Loans
Baltimore-Council for Economic Business Opportunities   (410) 576-2326

MASSACHUSETTS

Statewide Financing Information and Resources: www.state.ma.us

Office of Business Development   (617) 727-3206
One Ashburton Place, Room 2101, Boston, MA 02108

Economic Development
• Massachusetts Business Development Corporation   617) 350-8877

Financial Assistance
• Massachusetts Industrial Finance Authority   (617) 451-2477
• Capital Formation Service   (617) 552-4091
• Technology Capital Network, Inc.   (617) 253-7163

Minority/Women
State Office of Minority and Women's Business Assistance   (617) 727-8692

West Suburban Chamber of Commerce   (617) 894-4700
One Moody Street, Suite 301, Waltham, MA 02154
SBA District Office -Boston   (617) 565-5590
10 Causeway Street, Room 265, Boston, MA 02222-1093
Springfield (Branch Office)   (413) 785-0268
1550 Main Street, Room 212, Boston, MA01103

Massachusetts Small Business Development Centers
University of Massachusetts   (413) 545-6301
Room 205, School of Management, Amherst, MA 01003

Boston (Minority Business Assistance Center)	(617) 287-7750
Springfield	(413) 737-6712
Chestnut Hill	(617) 552-4091
Worcester	(508) 793-7615

Massachusetts Small Business Investment Companies
Boston-BancBoston Ventures, Inc.	(617) 434-2442
Boston-Chestnut Street Partners, Inc.	(617) 345-7200
Boston-Commonwealth Enterprise Fund, Inc.	(617) 482-1881
Boston-Northeast SBI Corp.	(617) 445-2100
Boston-Pioneer Ventures Limited Partnership	(617) 742-7825
Boston-Pioneer Ventures Limited Partnership II	(617) 422-4947
Boston-Transportation Capital Corporation	(617) 536-0344
Boston-U.S. Trust Capital Corporation	(617) 726-7000
Cambridge-Zero Stage Capital V, LP (617) 876-5355	
Danvers-Seacoast, LP	(508) 777-3866
Farmington-Argonauts MESBIC Corporation	(508) 820-3430
Newton-Business Achievement Corporation	(617) 965-0550

Massachusetts Certified Development Companies
Boston-Massachusetts Certified Development Corporation	(617) 350-8877
Holyoke-Riverside Development Corporation	(413) 533-7102
Leominster-North Central Mass. Development Corp.	(508) 840-4300 x236
Lynn-Lynn Capital Investment Corporation	(617) 592-2361
Peabody-Northeastern Mass. Economic Development Co.	(508) 531-0454
Pittsfield-Pittsfield Economic Revitalization Corporation	(413) 499-9371
Quincy-South Shore Economic Development Corporation	(617) 479-1111
Springfield-Western Mass. Small Business Assistance, Inc.	(413) 787-1553
Taunton-South Eastern Economic Development Corporation	(508) 822-1020
Waltham-Bay Colony Development	(617) 891-3594
Worcester-Worcester Business Development Corporation	(508) 753-2924

Micro Loans
Boston-Jewish Vocational Service	(617) 451-8147
Springfield-Springfield Business Development	(413) 787-6050

MICHIGAN

Statewide Financing Information and Resources: www.state.mi.us

Michigan Jobs Commission   (517) 373-9808
Victor Office Center, Fourth Floor, 201 N. Washington Square
Lansing, MI 48913

Economic Development
- Business Start-up Assistance   (517) 373-9808
- Economic/Labor Market Information   (517) 373-9808

Financial Assistance
- Business Operating Cost Estimating Service   (517) 373-9808
- Joint Venture Assistance   (517) 373-9808
- Private Financing Referral Service   (517) 373-9808
- Public Financing Programs   (517) 373-9808

Minority/Women
- Minority and Women-Owner Business Services   (517) 373-9808

Michigan Chamber of Commerce   (517) 371-2100
600 South Walnut Street, Lansing, MI 48933

SBA District Offices-Detroit   (313) 226-6075
477 Michigan Avenue, Room 515, Detroit, MI 48226
Marquette (Branch Office)   (906) 225-1108
228 West Washington, Suite 11, Marquette, MI 49885

Michigan Small Business Development Centers
Wayne State University   (313) 964-1798
2727 Second Avenue, Room 107, Detroit, MI 48201

Allendale	(616) 892-4120	Howell	(517) 546-4020
Ann Arbor	(313) 930-0033	Bad Axe	(517) 269-6431
Lansing	(517) 483-1921	Benton Harbor	(616) 927-8179
Lapeer	(810) 667-0080	Big Rapids	(616) 592-3553
Brighton	(810) 227-3556	Mt. Pleasant	(517) 774-3270
Cadillac	(616) 775-9776	Muskegon	(616) 722-3751
Caro	(517) 673-2849	Detroit	(313) 993-1115
Saline	(313) 944-1016	Escanaba	(906) 786-9234
Traverse City	(616) 929-5000	Flint	(810) 239-5847
Grand Haven	(616) 846-3153	Troy	(810) 952-5800
Grand Rapids	(616) 771-6693	Hart	(616) 873-7141
Warren	(810) 751-3939	Highland Park	(313) 222-2956

Michigan Small Business Investment Companies
Ann Arbor-White Pines Capital Corporation   (313) 747-9401
Dearborn-Dearborn Capital Corporation   (313) 337-8577
Farmington Hills-Metro District Investments   (810) 851-6300
Lansing-The Capital Fund   (517) 323-7772

Michigan Certified Development Companies
Big Rapids-Growth Finance Corporation   (616) 592-2082
Detroit-Detroit Economic Growth Corporation   (313) 963-2940
Detroit-Metropolitan Growth and Development Corporation   (313) 224-0749

Grand Rapids-Economic Development Foundation	(616) 785-4333
Holland-Ottawa County Development Company, Inc.	(616) 892-4120
Lansing-Michigan Certified Development	(517) 373-6379
Lapeer-Lapeer Development Corporation	(810) 667-0080
Saginaw-East Central Michigan Development Corporation	(517) 797-0800

Micro Loans
Detroit-Detroit Economic Growth	(312) 963-2940
Flint-Community Capital	(810) 239-5847

MINNESOTA

Statewide Financing Information and Resources:　　www.state.mn.us

Small Business Assistance Office　　(612) 296-3871
500 Metro Square, 121 7th Place East, St. Paul, MN 55101-2146

Economic Development
• Bureau of Small Business　　(612) 296-3871
• Small Business Development Center (Administrative Ofc.)　　(612) 297-5770

Financial Assistance
• Department of Trade and Economic Development　　(612) 297-1391
  Office of Business Development & Finance

Minnesota Chamber of Commerce　　(612) 292-4650
30 East Seventh Street, Suite 1700, St. Paul, MN 55101

SBA District Office　　(612) 370-2324
100 North Sixth Street, Suite 610-C, Minneapolis, MN 55403-1563

Minneapolis Small Business Development Centers
Department of Trade and Economic Development　　(612) 297-5770
500 Metro Square, 121 Seventh Place East, St. Paul, MN 55101-2146

Bemidji	(218) 755-4286	Moorhead	(218) 236-2289
Bloomington	(612) 832-6221	Brainerd	(218) 828-2528
Pine City	(612) 629-7340	Duluth	(218) 726-6192
Plymouth	(612) 550-7218	Grand Rapids	(218) 327-2241
Hibbing	(218) 262-6703	Rochester	(507) 285-7536
International Falls	(218) 285-2255	Rosemount	(612) 423-8262
Mankato	(507) 389-8863	Marshall	(507) 537-7386
St. Cloud	(320) 255-4842	Minneapolis	(612) 338-3280
Virginia	(218) 741-4251		

Minnesota Small Business Investment Companies
Duluth-Northland Capital Venture Partnership	(218) 722-0545
Minneapolis-Agio Capital	(612) 339-8408
Minneapolis-Capital Dimensions Venture Fund, Inc.	(612) 854-3007
Minneapolis-Milestone Growth Fund, Inc	(612) 338-0090
Minneapolis-Norwest Equity Partners, IV, LP	(612) 667-1650
Minneapolis-Norwest Equity Partners V, LP	(612) 667-1650
Minneapolis-Piper Jaffray Healthcare Capital LP	(612) 342-6335

Minnesota Certified Development Companies
Arden Hills-Twin Cities Metro Certified Development Co.	(612) 481-8081
Coon Rapids-Central Minnesota Development Company	(612) 755-2304
Mankato-Region Nine Development Corporation	(507) 387-5643
Minneapolis-Economic Development Company	(612) 673-5176
Rochester-Southeastern Minnesota 504 Development, Inc.	(612) 288-6442
St. Cloud-Minnesota Business Finance, Inc.	(320) 255-1685
St. Paul-Saint Paul/Metro East Development Corporation	(612) 225-4900
Slayton-Prairieland Economic Development Corporation	(507) 836-6656

Micro Loans
Minneapolis-Women Venture	(612) 646-3808
Minneapolis-Consortium of Community Development	(612) 371-9986

MISSISSIPPI

Statewide Financing Information and Resources:	www.state.ms.us

Mississippi Department of Economic and
   Community Development   (601) 359-3449
P.O. Box 849, Jackson MS 39205-0849
Economic Development
• Business Incubator	(601) 352-0957
• Existing Business and Industry Assistance Division	(601) 359-3593
• Mississippi Enterprise for Technology	(601) 688-3144

Financial Assistance
• Mississippi Business Finance Corporation	(601) 359-3552

Minority/Women
• Jackson Minority Business Development Center	(601) 362-2260
• Minority Business Enterprise	(601) 359-3448

Mississippi Economic Council   (601) 969-0022
620 North Street, P.O. Box 23276, Jackson, MS39225-3276

SBA District Office   (601) 863-4449
  One Hancock Plaza, Gulfport, MS 39501-7758
Jackson   (601) 965-4378
  101 West Capitol Street, Suite 400, Jackson, MS 39201

Mississippi Small Business Development Centers
University of Mississippi   (601) 232-5001
Old Chemistry Building, Suite 216 University, MS 38677

Biloxi	(601) 396-1288	Booneville	(601) 720-7448
Cleveland	(601) 846-4236	Decatur	(601) 635-2111
Ellisville	(601) 477-4165	Gautier	(601) 497-7723
Greenville	(601) 378-8183	Hattiesburg	(601) 544-0030
Itta Bena	(601) 254-3601	Jackson	(601) 968-2795
Long Beach	(601) 865-4578	Lorman	(601) 877-6684
Meridan	(601) 482-7445	Mississippi State	(601) 325-8684
Natchez	(601) 445-5254	Raymond	(601) 857-3536
Ridgeland	(601) 865-4578	Southaven	(601) 342-7648
Summit	(601) 276-3890	Tupelo	(601) 680-8515
University	(601) 234-2120		

Mississippi Small Business Investment Company
Greenville-Sun Delta Access Center, Inc.   (601) 335-5291
Mississippi Certified Development Companies
Gulfport-Southern Mississippi Economic Devel. Co., Inc.   (601) 868-2311
Jackson-Mississippi Development Company   (601) 981-1625
Pontotoc-Three Rivers local Development Company, Inc.   (601) 489-2415

Micro Loans
Greenville-Delta Foundation   (601) 335-5291
Jackson-Friends at Children of Mississippi   (601) 362-1541

MISSOURI

Statewide Financing Information and Resources: www.state.mo.us

Missouri Department of Economic Development   (573) 751-4962
Truman State Office Building
301 West High Street, P.O. Box 1157
Jefferson City, MO 65102

Economic Development
• Business Development Section   (573) 751-9045

- Business Information Programs   (573) 751-4982

Financial Assistance
- Community and Economic Development   (573) 751-0717
  Finance Program

Minority/Women
- Office of Minority Business   (573) 751-3237
- Women's Council   (573) 751-0810

Missouri Chamber of Commerce   (573) 634-3511
P.O. Box 149, Jefferson City, MO 65102

SBA District Offices-Kansas City   (816) 374-6708
   Lucas Place, 323 West Eighth St, Suite 501, Kansas City, MO 64105
St. Louis   (314) 539-6600
   815 Olive Street, Room 242, St. Louis, MO63101
Springfield (Branch Office)   (417) 864-7670
   620 South Glenstone St., Suite 110, Springfield, MO 65802-3200

Missouri Small Business Development Centers
University of Missouri   (573) 882-0344
300 University Place, Columbia, MO 65211

Cape Girardeau	(573) 290-5965	Chillicothe	(816) 646-6920
Columbia	(314) 882-7096	Flat River	(573) 431-4593
Joplin	(417) 625-9313	Kansas City	(816) 501-4572
Kirksville	(816) 785-4307	Rolla	(573) 341-4559
Springfield			(417) 836-5685
St. Louis			(314) 977-7232
Warrensburg			(816) 543-4402

Missouri Small Business Investment Companies
Clayton Enterprise Fund   (314) 725-5500
Kansas City-Bankers Capital Corporation   (816) 531-1600
Kansas City-Capital for Business Venture Fund II,LP   (816) 234-2357
Kansas City-KCEP   (816) 960-1771
Kansas City-MorAmerica Capital Corporation   (816) 842-0114
Kansas City-United Missouri Capital Corporation   (816) 860-7914
St. Louis-Capital for Business Venture Fund I, Inc.   (314) 746-7427
St. Louis-Gateway Partners, LP   (314) 721-5707

Missouri Certified Development Companies
Camdenton-Central Ozarks Development, Inc.   (573) 346-5692
Clayton-Business Finance Corporation of St. Louis County (314) 889-7663
Columbia-Enterprise Development Corporation   (573) 875-8117
Jefferson City-Rural Missouri, Inc.   (573) 635-0136

Kansas City-Clay Development Corporation	(816) 468-4989
Kansas City-Economic Development Corp. of Kansas City	(816) 221-0636
Hillsboro-Economic Development Corp. of Jefferson County	(314) 789-5336
Rolla-Meramec Regional Development	(573) 364-2993
St. Charles-St. Charles EDC	(314) 441-6880
St. Joseph-Mo-Kan Development, Inc.	(816) 233-3144
St. Louis-St. Louis Local Development Company	(314) 622-3400
Trenton-Green Hills Rural Development. Inc.	(816) 359-5086

Micro Loans
Kansas City-Center for Business Innovation   (816) 561-8567

MONTANA

Statewide Financing Information and Resources: www.state.mt.us

Department of Commerce   (406) 444-3494
1424 Ninth Avenue, Helena, MT 59620-0501

Economic Development
• Economic Development Division   (406) 444-3814
• Business Recruitment Program   (406) 444-4187

Financial Assistance
• Microbusiness Finance Program   (406) 444-4187
• Board of Investments   (406) 444-0001
• CDBG Economic Development Program   (406) 444-2787
Minority/Women
• Disadvantaged Business and Women's
  Business Procurement Assistance   (406) 444-6337

SBA District Office   (406) 441-1081
301 South Park, Drawer 10054, Room 334, Helena, MT 59626

Montana Small Business Development Centers
Montana Department of Commerce   (406) 444-4780
1424 North Avenue, Helena, MT 59620

Billings	(406) 256-6875	Kalispell	(406) 756-3833
Bozeman	(406) 587-3113	Missoula	(406) 543-3550
Butte	(406) 782-7333	Sidney	(406) 482-5024
Cedar Falls-High Plains Development			(406) 454-1934
Havre			(406) 265-9226
Helena-Small Business Development Service			(406) 444-4780

Montana Certified Development Companies
Billings-Economic Devel. Corp. of Yellowstone County   (406) 245-0415
Helena-Montana community Finance Corp.   (406) 443-3261

NEBRASKA

Statewide Financing Information and Resources:	www.state.ne.us

Nebraska Department of Economic Development   (402) 471-3111
P.O. Box 94666, 301 Centennial Mall South, Lincoln, NE 68509-4666

Economic Development
- Existing Business Assistance Division   (402) 471-4167
- One-Stop Business Assistance Center   (402) 471-3782
- Nebraska Business Development Center   (402) 595-2381
- Entrepreneurship Projects   (402) 471-4803

Financial Assistance
- Export Promotion   (402) 471-4668
- Nebraska investment Finance Authority   (402) 434-3900
Minority/Women
- Office of Women's Business Ownership   (402) 221-3622

Nebraska Chamber of Commerce & Industry   (402) 474-4422
1320 Lincoln Mall, P.O. Box 95128, Lincoln, NE 68509

SBA District Office   (402) 221-3622
11141 Mill Valley Road, Omaha, NE 68154

Nebraska Small Business Development Centers
University of Nebraska at Omaha   (402) 554-2541
College of Business Administration Bldg.
60th & Dodge Streets, Room 407, Omaha, NE 68182

Chadron	(308) 432-6286	Omaha	(402) 595-3511
Kearney	(308) 865-8344	Omaha (U. of NE)	(402) 595-2391
Lincoln	(402) 472-3358	Peru	(402) 872-2274
North Platte	(308) 635-7513	Scottsbluff	(308) 635-7513
Wayne	(402) 375-7575		

Nebraska Certified Development Company
Lincoln-Nebraska Economic Development Corporation   (402) 475-2795

Micro Loans
Omaha-Small Business Network   (402) 346-8262

NEVADA

Statewide Financing Information and Resources:	www.state.nv.us

Nevada State Development Corporation   (702) 323-3625
350 South Central Street, Suite 310, Reno, NV 89501

Economic Development
- Nevada Department of Business and Industry   (702) 486-2750
- Nevada State Development Corporation   (702) 323-3625
- Nevada Self-Employment Trust (NSET)   (702) 329-6789

Financial Assistance
- Department of Business and Industry   (702) 687-4250
  Industrial Development Revenue Bond Program
- Southern Nevada Certified Development Company   (702) 732-3998
- Nevada Revolving Loan Fund Program   (702) 882-3882 or (702) 687-1812
- Nevada State Development Corporation   (702) 323-3625
- Commission on Economic Development   (702) 687-4325
- Nevada Development Capital Corporation   (702) 323-3625

Minority/Women
- Nevada Department of Business and Industry   (702) 486-2750

Nevada State Chamber of Commerce   (702) 686-3030
405 Marsh Avenue, P.O. Box 3499, Reno, NV 89505
SBA District Office   (702) 388-6611
301 E. Stewart St., Rm. 301, P.O. Box 7527, Las Vegas, NV 89125-2527

Nevada Small Business Development Centers
University of Nevada at Reno   (702) 784-1717
College of Business Administration
Mail Stop 032, 1664 N. Virginia Street, Reno, NV 89503

Winnemucca	(702) 623-5777	Carson City (CoC)	(702) 882-1565
Las Vegas	(702) 895-0852	Elko (CC)	(702) 753-2245
North Las Vegas	(702) 399-6300	Incline Village (CoC)	(702) 831-4440

Small Business Investment Companies

Nevada Certified Development Companies
Las Vegas-New Ventures Capital Development   (702) 382-9522
Las Vegas-Southern Nevada Certified Development Corp.   (702) 732-3998
Reno-Nevada State Development Corporation   (702) 323-3625

NEW HAMPSHIRE

Statewide Financing Information and Resources: www.state.nh.us

Business Finance Authority   (603) 271-2391
New Hampshire Industrial Development Authority
Four Park Street, Suite 302, Concord, NH 03301

Business Development
- Business Visitation Program .... (603) 271-2591
- Corporate Division .... (603) 271-3244
- New Hampshire Business Development Corporation ... (603) 623-5500
- Office of Business and Industrial Development ... (603) 271-2591

Financial Assistance
- Business Finance Authority .... (603) 271-2391
  Industrial Revenue Bonds
  Credit Enhancement Programs
- Office of Business and Industrial Development ... (603) 271-2591
- Technology Capital Network, Inc. .... (617) 253-7163

Business and Industry Association of New Hampshire ... (603) 224-5388
122 North Main Street, Concord, NH 03301

SBA District Office
143 North Main St., Suite 202, P.O. Box 1258, Concord, NH 03302-1258

New Hampshire Small Business Development Centers
University of New Hampshire .... (603) 862-2200
108 McConnell Hall, Durham, NH 03824

Keene	(603) 358-2602	Littleton	(603) 444-1053
Manchester	(603) 624-2000	Nashua	(603) 886-1233
Plymouth	(603) 535-2526		

New Hampshire Certified Development Companies
Concord-Concord Regional Development corporation ... (603) 228-1872
Portsmouth-Granite State Economic Development Corp. ... (603) 436-0009

Micro Loans
Concord-Capital Regional Development .... (603) 228-1872
Portsmouth-Granite State EDC .... (603) 436-0009

NEW JERSEY

Statewide Financing Information and Resources: .... www.state.nj.us

New Jersey Department of Commerce and Economic Development
20 West State Street, CN 835, Trenton, NJ 08625 ... (609) 292-2444

Economic Development
- Prospect Marketing .... (609) 292-0700

Financial Assistance
- New Jersey Economic Development Authority ...... (609) 292-1800
  -Commercial Lending .... (609) 292-0187

Minority/Women
• Division of Development for Small Business and
  Women's and Minority Businesses   (609) 292-3860

New Jersey State Chamber of Commerce   (609) 989-7888
50 W. State Street, Suite 1310, Trenton, NJ 08608

SBA District Office   (201) 645-2434
2 Gateway Center, Fourth Floor, Newark, NJ 07102

New Jersey Small Business Development Centers
Rutgers University   (201) 648-5950
Graduate School of Management   (201) 648-5950
University Heights, 180 University Ave, Newark, NJ 07102
Atlantic City   (609) 345-5600   Trenton   (609) 586-4800
Camden   (609) 757-6221   Union   (908) 527-2946
Lincroft   (908) 842-8685   Washington   (908) 689-9620
Paramus   (201) 447-7841

New Jersey Small Business Investment Companies
Chatham-MidMark Capital, LP   (201) 822-2999
Fort Lee-Capital Circulation Corporation   (201) 947-8637
Little Falls-Tappan Zee Capital Corporation   (201) 256-8280
Livingston-CIT Group/Venture Capital, Inc.   (201) 740-5429
Newark-ESLO Capital Corporation   (201) 242-4488
Newark-Rutgers Minority Investment Company   (201) 648-5287
Summit-First Fidelity Capital   (908) 598-3363
Teaneck-DFW Capital Partners, LP   (201) 836-2233

New Jersey Certified Development Companies
Newark-Union County Economic Development Corporation   (908) 527-1166
Trenton-Corporation for Business Assistance in New Jersey (609) 633-2631
West Orange- Economic Development Ciro, Essex County   (201) 731-2772

Micro Loans
Newark-Greater Newark Business Development   (201) 242-6237
Trenton-Trenton Business Asst.   (609) 989-3509

NEW MEXICO

Statewide Financing Information and Resources: www.state.nm.us

Economic Development Department   (505) 827-0300
P.O. Box 20003, Santa Fe, NM 87504-5003

Economic Development
• New Mexico Small Business Development Center   (505) 438-1362

Financial Assistance
• Economic Development Division (505) 827-0300

Minority/Women
• Governor's Commission on the Status of Women   (505) 841-8920

Association of Commerce & Industry of New Mexico   (505) 842-0644
2309 Renard Place, SE, Suite 402, Albuquerque, NM 87106

SBA District Office   (505) 766-1870
625 Silver Avenue, SW, Suite 320, Albuquerque, NM 87102

New Mexico Small Business Development Centers
Santa Fe Community College   (505) 438-1362
P.O. Box 4187, South Richards Avenue, Santa Fe, NM 87502-4187

Alamogondo	(505) 434-5272	Los Alamos	(505) 662-0001
Albuquerque	(505) 248-0132	Los Lunas	(505) 925-8980
Carlsbad	(505) 887-6562	Las Vegas	(505) 454-2595
Clovis	(505) 769-4136	Roswell	(505) 624 7133
Espanola	(505) 747-2236	Silver City	(505) 538-6320
Farmington	(505) 599-0528	Gallup	(505) 722-2220
Tucumcaru	(505) 461-4413	Grants	(505) 287-8221
Las Cruces	(505) 527-7606	Hobbs	(505) 392-5549

New Mexico Certified Development Company
Albuquerque-Enchantment Land Certified Devel. Corp.   (505) 843-9232

Micro Loans
Albuquerque-Women's Economic Self-Sufficiency   (505) 848-4760

NEW YORK

Statewide Financing Information and Resources: www.state.ny.us

New York Empire State Development   (518) 473-0499

Division for Small Business
One Commerce Plaza, Albany, NY 12245

Business Development
• Business Assistance Hot Line   (800) 782-8369
• Business Service Ombudsman   (518) 473-0499 or (212) 803-2289
• Division for Small Business   (518) 473-0499
• New York State Small Business Advisory Board   (518) 473-0499
• Small Business Advocacy Program   (518) 473-0499 or (212) 803-2200

Financial Assistance
• Empire State Development Corporation   (212) 803-3100

Minority Women
• Entrepreneurial Assistance Program   (212) 803-2410
• Minority and Women's Business Division   (212) 803-2410

Other Key New York Phone Numbers

Business Council of New York State (518) 465-7511
125 Washington Avenue, Albany, NY 12210

SBA District Offices
Buffalo   (716) 551-4301
   111 West Huron Street, Room 1311, Buffalo, NY 14202
Elmira (Branch Office)   (607) 734-8130
   333 East Water Street, Fourth Floor, Elmira, NY 14901
Melville (Branch Office)   (516) 454-0750
   35 Pinelawn Road, Suite 207W, Melville, NY 11747
New York City   (212) 264-4355
   26 Federal Plaza, Room, 3100, New York, NY 10278
Rochester (Branch Office)   (716) 263-6700
   100 State Street, Suite 410, Rochester, NY 14614
Syracuse   (315) 448-0423
   100 South Clinton Street, Room 1073, Syracuse, NY 13261

New York Small Business Development Centers
State University of New York (SUNY)   (518) 443-5398
SUNY Plaza S-523, Albany, NY 12246   (800) 732-SBDC

Location	Phone	Location	Phone
Albany	(518) 442-5577	New York City	(212) 346-1900
Binghamton	(607) 777-4024	Niagara Falls	(716) 285-4793
Bronx	(718) 563-3570	Oswego	(315) 343-1545
Brooklyn	(718) 368-4619	Plattsburgh	(518) 562-4260
Buffalo	(716) 878-4030	Rochester	(716) 232-7310
Canton	(315) 386-7312	Sanborn	(716) 693-1910
Corning	(607) 962-9461	Southhampton	(516) 287-0059
Dobbs Ferry	(914) 674-7485	Staten Island	(718) 390-7645
Farmington	(516) 420-2765	Stony Brook	(516) 632-9070
Fishkill	(914) 897-2607	Suffern	(914) 356-0370
Geneseo	(716) 245-5429	Syracuse	(315) 492-3029
Geneva	(315) 781-1253	Utica	(315) 792-7546
Hempstead	(516) 564-8672	Waterton	(315) 782-9262
Jamaica	(718) 262-2880	White Plains	(914) 644-4116
Jamestown	(716) 665-5754	Kingston	(914) 339-0025

New York Small Business Investment Companies

Albany-NYBDC Capital Corporation	(518) 463-2268
Buffalo-M&T capital Corporation	(716) 848-3800
Flushing-FirstCounty Capital, Inc.	(718) 461-1778
Flushing-Flushing Capital Corporation	(718) 886-5866
Great Neck-Sterling Commercial Capital, Inc.	(516) 482-7374
Mount Kisco-KOCO Capital Co.	(914) 241-7430
New York-American Asian Capital Corporation	(212) 422-6880
New York-Argentum Capital Partners, LP	(212) 949-8272
New York-BT Capital Corporation	(212) 250-8082
New York-Barclays Capital	(212) 412-3937
New York-Capital Investors & Management Corporation	(212) 964-2480
New York-Chase Manhattan Capital Partners	(212) 662-3100
New York-Citicorp Venture Capital, LTD	(212) 559-1127
New York-Creditanstalt	(203) 861-1410
New York-East Coast Venture Capital, Inc.	(212) 245-6460
New York-Edwards Capitak Co. (Medallion Fin. Corp.)	(212) 682-3300
New York-Elk Associates Funding Corporation	(212) 355-2449
New York-Empire State Capital Corporation	(212) 513-1799
New York-Eos Partners SBIC, LP	(212) 832-5814
New York-Esquire Capital	(516) 462-6944
New York-Exeter Equity Partners, LP	(212) 872-1170
New York-Exeter Venture Lenders, LP	(212) 872-1170
New York-Exim Capital Corporation	(212) 683-3375
New York-Fair Capital Corporation	(212) 964-2480
New York-First Wall Street SBIC, LP	(212) 742-3770
New York-Freshstart Venture Capital Corporation	(212) 265-2249
New York-Furman Selz SBIC, LP	(212) 309-8200
New York-Hanam Capital Corporation	(212) 564-5225
New York-Inter Equity Capital Partners, LP	(212) 779-2022
New York-LEG Partners SBIC, LP	(212) 207-1585
New York-Medallion Funding Corporation	(212) 682-3300
New York-NatWest Capital	(212) 602-1200
New York-Norwood Venture Corporation	(212) 869-5075
New York-Paribas Principal, Inc.	(212) 841-2115
New York-Pierre Funding Corportion	(212) 888-1515
New York-Prospect Street	(212) 490-0480
New York-Pyramid Ventures, Inc.	(212) 250-9571
New York-Transportation Capital Corp. (Medallion Fin.)	(212) 682-3300
New York-Trusty Capital, Inc.	(212) 629-3011
New York-UBS Partners, Inc.	(212) 821-6490
New York-United Capital Investment Corporation	(212) 682-7210
New York-Venture Opportunities Corportion	(212) 832-3737
Purchase-International Paper Capital Formation, Inc.	(914) 397-1579
Rochester-Ibero American Investors Corporation	(716) 262-3440
Rye-Fundex Capital	(914) 967-2227
Tarrytown-TLC Funding Corporation	(914) 332-5200

New York Certified Development Companies
Albany-Albany Local Development Corporation	(518) 434-5192
Albany-Empire State Certified Development Corporation	(518) 463-2268
Binghamton Tier Information & Enterprises Resources, Inc.	(607) 724-1327
Buffalo-Buffalo Enterprise Development Corporation	(716) 842-6923
Carle Place-Long Island Development Corporation	(516) 349-7800
Hudson-Hudson Development Company	(518) 828-4718
Jamestown-Chautauqua Region Industrial Development Corp.	(716) 664-3262
Mohawk-Mohawk Valley Certified Development Corp.	(315) 866-4671
Oswego-Operation Oswego County, Inc.	(315) 343-1545
Port Jervis-Progress Development Corporation	(914) 858-8358
Rochester-Monroe County Industrial Development Corp.	(716) 428-5060
Rochester-Rochester Economic Development Corporation	(716) 428-6966
Saranac Lake-Adirondack Economic Development Corp.	(518) 891-5523
Syracuse-Greater Syracuse Business Development Corp.	(315) 470-1887

Micro Loans
New York-Manhattan BoroughDevelopment	(212) 791-3660
Rochester-Rural Opportunities	(716) 546-7180

NORTH CAROLINA

Statewide Financing Information and Resources:	www.state.nc.us

North Carolina Small Business and Technology (919) 715-7272
Development Center
333 Fayetteville Street Mall, Raleigh, NC 27603

Economic Development
• North Carolina Small Business and Technology (919) 715-7272
Development Center

Financial Assistance
• North Carolina Small Business and Technology (919) 715-7272
Development Center

North Carolina Citizens for Business & Industry (919) 836-1400
225 Hillsborough Street, Suite 460, P.O. Box 2508, Raleigh, NC 27602

SBA District Office (704) 344-6563
208 North College St., Suite A2015, Charlotte, NC 28202-2137

North Carolina Small Business Development Centers
University of North Carolina			(919) 715-7272
333 Fayette Street Mall, Suite 1150, Raleigh, NC 27601-1742			(800) 258-0862
Ashville	(704) 251-6025	Greensboro	(910) 334-7005
Boone	(704) 262-2492	Greenville	(919) 328-6183

Chapel Hill	(919) 962-0389	Hickory	(704) 345-1110
Charlotte	(704) 548-1090	Pembroke	(910) 521-6603
Cullowhee	(704) 227-7494	Rocky Mount	(919) 985-5130
Elizabeth City	(919) 335-3247	Wilmington	(910) 395-3744
Fayetteville	(910) 486-1727	Winston-Salem	(910) 750-2030

North Carolina Small Business Investment Companies
Charlotte-NationsBanc Capital Corporation	(704) 386-8063
Greensboro-Blue Ridge Investors	(910) 370-0576
Raleigh-Oberlin	(914) 743-2544

North Carolina Certified Development Companies
Charlotte-Centralina Development Corporation, Inc.	(704) 372-2416
Charlotte-Charlotte Certified Development Corporation	(704) 373-0160
Durham-Self-Help Ventures Fund	(919) 956-4400
Henderson-Region K Certified Development Company, Inc.	(919) 492-2531
Hertford-Abemaele Development Authority	(919) 426-5755
Hickory-Region E Development Corporation	(704) 322-9191
New Bern-Neuse River Development Authority, Inc.	(919) 638-6724
Raleigh-Capital Economic Development Corporation	(919) 832-4524
Rutherfordton-Region C Development Corporation, Inc.	(704) 287-2281
Waynesville-Smokey Mountain Development Corporation	(704) 452-1967
Wilmington-Wilmington Industrial Development, Inc.	(910) 763-8414
Winston-Salem-Northwest Piedmont Development Corp.	(910) 761-2108

Micro Loans
Boone-W.A.M.Y. Community Action	(704) 264-2421
Durham-Self-Help Ventures	(919) 956-8526

NORTH DAKOTA

Statewide Financing Information and Resources:	www.state.nd.us

Department of Economic Development and Finance	(701) 328-5300
1833 East Dismarck Expresseway, Bismarck, ND 58504	

Economic Development
• Business and Community Assistance Center	
Minot State University	(701) 858-3825
• Institute for Business and Industry Development	(701) 231-1001
• Center for Innovation and Business Development	(701) 777-3132

Financial Assistance
• Economic Development & Finance	(701) 328-5300

Minority/Women
- Native American Business Assistance   (701) 328-5300
- Women's Business Development   (701) 328-5300

Greater North Dakota Assn./State Chamber of Commerce   (701) 222-0929
2000 Schafer Street, P.O. Box 2639, Bismarck, ND 58502

SBA District Office   (701) 239-5131
657 2nd Avenue, North, Room 219, P.O. Box 3086, Fargo, ND 58108-3086

North Dakota Small Business Development Centers
University of North Dakota   (701) 777-3700
118 Gamble Hall, Grand Forks, ND 58202-7308   (800) 445-7232

Bismarck	(701) 223-8583	Dickinson	(701) 227-2096
Grand Forks	(701) 772-8502	Fargo (Regional)	(701) 237-0986
Minot	(701) 852-8861	Grafton	(800) 445-7232

North Dakota Small Business Investment Company
Fargo-North Dakota SBIC, LP   (701) 298-0003

North Dakota Certified Development Company
Fargo-Fargo-Cass Economic Development Center   (701) 237-6132

Micro Loans
Fargo-Lake Agassiz Regional   (701) 239-5373

OHIO

Statewide Financing Information and Resources: www.state.oh.us
Office of Small Business   (614) 466-2718
Ohio Department of Development
77 South High Street, P.O. Box 1001, Columbus, OH 43216-1001

Economic Development   (419) 332-2882
- One-Stop Business Permit Center

Financial Assistance
- Office of Minority Financial Incentives   (614) 644-7708
- Business Loans   (614) 466-5420

Minority/Women
- Women's Business Resource Program   (614) 466-4945
- Minority Business Development Program   (614) 466-5700

Ohio Chamber of Commerce   (614) 228-4201
230 East Town Street, P.O. Box 15159, Columbus, OH 43215-0154

SBA District Offices
Cincinnati (Branch Office)   (513) 684-2814
    525 Vine Street, Suite 870, Cincinnati, OH 45202
Cleveland   (216) 522-4180
    1111 Superior Avenue, Suite 630, Cleveland, OH 44114-2507
Columbus   (614) 469-6860
    2 Nationwide Plaza, Suite 1400, Columbus, OH 43215-2542
Ohio Small Business Development Centers
Ohio Department of Development   (614) 466-2711
77 South High Street, P.O. Box 1001, Columbus, OH 43226-1001

Akron	(330) 379-3170	Lima	(419) 229-5320
Athens	(614) 592-1188	Lorian	(216) 233-6500
Bowling	(419) 352-3817	Marietta	(614) 376-4832
Canton	(216) 499-9600	Marion	(614) 387-0188
Celina	(419) 586-0355	New Philadelphia	(216) 339-9070
Cincinnati	(513) 753-7141	Portsmouth	(614) 355-2316
Cleveland	(216) 621-3300	Salem	(216) 332-0361
Cleveland	(216) 432-5364	Southpoint	(614) 894-3838
Columbus	(614) 225-6081	Springfield	(513) 322-7821
Dayton	(513) 226-8230	St. Clairsville	(614) 695-9678
Dayton	(513) 873-3503	Steubenville	(614) 282-6226
Defiance	(419) 784-3777	Toledo	(419) 243-8191
Fremont	(419) 334-8400	Youngstown	(216) 746-3350
Hillsboro	(513) 393-9599	Zanesville	(614) 452-4868
Jefferson	(216) 576-9134	Kettering	(513) 258-6180

Ohio Small Business Investment Companies
Cincinnati-River Cities Capital Fund, LP   (513) 621-9700
Cleveland-Clarion Capital Corporation   (216) 687-1096
Cleveland-Key Equity Capital Corporation   (216) 689-5776
Cleveland-National City Capital Corporation   (216) 575-2491
Columbus-Banc One Capital   (614) 227-4209
Dayton-Enterprise Ohio   (513) 226-0457
Worthington-Cactus Capital Company   (614) 436-4060

Ohio Certified Development Companies
Akron-Cascade Capital   (216) 376-5550
Canton-Stark Development Board Fianace Corporation   (330) 453-5900
Cincinnati-Cincinnati Local Development Company   (513) 352-1958
Cincinnati-Hamilton County Development Company, Inc.   (513) 632-8292
Cleveland-Cleveland Area Development Finance Corp.   (216) 621-3300
Columbus-Columbus Countywide Development Corp.   (614) 645-6171
Columbus-Ohio Statewide Development Corporation   (614) 466-5043
Dayton-Citywide Small Business Development Corp.   (513) 226-0457
Dayton-County Corp Development   (513) 225-6328
Franklin-Certified Devel. Corp. of Warren County, Inc.   (513) 748-4359

Hamilton-Certified Development Co. of Butler County, Inc.	(513) 887-3404
Mentor-Lake County Small Business Assistance Corporation	(216) 951-1290
Mentor-Mentor Economic Assistance Corporation	(216) 974-5739
Springfield-Clark County Development Corporation	(419) 243-8251
Xenia-Xenia-Greene County Small Business Devel. Co., Inc.	(513) 372-0444
Youngstown-Mahoning Valley Economic Development Corp.	(330) 759-3668

Micro Loans

Akron-Women's Entrepreneurial Growth	(330) 379-9280
Columbus-Columbus Countywide Development	(614) 645-6171

OKLAHOMA

Statewide Financing Information and Resources: www.state.ok.us

Oklahoma Department of Commerce   (405) 843-9770
6601 Broadway Extension, Building 5, Oklahoma City, OK 73116

Economic Development
- Business Development Division   (405) 841-5167
- Business Service Program   (405) 841-5227
- Research and Planning Division   (405) 841-5170
- Community Affairs and Development Division   (405) 841-9326

Financial Assistance
- Capital Resources Network   (405) 841-5140
- Oklahoma Development Finance Authority   (405) 848-9761

Minority/Women
- Minority Business Assistance   (405) 841-5227
- Women-Owned Certification   (405) 841-5242

Oklahoma State Chamber of Commerce & Industry   (405) 235-3669
330 NE 10th Street, Oklahoma City, OK 73104

SBA District Office   (405) 231-5521
210 West Park Avenue, Suite 1300, Oklahoma City, OK 73102

Oklahoma Small Business Development Centers
Southern State University   (405) 924-0277
517 West University, Durant, OK 74730   (800) 522-6154

Ada	(405) 436-3190	Midwest City	(405) 733-7348
Alva	(405) 327-8608	Oklahoma City	(405) 232-1968
Durant	(405) 924-0277	Poteau	(918) 647-4019
Enid	(405) 242-7989	Tahlequah	(918) 458-0802
Langston	(405) 466-3256	Tulsa	(918) 583-2600
Lawton	(405) 248-4946	Weatherford	(405) 774-1040
Miami	(918) 540-0575		

Oklahoma Small Business Investment Companies
Oklahoma City-BancFirst Investment Corporation   (405) 270-1000

Oklahoma Certified Development Companies

Burnes Flat-SWODA Development Corporation	(405) 562-4882
Durant-Rural Enterprises, Inc.	(405) 924-5094
Muskogee-Verd-Ark-Ca Developemtn Corporation	(918) 683-4634
Oklahoma City-Metro Area Development Corporation	(405) 424-5181
Tulsa-Small Business Capital Corporation	(918) 599-6112
Tulsa-Tulsa Economic Development Corporation	(918) 585-8332
Tulsa-Tulsa Economic Development	(918) 585-8332

OREGON

Statewide Financing Information and Resources: www.state.or.us

Economic Development Office   (503) 986-0123
775 Summer Street, NE, Salem, OR 97310

Economic Development
• Marketing Services   (503) 986-0111
• Business Inforamation Center   (503) 986-2222
    Business Start-ups Packets

Financial Assistance
• Business Finance Section   (503) 986-0160

Minority/Women
• Oregon Department of Transportation   (503) 986-2643
    Office of Minority, Women's & Emerging Small Businesses   (503) 378-5651

Associated Oregon Industries, Inc.   (503) 588-0050
1149 Court Street, NE, P.O. Box 12519, Salem, OR 97309

SBA District Office   (503) 326-2682
222 South West Columbia St., Suite 500, Portland, OR 97201-6605

Oregon Small Business Development Centers
Lane Community College   (541) 726-2250

44 West Broadway, Suite 501, Eugene, OR 97401-3021

Albany	(541) 917-4923	Milwaukie	(503) 656-4447
Ashland	(541) 772-3478	Ontario	(541) 889-2617
Bend	(541) 383-7290	Pendleton	(541) 276-6233
Coos Bay	(541) 888-7100	Portland	(503) 274-7482
Eugene	(541) 726-2255	Roseburg	(541) 672-2535
Grants Pass	(541) 471-3515	Salem	(503) 399-5088
Gresham	(503) 667-7658	Seaside	(503) 738-3347
Klamath Falls	(541) 885-1760	The Dalles	(541) 298-3118
LaGrande	(541) 962-3391	Tillamook	(503) 842-2551
Lincoln City	(541) 994-4166	Medford	(541) 772-3478

Oregon Small Business Investment Companies
Portland-Northern Pacifice Capital Corporation   (503) 241-1255
Portland-Shaw Venture Partners III, LP   (503) 228-4884

Oregon Certified Development Companies
Albany-Cascades West Financial Services, Inc.   (541) 967-8551
Beaverton-Northwest Small Business Finance Corporation   (503) 629-9662
Pendleton-Greater Eastern Oregon Development Corp.   (541) 276-6745
Redmond-Oregon Certified Business Development Corp.   (541) 672-6728

Micro Loans
Albany-Cascades West   (541) 967-8551

PENNSYLVANIA

Statewide Financing Information and Resources: www.state.pa.us

Department of Commerce   (717) 783-8950
400 Forum Building, Harrisburg, PA 17120

Economic Development
• Small Business Resource Center   (717) 783-5700
• Office of Entrepreneurial Assistance (ARC Program)   (717) 783-8950
• Office of Small Business Advocate (717) 783-2525

Financial Assistance
• Machine and Equipment Loan Fund   (717) 783-5046
• Pennsylvania Capital Access Program   (717) 783-1109
• Pennsylvania Capital Loan Fund   (717) 783-1768
• Pennsylvania Economic Development Financing Authority   (717) 783-1108
• Pennsylvania Industrial Development Authority   (717) 787-6245

- Pennsylvania Minority Business Development Authority   (717) 783-1127
- Revenue Bond and Mortgage Program   (717) 783-1108

Minority/Women
- Women's Business Advocate and
  Entrepreneurial Assistance Office   (717) 787-3339
- Governor's Advisory Commission on
  African American Affairs   (717) 772-5085
- Governor's Advisory Commission on Latino Affairs   (717) 783-3877

Pennsylvania Chamber of Business & Industry   (717) 255-3252
One Commerce Square, 417 Walnut streeet, Harrisburg, PA 17101

SBA District Offices
Harrisburg (Branch Office)   (717) 782-3840
   100 Chrstnut Street, Room309, Harrisburg, PA 17101
King of Prussia   (610) 962-3800
   475 Allendale Road, Sute 201, King of Prusia, PA 19406
Pittsburgh   (412) 644-2780
   960 Penn Avenue, 5th Floor, Pittsburgh, PA 15222
Wiles-Barre (Branch Office)   (717) 826-6497
   20 N. Pennsylvania Ave, Room 2327, Wilkes-Barre, PA 18701-3589

Pennslyvania Small Business Development Centers
University of Pennsylvania, the Wharton School   (215) 898-1219
Vance Hall, 4th Floor, 3733 Spruce St., Philadelphia, PA 19104-6374

Bethlehem	(610) 758-3980	Loretto	(814) 472-3200
Clarion	(814) 226-2060	Philadelphia	(215) 204-7282
Erie	(814) 871-7714	Pittsburgh	(412) 396-6233
Harrisburgh	(717) 720-4230	Scanton	(717) 941-7588
Latrobe	(412) 537-4572	Wilkes-Barre	(717) 831-4340
Lewisburg	(717) 524-1249		

Pennsylvania Small Business Investment Companies
Malvern-CIP Capital, LP   (610) 695-2066
Philadelphia-Core State Enerprises   (215) 973-6519
Radnor-Meridian enture Partners   (610) 254-2999
Wayne-Grater Philadelphia Venture Capital Corp. Inc.   (610) 688-6829
Wayne-CIP Capital   (610) 964-7860

Pennsylvania Certified Development Companies
Allentown-Allentown Economic Development Corporation   (610) 435-8890
Altoona-Altoona-Blair County Development Corp.   (814) 944-6113
Butler-Community Development Corp. of Butler County   (412) 283-1961
Exton-South Eastern Econ. Development Co. of Pennsylvania   (610) 363-6110
Lewisburg-SEDA-COG Local Development Corporation   (717) 524-4491

Philadelphia-DelVal Business Fiance Corporation	(215) 871-3770
Philadelphia-PIDC Local Develoment Corporation	(215) 496-8020
Pittsburg-Pittsburg Countywide Corporation Inc.	(412) 471-1030

Micro Loans
Philadelphia-Ben Franklin Tech Center	(215) 382-0380
York-York County Industrial Dev.	(717) 846-8879

PUERTO RICO

Statewide Financing Information and Resources:	www.state.pr.us
Department of Economic Development & Commerce	(787) 721-2898
P.O. Box 4435, San Juan, PR 00902-4435	

Economic Development
• Office of Ombudsman	(787) 724-7373
• Commercial Development Administration	(787) 721-3290

Financial Assistance
• Economic Development Bank for Puerto Rico	(787) 766-4300
• Economic Development Administration	(787) 758-4747
• Government Bank for Puerto Rico	(787) 722-3760

Chamber of Commerce of Puerto Rico	(787) 721-3290
100 Tetuan Street, Old San Juan, PR 00901	

SBA District Office	(787) 766-5572
Citibank Bldg, 252 Ponce de Leon Ave., Sutie 201, Hato Rey, PR 00918	

Puerto Rico Small Business Development Centers
Edifico Union Plaza (787) 763-6811
Suite 701, 416 Ponca De Leon Ave., Hato Rey, PR 00918

Humacao	(809) 850-2500	Ponce	(809) 841-2641
San Juan	(809) 765-2335	Rio Piedras	(809) 763-5880

Pureto Rico Small Business Investment Company
Hato Rey-North America Investment Corporation	(787) 754-6178

Puerto Rico Certified Development Companies
Hato Rey- Corp. para el Fomento Econ. de la Ciudad Capital	(787) 756-5080
Hato Rey-North Puerto Rico Local Developemnt Co., Inc.	(787) 754-7474
Orocvis-Caciques Development Corporations	(787) 876-2520
San Juan-La Marketing Development Corporation	(787) 765-0801
Santurce-Advancer Local Developoment Corporation	(787) 721-6797

Micro Loans
Rio Piedras-Corp. for the Economic Devleopment	
of the City of San Juan	(787) 756-5080

RHODE ISLAND	
Statewide Financing Information and Resources:	www.state.ri.us
Rhode Island Economic Development Corporation 1 West Exchange Street, Providence, RI 02903	(401) 277-2601
Economic Development • Business Development Division	(401) 277-2601
Financial Assistance • Financing Programs • Small Business Loan Fund	(401) 277-2601 (401) 277-2601
Greater Providence Chamber of Commerce 30 Exchange Terrace, Providence, RI 02903	(401) 521-5000
SBA District Office 380 Westminister Street, Providence, RI 02903	(401) 528-4584

Rhode Island Small Business Development Centers
Bryant College SBDC   (401) 232-6111
1150 Douglas Pike, Smithfield, RI 02917-1282
Lincoln   (401) 334-1000   Middletown   (401) 849-6900
North Kingstown (401) 294-1228   Newport   (401) 849-6900
Providence   (401) 831-1330

Rhode Island Small Business Investment Companies
Cranston-Domestic Capital Corporation   (401) 946-3310
Providence-Fleet Equity Partners VI, LP   (401) 278-6770
Providence-Fllet Venture Resources, Inc.   (401) 278-6770
Providence-Moneta Capital Corporation   (401) 454-7500
Rhode Island Certified Development Company
Providence-Ocean State Business Development Authority   (401) 454-4560

Micro Loans
None

SOUTH CAROLINA	
Statewide Financing and Information Resources:	www.state.sc.us
Governor's Office-Small and Minority Business Assistance 1205 Pendleton Street, Columbia , SC 29201	(803) 734-0657

Economic Development
* Existing Business and Industry Services Department   (803) 737-0400

Financial Assistance
* Jobs Economic Develpment Authority   (803) 737-0079

Minority/Women
* Office of Small and Minority Business Assistance   (803) 734-0657

South Carolina Chamber of Commerce   (803) 799-4601
1201 Main Street, Suite 1810, Columbia, SC 29201

SBA District Office   (803) 765-5377
1835 Assembly Street, Room 358, Columbia, SC 29201

South Carolina Small Business Development Centers
University of South Carolina   (803) 777-4907
College of Business Administration, Columbia, SC 29208

Aiken	(803) 64103646	Florence	(803) 661-8256
Beaufort	(803) 521-4143	Greenville	(864) 250-8894
Charleston	(803) 740-6160	Greenwood	(803) 941-8071
Clemson	(803) 656-3227	Orangeburg	(803) 536-8445
Columbia	(803) 777-5118	Rock Hill	(803) 323-2283
Conway	(803) 349-2170	Spartanburg	(864) 594-5080

South Carolina Small Business Investment Companies
Charleston-Charleston Capital Corporation   (803) 723-6464
Greenville-Reedy River Ventures   (864) 232-6198

South Carolina Certified Development Companies
Columbia-Certified Development Corp. of South Carolina   (803) 798-4064
Rock Hill-Catawaba Regional Dev.   (803) 327-9041
Spartanburg-Cit of Spartanburg Development Corporation   (864) 596-2108
Sumter-Santee-Lynches Regional Development Corporation   (803) 775-7381

Micro Loans
Charleston-Charlesto Citywide Local Dev. Corp.   (803) 724-3796

SOUTH DAKOTA

Statewide Financing Information and Resources: www.state.sd.us

Governor's Office of Economic Development   (605) 773-5032
711 East Wells Avenue, Pierre, SD 57501-3369

Economic Development
- Economic Locaiton Services   (605) 773-5032
- Business Research Bureau   (605) 677-5287

Financial Assistance
- Financial Packaging   (605) 773-5032
- Economic Development Finance Authority   (605) 773-5032
- Revolving Economic Development and Initiative Fund   (605) 773-5032

Industry & Commerce Association of South Dakota   (605) 224-6161
108 North Euclid Avenue, P.O. Box 190, Pierre, SD 57501

SBA District Office   (605) 330-4231
110 South Phillips, Suite 200, Sioux Falls, SD 57102-1109

South Dakota Small Business Development Centers
University of South Dakota   (605) 677-5498
School of Business
Patterson Hall 115, 414 EAst Clarke Street, Vermillion, SD 57069
Aberdeen   (605) 626-2565   Sioux Falls   (605) 367-5753
Rapid City   (605) 394-5311

South Dakota Certified Development Companies
Pierre-South Dakota Development Corporation   (605) 773-5032
Speanfish-Northern Hills Community Dev.   (605) 642-7106
Watertown-First District Development Company   (605) 886-7225
Micro Loans
Kyle-Lakota Fund   (605) 455-2500

TENNESSEE

Statewide Financing Information and Resource: www.state.tn.us

Department of Econmic and Community Development   (800) 872-7201
320 Sixth Avenue North, Nashville, TN 37243

Economic Development
- Small Business Office   (615) 741-2626
- Center for Industrial Services   (615) 532-8657
- SCORE   (615) 736-7621

Minority/Women
- Office of Minority Business Enterprise   (615) 741-2545
- Women Business Owners   (615) 741-2545
- Minority Business Deveelopment Center   (615) 255-0432

Tennessee Assocaition of Business   (615) 256-5141
611 Commerce Street, Suite 3030, Nashville, TN 37203-3742

SBA District Office   (615) 736-5881
50 Advantage Way, Suite 201, Nashville, TN 37228-1500

Tennessee Small Business Development Centers
Unviersity of Memphis   (901) 678-2500
South Campus (Getwell Road), Building #1, Memphis, TN 38152

Chattanooga	(423) 266-5781	Johnson City	(423) 439-5630
Chattanooga	(423) 752-1774	Kingsport	(423) 392-8017
Clarksville	(615) 648-7764	Knoxville	(423) 525-0277
Cleveland	(423) 478-6247	Memphis	(901) 527-1041
Columbia	(615) 898-2745	Morristown	(423) 585-2675
Dyersburg	(901) 286-3201	Murfreesboro	(615) 898-2745
Hartsville	(615) 374-9521	Nashville	(615) 963-7179
Jackson	(901) 424-5389		

Tennessee Small business Investment Companies
Chattanooga-Valley Capital Corporation   (423) 265-1557
Memphis-West Tennessee Venture Capital Corporation   (901) 522-9237
Nashville-Equitas   (615) 383-8673
Nashville-Pacific Capital, LP   (615) 292-3166
Nashville-Sirrom Capital Corporation   (615) 256-0701

Tennessee Certified Development Companies
Chattanooga-Southeast Local Development Corporation   (423) 266-5781
Columbia-Sout Central Tennessee Business
    Development Corp.   (615) 381-2041
Knoxville-Areawide Development Corporation   (423) 588-7972
Nashville-Mid-Cumberland Area Development Corporation   (615) 862-8831

TEXAS

Statewide Financing Information and Resources: www.state.tx.us

Texas Department of Commerce   (512) 936-0100
1700 North Congress Avenue, P.O. Box 12728, Austin, TX 78711

Economic Development
- Texas One   (512) 936-0237
- Business Development Division   (512) 936-0223
- Information and Research   (512) 936-0081
- Business Information and Referral   (800) 888-0581

• Growth-Retention	(512) 936-0254
• Community Assistance/Small Business	(512) 936-0223

Financial Assistance

• Business Services	(512) 936-0282
• Capital Development	(512) 936-0260
• Enterprise Zone	(512) 936-0270
• Smart Jobs	(512) 936-0500
• Texas Manufacturing Assistance Center	(512) 936-0235

Minority/Women

• Community assistance/Small Business	(512) 936-0223

Other Key Texas Phone Numbers

Texas Association of Business and Chambers of Commerce   (512) 472-1594
1209 Nueces, Austin, TX 78701

SBA District Offices
Corpus Christi (Branch Office)   (512) 888-3331
   606 N. Carancahua, Suite 1200, Corpus Christi, TX 78476
El Paso   (915) 540-5155
   10737 Gateway West, Suite 114, Ft. Worth, TX 76155
Harlingen   (210) 427-8625
   222 E. Van Buren Street, Room 500, Harlingen, TX 78550-6855
Houston   (713) 773-6500
   9301 Southwest Freeway, Suite 550, Houston, TX 77074-1591
Lubbock   (806) 743-7462
   1611 Tenth Street   , Suite 200, Lubbock, TX 79401-2693
San Antonio   (210) 472-5900
   727 E. Durango Blve. Suite A-527, San Antonio, TX 78206-1204
Texas Small Business Develoment Centers
Dallas County Community College, North Texas SBDC   (214) 565-5831
   1402 Corinth Street, Suite3 2111, Dallas, TX 75215
Houston Small Business Development Center   (713) 752-8400
   1100 Louisiana, Suite 500, Houston, TX 77002
Lubbock Small Business Development Center   (806) 745-3973
   2579 South Loop 289, Lubbock, TX 79423
University of Texas, San Antionio   (210) 558-2460
   1222 North Main, San Antonio, TX 78212

Abilene	(915) 670-0300	Alpine	(915) 837-8694
Alvin	(713) 388-4686	Huntsville	(409) 294-3737
Amarillo	(806) 372-5151	Kingsville	(512) 595-5088
Athens	(903) 675-7403	Lake Jackson	(409) 266-3380
Austin	(512) 473-3510	Laredo	(210) 722-0563

Baytown	(713) 425-6309	Longview	(903) 757-5857
Beaumont	(409) 880-2367	Lubbock	(806) 745-1637
Bonham	(903) 583-4811	Brenham	(409) 830-4137
Lufkin	(409) 639-1887	Bryan	(409) 260-5222
Mt. Pleasant	(800) 357-7232	Corpus Christi	(512) 881-1888
Odessa	(915) 552-2455	Corsicana	(903) 874-0658
Paris	(903) 784-1802	Dallas	(214) 565-5842
Plano	(214) 985-3770	San Angelo	(915) 942-2098
San Antonio	(210) 558-2458	Stafford	(713) 933-7932
Dension	(903) 786-3551	Stephenville	(817) 968-9330
Houston-Charter Venture			(713) 692-6121
Duncanville	(214) 709-5878	Edinburg	(210) 316-2610
Tyler	(903) 510-2975	El Paso	(915) 534-3410
Uvalde	(210) 278-2527	Fort Worth	(817) 794-5978
Victoria	(512) 575-8944	Gainesville	(817) 668-4220
Waco	(817) 750-3600	Galveston	(409) 740-7380
Wichita Falls	(817) 689-4373	Grand Prairie	(214) 565-5850
Houston	(713) 591-9320		

Texas Small Business Investment Companies

Dallas-alliance Enterprise Corporation	(972) 991-1597
Dallas-AMT Capital	(214) 905-9760
Dallas-Banc One Capital Partners Corpoation	(214) 979-4360
Dallas-Capotal Southwest Venture Corporaation	(214) 233-8242
Dallas-Mapleleaf Capital, Ltd. (214) 239-5650	
Dallas-NationsBanc Capital Corporation	(214) 508-0900
Dallas-North Texas MESBIC, Inc.	(214) 991-8060
Dallas-PMC Investment Corporation (214) 380-0044	
Dallas-Stratford Capital Parnters, LP (214) 740-7377	
Dallas-Western Financial Capital Corporation	(214) 380-0044
Fort Worth-HCT Capital Corporation	(817) 763-8706
Fort Worth-SBIC Partners, LP	(817) 339-7020
Houston-Alliance Business Investment Co.	(713) 659-3131
Houston-The Catalyst Fund, Inc.	(713) 623-8133
Houston-Charter Venture	(713) 692-6121
Houston-Chen's Financial Group, Inc.	(713) 772-8868
Houston-Houston Partners, SBIP	(713) 222-8600
Houston-MSBIC Financial Corporation of Houston	(713) 869-4061
Houston-SBI Capital Corporation	(713) 975-1188
Houston-UNCO Ventures, Ltd.	(713) 622-9595
Houston-Ventex Partners, Ltd.	(713) 659-7860
San Antonio-First Capital Group	(210) 736-4233

Texas Certified Development Companies

Abilene-Council Finance	(915) 672-8544
Amarillo-Texas Panhandle Regional Development Corp.	(806) 372-3381
Austin-Capital Certified Development Corporation	(512) 936-0223

Austin-Cen-Tex Certified Development Corporation	(512) 473-3500
Austin-Texas Certified Development Company	(512) 476-8939
Beaumont-Southeast Texas Economic Devel. Foundation	(409) 838-6581
Brownsville-Brownsville Local Development Company Inc.	(210) 548-6150
Bryan-Bryan College Station Certified Development Co.	(409) 775-3699
Dallas-Dallas Business Finance	(214) 428-7332
El Paso-Upper Rio Grande Development Company	(915) 533-0998
Fort Worth-Fort Worth Economic Development Corporation	(817) 336-6420
Houston-Houston-Galveston Area Local Development Corp.	(713) 627-3200
Kilgore-East Texas Regional Development Company, Inc.	(903) 984-3989
Lubbock-Caprock Business Finance Corporation, Inc.	(806) 762-8721
McAllen-Lower Rio Grande Valley Certified Devel. Corp.	(210) 682-3481
Plano-North Texas Certified Development Corporation	(241) 516-0514
San Antonio-San Antonio Local Development Corporation	(210) 207-3932
Texarkana-Ark-Tex Regional Development Company, Inc.	(903) 798-3955
Waco-Central Texas Certified Development Company	(871) 799-0259

Micro Loans

Dallas-Southern Dallas Development Corp.	(214) 428-7332

UTAH

Statwide Financing Information and Resources:	www.state.ut.us
Community and Economic Development 324 South State Street, Sutie 500, Salt Lake City, UT 84111	(801) 538-8700

Economic Development
• Business Expansion & Retention	(801) 538-8775
• Small Business Development Center	(801) 255-5991

Financial Assistance
• Economic Development Corporation of Utah	(801) 538-8775
• Utah Capital Access Act	(801) 538-8776
• Utah Microenterprise Loan Fund	(801) 269-8408
• Utah Technology Finance Corporation	(801) 364-4346

Minority Opportunities
• Office of Black Affairs	(801) 538-8829
• Office of Hispanic Affairs	(801) 538-8850
• Office of Indian Affairs	(801) 538-8808

Utah State Chamber of Commerce Association c/o Sugar House Area Chamber of Commerce 1095 East 2100 South, Salt Lake City, UT 8413	(801) 467-0844

SBA District Office   (801) 524-3209
125 South State St., Room 2237, Salt Lake City, UT 84138-1195

Utah Small Business Development Centers
Salt Lake Community College   (801) 957-3480
1623 State St., Salt Lake City, UT 84115

Cedar City	(801) 586-5400	Orem	(801) 222-8230
Ephraim	(801) 283-4021	Price	(801) 637-5032
Logan	(801) 797-2277	Roosevelt	(801) 722-4523
Ogden	(801) 626-7232	St. George	(801) 652-7732
Moab	(801) 626-6070		

Utah Small Business Investment Companies
Salt Lake City-First Security Business Investment Corp.   (801) 246-5737
Salt Lake City-Wasatch Venture   (801) 524-8939

Utah Certified Development Company
Midvale-Deseret Certified Development Company   (801) 566-1163
Ogden-Northern Utah Capital   (801) 627-1333

Micro Loans
Salt Lake City-Utah Tech, Finance   (801) 364-4346

VERMONT

Statewide Financing Information and Resources: www.state.vt.us

Vermont Department of Economic Development   (802) 828-3221
109 State Street, Montpelier, VT 05602

Economic Development
• Small Business Development Center   (802) 728-9101

Financial Assistance
• Vermont Economic Development Authority   (802) 223-7226

Minority/Women
• Government Assistance Prgram   (802) 828-3221

Vermont Chamber of Commerce   (802) 223-3443
P.O. Box 37, Montpelier, VT 05601

SBA District Office   (802) 828-4422
87 State Street, Room 205, P.O. Box 605, Montpelier, VT 05601

Vermont Small Business Development Centers
Vermont Technical College   (802) 728-9101
P.O. Box 422, Randolph, VT0 5060-0422   (800) 464-SBDC
Brattleboro   (802) 258-3886   North Bennington   (802) 422-8975
Burlington   (802) 658-9228   Rutland   (802) 773-9147
Middlebury   (802) 388-7953   Springfield   (802) 885-2071
Montpelier (EDC)   (802) 223-4654
St. Johnsbury   (802) 748-1014

Vermont Small Business Investment Company
Waterbury-Green Mountain Capital, LP   (802) 244-8981

Vermont Certified Development Companies
Montpelier-Central Vermont Economic Development Corp.   (802) 223-4654
Montpelier-Vermont 503 Corporation   (802) 828-5627
St. Johnsbury-Northern Community Investment Corp.   (802) 748-5101

Micro-Loans
St. Albams-economic Development Council
    of Northern Vermont   (802) 524-4546

VIRGINIA

Statewide Financing Information and Resources: www.stae.va.us

Virginia Small Business Development Network
Virginia Department of Economic Development   (804) 371-8253
P.O. Box 798, Richmond, VA 23206-0798

Economic Development
• Small Business Development Center   (804) 371-8253

Financial Assistance
• Virginia Small Business Financing Authority   (804) 371-8254

Minority/Womens
• Department of Minority Business Enterprise   (804) 786-5560

The Virginia Chamber of Commerce   (804) 644-1607
9 South Fifth Street, Richmond, VA 23219

SBA District Office   (804) 771-2400
1504 Santa Rosa Road, Suite 200, Richmond, VA 23229

Virginia Small Business Development Centers
Commonwealth of Virginia Dept. of Economic Devel.   (804) 371-8253

Virginia Business Development Network
901 East Byrd Street, West Tower, 19th Floor, Richmond, VA 23206

Abingdon	(540) 676-5615	Lynchburg	(804) 582-6170
Alexandria	(703) 299-9146	Manassas	(703) 335-2500
Arlington	(703) 993-8182	Middletown	(540) 869-6649
Belle Haven	(757) 442-7179	Richlands	(540) 964-7345
Charlottesville	(804) 295-8198	Richmond	(800) 646-7232
Fairfax	(703) 277-7700	Roanoke	(540) 983-0717
Farmville	(804) 395-2086	South Boston	(804) 575-0044
Fredericksburg	(540) 654-1060	Sterling	(703) 430-7222
Hampton	(757) 825-295	Warsaw	(804) 333-0286
Harrisonburg	(540) 568-3227	Wytheville	(540) 223-4798

Virginia Small Business Investment Companies
Arlington-Continental SBIC (703) 527-5200
McLean-East West United Investment Company (703) 442-0150
Virginia Beach-Eastern Virginia SBIC (757) 626-1111
Vienna-Walnut Capital Corporation (703) 448-3771

Virginia Certified Development Companies
Charlottesville-Virginia Economic Development Corporation (804) 979-0114
Fredericksburg-Rappahannock Economic Development Corp. (800) 627-2892
Norfolk-Urban Business Development Corporation (757) 623-2691
Petersburg-Crater Development Company (804) 861-1666
Portsmouth-Portsmouth Certified Development Corporation (757) 393-8989
Richmond-James River Certified Development Corporation (804) 788-6966
South Hill-Lake Country Development Corporation (804) 447-7101
Sterling-Virginia Asset Financing (703) 421-0504

Micro Loans
Arlington-Ethiopian Community Development (703) 685—510
Lynchburg-Business Development Center (804) 582-6100

WASHINGTON

Statewide Financing Information and Resources: www.state.wa.us

Business Assistance Center
Department of Community, Trade and Economic Development (360) 753-4900
906 Columbia Street SW, P.O. Box 48300, Olympia, WA 98504-8300

Economic Development
• Business Assistance Hotline (800) 237-1233
• Business Development (206) 464-7255

- Innovation and tech. Development Assistance Program   (206) 464-5450
- Small Business Development Center   (509) 335-1576
- Small Business Ombudsman   (360) 586-3022
- Small Business Hotline   (360) 664-9501

Financial Assistance
- Community Development Finance Program   (360) 753-4900
- Development Loan Fund   (360) 753-4900
- Small Business Finance Unit   (360) 753-4900
- Washington Economic Development Finance Authority   (206) 389-2559

Minority/Women
- Minority and Women's Business Development   (206) 389-2561

Association of Washington Business   (360) 943-1600
P.O. Box 658, 1414 South Cherry St., OLympia, WA 98507-0658

SBA District Offices
Seattle   (206) 553-7310
    1200 Sixth Avenue, Suite 1700, Seattle, WA 98101-1128
Spokane   (509) 353-2810
    West 601 First Avenue, Tenth Floor, Spokane, WA 99204-0317

Washington Small Business Development Centers
Washington State University   (509) 335-1576
Johnson Tower 501, Pullman, WA 99164-4851

Aberdeen	(360) 538-4021	Seattle	(206) 553-5615
Bellevue	(206) 643-2888	Spokane	(509) 358-7544
Bellingham	(360) 676-2170	Tacoma	(206) 272-7232
Centralia	(360) 736-9391	Vancouver	(360) 260-6372
Kennewick	(509) 735-6222	Walla Walla	(509) 527-4681
Lynwood	(206) 640-1435	Wenatchee	(509) 662-8016
Moses Lake	(509) 762-6289	Yakima	(509) 574-4940
Mt. Vernon	(360) 416-7872	Okanagan	(509) 826-5107
Olympia	(360) 753-5616	Port Angeles	(360) 457-7793

Washington Small Business Investment Companies
Bellevue-Pacific Northwest Partners   (206) 646-7357

Washington Certified Development Companies
Dennewick-Southeastern Washington Development Assoc.   (509) 735-1000
Seattle-Evergreen Community Development Association   (206) 622-3731
Spokane-Greater Spokane Business Devleopment Association   (509) 458-8555

Micro Lenders
Everett-Snohomish County Private Industry   (206) 743-9669

WEST VIRGINIA

Statewide Financing Information and Resources: www.state.wv.us

Development Office   (304) 558-2234
Department of Commerce
Capitol Complex, Bldg. 6, room 525, Charleston, WV 25305

Economic Development
• Small Business Development Center   (304) 558-3650

Financial Assistance
• West Virginia Economic Development Authority   (304) 558-3650

West Virginia Chamber of Commerce   (304) 342-1115
1314 Virginia Street East, P.O. Box 2789, Charleston, WV 25330-2789

SBA District Offices
Charleston (Branch Office)   (304) 347-5220
    550 Eagan Street, Room 309, Charleston, WV 25301
Clarksburg   (304) 623-5631
    168 West Main Street, Sixth Floor, Clarksburg, WV 26301

West Virginia Small Business Development Center
West Virginia Development Office   (304) 558-2960
950 Kanawha Blvd. East, Charleston, WV 25301

Beckley	(304)255-4022	Morgantown	(304) 293-5839
Fairmont	(304) 367-4125	Parkersburg	(304) 424-8277
Huntington	(304) 696-6789	Shepherdstown	(304) 876-5261
Montgomery	(304) 422-5501	Wheeling	(304) 233-5900 x4206

West Virginia Certified Development Companies
Charleston-West Virginia Certified Development Corp.   (304) 558-3691
Oak Hill-4-C Certified Development Corporation   (304) 469-3972
Wheeling-OVIBDC CDC, Inc.   (304) 232-7722

WISCONSIN

Statewide Financing Information and Resources: www.state.wi.us

Department of Development   (608) 266-1018
123 West Washington Avenue, P.O. Box 7970, Madison, WI 53707
Economic Development

- Bureau of Business Development (608) 266-1386
- Bureau of Business & Industry Services   (608) 267-0313
- Small Business Ombudsman   (608) 267-9384

Financial Assistance
- Wisconsin Business Development Finance Corporation   (608) 258-8830
- Wisconsin Development Fund   (608) 266-1018
- Wisconsin Housing and Economic Development Authority   (800) 334-6873

Minority/Women
- Bureau of Minority Business Development   (608) 267-9550
- Women's Business Liaison   (608) 266-9944
- Wisconsin Housing and Economic Development Authority   (800) 334-6873

Wisconsin Manufacturers and Commerce   (608) 258-3400
501 E. Washington Avenue, P.O. Box 352, Madison, WI 53701-0352

SBA District
Madison   (608) 264-5261
    212 East Washington Avenue, Room 213, Madison, WI 53703
Milwaukee (Branch Office)   (414) 297-3941
    310 West Wisconsin Avenue, Suite 400, Milwaukee, WI 53203

Wisconsin Small Business Development Centers
University of Wisconsin   (608) 263-7794
432 North Lake Street, Room 423, Madison, WI 53706

Eau Claire	(715) 836-5811	Milwaukee	(414) 227-3240
Green Bay	(414) 465-2089	Oshkosh	(414) 424-1453
Kenosha	(414) 595-2189	Stevens Point	(715) 346-2004
La Crosse	(608) 785-8782	Superior	(715) 394-8351
Madison	(608) 263-2221	Whitewater	(414) 472-3217

Wisconsin Small Business Investment Companies
Brookfield-Bando-McGlocklin SBIC   (414) 784-9010
Brokfield-Polaris Capital Corporation   (414) 637-8388 x127
Milwaukee-Banc One Venture Corporation   (414) 765-2274
Milwaukee-Future Value Ventures, Inc.   (414) 278-0377
Milwaukee-InvestAmerica Investment Advisors, Inc.   (414) 276-3839
Milwaukee-M & I Ventures Corporation   (414) 765-7910
Milwaukee-MorAmerica Capital Corporation   (414) 276-3839

Wisconsin Certified Development Companies
Almera-Western Wisconsin Development Corporations   (715) 357-6282
Eau-Claire-Wisconsin Business Development Finance Corp.   (715) 834-9474
Green Bay-Great Lakes Asset Corproation   (414) 499-6444
Kenosha-Kenosha Area Development Corporation   (414) 605-1101
Madison-Madison Development Corporation   (608) 256-2799

Madison-Wisconsin Business Development Finance Corp.	(608) 258-8830
Milwaukee-Milwaukee Economic Development Corporation	(414) 286-5840
Racine-Racine County Business Development Corporation	(414) 638-0234
Waukesha-Waukesha County Associate Development Corp.	(414) 695-7900

WYOMING

Statewide Financing Information and Resources:	www.state.wy.us
Division of Economic and Community Development 6101 Yellowstone Road, Fourth Floor, Cheyenne, WY 82002	(307) 777-7284

Economic Development
- DECD Business Development Section — (307) 777-7284
- Business/Enterpreneur Assistance — (307) 777-7133

Financial Assistance
- Wyomic Industrial Development Corporation (WIDC) — (307) 234-5351
- DECD Small Grants Program — (307) 777-7284

Wyoming Department of Transportation -Disadvantaged Business Assistance	(307) 777-4457
Wyoming Department of Employment	(307) 777-7672
SBA District Office 100 East B Street, Federal Bldg., Room 4001, P.O. Box 2839, Casper, WY 82602-2839	(307) 261-6500

Wyoming Small Business Development Centers

University of Wyoming	(307) 766-3505
P.O. Box 3622, Laramie, WY 82071-3622	(800) 348-5194
Casper	(307) 234-6683
Powell	(307) 754-2139
Cheyenne	(307) 632-6141
Rock Springs	(307) 352-6894

Micro Loans
None

Bibliography

Bel Air, Roger. *How to Borrow Money From A Banker*. New York: AMACOM, 1988.

DeThomas, Art. *Financing Your Small Business*. Oasis Press, 1992.

Langstaff, Margot: *The Colorado Guide To Financing Sources*. Financial Education Publishers, 1995.

Nicholas, Ted. *43 Proven Ways To Raise Capital For Your Small Business*. Enterprise Printing, 1991.

SBA Office of Advocacy. *Small Business Assistance*. U.S. Government Printing Office, 1997.

How to save on attorney fees

How to save on attorney fees

Millions of Americans know they need legal protection, whether it's to get agreements in writing, protect themselves from lawsuits, or document business transactions. But too often these basic but important legal matters are neglected because of something else millions of Americans know: legal services are expensive.

They don't have to be. In response to the demand for affordable legal protection and services, there are now specialized clinics that process simple documents. Paralegals help people prepare legal claims on a freelance basis. People find they can handle their own legal affairs with do-it-yourself legal guides and kits. Indeed, this book is a part of this growing trend.

When are these alternatives to a lawyer appropriate? If you hire an attorney, how can you make sure you're getting good advice for a reasonable fee? Most importantly, do you know how to lower your legal expenses?

When there is no alternative

Make no mistake: serious legal matters require a lawyer. The tips in this book can help you reduce your legal fees, but there is no alternative to good professional legal services in certain circumstances:

- when you are charged with a felony, you are a repeat offender, or jail is possible

- when a substantial amount of money or property is at stake in a lawsuit

- when you are a party in an adversarial divorce or custody case

- when you are an alien facing deportation

- when you are the plaintiff in a personal injury suit that involves large sums of money

- when you're involved in very important transactions

Are you sure you want to take it to court?

Consider the following questions before you pursue legal action:

What are your financial resources?

Money buys experienced attorneys, and experience wins over first-year lawyers and public defenders. Even with a strong case, you may save money by not going to court. Yes, people win millions in court. But for every big winner there are ten plaintiffs who either lose or win so little that litigation wasn't worth their effort.

Do you have the time and energy for a trial?

Courts are overbooked, and by the time your case is heard your initial zeal may have grown cold. If you can, make a reasonable settlement out of court. On personal matters, like a divorce or custody case, consider the emotional toll on all parties. Any legal case will affect you in some way. You will need time away from work. A newsworthy case may bring press coverage. Your loved ones, too, may face publicity. There is usually good reason to settle most cases quickly, quietly, and economically.

How can you settle disputes without litigation?

Consider *mediation*. In mediation, each party pays half the mediator's fee and, together, they attempt to work out a compromise informally. *Binding arbitration* is another alternative. For a small fee, a trained specialist serves as judge, hears both sides, and hands down a ruling that both parties have agreed to accept.

So you need an attorney

Having done your best to avoid litigation, if you still find yourself headed for court, you will need an attorney. To get the right attorney at a reasonable cost, be guided by these four questions:

What type of case is it?

You don't seek a foot doctor for a toothache. Find an attorney experienced in your type of legal problem. If you can get recommendations from clients who have recently won similar cases, do so.

Where will the trial be held?

You want a lawyer familiar with that court system and one who knows the court personnel and the local protocol—which can vary from one locality to another.

Should you hire a large or small firm?

Hiring a senior partner at a large and prestigious law firm sounds reassuring, but chances are the actual work will be handled by associates—at high rates. Small firms may give your case more attention but, with fewer resources, take longer to get the work done.

What can you afford?

Hire an attorney you can afford, of course, but know what a fee quote includes. High fees may reflect a firm's luxurious offices, high-paid staff and unmonitored expenses, while low estimates may mean "unexpected" costs later. Ask for a written estimate of all costs and anticipated expenses.

How to find a good lawyer

Whether you need an attorney quickly or you're simply open to future possibilities, here are seven nontraditional methods for finding your lawyer:

1) **Word of mouth**: Successful lawyers develop reputations. Your friends, business associates and other professionals are potential referral sources. But beware of hiring a friend. Keep the client-attorney relationship strictly business.

2) **Directories**: The Yellow Pages and the Martin-Hubbell Lawyer Directory (in your local library) can help you locate a lawyer with the right education, background and expertise for your case.

3) **Databases**: A paralegal should be able to run a quick computer search of local attorneys for you using the Westlaw or Lexis database.

4) **State bar associations**: Bar associations are listed in phone books. Along with lawyer referrals, your bar association can direct you to low-cost legal clinics or specialists in your area.

5) **Law schools**: Did you know that a legal clinic run by a law school gives law students hands-on experience? This may fit your legal needs. A third-year law student loaded with enthusiasm and a little experience might fill the bill quite inexpensively—or even for free.

6) **Advertisements**: Ads are a lawyer's business card. If a "TV attorney" seems to have a good track record with your kind of case, why not call? Just don't be swayed by the glamour of a high-profile attorney.

7) **Your own ad**: A small ad describing the qualifications and legal expertise you're seeking, placed in a local bar association journal, may get you just the lead you need.

How to hire and work with your attorney

No matter how you hear about an attorney, you must interview him or her in person. Call the office during business hours and ask to speak to the attorney directly. Then explain your case briefly and mention how you obtained the attorney's name. If the attorney sounds interested and knowledgeable, arrange for a visit.

The ten-point visit

1) Note the address. This is a good indication of the rates to expect.

2) Note the condition of the offices. File-laden desks and poorly maintained work space may indicate a poorly run firm.

3) Look for up-to-date computer equipment and an adequate complement of support personnel.

4) Note the appearance of the attorney. How will he or she impress a judge or jury?

5) Is the attorney attentive? Does the attorney take notes, ask questions, follow up on points you've mentioned?

6) Ask what schools he or she has graduated from, and feel free to check credentials with the state bar association.

7) Does the attorney have a good track record with your type of case?

8) Does he or she explain legal terms to you in plain English?

9) Are the firm's costs reasonable?

10) Will the attorney provide references?

Hiring the attorney

Having chosen your attorney, make sure all the terms are agreeable. Send letters to any other attorneys you have interviewed, thanking them for their time and interest in your case and explaining that you have retained another attorney's services.

Request a letter from your new attorney outlining your retainer agreement. The letter should list all fees you will be responsible for as well as the billing arrangement. Did you arrange to pay in installments? This should be noted in your retainer agreement.

Controlling legal costs

Legal fees and expenses can get out of control easily, but the client who is willing to put in the effort can keep legal costs manageable. Work out a budget with your attorney. Create a timeline for your case. Estimate the costs involved in each step.

Legal fees can be straightforward. Some lawyers charge a fixed rate for a specific project. Others charge contingency fees (they collect a percentage of your recovery, usually 35-50 percent if you win and nothing if you lose). But most attorneys prefer to bill by the hour. Expenses can run the gamut, with one hourly charge for taking depositions and another for making copies.

Have your attorney give you a list of charges for services rendered and an itemized monthly bill. The bill should explain the service performed, who performed the work, when the service was provided, how long it took, and how the service benefits your case.

Ample opportunity abounds in legal billing for dishonesty and greed. There is also plenty of opportunity for knowledgeable clients to cut their bills significantly if they know what to look for. Asking the right questions and setting limits on fees is smart and can save you a bundle. Don't be afraid to question legal bills. It's your case and your money!

When the bill arrives

- **Retainer fees**: You should already have a written retainer agreement. Ideally, the retainer fee applies toward case costs, and your agreement puts that in writing. Protect yourself by escrowing the retainer fee until the case has been handled to your satisfaction.

- **Office visit charges**: Track your case and all documents, correspondence, and bills. Diary all dates, deadlines and questions you want to ask your attorney during your next office visit. This keeps expensive office visits focused and productive, with more accomplished in less time. If your attorney charges less for phone consultations than office visits, reserve visits for those tasks that must be done in person.

- **Phone bills**: This is where itemized bills are essential. Who made the call, who was spoken to, what was discussed, when was the call made, and how long did it last? Question any charges that seem unnecessary or excessive (over 60 minutes).

- **Administrative costs**: Your case may involve hundreds, if not thousands, of documents: motions, affidavits, depositions, interrogatories, bills, memoranda, and letters. Are they all necessary? Understand your attorney's case strategy before paying for an endless stream of costly documents.

- **Associate and paralegal fees**: Note in your retainer agreement which staff people will have access to your file. Then you'll have an informed and efficient staff working on your case, and you'll recognize their names on your bill. Of course, your attorney should handle the important part of your case, but less costly paralegals or associates may handle routine matters more economically. Note: Some firms expect their associates to meet a quota of billable hours, although the time spent is not always warranted. Review your bill. Does the time spent make sense for the document in question? Are several staff involved in matters that should be handled by one person? Don't be afraid to ask questions. And withhold payment until you have satisfactory answers.

- **Court stenographer fees**: Depositions and court hearings require costly transcripts and stenographers. This means added expenses. Keep an eye on these costs.

- **Copying charges**: Your retainer fee should limit the number of copies made of your complete file. This is in your legal interest, because multiple files mean multiple chances others may access your confidential information. It is also in your financial interest, because copying costs can be astronomical.

- **Fax costs**: As with the phone and copier, the fax can easily run up costs. Set a limit.

- **Postage charges**: Be aware of how much it costs to send a legal document overnight, or a registered letter. Offer to pick up or deliver expensive items when it makes sense.

- **Filing fees**: Make it clear to your attorney that you want to minimize the number of court filings in your case. Watch your bill and question any filing that seems unnecessary.

- **Document production fee**: Turning over documents to your opponent is mandatory and expensive. If you're faced with reproducing boxes of documents, consider having the job done by a commercial firm rather than your attorney's office.

- **Research and investigations**: Pay only for photographs that can be used in court. Can you hire a photographer at a lower rate than what your attorney charges? Reserve that right in your retainer agreement. Database research can also be extensive and expensive; if your attorney uses Westlaw or Nexis, set limits on the research you will pay for.

- **Expert witnesses**: Question your attorney if you are expected to pay for more than a reasonable number of expert witnesses. Limit the number to what is essential to your case.

- **Technology costs**: Avoid videos, tape recordings, and graphics if you can use old-fashioned diagrams to illustrate your case.

- **Travel expenses**: Travel expenses for those connected to your case can be quite costly unless you set a maximum budget. Check all travel-related items on your bill, and make sure they are appropriate. Always question why the travel is necessary before you agree to pay for it.

- **Appeals costs**: Losing a case often means an appeal, but weigh the costs involved before you make that decision. If money is at stake, do a cost-benefit analysis to see if an appeal is financially justified.

- **Monetary damages**: Your attorney should be able to help you estimate the total damages you will have to pay if you lose a civil case. Always consider settling out of court rather than proceeding to trial when the trial costs will be high.

- **Surprise costs**: Surprise costs are so routine they're predictable. The judge may impose unexpected court orders on one or both sides, or the opposition will file an unexpected motion that increases your legal costs. Budget a few thousand dollars over what you estimate your case will cost. It usually is needed.

- **Padded expenses**: Assume your costs and expenses are legitimate. But some firms do inflate expenses—office supplies, database searches, copying, postage, phone bills—to bolster their bottom line. Request copies of bills your law firm receives from support services. If you are not the only client represented on a bill, determine those charges related to your case.

Keeping it legal without a lawyer

The best way to save legal costs is to avoid legal problems. There are hundreds of ways to decrease your chances of lawsuits and other nasty legal encounters. Most simply involve a little common sense. You can also use your own initiative to find and use the variety of self-help legal aid available to consumers.

11 situations in which you may not need a lawyer

1) **No-fault divorce**: Married couples with no children, minimal property, and no demands for alimony can take advantage of divorce mediation services. A lawyer should review your divorce agreement before you sign it, but you will have saved a fortune in attorney fees. A marital or family counselor may save a seemingly doomed marriage, or help both parties move beyond anger to a calm settlement. Either way, counseling can save you money.

2) **Wills**: Do-it-yourself wills and living trusts are ideal for people with estates of less than $600,000. Even if an attorney reviews your final documents, a will kit allows you to read the documents, ponder your bequests, fill out sample forms, and discuss your wishes with your family at your leisure, without a lawyer's meter running.

3) **Incorporating**: Incorporating a small business can be done by any business owner. Your state government office provides the forms and instructions necessary. A visit to your state office will probably be

necessary to perform a business name check. A fee of $100-$200 is usually charged for processing your Articles of Incorporation. The rest is paperwork: filling out forms correctly; holding regular, official meetings; and maintaining accurate records.

4) **Routine business transactions**: Copyrights, for example, can be applied for by asking the U.S. Copyright Office for the appropriate forms and brochures. The same is true of the U.S. Patent and Trademark Office. If your business does a great deal of document preparation and research, hire a certified paralegal rather than paying an attorney's rates. Consider mediation or binding arbitration rather than going to court for a business dispute. Hire a human resources/benefits administrator to head off disputes concerning discrimination or other employee charges.

5) **Repairing bad credit**: When money matters get out of hand, attorneys and bankruptcy should not be your first solution. Contact a credit counseling organization that will help you work out manageable payment plans so that everyone wins. It can also help you learn to manage your money better. A good company to start with is the Consumer Credit Counseling Service, 1-800-388-2227.

6) **Small Claims Court**: For legal grievances amounting to a few thousand dollars in damages, represent yourself in Small Claims Court. There is a small filing fee, forms to fill out, and several court visits necessary. If you can collect evidence, state your case in a clear and logical presentation, and come across as neat, respectful and sincere, you can succeed in Small Claims Court.

7) **Traffic Court**: Like Small Claims Court, Traffic Court may show more compassion to a defendant appearing without an attorney. If you are ticketed for a minor offense and want to take it to court, you will be asked to plead guilty or not guilty. If you plead guilty, you can ask for leniency in sentencing by presenting mitigating circumstances. Bring any witnesses who can support your story, and remember that presentation (some would call it acting ability) is as important as fact.

8) **Residential zoning petition**: If a homeowner wants to open a home business, build an addition, or make other changes that may affect his or her neighborhood, town approval is required. But you don't need a lawyer to fill out a zoning variance application, turn it in, and present your story at a public hearing. Getting local support before the hearing is the best way to assure a positive vote; contact as many neighbors as possible to reassure them that your plans won't adversely affect them or the neighborhood.

9) **Government benefit applications**: Applying for veterans' or unemployment benefits may be daunting, but the process doesn't require legal help. Apply for either immediately upon becoming eligible. Note: If your former employer contests your application for unemployment benefits and you have to defend yourself at a hearing, you may want to consider hiring an attorney.

10) **Receiving government files**: The Freedom of Information Act gives every American the right to receive copies of government information about him or her. Write a letter to the appropriate state or federal agency, noting the precise information you want. List each document in a separate paragraph. Mention the Freedom of Information Act, and state that you will pay any expenses. Close with your signature and the address the documents should be sent to. An approved request may take six months to arrive. If it is refused on the grounds that the information is classified or violates another's privacy, send a letter of appeal explaining why the released information would not endanger anyone. Enlist the support of your local state or federal representative, if possible, to smooth the approval process.

11) **Citizenship**: Arriving in the United States to work and become a citizen is a process tangled in bureaucratic red tape, but it requires more perseverance than legal assistance. Immigrants can learn how to obtain a "Green Card," under what circumstances they can work, and what the requirements of citizenship are by contacting the Immigration Services or reading a good self-help book.

Save more; it's E-Z

When it comes to saving attorneys' fees, Made E-Z Products is the consumer's best friend. America's largest publisher of self-help legal products offers legally valid forms for virtually every situation. E-Z Legal Kits and the Made E-Z Guides which cover legal topics include all necessary forms and a simple-to-follow manual of instructions or a layman's book. Made E-Z Books are a library of forms and documents for everyday business and personal needs. Made E-Z Software provides those same forms on disk and CD for customized documents at the touch of the keyboard.

You can add to your legal savvy and your ability to protect yourself, your loved ones, your business and your property with a range of self-help legal titles available through Made E-Z Products.

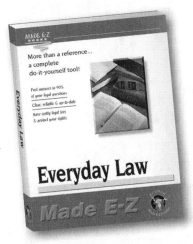

FEDERAL & STATE
Labor Law Posters

By the book...

Whatever you need to know, we've made it E-Z!

Informative text and forms you can fill out on-screen.* From personal to business, legal to leisure—we've made it E-Z!

Get Out Of Debt

Credit Repair

Vital Records

Living Wills

Asset Protection

Buying/Selling Your Home

Personal & Family

For all your family's needs, we have titles that will help keep you organized and guide you through most every aspect of your personal life.

Business

Whether you're starting from scratch with a home business or you just want to keep your corporate records in shape, we've got the programs for you.

Incorporation

Corporate Records

Accounting

Your Profitable Home Business

Selling on the Web

Advertising Your Business

 ss 2001.r1

	ITEM #	QTY.	PRICE‡	EXTENSION
Made E-Z Software				
E-Z Construction Estimator	SS4300		$24.95	
E-Z Contractors' Forms	SS4301		$24.95	
Contractors' Business Builder Software Bundle	SS4002		$49.95	
Corporate Secretary	SS4003		$24.95	
Asset Protection Made E-Z	SS4304		$24.95	
Corporate Records Made E-Z	SS4305		$24.95	
Vital Records Made E-Z	SS4306		$24.95	
Managing Employees	SS4307		$24.95	
Accounting Made E-Z	SS4308		$24.95	
Limited Liability Companies (LLC)	SS4309		$24.95	
Partnerships	SS4310		$24.95	
Solving IRS Problems	SS4311		$24.95	
Winning In Small Claims Court	SS4312		$24.95	
Collecting Unpaid Bills Made E-Z	SS4313		$24.95	
Selling On The Web (E-Commerce)	SS4314		$24.95	
Your Profitable Home Business Made E-Z	SS4315		$24.95	
Get Out Of Debt Made E-Z	SS4317		$24.95	
E-Z Business Lawyer Library	SS4318		$49.95	
E-Z Estate Planner	SS4319		$49.95	
E-Z Personal Lawyer Library	SS4320		$49.95	
Payroll Made E-Z	SS4321		$24.95	
Personal Legal Forms and Agreements	SS4322		$24.95	
Business Legal Forms and Agreements	SS4323		$24.95	
Employee Policies and Manuals	SS4324		$24.95	
Incorporation Made E-Z	SW1176		$24.95	
Last Wills Made E-Z	SW1177		$24.95	
Everyday Law Made E-Z	SW1185		$24.95	
Everyday Legal Forms & Agreements Made E-Z	SW1186		$24.95	
Business Startups Made E-Z	SW1192		$24.95	
Credit Repair Made E-Z	SW2211		$24.95	
Business Forms Made E-Z	SW2223		$24.95	
Buying and Selling A Business Made E-Z	SW2242		$24.95	
Marketing Your Small Business Made E-Z	SW2245		$24.95	
Get Out Of Debt Made E-Z	SW2246		$24.95	
Winning Business Plans Made E-Z	SW2247		$24.95	
Successful Resumes Made E-Z	SW2248		$24.95	
Solving Business Problems Made E-Z	SW2249		$24.95	
Profitable Mail Order Made E-Z	SW2250		$24.95	
Deluxe Business Forms	SW2251		$49.95	
E-Z Small Business Library	SW2252		$49.95	
Sub-total for Software			$	
Made E-Z Guides				
Bankruptcy Made E-Z	G300		$14.95	
Incorporation Made E-Z	G301		$14.95	
Divorce Made E-Z	G302		$14.95	
Credit Repair Made E-Z	G303		$14.95	
Living Trusts Made E-Z	G305		$14.95	
Living Wills Made E-Z	G306		$14.95	
Last Will & Testament Made E-Z	G307		$14.95	
Buying/Selling Your Home Made E-Z	G311		$14.95	
Employment Law Made E-Z	G312		$14.95	
Collecting Child Support Made E-Z	G315		$14.95	
Limited Liability Companies Made E-Z	G316		$14.95	
Partnerships Made E-Z	G318		$14.95	
Solving IRS Problems Made E-Z	G319		$14.95	
Asset Protection Made E-Z	G320		$14.95	
Buying/Selling A Business Made E-Z	G321		$14.95	
Financing Your Business Made E-Z	G322		$14.95	
Profitable Mail Order Made E-Z	G323		$14.95	
Selling On The Web Made E-Z	G324		$14.95	
SBA Loans Made E-Z	G325		$14.95	
Solving Business Problems Made E-Z	G326		$14.95	
Advertising Your Business Made E-Z	G327		$14.95	
Shoestring Investing Made E-Z	G330		$14.95	
Stock Market Investing Made E-Z	G331		$14.95	
Fund Raising Made E-Z	G332		$14.95	
Money For College Made E-Z	G334		$14.95	
Marketing Your Small Business Made E-Z	G335		$14.95	

‡ Prices are for a single item, and are subject to change without notice.

See an item in this book you would like to order?

1. Photocopy this order form.
2. Complete your order and mail to:

MADE E◆Z PRODUCTS

384 S Military Trail
Deerfield Beach, FL 33442
www.MadeE-Z.com

CONTRACTORS' CORNER

...when contractors need it in writing!

All the forms and software
for builders, electricians,
plumbers, sub-contractors,
painters, and other trades.

www.contractorsforms.com

Company Purchase Orders welcome
with approved credit.
All orders ship UPS Ground unless
otherwise specified.

continued on next page

MADE E-Z™ PRODUCTS

	ITEM #	QTY.	PRICE‡	EXTENSION
Owning A No-Cash-Down Business Made E-Z	G336		$14.95	
Offshore Investing Made E-Z	G337		$14.95	
Multi-level Marketing Made E-Z	G338		$14.95	
Get Out Of Debt Made E-Z	G340		$14.95	
Your Profitable Home Business Made E-Z	G341		$14.95	
Winning Business Plans Made E-Z	G342		$14.95	
Mutual Fund Investing Made E-Z	G343		$14.95	
Business Startups Made E-Z	G344		$14.95	
Successful Resumes Made E-Z	G346		$14.95	
Free Stuff For Everyone Made E-Z	G347		$14.95	
Sub-total for Guides			$	
Made E-Z Kits				
Bankruptcy Kit	K300		$24.95	
Incorporation Kit	K301		$24.95	
Divorce Kit	K302		$24.95	
Credit Repair Kit	K303		$24.95	
Living Trust Kit	K305		$24.95	
Living Will Kit	K306		$24.95	
Last Will & Testament Kit	K307		$19.95	
Buying and Selling Your Home Kit	K311		$24.95	
Employment Law Kit	K312		$24.95	
Limited Liability Company Kit	K316		$24.95	
Business Startups Kit	K320		$24.95	
Small Business/Home Business Kit	K321		$24.95	
Sub-total for Kits			$	
Made E-Z Books				
Everyday Legal Forms & Agreements Made E-Z	BK407		$24.95	
Personnel Forms Made E-Z	BK408		$24.95	
Collecting Unpaid Bills Made E-Z	BK409		$24.95	
Corporate Records Made E-Z	BK410		$24.95	
Everyday Law Made E-Z	BK411		$24.95	
Vital Records Made E-Z	BK412		$24.95	
Business Forms Made E-Z	BK414		$24.95	
Sub-total for Books			$	
Labor Law Posters				
☆ Federal Labor Law	LP001		$14.95	
☆ State Specific Labor Law see state listings below			$39.95	

State	Item#	QTY	State	Item#	QTY	State	Item#	QTY
AL	83801		KY	83817		ND	83834	
AK	83802		LA	83818		OH	83835	
AZ	83803		ME	83819		OK	83836	
AR	83804		MD	83820		OR	83837	
CA	83805		MA	83821		PA	83838	
CO	83806		MI	83822		RI	83839	
CT	83807		MN	83823		SC	83840	
DE	83808		MS	83824		S. Dakota not available		
DC	83848		MO	83825		TN	83842	
FL	83809		MT	83826		TX	83843	
GA	83810		NE	83827		UT	83844	
HI	83811		NV	83828		VT	83845	
ID	83812		NH	83829		VA	83846	
IL	83813		NJ	83830		WA	83847	
IN	83814		NM	83831		WV	83849	
IO	83815		NY	83832		WI	83850	
KS	83816		NC	83833		WY	83851	

☆ Required by Federal & State Laws

Sub-total for Posters	$
TOTAL FOR ALL PRODUCTS	$
Add Shipping & Handling $3.50 for first item, $1.50 for each additional item	$
TOTAL PRODUCTS and S & H	$
Florida Residents add 6% sales tax	$
TOTAL OF ORDER	$

‡ Prices are for a single item, and are subject to change without notice.

❖ **FOR FASTER SERVICE** ❖

Order by phone:
(954) 480-8933

Order by fax:
(954) 480-8906

SS 2001 r3

Name

Company

Position

Address

City

State   Zip

Phone
(   )

PAYMENT
❏ check enclosed, payable to:
Made E-Z Products, Inc.
384 S. Military Trail
Deerfield Beach, FL 33442

❏ charge my credit card: ❏ MasterCard ❏ VISA

ACCOUNT NO.   EXP. DATE

Signature: (required for credit card purchases)

MADE E·Z® LIBRARY

Credit Repair

Buying & Selling a Business

Bankruptcy

MADE E-Z GUIDES

Each comprehensive guide contains all the information you need to master one of dozens of topics, plus sample forms (if applicable).

Most guides also include an appendix of valuable resources, a handy glossary, and the valuable 14-page supplement "How to Save on Attorney Fees."

Index

N-W•••••

100 BEST FAMILY RESORTS IN NORTH AMERICA

"Unlike usual 'family' (mostly just tantrum-tolerant) guides,
this gives equal time to grown up gimmes, miraculously pinpointing
spots that combine kidstuff and capital 'C' Class."

—Pamela Robin Brandt,
New York Daily News

"Are you tired of family vacations that offer limited activities?
Bored with the usual tourist-trap destinations? Then pick up a copy of
100 Best Family Resorts in North America . . . and start planning
the best family vacation ever."

—*BCP Parent Pages*

"Gives parents scores of options for family travel . . . from
charming country lodges and mountain getaways to the big hotels. A great
place to start when you're looking for the ultimate family destination."

—Felice H. Shapiro, Publisher,
New York Family Publications

Help Us Keep This Guide Up to Date

Every effort has been made by the author and editors to make this guide as accurate and useful as possible. However, many things can change after a guide is published—establishments close, phone numbers change, facilities come under new management, and so on.

We would love to hear from you concerning your experiences with this guide and how you feel it could be improved and be kept up to date. While we may not be able to respond to all comments and suggestions, we'll take them to heart and we'll also make sure to share them with the author. Please send your comments and suggestions to the following address:

The Globe Pequot Press
Reader Response/Editorial Department
P.O. Box 480
Guilford, CT 06437

Or you can e-mail us at:
editorial@globe-pequot.com

Thanks for your input, and happy travels!

100 BEST FAMILY RESORTS IN NORTH AMERICA

100 Quality Resorts with Leisure Activities for Children and Adults

Fifth Edition

by

Janet Tice and Jane Wilford

Revised by Becky Danley

The Globe Pequot Press

GUILFORD, CONNECTICUT

Cover photos courtesy of Palmetto Dunes Resort
Cover design by Lana Mullen
Text design by Nancy Freeborn/Freeborn Design

Library of Congress Cataloging-in-Publication Data is available.
ISBN 0-7627-0504-3

Manufactured in the United States of America
Fifth Edition/First Printing

To Fabiana and Sykes, who first provided the inspiration,
and to Paul and Sarah, who continue to share the adventure.
Our wonderful children and our best family travel critics!

Contents

Preface

"Best" is a curious adjective, one that is entirely subjective. So let us define our sense of best—both what it does and what it doesn't mean.

Best is not necessarily the fanciest, the biggest, the most expensive.

Best is not always the sleekest, the poshest, or the newest.

Best, in the context of this book, is what is best for families.

Best is variety—in setting and atmosphere.

Best is variety in recreational interests and in prices.

Best is variety in geographical location. A broad selection allows you to have choices whether you want to travel far or near.

We searched for the most extensive children's programs, yet balanced this with an interest in presenting a good cross-section of North America. If we have overlooked your favorite, let us know. Please write to us in care of The Globe Pequot Press, P.O. Box 480, Guilford, CT 06437.

Janet Tice
Jane Wilford

Acknowledgments

Many thanks to D. Sykes Wilford, who shared his travels and his travails during the production of this manuscript.

Introduction

Although traveling with children is not a new phenomenon, many Americans these days are viewing the traditional family vacation in a different light. In past decades family vacations have most frequently been determined by the needs and wants of the children. Planning the entire vacation around the kids often left Mom and Dad with the sense that they had not had a vacation at all but, rather, a trial by fire. The only option was to leave Junior behind in the care of grandparents or close family friends while the parents ventured off on their own. In an attempt to share experiences with their children, many parents, seeking middle ground, are adjusting the focus of their leisure-time plans.

Vacations these days often mean shorter and more frequent jaunts. Increasingly, they involve flying rather than loading up the family car and driving. Mini vacations are becoming popular and are frequently planned to coincide with one or the other parent's business trips. On the philosophical side, current trends in child care emphasize the importance of a parent's presence, especially for the first three years, and many parents are reluctant to leave their infants and toddlers for extended periods.

The intent of this book is to identify those places where adults and children can enjoy interesting and age-appropriate activities. Baby-sitting services for infants, a ski school for three-year-olds, and a supervised recreational program for older children are some of the possibilities explored. In selecting resorts we have taken into consideration different styles, price ranges, and diverse geographic locations. It is a representative sampling rather than an all-inclusive listing. Often we have been limited by lack of space and lack of information. This book does not highlight every Disney World and Six Flags Over Somewhere establishment in the United States. While these certainly serve an important educational function in a pleasant and exciting atmosphere for children, therein lies the catch: They are directed primarily toward children. But parents deserve vacations too—adult vacations with grown-up activities.

This is not, then, a book about vacations *for* kids. Rather, it is a book about vacations *with* kids, about family adventures in which adults can be adults and children can be children and in which there is common ground for sharing.

In general we are pleased with the progress we've noted in the resorts we have chosen from our previous editions. They are not resting on their laurels but seem to be enthusiastic and dedicated to making more and more improvements and providing better and better facilities and programs for families. In addition, new resorts developing exciting agendas are constantly entering this family-oriented market.

If we've left out your favorite family spot, or if you own a resort and feel slighted, please write to us in care of The Globe Pequot Press. We're always glad to know of places where families find special treatment.

Costs and Caveats

Prices are noted throughout the book in the accommodations section of each resort's description. They are current as of 1999. But, just like the new car that depreciates the minute you drive away from the showroom, prices have to be adjusted for inflation the minute they're stated. Keep this in mind if your travel plans do not materialize right away but instead are put on the back burner for a couple of years. Inflation takes its toll simultaneously and universally; however, the prices quoted here can serve as a basis for comparison among resorts regardless of the year in which you consult this guide.

The problem most commonly caused by prices is sorting out just what a given price includes. In the travel industry, various pricing schedules are frequently used to identify the relationship between lodging and meals. For example:

European plan means the rate quoted is for lodging only.

Modified American plan means two meals a day (usually breakfast and dinner) as well as lodging are included in the daily rate.

Full American plan means three meals a day and lodging are covered in the daily rate.

The extent of what else is included in the daily room rate, such as use of the recreational facilities, varies widely from one resort to another. Every effort has been made to identify the extras for which no additional charge is required. If "complimentary" or "free" is not clearly stated for a service or activity, you can safely assume that there is a fee.

Besides lodging and meals, prices are specifically noted for children's programs. As a well-seasoned traveler, you already have a ballpark idea of the prices of lift tickets for skiing and greens fees for golf. Emphasis here is on costs of the children's activities because now you're trying to become well seasoned as a traveling parent.

The prices and rates listed in this guidebook were confirmed at press time. We recommend, however, that you call establishments to obtain current information before traveling.

Planning Family Vacations

How This Book Can Help You

As your vacation rolls around, you start weighing the pros and cons of bringing the children along. You feel that you desperately need exclusive time for adult conversation with your spouse or other grown-ups. Yet you wonder if following through on that idea is fair to your kids. Vacations need not be an either/or proposition—either resigning yourself to a week or two of nonstop "Sesame Street" activities with no relief in sight or excluding the children from the few leisure weeks you have away from a demanding career. The former scenario almost always requires relinquishing your own interests, while the latter is complicated by worry and guilt over little Johnny or Susie left behind at Grandma's as you're off footloose and fancy-free. It is possible, however, to have a vacation that is fair to both you and your children.

So you're ready to plan a vacation with the kids. Though this sounds like what parents have been doing for generations, you're different from previous generations. You're better educated and fairly well traveled; you've delayed getting married and having children until your career was launched; and most likely you're older as you reach this phase of family life than were your parents. In addition, you probably have different expectations for both yourself and your children, expectations that influence how you want to spend your leisure time. While you're devoted to your children and conscious of the importance of your input into their intellectual, emotional, and social growth, you also realize that part of being a good parent is tending to your own physical and psychological well-being. You imagine that it must be feasible to share a pleasurable vacation experience with your children without denying your own interests and concerns. Well, it is!

When you've made the decision that the kids should come along this time and you know that one more carousel or one more pair of Mickey Mouse ears just might drive you crazy, then let this book help you discover the perfect vacation spot, where the whole family can be happy together.

Whether you are considering a few relaxing days at a country hideaway or a week of fun in the sun on a beach, rest assured that there are accommodations with facilities and activities that will delight you and your children. A family vacation doesn't have to mean settling for renting the same house at the nearest beach each season for the next several years or the proverbial visit to Grandma's house year after year. Variety can be found, and if you're itching for a good game of golf, you don't have to fret over whether your three-year-old can manage walking eighteen holes or what antics he'll perform along the way. These concerns can be resolved by choosing the proper surroundings and conditions.

When a young parent once inquired about children's activities at one resort, the staff member gave her a bottle of bubbles. That would last about thirty seconds, right? Thank goodness many resorts are more enlightened, and those you'll find here.

Explore in the following pages a selection of hotels, condominiums, and resorts that offer conveniences to accommodate the needs and wishes of both adults and children. So that you can gratify your diverse and periodically changing geographical interests, you will discover that this guide includes establishments throughout the United States, with a few in Canada. The United States is at the forefront of the new approach to family vacations.

In compiling this collection several criteria were considered: attractive surroundings; good dining facilities, including comfortable lounges and bars; babysitting services; and recreational activities for both parents and children. Needless to say, some of the establishments listed here meet more of the criteria or meet them better than others. But then, your wishes and requirements may vary from one trip to the next: One year you may need just a competent baby-sitter to stay in your hotel room with your infant while you enjoy an elegant, leisurely dinner, and the next year you may need a complete day-care center/nursery school for your energetic toddler while you spend the day out on the slopes. This book does not rank resorts on how well the criteria are met; it simply describes them and all their available services. You can then pick and choose according to your personal preferences and current needs.

To make it easier to find your ideal vacation spot, the descriptive entries are grouped by geographical location, then alphabetically within these divisions; addresses and telephone numbers are included in the descriptions.

Following the descriptions is a standard alphabetical index of resort names to help you pull out the perfect place that a friend recently mentioned at a dinner party, the location of which eludes your recollective powers. This arrangement should afford you easiest access to the required information regardless of your perspective when designing your vacation.

Finally, a special categories index is given that lists resorts by type, such as seaside resorts or resorts with skiing. A resort may appear under more than one heading—it may, for example, shine for its golf course as well as for its beach. Conversely, a resort will not appear under every heading for which it has attractions, only for those that particularly distinguish it.

While probably the foremost concern for your next trip is simply to make that perfect match between your personal circumstances and the most suitable resort, you may occasionally feel a bit nervous about some of the practical logistics of traveling with kids. The section on helpful hints when traveling with children may forestall a few inconveniences that may arise when away from home; the medical information should allay some fears about illnesses and emergencies; and the segments on educating yourself and the advantages of a good travel agent may assist in ironing out the details of your vacation arrangements. In any case, they will stimulate you to analyze your own and your children's habits so that you can anticipate some of the problems and joys of traveling with youngsters.

So you're off. Good luck and happy vacation!

Helpful Hints for Traveling with Children

It can be a joy to travel with children. Sure, sometimes the preparations may seem exhausting and spurts of parental anxiety en route may be tiring as well, but the excitement and wonder of children as they encounter new experiences are worth the price of admission.

On the following pages you'll find some helpful hints for traveling with kids. Many of these suggestions may seem incredibly obvious, but stating the obvious is not always a disadvantage. And a little repetitive reinforcement may help you react more quickly or think better on your feet. An excellent resource book is *Trouble-free Travel with Children* (The Book Peddler, 1991) by Vicki Lansky, author of more than twenty books for new parents.

The first trick to traveling with kids is preparing them for the adventure. Talk to your child in advance; advise her where you're going and what you'll be doing. Infants (in spite of the mounds of disposable diapers you must tote) are very portable. Even toddlers whose whole world revolves around Mom and Dad are happy as long as familiar faces are near at hand. But as a child's world expands to include friends and a wider realm of belongings, verbal preparation becomes very important. Sometimes it's easy to assume that your youngster will pick up on things by osmosis, but children don't always assimilate information about vacation plans that floats around the house in chitchat. It's necessary to explain directly to them what is in store. Books and maps about your destination and route can be shared; even for very young children, maps translate the excitement of travel into a tangible form.

Besides detailing the fun of this new experience, reassure your child that you'll be returning home; that although your daughter may not bring along every Barbie doll and Raggedy Ann, her dolls will still be here when she gets back; and that even though your son may miss his best friends, they won't forget him. Even three- and four-year-olds can "write" postcards along the way as a means of staying connected with friends back home.

As an experienced traveler, you know the ropes of appropriate packing for trips. As a conscientious parent, you are most familiar with what your child will want or need away from home. The standard rule of thumb—don't overpack—applies just as well for children as it does for adults. The length of the trip adjusted for the dirt factor of your own child (how many outfits can he go through in a day?) should give you a reasonable handle on the amount of clothes to pack. Laundromats are never that far away, many hotels have laundry services, and kids' clothes (just by virtue of their size) are fairly easy to hand wash in a hotel bathroom. And don't take along what your child isn't happy with. No matter how much time dear Aunt Josie spent crocheting that sweet little dress, if your daughter doesn't like it, if it's uncomfortable, it will be nothing more than an unnecessary bulge in your suitcase.

If your child uses a bottle, a trip may not be the best time to nudge him out of it; a bottle may provide a bit of security in unfamiliar surroundings. Just be sure to pack a bottle brush: If a bottle gets lost at the bottom of a travel bag for a day or two, mysterious molds blossom, dispelled only by a little scrubbing.

Toys, too, have to fall under the "don't overpack" rule. Remember that for children, seemingly mundane objects in new surroundings often provide considerable amusement. It's a good idea to stash away a couple of new attention-getters, but don't forget the tried and true. A cuddly doll, even if it is beginning to look somewhat old and ratty, or a special pillow is often very comforting for a little one sleeping in a strange bed for the first time. Age-adjusted, of course, books, a small ball, crayons, coloring books, scissors, construction paper, a bean bag (remember them from when you were a kid?), and small games such as a pint-size checkerboard are all packable items. Even blocks like Duplos or Legos, if arranged in one compact cube, can be packed fairly easily. Some parents cherish a Fisher-Price tape recorder or a Walkman (with earphones, please) as something akin to a gift from the gods. Terrifically totable and accompanied by a selection of tapes (anything from Walt Disney stories to old radio shows to historical accounts of George Washington and Benjamin Franklin are on the market now), a tape recorder can effectively hold a child's attention.

For the preschooler or older child, you may consider investing in a backpack. Set down the rules with your child when packing: He can bring along whatever fits in the pack, and he has to carry it. This way you give your child a sense of participating in the preparations and obviate the almost inevitable whine about something Mom didn't include. And practically unnoticed you can sneak in a little lesson in responsibility.

A "surprise box" is also a fun way to generate excitement about a trip. Without divulging details, clue your child in to your preparations of the secrets and mysteries of this cache. Then watch the fun as he delves into the goodies (snacks and small toys) when the vacation adventure begins. A surprise box can entertain your youngster anywhere from two minutes to two hours; if you're particularly circumspect and shrewd, you'll be on the latter end of the spectrum.

When making plane reservations, try to secure seat assignments at the same time. Indicate the age of your young traveler, and request the bulkhead seats. These seats afford a little extra leg room and can be padded with blankets and pillows if your child decides to snooze (lucky you!). It may mean that your feet will be struck by paralysis if little Janie nestles down on her pillow and curls up on your toes, but it is an improvement over having her elbow in your drink. Also, without passengers in front of you in this seating arrangement, you won't fret over a rambunctious child's kicks disturbing other people.

If two parents are flying with a lap child, reserve an aisle seat and a window seat. Regular air travelers never request a center seat, so if the plane is not full, you'll wind up with that third seat in which to spread out; if a stranger does venture into your row, it's simple enough for one parent to move over a notch.

Many airlines stock on-board activity packs for children, and some even prepare special meals for their younger travelers. Sometimes airlines have a limited amount of baby food; usually you need to pack your own. Inquire about these services.

If you plan to rent a car during your vacation, be sure to request a car seat for a child four years old and younger. While many rental agencies take this in stride, the number of car seats is usually limited, so it's important to make a reservation for this accessory in advance. Whether your mode of transportation is your own car or a rental, plan frequent stops. Cramped legs and fidgetiness set in fast for youngsters. These factors are not unknown in air travel either; even a walk down the aisle of the plane to the bathroom is a change of pace for a child.

Airplanes pose additional problems: Small children often have greater difficulty than adults in adjusting to altitude changes. During takeoffs and landings, infants should be encouraged to nurse or drink a bottle; the sucking action combats blocked ear and painful sinus problems. Older children can use the same techniques as adults—yawning and chewing gum.

In car travel, a small ice chest in the backseat can be a real boon. Filled with milk, juice, and fruit, it provides a source of ready refreshment and relieves frantic searches for a fast-food stop or a corner grocery. Even when traveling by air, if your luggage allotment permits, check a small ice chest (empty) along with your other bags. Once you arrive at your hotel, it can be filled with ice and drinks and can be taken along in a rental car on side trips. Many accommodations include small refrigerators in the rooms, and some are equipped with kitchens, but if not, you've solved a problem before it arises. It's much easier to dig into an ice chest for a drink than to track down juice somewhere in the hotel facilities at nine o'clock at night. But if this seems too cumbersome and your child desperately needs something late at night, remember the hotel bar—it is the best place to hit, for it always has orange juice (for Screwdrivers), tomato juice (for Bloody Marys), and milk (for White Russians). It may be more expensive, but can you really afford to count pennies when Johnny refuses to go to sleep without his nightly cup of milk? It's an investment in your peace of mind.

When stocking up on drinks, buy the variety in cardboard cartons. Since they are unbreakable and need no refrigeration, they can be squirreled away in a suitcase or even tossed into a purse. On an airplane, the flight attendants never seem to pass by soon enough or often enough to satisfy little ones.

For edibles, small boxes of raisins, granola bars, and individually wrapped cheese chunks such as La Vache qui Rit (what child can resist a silly laughing cow in a red net bag?) make good nourishing snacks. Good old clever Mom can rack up some kudos when she pulls one of these treats from her bag before Susie even thinks about getting antsy.

Once you arrive at your destination and settle into your hotel, turn over an area, even if just a corner, to your child. His own space filled with his own stuff may mean a lot to him in terms of a sense of belonging, and with a bit of prodding you may avoid having toys strewn all about.

Collecting souvenirs on a trip is at best a time-consuming process or maybe even a headache or two. Either Joey wants everything in sight or he chooses the most inappropriate piece of junk you've ever seen. Sure, certain limits on buying have to be set, but who cares if he chooses the made-in-Japan pencil sharpener in the shape of a cannon during a visit to Valley Forge? With a nod from Lady Luck, it will be lost before you're homeward bound. Just as a cookbook containing three wonderful meat-pie recipes from Nova Scotia or an artistic ceramic tile made in the Southwest is something that you can't possibly do without, there are special reminders of a trip that a child feels he needs. They're just different. A few neat rocks and a couple of sticks may be the only things he wants to show off to his best buddy back home. Or if your little girl wants to take home a shiny red coin purse to her best friend, she doesn't care (and neither does her friend) that the same item is on the shelves in every Wal-Mart-type store across the country, so why should you? A smattering of understanding and patience can go a long way.

Recreational activities in your new surroundings must be evaluated with a clear head and a sharp eye. All of the resorts included here offer organized children's activities or baby-sitting services, so it's not necessary to drag kids along on every adult event you want to investigate. Antiques hunting and museum visits are usually not first-rate attractions for members of the kiddie league. Plan on a baby-sitter or a group activity for an afternoon that you want to spend on a grown-up outing.

And for those days that are devoted entirely to being together, alternate grown-up pursuits with juvenile ones. Remember that a child's attention span is not as refined or sophisticated as an adult's; variety is more than the spice of life— it's the key to sanity in some cases. Climbing on the cannons at an old fort is much more fun for a child than reading every historical marker; a mixture of both keeps everyone happy. All day on the beach may be too much for a three- or four-year-old, and you can take ten-to-one odds that he won't be content following your lead to relax and soak up the sunshine. Bargain with your child: a run on the beach and a few splashes in the waves, then quiet time building a sand castle.

Many resorts have lodging with fully equipped kitchens so that you can cook family meals in a homelike setting. Many resort restaurants make an attentive effort to please children; a special dining hour for families or a clever children's menu certainly helps make life more pleasant. But when you grow weary of dining in restaurants, a picnic may be a reasonable alternative. Many hotels can prepare box lunches, or you can pick up some cold cuts at a small grocery for a do-it-yourself picnic. Ordering a meal through room service can be a special treat for a child.

As you skim the descriptive entries of the resorts, you'll realize that most are self-contained vacation spots. Each offers a place to sleep, a place to eat, and something to do. This is intentional, as children seem to function best staying in one place. Establishing a home base, exploring the setting, and taking afternoon side trips are often preferable to being on the road constantly. Besides negating all the packing and unpacking of a traditional road trip (remember, this is not the newest rock star promoting his latest album that you're traveling with!), having a home base helps a child develop a sense of security as the new surroundings become familiar.

With a few tricks up your sleeve and some understanding forethought, traveling with kids can be a fun-filled family adventure. Your well-considered plans make the whole process workable and buy a lot of happiness for both you and your child.

Medical Information

Unless you can take your own family doctor or pediatrician with you, the best advice to follow is the old Girl Scout motto "Be Prepared." Keep in mind: (1) This adventure you're about to embark upon is not a trek along the shores of the East Siberian Sea, and (2) you are not the sole custodian of Band-Aids. As amazing as it may seem, doctors and pharmacies do exist out there in that twilight zone called family vacations.

Before starting your trip, consult your pediatrician for advice; she/he may even be able to supply names of colleagues where you'll be visiting. If you fear that your child is coming down with something as you depart on your vacation, or if she's particularly accident-prone, you can check with the resort staff upon arrival about the location of the nearest hospital and pharmacy and the availability of doctors and nurses (many resorts have medical personnel on call). Sometimes the best recommendations come from other parents, wherever you may find them. If the need is immediate, don't hesitate to ask a likely looking parent working in a car rental agency, a restaurant, a shop, or the airport. And without seeming alarmist, look up the telephone number of the local poison control center; anticipating the slim chance of ever needing it, you'll be gratified that it's handy should your child ingest a handful of your brightly colored vitamin pills. It is also a good idea to check with your medical insurance provider before you leave home for out-of-state or -country authorization/billing procedures.

Pack a medical emergency kit and try to envision the unexpected. If your child scrapes a knee at a playground or develops an earache in the middle of the night, you won't want to take time tracking down a drugstore to relieve his discomfort. You can purchase a ready-made medical kit that fits compactly in a car's glove compartment or carry-on bag, or you may prefer the do-it-yourself variety. The following list is merely suggestive; review your own medicine cabinet to fill in the gaps.

standard vitamins and medications your child normally takes

a thermometer

children's Tylenol

children's cough syrup

adhesive strips

nose drops (though most kids hate them)

a decongestant such as Dimetapp

an aspirator

ear drops

suppositories and anti-dirrheal medicine (change in water and altitude or
    sheer excitement can affect a child's system)

Desitin or A and D ointment

antibiotic ointment or spray such as Bacitracin or Bactine (for cuts
    and scrapes)

tweezers and a sterile needle (to remove splinters)

Ipecac (to induce vomiting if your child overdoses on peculiar substances)

Q-Tips and cotton balls

sterile gauze pads (for applying direct pressure to cuts)

insect repellent

Though this list seems long, the items take up very little space in a suitcase. Remember, you don't have to pack a lifetime supply of any of these things. A small box of adhesive strips and a small bottle of cough medicine will meet the immediate need and buy you time to find the drugstore.

Knowing What Questions to Ask

It seems as if there are almost as many pricing schedules, package plans, and special programs as there are resorts. There are EP, MAP, FAP, golf and tennis packages, weekend specials, and midweek discounts. Depending on geographical location, high season is winter at one resort and summer at another. Even the seasons are defined arbitrarily. Summer may be the end of June through Labor Day or, perhaps, Memorial Day through Labor Day. Christmas season starts December 15 at some places and a week later at others. All the jargon and variations on a theme can make you feel like a babe in the woods when contacting a resort about your plans. To avoid arriving someplace and getting halfway through your stay only to find out that you should have taken advantage of some special offer, you have to be savvy in the possibilities and the vocabulary. Even if you aren't familiar with the latest buzzwords, just knowing that different vacation configurations exist puts you a leg up; you can at least ask, "Are there any family discounts or package plans for _____ [fill in the blank—golf, tennis, skiing, etc.]?"

At some resorts, you walk in and pay one price. At others, every hour on the tennis court or every bicycle ride around the block is charged separately. Both approaches have redeeming aspects. To some folks, it's downright annoying to have to reach constantly for a wallet. After all, this is a vacation and they don't want to be troubled with mundane monetary matters. On the other hand, some people would rather pay as they go, laying down the cash for only the services they use. If you've had aquaphobia since childhood and don't care to be within 10 feet of a lake, much less out in the middle rocking a canoe, free boating privileges are worthless. As long as you're in the know as to a resort's practices and policies beforehand, you'll suffer no surprises and no aggravation or disappointment during your visit.

Much of a resort's terminology is self-explanatory, and for the experienced traveler, even the acronyms are no mysteries. The most commonly used abbreviations are EP, for European plan, meaning lodging only; MAP, for modified American plan, which includes two meals a day in the room rate; and FAP, for full American plan, which includes three meals a day.

Knowing a resort's designation of low and high season is also crucial to your planning. If you're not absolutely wedded to certain dates and you can juggle your schedule on the home front, you might land in the low season simply by altering your plans by a week.

Moving to more detailed information, you may want to ask a resort certain specific questions. The questions outlined here can be used on the resorts described in this book for elaboration on particular points, or you can test them out on places that you discover on your own.

Lodging

Are the accommodations hotel rooms, condominium units, or cottages with kitchens?

If they are hotel rooms:

- Are there connecting rooms?
- Is there a refrigerator in the room? (This is handy for chilling juice and milk and keeping snacks fresh.)
- What is the range of prices, and is there a reduced rate for children?
- Is there a charge for a crib or rollaway bed?

Dining

What types of dining areas are there? Is there a spot to get Joey a hot dog and a place that tantalizes more refined taste buds?

Is there a dress requirement? (What a disappointment to venture into a tempting restaurant only to learn that gentlemen are required to wear jackets and you packed nothing but golf shirts!)

Is there a meal plan? Is it mandatory or optional?

Kids

Is there a supervised program for children?

- What are the planned activities, and what are the ages of the children who participate?
- When is it held—times of the year, days of the week, and hours of the day? (The level of specificity may seem a little overboard, but consider a Monday-through-Friday-morning program: It's not going to be much help if you pull in at 1:00 P.M. on Friday and leave at 10:00 A.M. Tuesday.)

What is the daily or hourly fee?

- Is there a playground or game room? (Even if you're doing the supervision, if there's something amusing for the kids, they can release some energy and you can sit on the sidelines and read the newspaper.)

Are baby-sitting services available?

- Who makes the arrangements—you or the resort staff?
- What is the average rate? (You may linger a bit longer over that fine Cabernet if your baby-sitter receives $3.00 an hour rather than $6.00 an hour.)

And if you're skittish about your kid's health or proclivity toward disaster, inquire about local medical facilities.

- Is there a doctor or nurse in residence or on call?
- Where are the nearest hospital and pharmacy?

For You

If you're investigating a resort or have chosen it as a vacation destination, you no doubt have an inkling as to its recreational facilities. You're looking at it *because* of its beach, golf course, tennis center, or ski mountain. Besides its main attraction, you'll also want to know what secondary diversions are possible. You can't play golf sixteen hours a day—not even Jack Nicklaus does that. So ask:

- Is there a jogging path? parcourse fitness trail? hiking trails?
- Is there a spa or exercise room? sauna, steam room, whirlpool?
- Does the tennis complex also house racquetball courts?
- For golf, tennis, and fishing—is it possible to rent equipment, or is it necessary to bring your own?
- Are there any concerts, lectures, or classes?

Your interests will determine which questions to ask. Once you get a handle on what to ask, you'll find planning a vacation a lot more fun and a lot less time-consuming. You don't have to have all the answers; just being able to pose a few intelligent questions sets the ball in motion and can generate maybe even more information than you thought you wanted. As a knowledgeable consumer, you can pursue plans on your own or you can work quite effectively with a travel agent. In either case, a little self-education can certainly enhance the preparation and the end product: your leisure time.

Using a Travel Agent

Going to a travel agent has certain overtones of the classic Dr. Jekyll and Mr. Hyde story. Almost everyone has a friend or relative in the travel business; almost everyone has at least one horror story. Working conscientiously with a competent travel agent minimizes the possibility of frightful tales and increases the chances of very positive experiences.

Why should you use a travel agent? The main reasons are three: (1) Agents have the knowledge and expertise that come with training and experience (yours is not the only vacation ever planned); (2) they have access to comprehensive resources and services; and (3) it is convenient and economical, both in time and money.

Travel agents provide a service. They can book an airline flight, reserve a hotel room, and line up a rental car. There is generally no charge for this attention, as agents' commissions are paid by the supplier—either airlines, hotels, or car companies. An agent's success depends to a large extent on repeat business and referral, so pleasing the passenger is a top priority. Ideally, agents should be passenger advocates, defending "those who roam the world."

Travel, like so much else today, has become increasingly complicated. Since the deregulation of the airlines, the proliferation of airfares has been phenomenal. Any given pair of cities has up to sixty different fares, with as many rules and regulations. While this ultimately benefits the pleasure traveler, it also creates a certain amount of chaos. On a trip from New York to San Francisco, for example, the same seat in the airplane can cost anywhere between $299 and $750, depending on how far in advance you book, how long you're staying, and the promotional needs of the air carrier. When one adds other factors such as the day of the week, certain airports, one-stop versus nonstop flights, or whether you're wearing polka dots, more complications arise. While airlines generally give you their own lowest fares, they do not necessarily tell you about a competitor who may have even lower fares or more convenient flights.

This scenario supports all three reasons for using a travel agent. Save yourself time and money by turning over these problems to a travel agent. While you could spend literally days tracking down this information, a good travel agent with a talent for unraveling mysteries and a handy-dandy computer can accomplish miracles in anywhere from five minutes to an hour or so. Equipped with something called the "shoppers' fares," the computer allows a quick review of all the airlines that travel to a given destination and lists the fares beginning with the lowest. You can then work with the agent to figure out if saving $100 is really worth getting up at 3:00 A.M. Finally, you can capitalize on an agent's knowledge of the fares and facilities that each airline provides for children and of any special family-travel offers, such as "kids fly free" and discounts for spouses.

Even something as seemingly straightforward as a hotel reservation can be complicated by weekend specials, golf or tennis packages, seasons, midweek, and family offers. If there are many hotels on your agenda, it is a real pleasure to let the agent repeat the same information about your needs and desires sixteen times. A good agent is a whiz at interpreting brochures and deciphering the fine print. "Ocean view" does not mean on the beach; in fact, you may have to hang over the balcony with a pair of binoculars to see the ocean. "Secluded" may mean private, or it may mean you have to go 10 miles to find any other signs of life. In the air or on the ground, the knowledgeable agent saves you time and converts elusive information into something concrete in your vacation plans.

This is the age of information overkill; managing this information, sorting through the myriad possibilities, can be mind-boggling. Working with a professional travel agent can add several dimensions to this information process. An agent is a bountiful source of books, brochures, and maps; but more important are the agent's personal experience, the client base that gives feedback on pros and cons of trips, and close contact with colleagues in the travel agency who have traveled extensively. A good agent can pull all of this together, analyze your needs, and help make your vacation dream become a coherent reality.

While the savings in time have been illustrated, let's not forget how enlisting the services of a travel agent can save you money as well. This is an advantage not to be overlooked, for it is the travel agent who can find the most economical way of doing what you want to do. A good agent with appropriate input from you can match alternatives with your particular budget demands.

Now that you are aware of the joys of using a travel agent, how do you find this wonderful person? Travel agents are dealers in dreams—in charge of that very precious event, your vacation. You should pick your travel agent as carefully as you would your doctor—or your car mechanic! It's very nice to go to your Aunt Nelly or your neighbor's first cousin, but a smart consumer considers more substantial factors. Most important of these are the accessibility and policies of the agency and the personality and qualifications of the agent.

Working from the general to the specific, look first at the agency itself. Is it a pleasant environment; are the people animated? What are their policies on service charges, refunds, payments? Are they an appointed agency of the airlines, Amtrak, and the cruise lines? Airline appointments indicate a certain basic financial investment and preparation and the ability to write airline tickets. Most agencies are online nowadays and because of computerization have the capability to scan quickly for the best fares and most convenient flights, make seat assignments, and issue boarding passes. Another consideration is whether the agency is a member of the American Society of Travel Agents (ASTA). There are good agencies that may not be members, but affiliation with this professional organization of the travel industry indicates that an agency has been in operation for at least three years. ASTA also acts as a ready resource for problems and possible complaints.

The ability and personality of an individual agent are crucial factors in your selection. You should like and respect the person you entrust your pleasures to and have confidence in his/her ability and desire to look after your interests. A reliable, though subjective, way of choosing an agent is to ask friends whose opinion you trust and whose values you share. On a more objective level, you can check an agent's credentials. More and more agents are now becoming certified travel consultants, indicating at least five years' experience and completion of a two-year intensive study program. While this is a professional plus, it is not a requirement for a good agent. Personal compatibility, however, is of paramount importance. You should feel comfortable with the agent and able to ask questions—even the same one repeatedly or even the ones you're afraid may sound dumb.

The higher your level of involvement in planning, the more satisfaction you stand to gain from your trip. A good agent should be able to determine the broad outlines of your trip, to respond and listen to your ideas and needs, and to fill in with specific suggestions. The agent should have an idea of your lifestyle, your ideal vacation, and your budget. Your agent should ask, or you should volunteer, what seems to be personal information: How do you like to spend your days? Is shopping important to you? If you have a beach, are you happy? Will you die if you have no evening entertainment, or do you prefer a quiet stroll and a good book? What are your hobbies or special interests? Again, do not be afraid to discuss financial expectations. This can avoid a few nasty surprises—such as having to ransom one of the kids to pay for the trip! Also, be as specific as you can. "Sometime in August" does not get the same results as "one week, with a departure date between August 2 and August 8."

Even the best travel agent has a limited amount of time, and no one knows your expectations as well as you, so assume some of the legwork for detailed information yourself. Check with the tourist offices of the state or country you plan to visit for brochures and information on special events and attractions. The American Automobile Association (AAA), if you're a member and are driving for part or all of the trip, is an excellent resource for maps and detailed information. Travel books and articles are fun for the family and often have good advice on extras or little-known attractions in the area; check your local library for these. (Chinaberry Book Service, in San Diego, California, 800–776–2242, has a catalog of well-selected books and tapes for various ages and interests.) Also, talk to your friends who have been there for those real inside tips. In these ways, even if you're a do-it-yourselfer, you can comfortably join forces with a travel agent.

Several tour operators specialize in family travel, working with both travel agents and individual clients. Call them for their brochures. In Chevy Chase, Maryland, Grandtravel does escorted tours for grandparents and grandchildren, both in the United States and abroad (800–247–7651). In Durham, North Carolina, Families Welcome! offers families individually planned packages for travel in Europe as well as select destinations in the United States and Caribbean (800–326–0724). In San Francisco, California, Rascals in Paradise offers some resorts in the United States, some with their own personally directed children's programs during school holidays (800–U–RASCAL). Many local agencies are becoming aware of the family market and are beginning to specialize in this field; check your local parents' paper or the travel section of the local Sunday paper for these agencies in your area.

Finally, close your suitcase, lock the door, and take off—secure in the knowledge that your advance planning, plus professional help, will make this the best trip ever!

NEW ENGLAND

Connecticut

Maine

Massachusetts

New Hampshire

Vermont

The Balsams Grand Resort Hotel

Dixville Notch, New Hampshire 03576
(603) 255–3400, (800) 255–0600, (800) 255–0800 (in New Hampshire)
E-mail: thebalsams@aol.com
Web site: www.thebalsams.com

I n the fine tradition of grand old hotels, The Balsams has been graciously welcoming guests since 1866. The three main buildings are interconnected and quite impressive, with their white facades and red-tiled roofs. Two date from the late 1800s—the Dixville House and The Balsams Inn—and the newcomer, the Hampshire House, was added in 1917. At the foot of three very precipitous mountains—almost entirely surrounded by steep, 1,000-foot cliffs with the Notch Road the only way in or out—and overlooking Lake Gloriette, The Balsams offers a relaxed escape in a charming atmosphere. In summer Dixville Notch is a refreshing mountain retreat, in winter a delightful getaway for skiers.

The Balsams adds all the amenities for a fun-filled vacation in a worry-free atmosphere. Golf, tennis, swimming, hiking, mountain biking, lawn games, children's day camp, fine dining, and nightly entertainment are available and in keeping with an almost unique practice these days—no additional charges for use of any of the facilities. Winter activities include skiing, snowboarding, snowshoeing, and skating. Your needs are tended to, your interests can be pursued, and your cares can be dispelled. The resort is open from the third week in December until early April, reopening for the summer season from late May to mid-October.

Accommodations: There are 204 rooms at The Balsams, many with views of the mountains or the lake. Family suites with one or two bedrooms offer ample space for youngsters; these are quite popular. The Hampshire House is configured to provide convenient adjoining rooms for family accommodation. All the rooms have been restored, thus creating a comfortable ambience. Depending on the size of the room, its location and view, and the time of the year, prices range from $132 to $245 per person per night. Children's rates are on a graduated scale, calculated at $9.00 per day multiplied by the child's age, with a minimum charge of $35. So, infants to three-year-olds are $35 per day, four-years-olds are $36, and so on. These rates are based on a full American plan and include unlimited access to all the facilities. Cribs are provided.

Dining: The main dining room serves breakfast, lunch, and dinner during the summer season, breakfast and dinner only during the winter season. The summertime luncheon buffet is a sumptuous display of hot and cold entrees, cheeses, fruit, and desserts; you might sample the fried Maine shrimp or the Atlantic salmon. A menu luncheon is available at the Golf Clubhouse. The din-

Photo courtesy of The Balsams Grand Resort Hotel

ner menu offers an entirely different selection every evening, featuring seafood dishes as well as Long Island duckling, beef, and chicken. At the dinner hour jackets for men are appropriate. Parents are advised to bring appropriate dinner clothes for older children as well.

The Cafe is open year-round, 10:00 A.M.–midnight, and is perfect for lighter meals (sandwiches and grilled items). In the summer you might try The Panorama Golf Clubhouse or the poolside bar for refreshments; both offer delightful views and a chance to soak up the beautiful scenery. In the winter warm up with a cup of cider or hot buttered rum in La Cave. Also in winter you'll be shuttling over to The Balsams/Wilderness Ski Area, where breakfast and lunch are served at the Base Lodge and an a la carte luncheon is served in the dining room. Evening entertainment means cocktails and floor shows in the Switzerland of America Ballroom or dancing in the Wilderness Lounge; both are in the hotel.

Children's World: The Balsams is interested in providing excellent service for its younger guests as well as its adult visitors. For children this translates into a busy schedule of fun activities. Camp Wind Whistle is available from the Fourth of July through Labor Day (seven days a week); here children ages five through thirteen meet with counselors in The Balsams Playroom for sports, games, picnics, swimming, nature walks, arts and crafts, fishing, farm visits, and movies. Outdoor activities are stressed. Children have lunch with their counselors and then, after linking up with Mom and Dad around 4:00 P.M. to share their day's experiences, they can rejoin their young group for dinner at 6:30 P.M. There is no charge for this service. Age groups are divided as follows: five to seven years, eight to ten years, and eleven to thirteen years. Camp Wee Whistle is a special program for younger children, ages three and four, at no additional charge; during June, call for specific dates.

The outdoor children's area features a state-of-the art fiberglass and stainless steel play structure. The indoor game room (supervised) has an array of board games, video games, and Ping-Pong and pool tables. Open daily from 9:00 A.M. to midnight, the game room is a popular spot for youngsters to gather and make friends during both summer and winter seasons.

In winter children ages three to five can enroll in the Wee Whistle Ski School. Older children have their own morning and afternoon lessons. The cost is approximately $30 for two hours. Wintertime room rates for children at The Balsams include ski privileges.

A nursery at the Base Lodge takes nonskiing youngsters under six (who are out of diapers) while you're on the slopes. The experienced staff amuses children with a selection of games and toys from 9:00 A.M. to 4:00 P.M.; parents should join their children for lunch. This service is provided gratis to children of hotel guests. Individual baby-sitters (usually off-duty hotel employees) can be arranged at reasonable rates; sitters should be reserved when lodging reservations are made.

Recreation: At The Balsams you can spend busy days of back-to-back events from morning to night or just relax, set an unhurried pace, and enjoy the peace and beauty of the mountains. Two golf courses await golfers. The eighteen-hole championship course was designed by Donald Ross, an architect famous during the early twentieth century; set in the mountains, the undulating terrain can be challenging and the views truly stunning. The nine-hole course is just right for beginners or those who haven't tested their clubs in a while. There are pro shops at each course, putting greens, a practice fairway, and a pro staff on hand to help you polish your swing. The Centennial Golf School operates from May through early July and features a PGA professional for every four students.

Tennis enthusiasts can choose to play on either red-clay courts (three) or all-weather courts (three). Sign up with the pro for group or private lessons, and stop by the tennis shop to pick up those indispensable accessories.

Swim a few laps in the Olympic-size heated swimming pool overlooking Lake Gloriette. With the mountains in the background, this is an idyllic spot for sunbathing. You might try a refreshing dip in the lake or a relaxing excursion in a paddleboat, canoe, or rowboat. Fish in a crystal-clear mountain stream, hike in the wilderness (solo or with a guided group), or take a nature walk with the staff naturalist. The hotel's natural-history program combines tours, hikes, and discussions in a good introduction to the flora and fauna of the area. The mountain biking trails are well marked and offer fun at every level. Mountain bike rentals and repairs are available.

Lawn sports include badminton, horseshoes, croquet, volleyball, and shuffleboard; when you head indoors, there are billiards, Ping-Pong, bingo, an aerobic exercise room, and a movie theater. Take to the library/card room to snuggle up with a good book or play a few hands of bridge. To track down that essential souvenir, drop in at the gift shop, craft shop, gallery, balloon store, and fashion boutique.

In the wintertime this wonderland is draped in snow, and The Balsams/ Wilderness Ski Area (located on the property) is just a short shuttle ride from the hotel. There are thirteen downhill trails and 45 miles of packed and groomed trails for cross-country. Wintertime also means ice skating, snowshoeing on dedicated trails, and riding in horse-drawn sleighs. Whether you're seeking an escape from city crowds or want an active sports-oriented vacation, The Balsams offers the attention and service to make it all possible. ≋

Highland Lodge

Caspian Lake
RR 1, Box 1290
Greensboro, Vermont 05841
(802) 533–2647
E-mail: hlodge@connriver.net
Web site: www.pbpub.com/vermont/hiland.htm

C ross-country skiing in Vermont—it sounds so romantic and wholesome. You almost expect to see Bing Crosby round the corner of the inn. A lovely old white-frame building with a comfortable front porch, the lodge is set on 160 acres bordering Caspian Lake. Open from Christmas to mid-March, the lodge facilities make it easy to enjoy wintertime sports; open again from Memorial Day weekend until mid-October, the lodge is a perfect spot for enjoying the fall foliage colors or for enjoying a summer trip of swimming and boating.

Accommodations: Choose a guest room in the lodge or one of the cottages just behind the main building. Tastefully decorated with nice furnishings (some rooms have brass beds) and old-fashioned wallpaper, these accommodations can house approximately sixty guests. The cottages feature a living room, porch, bath, and one to three bedrooms; nine cottages include kitchenettes. Cribs are provided for little ones. Based on a modified American plan and double occupancy, rates are $95 to $128 per person per night. Children sharing a room or cottage with their parents are charged according to their ages, $20 to $65 a day.

Dining: Two connecting dining rooms in the lodge serve breakfast, lunch, and dinner. For entrees you may select fresh fish, lamb, duck, veal, or prime rib with vegetables from a local farm, and sample the homemade soups and breads, but be sure to save room for what the staff boasts are sinful desserts. You might sit near the fireplace in the dining room or by the large windows to take in the view; weather permitting, dining tables are set up on the porch. A modified American meal plan is offered, and there are children's portions and special items for youngsters.

Children's World: A swing set and a sandbox stocked with toys attract little ones. There are tennis and hiking for older children. For children of all ages, swimming at the supervised private beach is a great way to spend the afternoon. After a busy day kids may settle into the children's library, where they'll find books, games, and puzzles. In the mornings during July and August, youngsters ages four to nine link up with the Play Lady, who devises programs of crafts, swimming, and nature hikes; this is free of charge to guests. In addition, the staff can make arrangements for individual baby-sitters ($4.50 an hour).

Recreation: Thirty miles of groomed cross-country ski trails meander through fields and forests and across frozen lakes. You can line up a guided tour or pick up a little instruction. Bring your own equipment or rent the necessary para-phernalia at the ski shop.

In warmer weather hike or jog in the adjoining Barr Hill Nature Preserve, walk the Lodge's nature trail, or take to the water; swim at the beach or head out on the lake in a canoe, sailboat, or paddleboat provided by the lodge. The lake also means good fishing, particularly in early summer and fall; set your line for salmon, trout, or perch.

Back on land, challenge another guest to a tennis match on the clay court and then round up a game of badminton, volleyball, or croquet on the lawn. The nearby Green Mountains and White Mountains lure guests into afternoon driving excursions. ≋

Jay Peak Ski Resort
Jay, Vermont 05859
(802) 988–2611, (800) 451–4449

Way up in northern Vermont, just about 10 miles from the Canadian border, is the Jay Peak Ski Area. In a friendly, comfortable atmos-phere, skiing Montrealers who drift down this way add a bit of an international flair to Jay. The resort encompasses more than 300 acres of ski-able terrain, sometimes plummeting and sometimes meandering down from a 4,000-foot summit. With a ski season that lasts from November to late April or early May, a 332-inch average annual snowfall, and snowmaking on more than 80 percent of skiable terrain, skiing is serious business in this area of Vermont. Twenty glade and tree areas add to the uniqueness of skiing here.

Though primarily a winter holiday destination, many of the accommoda-tions in Jay are open year-round and can serve as a home base while you go off fishing, biking, hiking, picking wildflowers, and enjoying the clean mountain air. Plans are under way for the creation of a four-season recreational resort village designed with a deep commitment to environmental harmony.

Accommodations: Hotel Jay, located at the mountain base, has rooms with private balconies and also houses a restaurant and a lounge. Rates start at $227 per person for a two-night stay, including lifts, breakfast, and one dinner. When sharing a room with parents during the regular ski season, children (under age six) and juniors (seven to fourteen) stay and ski free. Teenagers stay for $30 per night when sharing parents' room.

At Slopeside condominiums, enjoy the convenience of ski-in/ski-out and the comfort of one to three bedrooms with balconies, kitchen, living room, and fireplace. The newest townhouses, whose number is limited, feature two floors of elegant space, with huge picture windows to enjoy the mountains. Jay has a variety of lodging; choose from small inns, lodges, and townhouses. Inglenook Lodge, located about a mile from the slopes, begins at $98 per night. Children ages five to sixteen pay $15; those under age five stay free. Inglenook has the only indoor swimming pool in the area, a big plus for kids. Call the resort's toll-free number for information on packages and lodging.

Dining: The dining room at Hotel Jay features international fare. The Inglenook Lodge and Jay Village Inn also have restaurants. Some evening you may wish to seek out the charm of an old country inn such as the Black Lantern.

Children's World: The Jay Peak Child Care Center provides indoor fun and games for two- to seven-year-olds from 9:00 A.M. to 4:00 P.M. at the Kinderschool, and from 4:00 to 9:00 P.M. at the Hotel Jay Family Room, with supervised dinner at 5:30 P.M. This service is free to guests of Jay Peak Condominiums or Hotel Jay; otherwise, the cost is $30 full-day and $15 half-day. For infants under age two, private care is available for $6.00 per hour, with a minimum of three hours. The Kinderschool Ski program is a special half-day morning ski program, followed by afternoon rest and activities; the cost is $25 for guests, $40 for nonguests. SKIwee, a nationally acclaimed children's program using fun and games to teach skiing skills, is an all-day program for children ages five to twelve. The cost is $47 for one day, $111 for three days, or $145 for five days. SKIwee kids have access to the Mountain Adventureland, a no-adult area in the woods with a snow hut and obstacle course for the more accomplished, and their own room with kid-size spaces and indoor ramp for a warmer practice. Older children, ten to sixteen years, can join the Mountain Adventurers and sample not only downhill skiing but also snowboarding, snowshoeing, cross-country skiing, or assisting the instructors with the smaller children and other snow activities. The cost of $141 for three days or $185 for five days includes rental of all equipment except downhill skis.

Preregistration is required for all programs. A large activity room in the base lodge gives kids a place to meet and play video games, pool, or Ping-Pong. Movies are shown regularly in the spacious family room, and families visiting midweek can enjoy such unique activities as a visit to a working dairy farm, night sledding and marshmallow roasts, and ice skating.

In the summertime Jay Peak offers a children's swim program and day camp. Activities include swimming instruction, arts and crafts, hiking, and more.

Recreation: The center of the wintertime attention and activity is Jay Peak, with its 2,100 vertical feet and thirty-five downhill runs. The aerial tram reaches from Hotel Jay up to the summit, and five other lifts keep skiers on the move. Lessons are offered at the ski school for all levels, from barely beginners to advanced skiers trying to perfect their mogul skiing. The 20 kilometers of groomed trails lead cross-country skiers over the hills and through the woods. Instruction is also available in cross-country techniques and telemarking—ever wonder how people do it? Here's your chance to find out.

While skiing is the reason for a winter holiday here, you may find yourself quite taken with the Jacuzzi and sauna facilities at Hotel Jay, especially after a tough day skiing (use is complimentary for Hotel Jay guests). The Inglenook has a sauna, an indoor swimming pool, and racquetball courts.

In the summer the emphasis is on relaxation and clean country living. Fishing and hiking in the mountains are favorite pastimes. Hotel Jay has an outdoor swimming pool and Har-Tru tennis courts (free for guests of the hotel). And to really appreciate the mountain scenery, take a ride on the aerial tram; on a clear day, views extend for 150 miles. ≋≋

Killington Ski and Summer Resort

Killington Road
Killington, Vermont 05751
(802) 773-1330, (800) 621-MTNS

K illington is the largest ski area in the eastern United States, and its vital statistics are indeed impressive: 212 runs on six interconnected mountains, plus Pico Mountain at Killington; more than 3,000 vertical feet; and a ski season that starts in mid-October and continues to June. Killington boasts an average annual snowfall of 250 inches. To ensure its earliest opening date and latest closing date in the East, sophisticated snowmaking techniques assist Mother Nature. Thirty-three lifts, including an eight-passenger heated gondola, get you quickly to the top.

A year-round resort, Killington is cradled in the Green Mountains of central Vermont, a setting whose beauty does not wane with the melting snow; in late spring and summer, the lush green landscape is the backdrop for tennis and golf holidays; in autumn the fall foliage colors take over.

Accommodations: There are almost 200 properties at Killington, ranging from small inns and lodges to condominium complexes. Killington Travel Services (800–621–6867) lists more than 115 of these and publishes helpful, descriptive information clearly outlining the many package plans available. Ski-in locations include Trailside Lodge, with standard rooms/bunk beds, and Trailside Village, Sunrise Village, and Spruce Glen condos. Rates are lower in summer and higher at holiday periods. Call for the latest rates.

Photo by Bob Perry, courtesy of Killington Ski and Summer Resort

Killington Resort Villages (800–343–0762) offers hotel-style and one-, two-, and three-bedroom condos, some within walking distance of the slopes, plus several other condominium complexes. The Villager nightly rates range from $52 to $92 in summer, $49 to $196 in winter. Condo summer rates are $89 to $240, rising to $112 to $688 in winter. Condominiums not within walking distance but right at the base of Killington Mountain include Edgemont, Whiffletree, Highridge, Mountain Green, and Pinnacle. Studio to four-bedroom units have fully equipped kitchens and fireplaces. Some condominiums have special features such as indoor pools or spa/exercise facilities (if you don't get enough on the slopes!).

Dining: In addition to the half dozen cafeterias at the bases of and on the mountains, The Clubhouse Grill is located across from Snowshed Base Lodge. In the area you'll find Italian, Chinese, Mexican, and German restaurants, or perhaps you'll sample French country dinners at the Red Clover Inn, typical New England dishes at the Vermont Inn, or continental cuisine at the Pittsfield Inn. Pubs and nightclubs provide late-evening entertainment.

Children's World: Whether your child is six weeks old or twelve years old, a first-time skier or a veteran, he or she will find a niche at Killington's Children's Center. Open daily from 8:00 A.M. to 4:30 P.M., the staff orchestrates indoor and outdoor play for infants to six-year-olds. First Tracks Ski School, for four- to five-year-olds, includes ski lessons as well as supervised play; the Superstars Ski Program groups six- to twelve-year-olds by ability for a full day of ski and play. Full-day fees include lunch; half-day sessions are available for the nonskiing and introductory skiing groups. For teenagers there's a weekly under-twenty-one disco with DJ or live bands, soda, and pizza. In December and March special weeks for teens are scheduled as well.

The Alpine Adventure Summer Camp offers age-grouped activities for youngsters six weeks to six years. The child-care ratio is four to one. Call for current cost of youth activities.

Recreation: Start your visit with a Meet the Mountain tour; skiers are grouped by ability and guided through a complimentary two-hour introduction to Killington's mountains. All seven mountains are accessed by the same lift ticket. All have beginner runs from their summits so that even novices can enjoy top-of-the-mountain views. From long lazy runs (one beginner's trail is 10 miles long) to steeply pitched expert terrain, every skier finds the appropriate challenge. This goes for ski clinics too, from classes for the newest beginner to workshops in racing for the advanced skier.

Après-ski activities include sleigh rides in the country and movies in the village, but maybe most appropriate for the end of an active day is a quiet rest in a sauna.

Summertime brings golf on an eighteen-hole course; tennis at the Killington School for Tennis; fishing, hiking, mountain biking, and horseback riding (Sunrise Stables) in the mountains. ≋

The Lighthouse Inn

Lighthouse Road
West Dennis, Massachusetts 02670
(508) 398-2244
Web site: www.lighthouseinn.com

An old-fashioned country inn, The Lighthouse Inn sits on the shores of Nantucket Sound. The core of the main building is aptly named as the historic Bass River Lighthouse. The inn recalls an easier pace of past times. The classic Cape Cod–style main house provides a beautiful view of the ocean; sprawling out behind are nine secluded acres with additional accommodations and recreational facilities.

Accommodations: The main house offers individual rooms and suites. Alternatively, you might choose one of the cottages with one to three bedrooms. Prices begin at $196 a night (including breakfast) in the summer season, $134

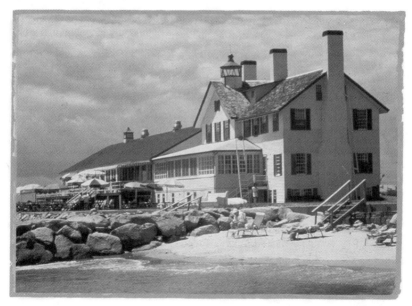

Photo courtesy of The Lighthouse Inn

a night (including breakfast) in the spring and fall. Children sharing a room or cottage with their parents are charged a graduated rate depending on their ages: ages three to five years, $30 a day; ages six to eight, $35 a day; nine to twelve, $45 a day; and thirteen-year-olds and older, $55 a day. For children the daily rate includes breakfast. Rates that include dinner are available.

Dining: The dining room in the main house entices guests with fresh fish and lobster dinners and lovely views over the water. Outdoors, the oceanside deck is the setting for lunch. A snack bar adjoins the pool. Once a week a poolside cookout is planned.

Children's World: Games, swimming, arts and crafts, sandcastle building, kite flying, miniature golf, and nature walks fill the days for InnKids. Three- and four-year-olds participate from 9:30 A.M. to noon, while children ages five and older carry on until 3:00 P.M. In the evening both groups are invited to get together from 5:30 to 8:30 P.M. for dinner and entertainment, perhaps a movie or a magician's show. The InnKids program runs from late June through August and is included in the fees for children noted above. Individual baby-sitting costs $6.00 an hour.

Recreation: Enjoying the soft ocean breezes may be all the activity you want during your first couple of days at Lighthouse Inn. Renewed and refreshed, you can then jump into the swimming pool, splash in the gentle waters of Nantucket Sound, and stroll along the beach. The outdoor tennis court awaits you when you turn energetic, and fishing can be a pleasant morning outing. You can also play Ping-Pong, pool, and shuffleboard or pursue quieter interests in the library/game room. ≋

Mount Snow

Mount Snow, Vermont 05356
(802) 464–8501, (800) 245–7669
E-mail: info@mountsnow.com
Web site: www.mountsnow.com

A very popular New England ski resort, Mount Snow is situated in the beautiful Green Mountains of southern Vermont. Much of its popularity is, no doubt, due to its accessibility and proximity to major Northeast metropolitan areas; a four-and-a-half-hour drive from New York, two-and-a-half hours from Boston, makes this a very manageable weekend trip for residents of these cities. But Mount Snow's size and variety also account for its appeal. From gentle beginner and broad intermediate slopes to some of the steepest expert runs in the Northeast, 135 trails in all drop down from a 3,600-foot summit for 1,700 vertical feet. The average annual snowfall is about 157 inches. It is supplemented by sophisticated snowmaking that covers 85 percent of the skiable terrain; the ski season runs from about early November to late April.

Accommodations: Lodging, in atmosphere, style, price, and location, runs the gamut of possibilities. From modern condominium complexes to quaint country inns, more than fifty options are within 10 miles of the mountain base. The lodging bureau issues descriptive booklets to help you choose the right spot, and various package plans for lodging and lift tickets are offered.

A full-service hotel at the edge of a small lake, Snow Lake Lodge is very close to the base of the mountain; with its own restaurant, game room, and spa, a two-day weekend rate is $390 on a modified American plan; reduced rates apply for children. Seasons and Snow Mountain Village are condominiums near the base, where two-bedroom units start at $722 for a two-day weekend. These units have kitchens and fireplaces; some have balconies and mountain views.

The new 199-room Grand Summit Resort Hotel is located slopeside in Mount Snow's main base area and offers a variety of rooms, ranging from standard hotel-style rooms to three-bedroom condos. Amenities include ski-in/ski-out accommodations, valet parking, a health club, spa and fitness programs, a year-round heated outdoor pool, Harriman's Restaurant, and more. A two-day weekend starts at $450.

Photo © Jeff Baird, courtesy of Mount Snow

The many country inns around the area can add a distinctly New England flavor to a ski holiday. The charming Hermitage Inn, 3 miles from Mount Snow, maintains 40 miles of cross-country ski trails; a two-day weekend is $500, which includes breakfast and dinner.

Dining: At the base of Mount Snow are five cafeterias, six lounges, and six restaurants; at the Summit Lodge, views over the mountains complement cafeteria-style lunches. Also near the base is Walter's restaurant in the Snow Lake Lodge. Most of the inns and lodges of the area have their own restaurants and feature a variety, from hearty home-style cooking to the continental cuisine typical of the Hermitage and the White House of Wilmington.

Children's World: Throughout the ski season, kids have a place at Mount Snow. Child Care, a quality program for ages six weeks to six years, is located in the heart of the main base area. The program is fully licensed by the state of Vermont and is designed to be interactive, fun, and developmentally appropriate for each child's needs. Child Care is open weekdays from 8:30 A.M. to 4:30 P.M.; weekends and holidays, 8:00 A.M. to 4:30 P.M. Reservations are required. A two-day package is $115; snacks and lunch are provided. A list of baby-sitters is available through Child Care.

For three-year-olds enrolled in full-day Child Care, PreSki offers an introduction to the fun sport of skiing through games and activities both on and off the snow. Cost per one-day clinic, including equipment, is $18. For children four to twelve, Mount Snow offers Perfect Kids ski and snowboard clinics. Snow Camp is for ages four through six; Mountain Riders or Mountain Camp is for ages seven to twelve. Children new to skiing or snowboarding can enjoy expanded, private learning terrain. All Perfect Kids programs are centrally located in the main base area.

Kids ages twelve and under ski/ride free when their parents purchase a five-day nonholiday lift ticket. During "Fun Factor Five" weeks (mid-January through mid-March), free family activities include an ice-cream sundae party with costume parade, grooming machines rides, and animal puppet theater. Summer Kids camp is offered June through Labor Day weekend.

Mount Snow also offers a new lift-served snow tubing park open both day and night. Free sledding is available on the Ski Baba slope under lights from 5:00 to 9:00 P.M. An outdoor ice skating pond is adjacent to the sledding slope and is open day and night. Snow tube, sled, and skate rentals are available. The Galaxy Arcade is open daily in the main base area and features video games, recreational games, a penny candy counter, and a lounge area.

Recreation: Almost 75 percent of the runs at Mount Snow are ranked intermediate. The rest are just about evenly split between beginner and expert. The Main Mountain has forty beginner and intermediate trails, the North Face with its steeper terrain and moguls attracts advanced skiers, and the Sunbrook area with sunny southern exposure supports a couple of long lazy runs. The teaching staff is prepared to show you the way to improved techniques, and you have your pick of packages for various combinations of lifts, lessons, and equipment.

For cross-country skiers, four touring centers are within 10 miles of Mount Snow at the Hermitage, Sitzmark, Timber Creek, and White House. Also within this distance are three stables—Beaver Brook, Flames, and Adam's Farm—where you can arrange sleigh rides.

When these mountains turn green, the big event is the Golf School, held on the championship Geoffrey Cornish course. Other warm-weather activities include swimming, fishing, hiking, biking, and horseback riding.

The Mount Washington Hotel and Resort

Route 302
Bretton Woods, New Hampshire 03575
(603) 278–1000, (800) 258–0330

Majestic Mount Washington presides over this resort, a massive complex of lodging, dining, and recreational facilities on 2,600 acres of wooded New Hampshire countryside in the White Mountains. Voted a *Better Homes and Gardens* "Favorite Family Resort," the architectural gem and focal point of this New England resort is the gracious and stately hotel. Built in 1902 by the industrialist and railroad tycoon Joseph Stickney, the hotel began welcoming visitors to a lifestyle of classic elegance and soon claimed its status among prime vacation retreats of the Northeast.

International fame came to Bretton Woods in 1944 when the hotel hosted financiers from forty-four countries who created the World Bank and the International Monetary Fund and set the gold standard at $35 an ounce (ah—the good old days). In 1978 this fine old structure—with its glimmering white facade topped by red-tiled roofs, its wonderfully spacious veranda furnished with white wicker chairs and settees, and its 150-foot-long lobby—was added to the National Register of Historic Places. Since 1986 it has held the distinction of being a National Historic Landmark.

A multiyear winterization project was implemented in 1991, with a goal of offering this world-class grand resort on a year-round basis by the end of the twentieth century. The goal has been realized with the resort's purchase of the popular Bretton Woods Ski Area in 1997 and the winter opening of The Mount Washington Hotel in 1999.

Accommodations: The 200-room hotel offers standard to deluxe lodging with a number of two-bedroom family suites. Nearly all have views of Mount Washington, the Willey-Rosebrook Mountain range, or the well-tended gardens. All guests in the hotel participate in a modified American plan, and prices range from $210 to $495 for double occupancy. Children under age four are free; ages five to twelve are $35; and over twelve are $70. A family chamber costs $370–$405 a night and accommodates up to four persons. The Bretton Arms, also a National Historic Landmark, offers accommodations in the atmosphere of an English country home. Guests here enjoy all the facilities of the main hotel. Based on a European plan, prices range from $90 to $209 per night. The Bretton Arms is open year-round.

Also open year-round, The Bretton Woods Motor Inn, located across from the hotel's entrance, offers contemporary accommodations at rates of $70 to $139 per night.

Photo courtesy of The Mount Washington Hotel and Resort

For an economical alternative, The Townhomes at Bretton Woods provide ample space for parties of two to twelve people; situated on the mountainside, these one- to five-bedroom units (with full kitchens) run from $129 to $369 per night, depending on the size of the unit and the season. All guests have access to all resort recreational facilities at established guest rates. Cribs and cots are available at $10 a night. Inquire also about special packages.

Dining: With all the different dining arrangements, your biggest problem will be deciding where to pick up your napkin. From casual, light meals to gracious, formal dinners, it just depends on how the spirit moves you. The main dining room of The Mount Washington Hotel is a large octagonal space (heaven forbid anyone should be relegated to a corner!) glimmering with crystal chandeliers and stained-glass windows. The menu changes nightly and features continental cuisine and regional American dishes. In this elegant setting, with views of Mount Washington, guests are invited to regard dinner as a dress-up affair; jackets are required for men, and ladies and children should dress appropriately. Sumptuous breakfasts are also served in the dining room.

The Bretton Arms dining room is also open for breakfast and dinner; here the evening meal features classic New England cuisine. For lunch and dinner Stickney's Restaurant (located on the lower concourse of the hotel) has a cafe atmosphere and specializes in lighter fare—salads, sandwiches, and light entrees; afternoon cocktails are also served here. Darby's Restaurant in the Motor Inn serves breakfast and dinner; here guests enjoy continental cuisine, along with scenic views of the mountains and the hotel. For sandwiches, Italian fare, and seafood, Fabyans Station is open for lunch and dinner. A restored railroad depot from the Victorian era, Fabyans is near the base of the ski area about a mile from the hotel. The base lodge at the ski area offers full lunch and dinner at the Slopeside Restaurant and Lounge as well as quick breakfasts and lunches cafeteria-style for those eager to hit the slopes. The midmountain Top O' Quad restaurant serves lunch with spectacular mountain views in winter.

For sipping cocktails, you may want to linger at Stickney's, Darby's, or Fabyans. Or perhaps you'll discover the Cave Lounge; located in the lower lobby of the hotel, the speakeasy atmosphere and nightly live entertainment transport you to the days of Prohibition. The elegant Princess Lounge is perfect for before- and after-dinner cocktails. The Pool Bar offers refreshments on warm summer days.

Children's World: Mid-June through Labor Day, and on weekends in spring and fall, the hotel sponsors the King of the Mountain Kids Kamp for children five to twelve. Enroll your child for a full- or half-day program with adventures like hiking in the woods, treks to the stables, swimming, tennis, "Cooking with the Chef," "Putting with the Pro," and crafts sessions. The program is from 9:00 A.M. to noon and from 1:00 to 4:30 P.M. The cost is $15 full-day, $10 half-day. Lunch is available for $7.25. There's also an evening program ($10) from 7:00 to 9:00 P.M. so that parents can dine quietly. Guests not on the modified American plan pay an additional $10 for dinner. Baby-sitting can be arranged for $5.50 per hour, plus 50 cents for each additional child.

In the wintertime, the nursery at the ski area lodge takes children from two months to five years for an indoor program costing $39 full-day or $29 half-day.

Children ages three to twelve participate in the Hobbit Children's Ski and Snowboard School. Rates for lifts, lessons, equipment, and lunch are $55 a day ($65 for snowboarding). Those children under age five who are new to the slopes can join a snow play and ski-readiness program, also $55 a day.

Recreation: You'll never be at a loss for things to do at Bretton Woods; your only dilemma may be trying to fit in all the activities. You may start your day jogging on one of the many marked trails ranging from 1 to 11 miles in length and graded by levels of difficulty.

Then stroll over to the first tee for a match on the eighteen-hole Donald Ross–designed championship golf course or challenging nine-hole course and take in the rolling terrain and mountain views, or sharpen your skills on the putting green and driving range. The Golf Club Pro Shop can meet all your needs for equipment and accessories (including attire) and can assist in scheduling lessons.

There are two heated pools at the hotel (one outdoor and a smaller indoor one) and another indoor heated pool at the motor inn; both locations have a sauna, and the motor inn facility includes a Jacuzzi as well.

Tennis buffs can head over to one of twelve well-groomed red-clay courts or join the tennis program for instruction (group and private lessons) at all levels of expertise.

The horseback-riding stables mean good fun for those who want their exercise sitting down. Set in an old Victorian building, the stables offer lessons and guided trail rides on the 50 miles of picturesque trails in the woods and fields. The woods are captivating whether you choose horseback riding or hiking (maybe you'll link up with a guided tour or a nature walk).

If fishing is your pleasure, some mighty fine trout are found in the Ammonoosuc River, which winds its way through the hotel grounds.

For other diversions you might consider a game of badminton, croquet, volleyball, or horseshoes; an afternoon of bicycling; or an hour in the game room for billiards, Ping-Pong, and video games (particularly big with the seven- to fourteen-year-old group). Your interests may take you to a night at the movies, a fashion show, an aerobics class, a bridge tournament, or a presentation of fine culinary techniques (these often include a bit of wine, sampling a dish, and a tour of the kitchen). The activities staff is on hand full-time to plan interesting and varied events. For some private, quiet time, wander into the library or relax under the nimble fingers of an expert masseur.

Music is special at Mount Washington. Chamber-music recitals are held frequently in the Conservatory; live music is featured in the Cave Lounge; the Mount Washington Orchestra will dance you off your toes nightly during dinner.

Kids love an excursion on the Mount Washington Cog Railway, the original "little train that could." Built in 1869, it was the world's first mountain-climbing cog railroad, and it remains the only one still powered entirely by steam. The (breathtaking!) round trip takes about three hours, and you can visit the mile-high park and observation center at the top.

Stickney Street, in the lower concourse of the hotel, is an array of shops featuring gifts, crafts, fashions, ice-cream delights, flowers, and the hotel's own post office.

Wintertime explodes in skiing events at Bretton Woods. The Bretton Woods Touring Center, housed in a Victorian-style building, is one of the finest cross-country skiing complexes in the East. There are approximately 100 kilometers of beautifully groomed trails among the firs and birches of the scenic countryside; three different trail systems are ranked in difficulty. Head out on your own, enroll for instruction, or join a daytime guided tour or a moonlight trek. Alpine skiers are delighted with the expansion done in the past decade. This once pleasant ski area of 1,100-foot vertical drop has added 400 vertical feet and now boasts thirty-three trails serviced by seven lifts. The ski season lasts from late November to early April; the average annual snowfall is 180 inches, and 98 percent of the trails are covered by snowmaking equipment to assist Mother Nature. In addition to the children's ski school, instruction for the more advanced is also available, accommodating all skiing levels in your family.

By the year 2002, the ski area will have tripled its skiable terrain, with the opening of the West Mountain in 1999 and the East Mountain, scheduled for 2002. Three new lifts and expanded base facilities will ensure an optimal ski experience for all! ≋

Smugglers' Notch Resort
4323 Vermont Route 108 South
Smugglers' Notch, Vermont 05464-9537
(802) 644–8851, (800) 451–8752

The Green Mountains of Vermont are not just beautiful foliage colors in the autumn and skiing fun in the winter. Smugglers' Notch Resort makes sure there's much more to enjoy all year long. Tucked in the rolling hills and mountains of northern Vermont, Smugglers' Notch is a self-contained resort village with sports facilities and getaway relaxation potential for the whole family. In winter, when Mother Nature blankets the region in snow, skiing on the three interconnected mountains is the primary activity. Tennis, hiking, swimming,

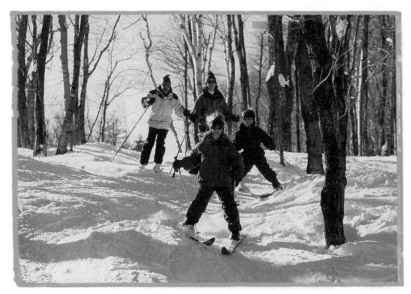

Photo courtesy of Smugglers' Notch Resort

and horseback riding are favorite pastimes when the weather warms. Any time of year one can explore the natural beauty and charm surrounding this mountain village and experience family fun—guaranteed! (Yes, the resort guarantees families will have fun or it refunds the activity portion of their stay.)

Accommodations: Approximately 460 condominium units are arranged in clusters of two- and three-story, modern but rustic buildings. From these all the amenities of the village are accessible by foot. Most of the units have fireplaces and private balconies, and all have completely equipped kitchens or kitchenettes. Size varies from studios to five-bedroom apartments.

The Club Smugglers' package plans cover lodging and most of the recreational activities. For example, the summertime FamilyFest program for five days and five nights includes accommodation in a one-bedroom condo (which sleeps four), the children's day camp, guided walks and hikes, swimming and water sliding, and family game nights, from $1,199 (rates based on dates of stay and size of accommodation). A winter five-day package for a family of four in the same type of lodging runs about $1,640; this includes lift tickets, lessons (Nordic, Alpine, snowboard, cross-country, telemark, and shaped skis), outdoor ice skating, limited tennis, welcome parties, swimming pool, sauna, and après-ski activities. A crib or extra futon cot for two- to seven-year-olds can be provided for $20 for the entire stay.

New England 〰 **37**

Dining: Though you may opt to cook in your condo, there are several restaurants in the village when dining out seems better than facing a skillet. In winter The Green Mountain Cafe and Bakery serves home-baked breakfast treats and hot lunches with fresh-roasted specialty coffees. The Mountain Grille is open for all three meals, including light fare available well into the evening and a special buffet for children. At the Hearth & Candle parents enjoy nouveau cuisine, and at Riga-Bello's all ages savor the ever-popular Italian favorites—pizza, calzones, salads, and beverages—to eat in or have delivered to their condo. For summertime ice-cream treats, there's the Village Creamery, or choose refreshing drinks at the Sports Bar, with its big-screen TV.

The Poolside Cafe and Mountainside Cabana are relaxing summertime spots for lunch and cocktails. And teenagers even have their own clubhouse, The Outer Limits, open daily from 5:00 P.M. to midnight, serving juice and soda. For extras and snacks stop by the Village Grocery, with Deli and Wine Shop.

Children's World: The Little Smugglers' Discovery Dynamos Camp operates from mid-December to the beginning of April. Three- to five-year-olds join their ski host for morning and afternoon ski lessons, sleigh rides, movies, and arts and crafts. Skiers and boarders ages six to twelve meet with the Smugglers' Adventure Ski and Snowboard Camp for lessons, snow soccer, and races. Après-ski activities include a daily bonfire at 3:30 P.M. with storytelling and hot chocolate for parents and children. With lunch included, the daily rate for these programs, 9:30 A.M.–4:00 P.M., is $60. The program, however, is included in the FamilyFest packages.

For teens ages thirteen to seventeen, the Explorer Ski and Snowboard Program offers challenging instruction and techniques, racing development, and a great way to make new friends. With the Outer Limits teen center and scheduled daily activities at 7:00 and 9:00 P.M., teenagers have plenty to do.

For younger, nonskiing children (newborn to three years), Alice's Wonderland is just that. Located in a quiet, sunlit corner of the resort, Alice's is 6,900 square feet or ten rooms of real state-of-the-art facilities. There are kid-size bathrooms, a complete kitchen, an infant "crawler room" equipped with mirrors and soft-sculpture gym, a separate crib room for naps, a closet of costumes, and an indoor jungle gym—one could go on and on. Open from 9:00 A.M. to 4:00 P.M. (8:30 A.M. to 4:30 P.M. during ski season), staffed with professionals, and boasting a ratio of one to four, it's a steal at $15 an hour ($50 for a full day).

During the summer season, from the end of June through Labor Day, the Discovery and Adventure Day Camps offer daily activities for three- to twelve-year-olds. Fun events include outdoor games, fishing, arts and crafts, hiking, treasure hunts, and swimming. At the playground are swings, climbing equipment, and a sandbox. Tennis, movies, hayrides, dances, and scavenger hunts/overnight hikes are scheduled for teenagers. The day camp is included in the price of the family vacation. For the really wee ones, individual baby-sitters can be booked for $7.00 an hour. A really nice feature is Parents Night Out, when children ages three to twelve are invited to dinner and a fun evening from 6:00 to 10:00 P.M. The cost is $20 per child. A similar program is free with the FamilyFest program.

Recreation: A network of sixty runs on three interconnected mountains is the focus of wintertime play. The ski season runs from mid-December to mid-April, and the average annual snowfall of 286 inches is supplemented by snowmaking equipment. The three mountains fall more or less into novice, intermediate, and advanced runs, but each mountain offers skiing for all levels of expertise. The total vertical drop is just over 2,600 feet. For the cross-country skier, 14 miles of trails roam through the mountains. Lessons in cross-country skiing, downhill skiing, and snowboarding can help you learn as a beginner or improve your skills. You might also try ice skating with the kids or a sleigh-ride adventure.

Turning indoors, you can enjoy the benefits of The Tub Club; with an exercise room and whirlpool and sauna facilities, you learn the proper regimen for a spa experience. With the resort's two indoor courts, tennis can be a wintertime sport; also in winter the large, heated swimming pool is covered with a bubble, so pack your swimsuit along with your ski sweater. In summer the bubble comes down. There's a water slide, called the Flume; a baby wading pool; and a seventeen-person outdoor Jacuzzi. Free swimming instruction is provided as part of the day-camp program, and adults can join the Aqua Aerobics for a good workout.

Notchville Park, Smugglers' newest water playground, encompasses three acres with three pools in a unique, tiered hillside setting. In addition to 5,000 square feet of water, the park includes Raven's Roost Climbing Tower, Catbird's Croquet Court, Sand Swallow's Volleyball Court, Peregrine's Picnic Pavilion, and the Half-Moon Bath House.

The Family Water Playground is a third, separate water facility that includes a turtle slide (for children ages three to eight years), the Little Smugglers' Lagoon (a large splash pool with waterfall, tunnels, fountains, and a lazy river ride), a lap pool, and every parent's delight, the Giant Rapid River Ride—306 feet of twists and thrills on an inner tube beginning 26 feet up in the air. Bathhouse, snack bar, and lounging deck with gorgeous mountain views help one recover.

Also a favorite with families is Rum Runner's Hideaway, a beautiful swimming lake tucked in the mountains, a short hike or hay-wagon ride away from the Village. Access is free to resort guests for swimming, fishing, picnicking, and relaxing; canoes and paddleboats are available for rent. It's a great way to relive the old days and introduce your kids to the joys of summer days at the ole swimmin' hole.

In addition to the two indoor courts, there are eight outdoor clay courts; six are lighted for evening play. The Ten Pro Tennis School, which has videotape review, just about guarantees improvement in your game.

Hiking and biking are popular ways to enjoy the mountain countryside, or try jogging on one of the cross-country trails. Head to a mountain stream for perch, pike, and trout fishing. Outdoor lawn games include softball, volleyball, soccer, and shuffleboard. And reserve time for a session in the spa or a horseback ride at the Vermont Horse Park (services here are not included in the package plans). For those who can't possibly leave home without their golf clubs, courses in nearby Stowe and Morrisville are open to Smugglers' guests. ≋

Stratton Mountain Resort

Stratton Mountain, Vermont 05155
(802) 297–4137, (800) 843–6867, or (800) STRATTON

Lessons, lessons, lessons! At Stratton Mountain Resort you can have instruction and training in several major sports. Whether your interests lead you to golf, tennis, swimming, racquetball, cross-country skiing, downhill skiing, telemark skiing, snowboarding, or snowshoeing, you can participate in classes for an introduction to a new sport or for polishing existing skills and techniques.

And where could you find a better place to get into shape and sharpen your sports expertise than in southern Vermont? Stratton Mountain Resort is set on 4,000 acres in the beautiful Green Mountains of Vermont. Since its opening in 1961, the resort has expanded a number of times to enhance the facilities and to attract sports-minded visitors to return again and again. Stratton Mountain is open year-round.

Accommodations: Choose a resort hotel, an alpine lodge, or your own villa. The Stratton Mountain Inn has 125 rooms and suites and also houses a restaurant, lounge, pool, sauna, and tennis courts. Stratton Village Lodge has ninety-one rooms and is in the heart of the village, just a few steps away from shops, and is considered ski-in/ski-out. The Birkenhaus and the Liftline Lodge offer more traditional accommodations, and each has its own restaurant. Winter rates at the Stratton Mountain Inn or Stratton Valley Lodge range from $119 to $169 a night; the Liftline Lodge is $85 to $135; the Birkenhaus, $99 to $149. Rates vary depending on date, midweek or weekend, packages, and so on. The

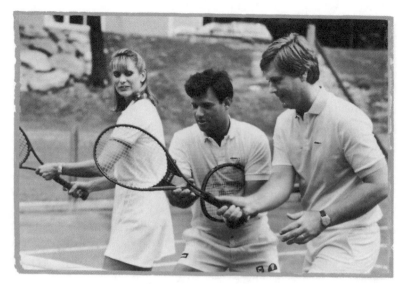

Photo by Hubert Schriebel, courtesy of Stratton Mountain Resort

Mountain Villas are one- to four-bedroom condominium apartments with fully equipped kitchens; many have fireplaces and private balconies. One-bedroom condos cost $90 to $230 per night, two bedrooms are $130 to $320, and three bedrooms are $170 to $400.

Two- to five-day/night Lifts and Lodging packages are available, from $49 to $99 based on a per person, per night rate. The popular Family Ski Week package includes five days' skiing and five nights' lodging, midweek (nonholiday), in a two-bedroom Valleyside condominium for families consisting of two adults and two children, all for $65 per person per night; children between the ages of four and twelve receive free KidsKamp. Call ahead for other available packages.

Summer rates at Mountain Villas range from $59 to $79 for hotel rooms, $90 to $150 for one-bedroom villas, and $110 to $170 for two-bedroom villas. Again, check for special-interest packages.

Dining: The Sage Hill Restaurant at the Stratton Mountain Inn serves hearty breakfasts, lunches, and New England cuisine dinners; savor cranberry duck or rack of lamb and pick up the recipe for your favorite dish, graciously shared by the chef. Also at the inn is The Tavern, a cozy spot to sip a hot toddy or your favorite cocktail. Tenderloins is the restaurant and lounge at the Clubhouse on the golf course.

In the winter start your day with breakfast at the Base Lodge, also fine for a quick lunch; the Mid-Mountain Restaurant (at 2,700 feet) is perfect for those who don't want to be off their skis long. Also at the mountain are the Birkenhaus Restaurant and the Liftline Lodge, which offer an old-world European atmosphere and cuisine, and the Partridge in a Pantry deli. Mulligan's Tavern is a great spot for families, with a good kids' menu, fireplaces, and live music. For terrific entertainment head back to the Base Lodge for live music at The Roost, a bar/restaurant.

Children's World: The ski season lasts from mid-November into April, and during this period youngsters are well cared for and find lots of entertainment. Seven- to twelve-year-olds join the Big Cub group for full-day supervision, lunch, and ski lessons, at $69 a day. Little Cubs take in ages four to six years for indoor games and fun as well as ski lessons (9:00 A.M.–3:45 P.M. daily); the fee is $69 a day, including lunch; a half-day is $45. And real tiny tots gather at the Stratton Childcare Center, a certified day-care facility for children six weeks to three years old. It operates year-round from 8:30 A.M. until 4:30 P.M. and offers indoor and outdoor activities. The cost is $69 a day in winter. The Stratton offers night skiing trails and extended nighttime childcare. Contact the resort for details.

The fun continues in summer with day-camp programs offered seven days a week during July and August. Kids between six and twelve years old spend from 8:30 A.M. to 4:00 P.M. busily engaged in art classes, swim and gymnastics lessons, group games, and field trips. The cost is $37 a day. The child-care center entertains ages six weeks to five years during the same hours for $40, including lunch. An intensive tennis camp for ages seven to seventeen focuses on lessons and tournaments but breaks up the day with hikes, games, and swim time. Its cost is $60 per day.

Recreation: Skiing at Stratton Mountain is a big event. Thirty-seven miles of trails add up to ninety-two runs for all levels of downhill skiers. Mother Nature drops an average annual 170 inches of snow on this mountain, at 3,875 feet the highest peak in southern Vermont, and is nudged along by rather sophisticated snowmaking equipment, covering 80 percent of the skiable terrain.

The Stratton Ski School holds classes for every level of ability. It prides itself on a full-day learning experience—five hours with an instructor. The Stratton Touring Center offers instruction in cross-country skiing for treks through the tall evergreens and across quiet meadows. Ice skating is another favorite winter sport.

If you're more inclined to warm-weather sports, enroll in the Stratton Golf School. Meet fellow students and your PGA instructors in a twenty-two-acre outdoor classroom where all playing conditions can be simulated, then head to the Stratton Mountain Country Club for a round on the twenty-seven-hole championship course.

Attend the Stratton Tennis School for private lessons or a group clinic. There are nineteen indoor and outdoor tennis courts at the Stratton Sports Center and two courts at the inn.

At the Sports Center are classes in swimming and aquacise in the 75-foot indoor pool, aerobics classes, Nautilus exercise, tennis, and three racquetball courts. During a recess from classes, sneak into the steam room or the whirlpool for some solitary relaxation. In addition, an outdoor pool, a sauna, and three whirlpools are located at the inn.

And don't forget to poke around the beautiful Vermont countryside. Hike in the hills and breathe that fresh clean air, jog or bicycle (rentals available) down country roads along fields of wildflowers, horseback ride on mountain trails, or try mountain biking from the summit. When you've had your fill of exercise, join bargain hunters at a local antiques auction or crafts fair. At the Stratton Arts Festival, in September and early October, you'll discover the fine wares of Vermont artists and craftspeople. Stratton Mountain Village, with the flair of an Alpine village, has lots of quaint shops, so finding the right memento of your trip will be an easy task. ≋

Sugarloaf/USA

RR 1, Box 5000
Kingfield, Maine 04947
(207) 237–2000, (800) THE–LOAF
E-mail: lodging@sugarloaf.com or info@sugarloaf.com
Web site: www.sugarloaf.com

Traditional New England reserve seems to be missing at Sugarloaf/USA. The prevailing attitude is friendly, upbeat, casually welcoming. While mainly associated with skiing and winter, Sugarloaf is fast becoming a four-season destination. All access is via Portland or Bangor, and once in western Maine, just about all roads lead to Sugarloaf. Route 27 is the main road to the ski area, and from the Carrabassett Valley, Sugarloaf literally stands out. You can distinguish the peak from 20 to 40 miles away, and once you leave the valley floor and start to climb, the panorama just gets better and better. Locals and repeat visitors have dubbed one particular spot "Oh-my-gosh corner," because it is so stunning as you round the corner and suddenly see the front of this impressive mountain with its seventy trails and an Alpine village set on the slope.

Accommodations: Sugarloaf has the capacity to sleep approximately 7,000 people on the mountainside. Condominiums, 912 of them, are set in various clusters of two to twenty-eight units and offer a wide selection of design. Styles include hotel rooms, studios, lofts, and up to five-bedroom, three-bath complexes. The thirty-six room Sugarloaf Inn and the Sugarloaf Mountain Hotel complete the lodging options. Custom-made packages are planned for each family's needs. Packages always include a health club pass, and a complimentary shuttle system gets you around the resort with ease.

Rates range from $100 to $220 for a hotel room, from $153 to $241 for a one-bedroom unit, and from $292 to $447 for a four-bedroom condominium. Cribs and rollaway beds are provided at a daily charge of $5.00.

Sugarloaf was one of the first ski areas to introduce the ski-in/ski-out concept; in fact, every accommodation is ski-in/ski-out. This is great for older children, as it gives them a sense of independence and it gives everyone a sense of freedom. If you want to sleep late or linger over coffee, others in your party need not delay their skiing. Gondola Village is the largest condominium and the heart of the development, and here you will find the nursery.

Dining: Dining in the Sugarloaf area is a fun adventure that is taken quite seriously. With fourteen on-mountain restaurants, you can have everything from burgers to bouillabaisse to haute cuisine.

Gepetto's is a slopeside restaurant with a greenhouse addition and a gourmet menu for lunch or dinner. The Seasons Restaurant at the Sugarloaf Inn offers innovative American cuisine in a relaxed atmosphere. A highlight of the

Seasons' menu is fresh Maine lobster. For après-ski the Widowmaker Lounge advertises "comfort with class," cocktails, and music you can hear yourself talk over. Upstairs at the base lodge, Avalanche provides a nonalcoholic teen center with lots of action. One of the more recent additions to Sugarloaf/USA is the Shipyard Brewhaus, located just at the base of the Birches slope. It serves fine Maine microbrews on tap, lunch daily, and pub fare after 2:00 P.M. During the summer six restaurants remain open, so there's still a wide choice.

Children's World: Sugarloaf has a terrific child-care program. A state-licensed child-care center at the base of the mountain accepts children from six weeks to six years of age. Hours are from 8:30 A.M. to 4:00 P.M. Advance reservations are a must. The charges are $42 for a full day or $27 for a half day. The night nursery is available from 6:00 to 9:00 P.M. on Thursday and Saturday for $15, $10 per additional sibling. Reservations are required. A fenced-in outdoor play area adds to winter fun, and inside are toys, movies, storytime, circletime, and arts and crafts—a developmentally appropriate program provided by caring professionals. The nap area is separate, with individual cribs, cots, and mats. A hot lunch is served, and snacks are given during the day. Introduction to skiing lessons for three-year-olds originate from the child-care center. For $54 a full day or $39 a half day, your child has the option of a thirty- to forty-minute private lesson or two-hour group experience. Price includes lifts, rental equipment, and all the components of the child-care program.

Evenings offer free supervised activities for five- to twelve-year-olds, six nights a week. Included in the offerings are game nights, Movie Night, Wild Card Night, and Turbo-tubing. Reservations are required.

Mountain Magic teaches skiing to children ages four to six years and stresses independence, safety, and fun. The system teaches walking on skis, side-stepping, wedge stops and turns, falling, and, of course, getting up. Mountain Adventure is a program for ages seven to sixteen, where skills are perfected. These programs run from 8:30 A.M. to 3:00 P.M.; the costs start at $54 a day and include lift ticket, lessons, lunch, and equipment rentals.

Summertime brings flowers and traditional July and August day camps. A five-week program provided by Carrabassett Valley begins in the second week in July. Kids ages four to fourteen enjoy lessons in swimming, tennis, golf, and fly-fishing, and an extensive arts program. At $65 a week, with daily rates also available, it's a great deal. On the mountain, Sugarloaf offers summer child-care for little ones, six weeks to six years. The facility is open daily from 8:00 A.M. to 5:00 P.M., and the cost is $40 a day. Reservations are required.

Recreation: The most impressive aspect of skiing Sugarloaf is that you are skiing a big mountain. It is a traditional mountain, in that it begins gently, goes to intermediate in the middle, and gets "durn hard at the top," as a local might say. Sugarloaf has the greatest vertical drop in the East. It is possible to come almost straight down the 2,820-foot vertical drop (and even do it in an upright position if you're good) having taken only two lifts. A good beginner or low intermediate skier can take Tote Road, a 3-mile trail from the top that follows the ridge and comes safely to the base, but gives that exciting feeling of skiing at the top of the world and surviving it. Cross-country skiers can explore 59 miles of trails, including some lighted for night skiing.

Other winter fun includes ice skating, snowshoeing, and cross-country skiing, with some scheduled night tours. The three Family Theme weeks offer additional family activities, and Holiday Weeks are chock-full of entertainment opportunities.

Come summer, when there is no snow on the ground, the Sugarloaf Golf Club opens. Designed by Robert Trent Jones Jr., this course is one of the best for wilderness golf and is one of the top 25 golf courses in the country, according to *Golf* magazine. Every tee has a spectacular view, and the mountain air is always cool. Tennis is limited to outside play, with two courts on the mountain and four in the town. The village has indoor racquetball courts, a sauna, hot tubs, a steam room, tanning beds, a climbing wall, and two swimming pools. But probably the most exciting summer sport is white-water rafting on the Kennebeck River. Sugarloaf also has a concentrated mountain-biking program. ≋

Sunrise Resort

Moodus, Connecticut 06469
(860) 873–8681, (800) 225–9033
Web site: www.sunriseresort.com

If cities or grand resorts aren't your style and you have fond memories of your own summer-camp days, Sunrise Resort may be just the place for you. This is a summer place for the whole family, in the rolling hills of rural Connecticut, on the banks of the Salmon River. It is open Memorial and Father's Day weekends, and the season is in full operation from late June through Labor Day. The office is open year-round; people are encouraged to call or visit ahead of the season. And since it's not open in winter, Sunrise schedules a "Christmas in July" week, complete with Santa and Rudolph. Activities go from 8:00 A.M. to midnight, and there's something for everyone in the family.

Accommodations: A wide variety of accommodations occupy the 200 acres. Across the river is another, undeveloped, 200 acres. All the 160 accommodations have names, and the style and number of beds vary in each—we recommend calling for a map and descriptions to help you decide between the

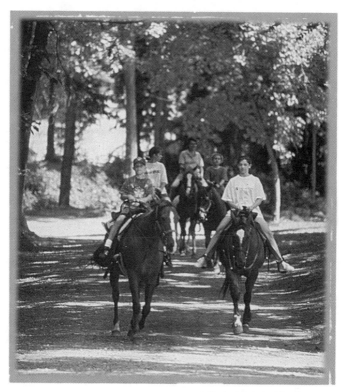

Waterfront cottages, the Rustic or Cabana rooms, and the Motel rooms. Rates are $79 to $99 per person per day, $395 to $495 per week. There are five-day (stay five days, pay for only four) and weekend special rates as well. Children ages five to fourteen pay two-thirds of the adult rate; children four and under pay one-third the adult rate. Meals and activities are included in these rates. For $49 per person per day, you can even bring your own recreational vehicle.

Dining: Described "as American as apple pie," meals are hearty. Select from five choices of entrees, three appetizers, and four or five desserts—and the menu changes daily. Three times per week dinner is served outdoors, with live music. The seven dining areas include two indoors and five outdoors, or partially outdoors. Children can choose from a menu especially geared to them.

Children's World: Outdoor fun is supervised from 9:30 A.M. to 5:00 P.M. in the fenced play area. Several areas, such as the School House, Playscape, and Western Village, complement the wading pool, swings, slides, and other playground equipment. The Merry-Go-Round Room is an enclosed area for when weather dictates, as well as for the 8:00 to 11:00 P.M. Fun Room activities. For younger children (under six), counselors are generally added as needed for the size of the group. For older children (either on their own or with Mom and Dad watching, participating, or taking pictures), activities are scheduled at various times throughout the day. Times change each day, perhaps beginning at 8:00 A.M. Tuesday with a paddle breakfast at the beach, or maybe at 2:30 P.M. Thursday for a scavenger hunt. A daily activity schedule is given to everyone, and the participation is up to each family member.

Such things as fire engine rides, diving for pennies, canoe races, a lollipop hunt, and rubber ducky games in the pool create a lot of laughter. There are family field events, softball and volleyball games, and dance lessons—aerobic, ballroom, and line dancing. A separate counselor for teens helps them plan activities they like, such as watching the movie *Jaws* while swimming (uh-oh), night hikes, and various sports and games (sometimes with kids challenging the parents).

Recreation: The opportunities for recreation form a long and familiar list, just like summer camp. The two main areas of activity are the pool and clubhouse at the top of the hill, and the waterfront at the Salmon River. Miles of trails are available to enjoy horseback riding and biking. There are canoes, rowboats, and watercycles on the river; and a children's pool, hot tubs, sauna, and exercise equipment on the hillside. Tennis and tennis lessons are free; this is a great chance to improve your game or get your child interested. Sports include softball, volleyball, shuffleboard, basketball, horseshoes, boccie, and, of course, Ping-Pong. A game room and two arcades provide a more sedentary, but not necessarily quieter, kind of action, and nearby are six golf courses for the enthusiast. Excursions in the area include Gillette's Castle, Essex Steam Train and Riverboat Ride, Lyman Orchard, two casinos, Broadway musicals at Goodspeed Opera House, and Echo Farm State Park—home of much wildlife, including the bald eagle. ≋

The Tyler Place on Lake Champlain

P.O. Box 66, Old Dock Road
Highgate Springs, Vermont 05460
(802) 868–4000, Fax (802) 868–7602
E-mail: tyler@together.net
Web site: www.tylerplace.com

Tucked away in the northwestern corner of Vermont, just minutes away from the Canadian border, Tyler Place boasts of its beautiful setting and family-friendly atmosphere. The Tyler Place was one of the first resorts to devote itself entirely to families. The original owners, Mr. and Mrs. Edward Tyler, developed a concept that includes family time and time for parents to rejuvenate as a couple. The Tyler family (second and third generation) continues to carry on the resort's family philosophy. Open from late May to mid-September, it's the kind of place that families return to again and again.

Accommodations: The Inn is the hub of activity, with its recreation rooms, main dining room, fireside lounge, deck, and glass-enclosed porches for visiting, relaxing, cocktails, and candlelight dining. Guest rooms—some are studios, some suites—are located in a separate wing. In addition, twenty-seven cottages, most with a fireplace in the living room and two or more bedrooms, are situated on and near the lake; these have kitchenettes and can sleep up to eight people. Many of the rooms include sleeping lofts or bunk beds; with these special attractions, it may not be difficult at all to get a youngster to go to sleep in a strange place. Cribs and high chairs for infants and toddlers are available at no extra charge.

In total, Tyler Place accommodates approximately fifty families. Based on a full American plan, the daily per person rate for each of the first two lodgers in a unit is $123 to $210 during July and August. Depending on the child's age, a rate of $45 to $84 a day applies; this covers lodging, meals, sports, and the activities program. Rates are 15 to 35 percent lower in May, early June, and September, during hands-on Learning Retreats for the Whole Family. The resort is closed the rest of the year.

Dining: The main dining room in the Inn serves a semibuffet breakfast, lunch, and dinner. New American country cuisine is the kitchen's specialty, and as a full American plan is in effect, you have only to decide which delicious entree to sample. Children have earlier dining hours with their counselors, allowing parents to relax over meals. A family breakfast room and family picnic lunch baskets are available.

Children's World: During the entire season there's an extensive program of events geared to eight different age groups, plus infant care. From the youngest Junior Toddlers (twelve to eighteen months) to Senior Teens (fourteen- to sixteen-year-olds), children are well entertained with morning and evening activities led by energetic and enthusiastic college students. Children take meals with their group leaders, and the hours between breakfast and lunch and after supper are filled with arts and crafts, nature walks, songs, games, storytime, volleyball, swimming, hayrides, fishing, movies, treasure hunts, sailing, tennis, sailboarding, kayaking, indoor pool parties—one gets out of breath just listing the activities! Busy and active, your child will no doubt be happy as well, with no chance of being "kid-starved." Afternoons are devoted to individual family time, with activities available if desired. If you can drag the kids away from friends and counselors, the staff will help you plan a day of sightseeing or fishing and send you off with a picnic lunch.

For the very young (newborns to two and one-half years), the resort features one-on-one "Parents' Helpers," (from high-school-age to mature adult), who will care for your young child and even prepare meals. The standard fee is $3.50 to $6.50 per hour. This is a real vacation for Mom and Dad, a break from wet diapers and baby food.

Recreation: Beautiful Lake Champlain is the source of much of the recreation and relaxation of Tyler Place. Take off in one of the resort's sailboats, canoes, kayaks, or sailboards. Try a little waterskiing (with instruction), guided canoe and bike trips, yoga, aerobics (step and water), and the workout facilities. Or bait your fishing line for bass and pike. The outdoor and indoor heated pools and Jacuzzi on the lakeshore provide hours of fun.

Learning retreats for the whole family were a popular addition started in 1998. They feature hands-on activities for all ages, including such topics as gardening, nature and outdoor skills, lakeshore studies, rural and farm life, and family wellness.

On land, six tennis courts and a fleet of bikes (one-speed, mountain, children's, tricycle, and child seats, all with helmets) are at your disposal, and the nature trails beckon hikers and joggers. For a change of pace, challenge another guest to an old-fashioned game of horseshoes, or try your hand at archery. Maybe you'll join a soccer game or start up a tennis round-robin with the folks in the neighboring cottage. Golf privileges are available at three golf courses within a fifteen- to forty-five-minute drive of the resort. Recreation fees are applied only for golf, outboard motors for fishing, waterskiing, lake cruises, and mountain bikes.

Nighttime brings other events, from dances and live jazz to guitar singalongs and Monte Carlo nights—pick your pleasure. What many guests like most is the hospitable atmosphere of the many and varied activities, with never any pressure to participate. ≋

Whitney's Inn
Box 822
Jackson, New Hampshire 03846
(603) 383–6886, (800) 677–5737

A holiday at a classic country inn does as much for the mind as for the body, and Whitney's Inn seems equally capable of repairing the spirit and rejuvenating the body. Located in the beautiful White Mountains of New Hampshire, the inn sits at the base of Black Mountain on fourteen acres of open fields and wooded hills, with a mountain pond and a brook. Drive into town across an old covered bridge, point your car toward the mountain, and at the end of the road, you'll find the welcoming charm of Whitney's Inn. Open year-round, this is a family operation, and the owners, the Bowmans, appreciate the special interests of families.

Accommodations: Standard and deluxe rooms are in the main inn, and family suites, particularly suited to parties with children, are close by in a separate building. The rate structure is a little complicated, as you have a choice between bed-and-breakfast or a modified American plan, with breakfast and gourmet dinner. Few standard rooms will accommodate families. B&B in deluxe rooms and family suites (more motel than inn style, but with more space also) cost $42 to $63 per person, double occupancy; children under twelve are $12 to $15, and older kids are $20. MAP rates are $62 to $83 per person; children are $17 to $25 midweek, $40 weekends. A good deal, and very popular, is one of the freestanding cottages (there are only two, so reserve early) with fireplace and two bedrooms: $124 to $165 per night, including breakfast. Weekend and holiday times are the higher rates. Children twelve and under stay and eat free during summer months in a Family Suite.

Dining: Breakfast and dinner will satisfy the best appetites. Breakfasts feature hearty fare, preparing you for an outdoor, athletic day. Dinners are relaxing affairs where you'll find such tasty items on the menu as smoked trout and roast turkey with an herb-sausage stuffing. The children's table at dinner offers grown-ups their much-needed quiet time and youngsters their favorite dishes, such as pizza, fried chicken, and fried fish. Try The Shovel Handle for lunch fare of salads, sandwiches, and hearty soups. Or stop by at the end of the day for a little après-ski.

Children's World: On weekends and during school vacations, six- to twelve-year-olds can participate in organized skiing at Black Mountain. The program runs daily from 8:30 A.M. to 3:00 P.M. The First Mountain Division is for experienced juniors; the $45 fee includes mountain skiing, instruction, snow sports, and lunch. The Second Mountain Division is for entry-level juniors; priced at $38, it includes the same activities, but surface lifts only. On weekends and holidays, half-days are available. Penguin Peak is for children ages three to five years and is a skiing-nursery program with one-on-one instruction. Open 9:00 A.M. to 4:00 P.M.; call (800) 475–4669 for details.

Recreation: Skiing at the Inn's back door is the primary wintertime activity. Of the twenty downhill trails, 34 percent are ranked intermediate. The vertical drop on this sunny side of Black Mountain is 1,100 feet. From the summit, skiers look out to Mount Washington and across picturesque New England farms. Snowmaking facilities on 98 percent of the mountain complement Mother Nature's efforts.

The Betty, a trail named in honor of longtime resident Betty Whitney, provides a 2-kilometer groomed loop connecting Whitney's Inn and Black Mountain Ski Area. This is a great starting point for families who ski both cross-country and downhill.

For cross-country skiers, the Jackson Ski Touring Center is located just 2 miles from the Inn; some of its 150 kilometers of trails crisscross the inn's property. Also on the wintertime calendar, the Inn has sledding, ice-skating parties, sleigh rides, and movies. The activities room offers games for the whole family, and the library is a peaceful hideaway.

In the summer, mountain biking, hiking, and jogging in these beautiful mountains are favorite activities. You can also fish, swim, join a cookout, and play a bit of tennis, badminton, croquet, volleyball, and shuffleboard. ≈≈≈

EAST

New York

Pennsylvania

Golden Acres Farm and Ranch

South Gilboa Road
Gilboa, New York 12076
(607) 588–7329, (800) 847–2151, (800) 252–7787 (in New York)
E-mail: farmresort@aol.com
Web site: www.upstateguide.com/goldenacres

"Old MacDonald had a farm, ee-i-ee-i-oh. And on that farm he had a cow." Well, the Gauthiers have a farm also, with at least as wide a variety of animals as Old Mac did—horses, goats, sheep, ducks, chickens, and a number of baby animals for cuddling and petting. If you like, you can begin your day by milking a cow, collecting eggs from the henhouse, or feeding the animals. The farm has always been family oriented and prides itself on a genuine "down-on-the-farm" experience with modern comforts. This 800-acre farm/resort is located on top of a 2,000-foot-high knoll in the Catskill Mountains and is open Memorial Day to Labor Day only.

Local sites of interest include Howe Caverns, Secret Caves, Hunter Mountain, game farms, and bird sanctuaries. Cooperstown, home of the Baseball Hall of Fame, is nearby, as is the Oneonta Soccer Hall of Fame. Golden Acres is in the center of numerous auction barns, flea markets, and roadside vegetable stands.

Accommodations: In the main house are the dining room, the nursery, an indoor playroom, and a teen lounge. Next door is a motel complex connected to game rooms, lounges, and the indoor pool and hot tub. Across the road (a short city block away) is Gilboa Ridge, with a farmhouse and farm cottage. There are ten connecting rooms and suites. Most rooms contain a double bed and a single bed, with space for rollaways or cribs ($25 per week per crib). Also at Gilboa Ridge are twenty-six "you cook" vacation apartments with kitchenettes and a campground area with water and electric hookups. The farm pays particular attention to single parents and has nondiscriminatory rates based on one adult traveling with a child. Rates are $60–$110 daily, with children paying $20–$35, depending on their age.

Dining: A modified American plan is optional and includes two meals for adults and three for children. Children and adults have a joint menu and dining room for breakfast and dinner, but no adults are allowed at lunch; then the children and teens and their counselors eat all those things that are so dear to their hearts—pizza and hamburgers, along with a few fruits and vegetables. Jewish dietary laws are observed. Two snacks daily are included for the young set, and the selection at the Snack Bar hits the spot between meals. Food is fresh and hearty, and you can eat all you wish. The evening menu includes appetizer, salad, soup, choice of two meats or one fish entree, side dishes, and desserts. All breads and pastries are freshly baked daily in the farm bakery.

Evening activities center on the Skylite Room and the Ragtime Lounge and include happy hour, bands, and entertainment; folk and square dancing; night at the races; and other activities—some for everyone, some for adults only, and a teen lounge for special programs. After the early evening entertainment, live music and dancing continue in the Ragtime Lounge.

Children's World: The program for children varies by age, takes advantage of the farm surroundings, and is offered from the end of May through the first week of September. For the under four set, a complete nursery service is scheduled from 10:00 A.M. to noon, 1:30 to 5:00 P.M., and 6:30 to 7:45 P.M. Parents collect their children for mealtimes.

For four- to twelve-year-olds, it is nonstop action throughout the day. For teens, informal activities emphasize meeting others and sharing things while maintaining freedom of action. The rec room, with its jukebox and video games, is popular with this group. Experienced and enthusiastic counselors (most of whom are studying to be teachers) supervise the events. The staff is international, with thirty-eight countries represented. It's great exposure for the children, who learn games and activities from around the world.

A typical day starts at 10:00 A.M., with a tour to feed the animals, collect eggs, or visit the gardens. Then come horseback riding (teaching beginners is a specialty here), swimming, lunch, and a rest period. Afternoon activities are geared to the children's interests—berry picking, frog hunts, hayrides, crafts, games, and perhaps an excursion to the caves or a hike and cookout in the woods. A snack of milk and cookies is followed by rounding up the cows for milking.

After a break for dinner and a quick hello to the parents, evening activities such as bonfires, talent shows, or cartoons start at 7:45 P.M. Kids have another snack, then head for bed about 9:00 P.M.—and well deserved it is! If parents want, they can go out, as a night patrol is on duty from 9:00 P.M. to 1:00 A.M., with a sign-in sheet on each room door. If you prefer, you can take a baby-sitter from either the staff or local listings at approximately $4.50 an hour, with a three-hour minimum.

Recreation: There is no charge for any of the activities. After catching your limit of fish, you might take off to one of the two tennis courts, the archery field, either of the two swimming pools, or the exercise room. The boats and floating docks at the lake make for a relaxing afternoon, or join a group for softball or volleyball. And grown-ups, too, can partake in the farm activities—feeding the animals, horseback riding, hopping aboard a hayride. A less active afternoon might include a class in macramé, copper enameling, pottery, or stained glass, or a stop by one of the recreation rooms for Ping-Pong and pool. If the weather is uncooperative, there's an indoor riding arena, five playrooms for rainy-day activities, and a complete workout room for adults. One nice feature at the Golden Acres is the policy of allowing an early check-in and late use of the facilities when checking out. ≈≈≈

Mohonk Mountain House

Lake Mohonk
New Paltz, New York 12561
(914) 255–1000, (800) 772–6646
Web site: www.mohonk.com

The wholesome peace and serenity of Mohonk Mountain House are not merely by-products of its setting in 2,200 acres of the Shawangunk Mountains, 90 miles north of New York City. The resort was founded in 1869 by twin brothers, Albert and Alfred Smiley, who, following their Quaker upbringing, regarded drinking, dancing, smoking, and card playing as unacceptable habits. Rather, they emphasized spiritual renewal as evidenced by the nature walks or prayer meetings planned for their proper clientele.

The times have indeed changed, but the gracious, quieter way of life of a bygone era still prevails at Mohonk. No discos swing until dawn here, and, in fact, no bar is on the premises, though guests may order cocktails with the midday and evening meals. Instead, you'll find cozy conversation lounges furnished with Victorian antiques, verandas lined with rocking chairs, miles of hiking trails, and extensive gardens. Open year-round, the rambling wood-and-stone Victorian structure appears almost like a castle, complete with turrets and towers, and sits on the edge of a clear mountain lake a half mile long.

Accommodations: The 261 guest rooms are spacious and tastefully and simply decorated with period furnishings. Most have private balconies overlooking the lake or looking across the valley to the mountains. Many have fireplaces. Some connecting rooms share a bath. On a full American plan (mandatory), daily rates are from $280 to $390 for a standard double guest room. The special Victorian and tower rooms command higher rates. For children occupying a room with their parents, the charge is $100 a day for those over twelve and $63 a day for four- to twelve-year-olds; children under age four are accommodated free. There is no charge for cribs or rollaway beds. Weekly rates and package plans are available. Ask about the "kids stay free" events held throughout the year.

Photo by Matthew Seaman, courtesy of Mohonk Mountain House

Dining: The main dining room where breakfast, lunch, and dinner are served is a large and elegantly simple room with highly polished woodwork and paneling rising 30 to 40 feet. The kitchen specializes in good American cuisine, from blueberry pancakes to fried chicken, steaks, fish, vegetarian dishes, and homemade breads and pastries. Jackets are standard attire for gentlemen at the evening meal. Cookouts and clambakes are occasionally planned. Afternoon tea is served daily at 4:00 P.M. Refreshments are also available in the Ice Cream Parlor and Soda Fountain and the Tee Room on the golf course.

Children's World: On weekends and holidays throughout the year and daily from mid-June through Labor Day, children are divided into four age groups: two- to four-year-olds, five- to six-year-olds, seven- to eight-year-olds, and nine- to twelve-year-olds. All groups have daily activities in the morning and, after lunch with the family, again in the afternoon. Typical events on the agenda are hikes, nature walks, scavenger hunts, shuffleboard contests, swimming, pony rides, rock scrambles, and frog hunts. Movies, square dances, and campfires are frequently planned for evenings. This is a complimentary service for hotel guests. Baby-sitters can be hired for younger children, with advance notice.

Recreation: Discovering nature's beauty is at the core of many of Mohonk's recreational activities. More than 85 miles of hiking trails wind through the woods and along the lake; dotting the paths are one hundred gazebos where you can sit to take in the views. Explore the grounds on horseback (Western and English style) or in a horse-drawn carriage ride, and leisurely meander through the award-winning gardens. Mohonk Lake has a small sandy beach at the west end and is stocked with trout; it is the location of swimming, fishing, and boating.

Traditional sports are tennis (lessons available) on the six courts (four clay, two Har-Tru) and the two platform tennis courts and golfing on the nine-hole Scottish-design course and the eighteen-hole putting green. There are tennis and golf pro shops for equipment and apparel. The fitness center offers exercise equipment, saunas, and spa services. Lawn games include shuffleboard, croquet, and lawn bowling.

During the winter months horse-drawn sleigh rides are popular, and when the lake freezes, ice skating is a favorite sport. And Mohonk maintains more than 35 miles of marked trails for cross-country skiing.

Throughout the year lectures, concerts, and slide shows are scheduled in the evening. Several three-day to weeklong programs are planned, covering topics such as bird-watching and identification, gardening, photography, foreign languages, cooking, music, mystery and sleuthing, and stargazing; professionals in the respective fields conduct these programs. ≈≈≈

Rocking Horse Ranch

Highland, New York 12528
(914) 691–2927, (800) 647–2624
E-mail: buckyrhr@aol.com
Web site: www.rhranch.com

"Giddy-up, ole paint" and, with a tip of your ten-gallon hat, off you ride into the sunset. Located only 75 miles from New York City and recently awarded a three-diamond rating by AAA, Rocking Horse Ranch has been owned and managed by the Turk family since 1958. They take pride in treating their guests as family; in fact, more than 80 percent of the guests are repeat clients. The 500 acres easily accommodate up to 350 guests while permitting a feeling of "wide open spaces." With a stable of 120 horses, mainly quarterhorse stock, Rocking Horse stakes a claim to being one of the best dude ranches around.

Accommodations: Rooms (120 in all) are located in either the Main Lodge or the Oklahoma Annex (motel-style units). The twenty-four connecting rooms and the ranchettes may be appropriate for large parties. The latter are similar to mini suites, with sitting areas and convertible sofa beds. Eighteen rooms have

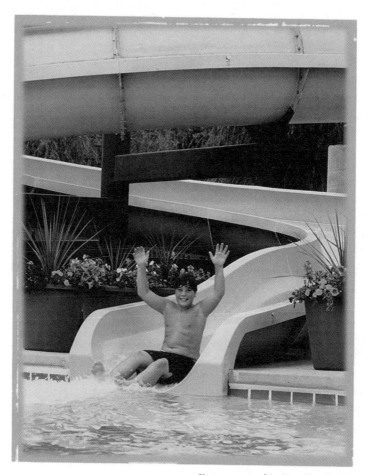

Photo courtesy of Rocking Horse Ranch

refrigerators. Daily rates based on double occupancy and a modified American plan are $75 to $195 per adult; children are charged at 50 percent of the adult rate, and weekly stays offer savings. In some package plans children stay free and are charged only for meals ($30 a day).

Dining: A modified American plan is mandatory at the resort and includes two meals for adults but three full meals for children. The three dining areas are the main dining room, an indoor snack bar, and, during the summer, an outdoor snack area by the pool. Meals are five to six courses, prepared by graduate chefs from the nearby Culinary Institute of America. Dinner selections include roast prime rib, barbecued steaks, or fillet of sole brought in fresh from a local market, complemented by a huge salad bar. At the dessert bar the chocolate blackout cake is not to be missed. The Round-Up Room Nightclub has floor shows and a live band. Two other cocktail lounges, each with a fireplace and a conversation area, are also quite inviting.

Children's World: The Fort Wilderness playground area, with swings and climbing equipment and the animal farm where Tony the Llama lives, is a favorite with kids. Year-round, children have a planned, supervised program seven days a week. The 9:00 A.M.–5:00 P.M. schedule is filled with horseback riding, swimming, waterskiing, crafts, and games. In the evening the fun continues with pizza parties, dances, and cookouts. On weekends during the winter, kids turn to skiing, tobogganing, and snow tubing.

There is no charge for the day's events, which include lunch and snacks with the counselors, or for the "nite patrol," set up to make rounds of corridors and, upon request, to check inside the room when parents are out. Baby-sitting can be arranged at $5.00 per hour.

Recreation: You might start your day with an early-morning horseback ride; invigorated by the sweet mountain air, lead your horse down a quiet trail through the woods. You can try both English- and Western-style riding. If you're a novice, you can link up with the experienced ranch staff for some basic instruction.

The rest of your day may be filled with waterskiing (instruction is free), enjoying more than 150 feet of water slide, swimming, fishing, and boating (paddleboats and rowboats) on the ten-acre lake. Play a game of tennis and hike or jog along the nature trails. A relaxing swim in one of three heated pools (two are outdoors, with one just for kids) can revive your spirits for a workout in the exercise room or a rousing game of volleyball, softball, basketball, or badminton. For an easier pace try a round of croquet, shuffleboard, or horseshoes. An archery field and an indoor shooting range are available for aspiring marksmen, and the eighteen holes of miniature golf are fun for kids and their parents.

In the fall the social director plans apple-picking trips, hayrides, and cookouts. In winter add cross-country skiing, tobogganing, snow tubing, and horseback riding in the snow; the 300-foot vertical ski slope is modest but has two new trails. At Rocking Horse all activities are free; the horseback riding, the use of all the sports equipment and facilities, and the entertainment are covered in the lodging rates.

The Sagamore

Lake George at Bolton Landing, New York 12814
(518) 644–9400, (800) 358–3585

The notion of an island hideaway usually involves images of thatch-roofed huts or oceanside condominiums, palm trees waving in a gentle breeze, miles of sandy beach, and golf, tennis, sailing, and swimming. The Sagamore will take you by surprise, for it is an island resort, and it grants its guests opportunities for golf, tennis, sailing, and swimming—and then it deviates from the image. You see, The Sagamore is on a seventy-acre island in Lake George in upstate New York. Surrounded by clear lake waters and the Adirondack Mountains, the tall evergreen trees and the clean mountain air set the stage here.

The Sagamore itself is different. Originally opened in 1883, it is part of another era, gracious and elegant. The main hotel building dates from 1930 and is listed on the National Register of Historic Places. After an extensive multimillion-dollar renovation, The Sagamore reopened as a year-round resort in 1985 and is a member of Preferred Hotels and Resorts Worldwide. The wings radiate from the main lobby and its semicircular, white-columned porch and seem to embrace the lawns, gardens, and lake views. Down the wings are more porches for sitting, strolling, and catching a different view of the lake. In the center, topping off this Victorian showplace, is the bell tower.

Accommodations: Of the 350 rooms and suites, 100 are in the main hotel and another 240 are distributed among the island's seven modern lodges (don't worry, modern does not denote a disturbance to The Sagamore's ambience). The remaining ten suites are part of a business executive complex. You will find attention to detail and historical accuracy in the decoration of the rooms and throughout the hotel. You'll think "charming, quaint, elegant, reserved" when you see Adirondack-stick or American-country furniture. Perhaps your room will be in mahogany and you'll draw a Queen Anne–style chair up to the desk when writing postcards. Rocking chairs and quilted bedspreads complete the picture in some rooms. In others fireplaces or balconies capture a guest's eye. Even the bathrooms are special and true to a grand era, with their pedestal-base sinks and mahogany towel bars.

Rates vary within the main hotel and the lodges, ranging from $120 to $630 depending on the season. While The Sagamore's European plan includes no meals, you are invited to dine on an a la carte basis. For added convenience and value, choose the modified American plan, priced at $49 per person per day, and enjoy a full breakfast and four-course dinner daily at any of The Sagamore's restaurants. Children five and younger dine free when the rest of the family is on the meal plan.

Dining: For a casual afternoon by the pool, you can have a light lunch and beverages at the Terrace. For a truly elegant and memorable dinner, the Trillium can transport you back through time in style (coats and ties required for gentlemen). Recipes for this restaurant have been carefully researched so that you can have an adventure in history as well as in dining. In between these options are the Sagamore Dining Room, where regional favorites are served at breakfast and dinner, and the Club Grill on the mainland, where views stretch out over the golf course and the lake. At the Verandah, in the lobby, guests can have continental breakfast in the morning, tea and finger sandwiches in the afternoon, and nightcaps before retiring. Mr. Brown's serves light meals in a publike setting. The touring vessel *Morgan* cruises the lake during lunch and dinner, offering its diners constantly changing scenic views. It is suggested that you make your dinner reservations when you book your room.

Children's World: Under the cheerful and watchful direction of the activities counselor, Sagamore kids take swimming lessons, play lawn games, dance, do face painting, go on boat rides, see clown shows, and unveil their hidden talents in crafts classes. In this one area The Sagamore does not follow nineteenth-century practices, which were somewhat restrictive when it came to children. Instead, in keeping with modern philosophies, The Sagamore wants its energized children to have a fun, athletic, and creative visit. The authentic 22-foot tepee gives the program its name: The Teepee Club. It runs from 8:00 A.M. to 4:00 P.M. daily during the summer and on major holidays and winter weekends for ages four to thirteen. The cost is $25 for each child, including lunch. From 5:00 until 9:00 P.M., four- to thirteen-year-olds can have dinner, play, or enjoy dress-ups and clown parties. A game room includes a Ping-Pong table, a pool table, video games, and a television. For children under age four, baby-sitting is offered at $7.50 an hour, with a three-hour minimum. Children ages three to five can join the evening program with a baby-sitter for $10.

Recreation: Just across the bridge from The Sagamore's island, Donald Ross designed an eighteen-hole championship golf course in the Adirondack foothills near the lake's edge, complemented by the restaurant and pro shop facilities at the course's attractive Tudor-style clubhouse.

The indoor swimming pool, tennis courts, and racquetball courts help guests stay busy and active year-round. The complete health spa offers its own form of indoor workout with its Nautilus equipment and then pampers with saunas, whirlpools, and massages. Spa packages include special diets, herbal wraps, and aromatherapy.

In warm weather swim in the beautiful, clean, freshwater lake; skim across its surface sailing, waterskiing, and sailboarding; or gently stroke the waters in a rowboat or fishing boat. Jog on the trails around the island or hike the foothills around the golf course. Take a horse out for an hour-long jaunt or stay close to home for a Sunday afternoon concert on the lawn.

In the wintertime Lake George freezes; hearty souls go ice fishing while others snuggle together during a horse-drawn sleigh ride. Ice skate over the frozen lake or go tobogganing and cross-country skiing on the snow-covered golf course. Downhill skiers can take advantage of nearby Gore Mountain and West Mountain, ski areas to which The Sagamore provides free bus transportation.

Saratoga is about 30 miles away and in summer shares its Performing Arts Center with interested visitors. ≋

Skytop Lodge
One Skytop
Skytop, Pennsylvania 18357
(717) 595–7401, (800) 345–7759
Web site: www.skytop.com

T he Pocono Mountains have long had a reputation as a romantic honeymoon destination. While this is certainly warranted, the Skytop Lodge will convince you that this area of northeast Pennsylvania is just right for a family vacation as well. Set on 5,500 acres of rolling hills, lakes, and rivers, the lodge is a large, rambling, stone building with a welcoming circular drive. Just 100 miles from either New York or Philadelphia, Skytop attracts many visitors with its relaxed atmosphere, hospitable charm, and recreational activities. It is open year-round.

Accommodations: Most of the rooms have views of the gardens and grounds; some will accommodate a family of four. If a large-enough room is not available, or if parents prefer, children are given their own room at $100 off the regular rate. Based on double occupancy, full American plan high-season (May through October) rates are $300–$425 weekends and $285–$375 Sunday through Thursday. Children under seventeen sharing the parents' room pay $20. November to April has special off-season rates and packages available; weekend and holiday rates, however, are more comparable to those in summer.

Dining: All meals are served in the main dining room, where gentlemen are requested to wear jackets in the evening. The Tea Room serves light fare such as soups and sandwiches, and the seasonal Golf Shop Grill is an alternate luncheon spot in warm weather. The Pine Room, an elegant and inviting area of the lobby with floor-to-ceiling windows, is the site of afternoon musical entertainment in the summer and cozy gatherings near the fireplace in the winter. The Tap Room serves cocktails and features dancing several nights a week.

Children's World: Camp-in-the-Clouds is in session for three- to twelve-year-olds daily from July 1 to Labor Day. The morning program runs from 9:30 A.M. to noon, the afternoon program from 2:00 to 5:00 P.M. Each session is $18, or $25 for the full day, and covers a program of swimming, boating, hiking, games, and crafts. Young children also enjoy the playground and the kiddie pool, while the older ones make the most of pool, Ping-Pong, and video games in the Recreation Room. The weekly Saturday night "Grand March" has become a tradition at Skytop. A combination parade, quadrille, and snake dance, it becomes hilarious at times, and guests and staff alike anticipate the fun. At holiday times during the rest of the year, the activities staff plans dinners and movies for children. Individual baby-sitters can be arranged for evenings only at $5.00 an hour.

Recreation: The Poconos make a lovely setting for sports activities. The eighteen-hole championship golf course is a combination of lush fairways and beautiful old trees on a rolling terrain. Putting greens and a pro shop round out the golfing facility. Tennis players are invigorated by the clean mountain air; of the seven outdoor courts, five are Har-Tru and two are an all-weather surface. Private lessons and clinics are offered.

Fishermen like the trout-filled stream and the three lakes full of bass and pickerel; novices will appreciate the fly-fishing instruction. Others take to these waters for swimming, boating, and canoeing. There's an outdoor swimming pool, and in cool weather swimmers enjoy the large indoor pool in its solarium setting.

You can work out in the exercise room, but outdoors you can have beautiful scenery *and* all the exercise you want. Try lawn bowling on well-tended greens (tournaments are held during the summer), or practice more conventional sports like badminton, croquet, archery, shuffleboard, softball, and miniature golf. The trails through the woods are perfect for hiking, biking, and jogging, and the gardens are suitable for relaxing strolls. Naturalists conduct tours of the local wildlife and vegetation. In the evening you might find a bridge game, play a little pool or billiards, take in a movie, or relax in the library.

In the winter Skytop has a few gentle slopes for downhill skiing; two poma lifts and seven trails with a vertical drop of just 275 feet make it ideal for learning. A ski pro can help with lessons. Several well-groomed trails cover acres of attractive territory for cross-country skiing. Rental equipment is available for both types of skiing, and larger ski areas are nearby at Alpine Mountain (8 miles) and Camelback (15 miles). Tobogganing, sledding, and ice skating are also wintertime favorites. ≋

SOUTHEAST

North Carolina

South Carolina

Virginia

West Virginia

Fairfield Sapphire Valley

70 Sapphire Valley Road
Sapphire, North Carolina 28774
(828) 743–3441, (800) 533–8268

The rolling foothills of the Blue Ridge Mountains provide the backdrop for Fairfield Sapphire Valley, a year-round resort community. The 5,700 acres, filled with the scent of pines and fresh mountain air, encompass three lakes, a golf course, a horseback-riding stable, and picturesque scenery for nature lovers and hikers. The serenity of a canoe ride on the lake, a relaxing afternoon fishing from the dock, or the rigors of a tennis clinic attract vacationers to this mountain setting tucked in the southwestern corner of North Carolina.

Accommodations: Hotel rooms, efficiencies, one- to three-bedroom condominiums, and three- and four-bedroom houses are clustered near the lakes or nestled among tall pines near the tennis center. Most of these lodgings have kitchens, and all have sundecks or balconies where you can sit to watch the sunset. Condominium rates begin at $90 for a room and go to $245 for a deluxe three-bedroom with view. Off-season (November–March) rates are $10 to $35 less.

Dining: Many families prepare meals in their villas, but if your idea of a vacation does not include cooking, the restaurants can relieve you of this chore. The Library Restaurant offers fine dining in a casual atmosphere, while Mica's Restaurant has an old-world charm and serves lunch and dinner daily. The club for the Sapphire Mountain Golf Course also houses a restaurant, which is open for lunch. There's no meal plan, so you're free to pick and choose as you please. The resort is located in a dry township; while no liquor, beer, or wine can be purchased, brown bagging is permitted and setups are available in the area restaurants.

Children's World: The children's program operates Monday through Friday from 9:00 A.M. to 4:00 P.M., mid-June through mid-August. Enroll your child for a full- or half-day session of events supervised by an enthusiastic staff. A full day with lunch is $20. The program is offered for ages six to twelve.

Swimming, boat rides, tennis, nature walks, fishing, and arts-and-crafts classes are on the agenda, as are an occasional puppet show and scavenger hunt. Video games are offered for the young computer whiz in your group. The recreation staff assists in making individual baby-sitting arrangements.

Recreation: The Sapphire Mountain Golf Course is an eighteen-hole championship course; views of the beautiful Blue Ridge Mountains provide ample

Photo courtesy of Fairfield Sapphire Valley

diversion if your game is not up to snuff. Water hazards on nine holes, including a waterfall, make it a memorable experience. If you're really serious about your performance, seek private instruction at the pro shop, which also accommodates your fashion and equipment needs.

Tennis enthusiasts enjoy the Tennis Center, which includes eight Har-Tru courts and two all-weather courts (two courts are lighted for evening play), as well as a well-stocked pro shop. The resident pro can assist in improving your swing in either private lessons or clinic programs.

For hikers and nature lovers, several trails wind around the lakes and through the woods; along the Fairfield Lake Trail, information plaques describe the plants and wildlife of the area. At the Equestrian Center you can engage a mount for a solo adventure or join a group for an escorted trail ride.

For an unusual afternoon outing, you might consider gem mining. In the late 1800s the land was mined quite successfully, and while you probably won't bring home a sapphire or a ruby, you'll no doubt have a good excursion. Check with the Recreation Department for mining tips and equipment.

Swimmers can opt for a dip in one of the lakes or in the indoor and outdoor heated pools located at the Recreation Center. Lake Fairfield is also the setting for boating expeditions; canoes, paddleboats, rowboats, and fishing boats can be acquired on a rental basis. Fishermen head to the lakes or a quiet mountain stream for fine trout fishing.

At the Recreation Center you'll also find basketball, volleyball, Ping-Pong, miniature golf, swimming pools, a weight room, Jacuzzi, and a sauna. In winter the Recreation Center becomes the focus of ski activities; three main trails are covered by snowmaking and lighted for evening skiing; group and private lessons are taught at the ski school. Many visitors reserve time for sightseeing in the area. The Biltmore House and Gardens, along with its winery, certainly warrant a side trip. Local mountain crafts can be purchased in Cashiers and Highlands. ≈≈≈

The Greenbrier

300 West Main Street
White Sulphur Springs, West Virginia 24986
(304) 536–1110, (800) 624–6070

The Greenbrier is a 6,500-acre estate in the beautiful Allegheny Mountains. Its history dates back to just after the Revolutionary War, when early settlers discovered the sulfur springs of this area. The grand Georgian architecture of The Greenbrier with its white columned porticoes, elaborate formal gardens, and friendly atmosphere set the scene for a memorable experience of fine dining, recreation, and relaxation.

The only problem at The Greenbrier may be deciding what to do first. With a list of recreational and social activities a mile long, you may need a personal secretary to help you get organized. When planning events for your stay, though, save time for an escape to discover nature's charms along the enticing woodland trails, well marked for joggers and walkers alike. And pause among the twelve acres of formal gardens, tended meticulously from spring through fall. With a reputation that has attracted presidents and royalty, The Greenbrier provides a level of elegant service and comfort that ensures an unforgettable vacation. It is open year-round.

Accommodations: With rooms and suites in the hotel as well as guest houses and cottages, you have a wide choice of accommodations. The rooms are large and bright, with comfortable, elegant furnishings. Based on a modified American plan, daily rates for a standard room start at $188 to $238 (depending on the season) per person, double occupancy; larger rooms and prime locations command slightly higher rates. There is no charge for children occupying the same room as their parents. The guest cottages include one to four bedrooms, a living room, and a porch or patio; many have fireplaces. The daily per person rate, based on an occupancy of two to eight people, is

Photo courtesy of The Greenbrier

$222–$377, modified American plan. The Creekside Cottages are available to guests visiting for a minimum of one week. Golf, tennis, and family package plans are offered. Cribs are provided at no extra charge.

Dining: The Greenbrier boasts exciting culinary experiences. Regional Southern specialties, such as spoon bread and fresh trout from the nearby mountain streams, as well as continental dishes, make dining a special part of a visit here. The sumptuous breakfasts, featuring homemade biscuits and country ham, are a real treat. A modified American plan is required for all guests. A coat and tie are standard attire for gentlemen at dinner.

The main dining room serves breakfast and six-course dinners; for a la carte dining April through October, the Tavern Room and Lounge provides a sophisticated setting. Sam Snead's at the Golf Club and Slammin' Sammy offer dining and entertainment during the summer season. At these spots diners enjoy views of the beautiful golf courses. Drapers Cafe—especially popular for its homemade ice cream—is convenient for light meals, snacks, and pastries throughout the day. Afternoon tea is served daily with musical accompaniment. In the elegant and warm Old White Club, guests gather at 5:00 P.M. for cocktails and complimentary hors d'oeuvres and later for music and dancing until closing.

Children's World: From Memorial Day through Labor Day and at the holiday times of Thanksgiving, Christmas, and Easter, the children's program more than fills the days of three- to twelve-year-olds. During the summer experienced counselors direct arts and crafts, picnics, nature hikes, croquet, shuffleboard, swimming, and games. Older children (six to twelve years) have tennis and golf instruction as well. The fee is $35 a day (10:00 A.M.–4:00 P.M.) for your first child and $25 a day for each additional child.

From 6:30 to 10:00 P.M., children ages six to twelve years old can join their counselors for dinner and an evening bowling or at the movies. So it's possible for grown-ups to arrange an evening or two for wining and dining. Baby-sitting services for younger children are also available at an average hourly rate of $5.00.

Recreation: Avid golf and tennis players are well satisfied at The Greenbrier. The Allegheny hills provide the beauty and the challenge of three eighteen-hole championship golf courses, one of which was redesigned in 1979 by Jack Nicklaus. The Greenbrier Sam Snead Golf Academy provides golfers of all skill levels the opportunity to improve their game. The academy provides professional teaching staff and state-of-the-art equipment and services.

Of the twenty tennis courts, fifteen are outdoors and five are indoors. The staff at the tennis pro shop can assist in finding partners. You may also confront the idiosyncrasies of your swing during instructional videotaped replays of your performance.

Kate's Mountain is the picturesque site of the Gun Club, with its four trap and skeet fields. Group tournaments can be organized, or perhaps you'll take in the action from the sidelines in the Clubhouse lounge.

Fishing enthusiasts head for the well-stocked streams and lakes, while swimmers can work out in the indoor or outdoor pool or relax at poolside. An exercise room is adjacent to the indoor swimming pool. The bowling center (eight lanes), table tennis, horseback riding, shuffleboard, horseshoes, croquet, bicycling, carriage rides, and movies offer additional diversions. The five hiking trails are graded by length and rise in elevation. One of the two jogging trails features twelve exercise stations. Winter sports include cross-country skiing, ice skating, and sleigh rides. Downhill skiing is ninety minutes away at the Snowshoe Ski Resort.

And when the body wearies and the spirits droop, the only respectable place to be is the Spa, which pampers guests with mineral baths, massage, steam, and sauna facilities—it was the sulfur water with its medicinal and recuperative powers that first attracted visitors to this region. For shoppers a fine selection of fashions, jewelry, handcrafts, and gifts is presented in the Gallery of Shops. ≋

The Grove Park Inn Resort

290 Macon Avenue
Asheville, North Carolina 28804-3799
(704) 252–2711, (800) 438–5800
Web site: www.groveparkinn.com

The scenery and climate of the Blue Ridge Mountains have long attracted visitors to Asheville. The Grove Park Inn, located on the western slope of Sunset Mountain, opened its doors to guests in 1913 and gives a feeling of pure country in the midst of the city, with grand vistas of mountains and green golf courses. Built of granite from the nearby mountains and dedicated to preserving a gracious turn-of-the-century atmosphere, the inn was named to the National Register of Historic Places in 1973. Its guest list over the years reads somewhat like a Who's Who: Thomas Edison, Henry Ford, Woodrow Wilson, Enrico Caruso, Béla Bartók, and President and Mrs. Franklin Roosevelt. History buffs will have a fine time wondering which room General Pershing slept in or if F. Scott Fitzgerald sat by the fireplace in the Great Hall sipping an after-dinner brandy. A fireplace there, by the way, is so huge that an adult can walk into it!

The resort's country club (originally the Swannanoa Hunt Club, begun in 1893) and the Inn were renovated in the late 1980s. Two wings, which com-

Photo courtesy of The Grove Park Inn Resort

plement the architectural style and materials of the main building, were added. The four-diamond, four-star Grove Park Inn is open year-round.

Accommodations: Both the historic main inn and the wings house guest rooms; those offering panoramic mountain views enchant many a guest. There are twelve suites and an exclusive club floor if your entourage warrants the space or additional amenities. In the regular rooms you can request a small refrigerator to keep children's drinks and snacks chilled and close at hand. During the low season, from January to April, the deluxe room rate is $149 a night in the main inn and $159 in the wings per double room. In the high season a deluxe double room is $200 in the main inn and $220 in the wings per night. Children under sixteen stay free in their parents' room; cribs and rollaway beds are available at no cost.

Dining: A full range of refreshments, from snacks and sandwiches to full-course meals, is offered. In the Blue Ridge Dining Room, buffet and table d'hote meals are served. At the Sunset Terrace enjoy mountain views from the veranda along with fine continental cuisine. The Carolina Cafe fills the bill for early lunches or late-afternoon snacks; it, too, attracts guests with its lovely views. For a change of pace, sample the gourmet cuisine at Horizons, a four-diamond-rated restaurant. In the evening you can enjoy your favorite beverage in the Great Hall Bar or take in the entertainment at Elaine's Nightclub (weekends).

Children's World: The Inn organizes children's activities throughout the year, tailor-made to the number of children visiting the hotel, for ages three to twelve years. The program is most active from Memorial Day to Labor Day, when a large number of families are vacationing at The Grove Park Inn.

From May through Labor Day, the resort offers Operation Kid-Nap, Monday through Saturday from 9:00 A.M. to 4:00 P.M. Saturday Operation Kid-Nap is offered year-round. The $27 fee includes lunch and a snack plus activities such as sports, arts and crafts, nature hikes, and swimming (yes, there is an indoor pool). From Monday to Thursday, 6:00 to 9:00 P.M. during the summer, a Dinner Club offers dinner and great activities for kids (and a chance for Mom and Dad to dine alone) for only $20. Kid's Night Out is a year-round program, held on Friday and Saturday nights from 6:00 to 10:30 P.M., which costs $25. If you prefer, the concierge desk will provide a list of individual baby-sitters, with varying fees.

Recreation: An eighteen-hole Donald Ross championship golf course meanders down the gentle mountain slope. Practice your backhand on one of the nine tennis courts (six outdoors, three indoors). The staff in the tennis and golf pro shops can assist you with your playing and fashion needs. An indoor Sports Center has racquetball, squash, and tennis courts; whirlpool; weight and exercise rooms; saunas; massages; and a fully equipped aerobics room with professionally taught classes. There are also indoor and outdoor pools available for hotel guests. But don't forget to take a walk down the garden paths and nature trails (also suitable when the urge to jog hits you).

Nearby you can explore the lake or try your hand at fishing, horseback riding, cycling, mountain biking, white-water rafting, ballooning, or llama trekking. In the winter a day of skiing (cross-country and downhill) is a popular excursion. For souvenirs you'll discover the six gift shops at the resort as well as many crafts shops and potteries in the area. The Biltmore Estate is only 8 miles from the inn; an afternoon can be well spent discovering the art, antiques, winery, and formal gardens of this magnificent old estate.

High Hampton Inn and Country Club

P.O. Box 338
Highway 107
Cashiers, North Carolina 28717
(704) 743–2411, (800) 334–2551
Web site: www.highhamptoninn.com

The verdant Blue Ridge Mountains provide a beautiful setting, and High Hampton, located in the Cashiers Valley at an altitude of 3,600 feet, allows its guests an escape to clean, crisp air, clear mountain lakes, and tall pine trees. Some people like the ambience of a country inn—quiet, friendly, with rustic accommodations and good home cooking. Others like the atmosphere of a resort, with lots of activities and events and busy days and nights. Happily, High Hampton has managed to blend the best of both these worlds. Roam over the 2,300 acres and explore the beauties of nature in the southwest corner of North Carolina. Dating from the mid-nineteenth century, High Hampton was once the summer home of Confederate General Wade Hampton and remained in the Hampton family until the 1920s.

For over seventy years, under the continuing ownership of the McKee family, the inn has welcomed guests to an informal atmosphere for golf, tennis, swimming, fishing, horseback riding, and simple relaxing. The architecture of the inn is charming and rustic, blending with the natural surroundings. The wide porches filled with plants and the lobby's stone chimney with four fireplaces hint at the warmth and friendly spirit within. The inn is open only from mid-April to mid-November, with a famous Thanksgiving Houseparty to close the season.

Accommodations: The 130 rooms at the inn (some of which are suites) are simple, warm, and rustic; the knotty pine walls and mountain-style furniture echo the landscape and the crafts of the region. Many of the rooms have very pleasant

Photo copyright © 1991 by Lavidge & Associates, courtesy of High Hampton Inn and Country Club

views of the grounds. Based on a full American plan, daily rates are $69 to $81 per person midweek, $75 to $88 on Friday and Saturday; children under six are $40, while older children are $49. Cribs are available for infants and toddlers at no charge. A number of privately owned homes are also available; these are fully equipped, with fireplace, deck, laundry, and kitchen. Choose from two to four bedrooms with no meals, but with daily maid service, for $184 to $334 a day. If you choose not to cook, a full American plan is available for $31 per person per day, or $20 for children under six years. Golf package plans are offered as well.

Dining: The one dining room at the Inn specializes in regional Southern cooking, and service is buffet style. Imagine down-home favorites like country ham, cream of peanut soup, homemade biscuits, and vegetables fresh from the garden. Afternoon tea is served daily in the lobby. Coats and ties are standard attire for men in the evening, as High Hampton is one of the few resorts that cling to traditional ways.

Wine and beer only are served in the dining room, but mixed drinks are served at the Rock Mountain Tavern, a popular spot to gather, listen to music, meet other guests, and line up partners for bridge or tennis. Movies, lobby games, dancing, and mountain hayrides fill the evening. Small groups of guests may gather on porches to compare notes, sip their own drinks, and talk about the day.

Children's World: Kids have their own building at High Hampton, called Noah's Ark, where youngsters ages five to twelve meet with counselors for daily activities such as arts and crafts, games, tennis, nature studies, and hiking.

Offered from June 1 through Labor Day, the program runs from 9:00 A.M. to 2:00 P.M. and includes lunch. After a free afternoon children can rejoin their group·at 6:00 P.M. for dinner (sometimes a hayride and cookout!) and games, movies, and stories until 9:00 P.M. The fee is $2.00 an hour per child. For wee ones and the hours after 9:00 P.M., baby-sitters are available.

The Play Group, for ages two, three, and four, is a fun experience where little ones do donkey-cart rides, bubble blowing, games, and crafts. The ratio of children to counselors is small, with lots of attention for each child.

While there's no swimming pool, a restricted, shallow area of the lake with a sandy beach is especially designed for young children. The area includes a toddlers' playhouse, swings, seesaw, and jungle gym, keeping the little ones amused for hours.

Rather than a teen club, High Hampton has The Gathering Place for Young Adults. Here, the next generation can gather to socialize and enjoy the pool table, Ping-Pong, and video games. Outdoor activities such as volleyball games, boating excursions, and picnics or mountain hikes are planned and enjoyed by all.

Recreation: The mountain terrain and picturesque scenery make golf a challenge and a pleasure. The eighteen-hole course, designed by George Cobb, is carved on a gently rolling plateau, skirting lakes and weaving through white pine and hemlock. There are two putting greens and a practice range; lessons are available. A new dining facility, The Overlook Cafe, is above the pro shop. It features light lunches and snacks, with continental breakfast for early birds.

The tennis center encompasses five outdoor courts, a pro shop, and an indoor practice area; clinics and private lessons are offered. You pay court fees and greens fees unless you are on a four- or seven-day golf or tennis package.

There are three mountain lakes for swimming and boating, but the thirty-five-acre Hampton Lake is the center of activity, where paddleboats, canoes, rowboats, and sailboats can be rented. But these clear waters are not just for invigorating swims and peaceful excursions. When the fishing mood strikes, you'll be happy to know that one of the lakes is stocked with rainbow and brook trout; bass and bream can also be lured from the waters.

Discover the rich natural beauty of these surroundings on one of the eight hiking trails. Or take to the mountain trails—in one and a half hours you can climb to the 4,618-foot summit of Chimney Rock for absolutely spectacular views. Take the ten-station Fitness Trail to the base of Rock Mountain. In a more leisurely manner, lawn sports such as badminton, croquet, shuffleboard, and archery may attract you, or maybe you'll be drawn to the gardens for a stroll among the dahlias, dogwoods, and azaleas.

The inn occasionally holds workshops in such diverse areas as bridge, fly-fishing, quilting, watercolor painting, and investments—what a pleasant way to glean helpful hints on a variety of topics! While proud of its facilities, the High Hampton Inn mostly boasts of its friendly atmosphere, its low-key pace, and the serenity and beauty of its natural setting. It is also proud that High Hampton "is not for everyone." But those who stay return year after year, and their children bring their own children. It's that kind of place. ≋

The Homestead

Hot Springs, Virginia 24445
(540) 839–1766, (800) 838–1766

A few classic institutions in the United States have captured the attention of vacationers for many years. With all its charm and grace, The Homestead ranks as one of these. Its fascinating history has roots in the 1700s, yet The Homestead has moved into this century with style, preserving an atmosphere of friendly elegance. As with several fine old resorts in this country, the medicinal quality of mineral springs first attracted people to the site of The Homestead. While The Spa is still a captivating diversion of many guests, many recreational facilities have been developed over the years, with golf being the premier sport here.

The current hotel was built in 1902, with additions continuing into the late 1920s. Despite those three decades of construction, The Homestead is a cohesive, majestic structure of red brick and white columns in Georgian style. At an elevation of 2,300 feet, the estate sprawls over 15,000 acres (yes—15,000!) of the Allegheny Mountains in western Virginia. It is open year-round.

Accommodations: The Homestead boasts more than 500 bright and spacious rooms. Sizes vary from traditional rooms to parlor rooms and suites; the rate is determined by the size of the room and its location. Based on a modified American plan, the rate for a standard double room during the April through October season is $179–$198 per person per day. From November through March the rates are slightly lower, except during the Christmas holidays, which more or less follow the high-season price schedule. Children over five sharing a room with their parents are extra; there is no charge for children under five and no additional charge for cribs and rollaways. The modified American plan rates include the room, two meals a day, swimming, afternoon tea, evening movies, and use of the supervised children's playground. Separate fees are charged for all other activities.

Dining: Dining at The Homestead is special. Executive chef Albert Schnarwyler ensures that every meal is a memorable experience. Imagine baked apples and

Photo courtesy of The Homestead

kippered herring for breakfast; consider lunches and dinners that feature local favorites such as Smithfield ham, rainbow trout from nearby mountain streams, and fresh turnip greens, as well as fine international cuisine. A selection that includes bluepoint oysters, grilled Dover sole with almonds, roast baby pheasant, and tournedos Rossini makes for difficult decisions; it's almost necessary to spend extended time at The Homestead just to sample the specialties. And the sublime creations of pastries, sorbets, and fresh fruit tarts should not be missed.

The dining room is open year-round. During the April through October season, The Homestead Grille serves dinner. Golfers enjoy lunch at the Cascades Club restaurant, and Sam Snead's Tavern is yet another alternative for dinner. Casual resort wear is expected for lunch in the dining room, and coats and ties are required for gentlemen in the evening. Picnic lunches can also be prepared if you choose to spend the day outdoors in the wooded mountains.

A time-honored custom at The Homestead is Afternoon Tea, served daily at 4:00 P.M. in the Great Hall. In an elegant setting graced by chandeliers and Corinthian columns, you can relax to soft piano music while sipping tea.

Children's World: Although The Homestead has traditionally catered to an older set, supervised children's activities are now offered year-round. Children are divided into groups—ages three to twelve years—to enjoy an active sports program of swimming, tennis, fishing, nature walks, and visits to the stables. The outdoor playground has been completely renovated, and children have their own fishing pond—great for kids of all ages. If bad weather precludes out-door play, children move inside the KidsClub for creative endeavors, stories, and educational games. The program operates Monday to Saturday from 9:00 A.M. to 4:00 P.M., and Sundays from 9:00 A.M. to 1:00 P.M. The cost is $45 for a full day with lunch; $26 for a half day.

During the winter children can learn to ski on The Homestead trails through Bunny School. Individual baby-sitters can be arranged for at any time (with proper advance notice); the rate is $6.00 an hour for one child; $1.00 more for each additional child.

Recreation: Even golf and tennis have hundred-year-old histories at The Homestead. There are three eighteen-hole golf courses, and the fact that native son Sam Snead started his golfing career here adds a certain panache to the atmosphere and lends credence to the caliber of play. The Old Course was opened in 1892 and revamped in the 1920s when a second course, the Cascades, was added. Robert Trent Jones designed the third course, the Lower Cascades, which opened in 1963. All three courses weave through a picturesque wooded landscape. With a putting green, a practice fairway, a pro shop, and lessons available, you have all the necessary ingredients to improve your game.

Tennis also got under way here in 1892; it has since expanded to seven courts. Lessons in tennis can be scheduled, and the tennis shop is well equipped.

The facilities at The Spa include massage, aromatherapy, mineral baths, aerobics classes, and indoor and outdoor swimming pools. There may be no proven miraculous powers in the famous mineral waters, but the benefits of a spa regimen to both body and spirit are not questioned. The Spa Salon offers complete hairstyling.

For fans of trap and skeet, there are four fields; instruction is offered so that even novices can try this sport. Other outdoor sports include falconry, horseback riding in the wooded countryside, trout fishing in the Cascades Stream, and hiking in the mountains. Or you may prefer to enjoy the scenery during a carriage ride. You might take your skills indoors to the eight bowling lanes. Or you might opt for Ping-Pong, billiards, or card and board games. In the evenings go dancing or take in a movie.

Winter sports are limited, but The Homestead does have nine downhill ski runs, open mid-December through March. With a vertical drop of just 700 feet, it cannot offer the diversity and challenge that a good skier seeks, but it may be a fun place for kids to learn, and it does provide an added dimension to a winter vacation. Near the lodge, which houses a restaurant, the ski school, and ski shops, is an Olympic-size skating rink; lessons are offered in ice skating. Cross-country skiers can explore acres of mountain meadows and trails, weather permitting, of course. ≋

Kiawah Island

12 Kiawah Beach Drive
Kiawah Island, South Carolina 29455
(803) 768-2121, (800) 845-2471 (South Carolina), (800) 654-2924

In climate and scenery, the islands off the coast of the Carolinas offer some of the finest resort living. At Kiawah Island the beauty of the natural setting has been carefully respected, while man-made amenities have been added to provide visitors with the best in comfort, relaxation, recreation, and fun. An island with 10 miles of beach on the Atlantic Ocean, Kiawah is actually two resort villages, each with its own lodging and recreational facilities; a shuttle-bus connects the villages.

West Beach Village (which dates from 1976) consists of the Kiawah Island Inn, condominiums, restaurants, a racquet club, shops, pools, and a golf course. At East Beach Village (the younger by five years), there are condominiums, restaurants, shops, a golf course, a tennis club, and Night Heron Park, a twenty-one-acre recreation area that encompasses a pool, lake, playgrounds, and picnic sites.

All these conveniences and amenities, and yet you still have the opportunity to feel close to nature, as only half the land will ever be developed. The sound ecological planning at Kiawah has preserved the lagoons and marshes and ensured homes for deer, raccoon, egrets, and brown pelicans; you might even get to see a loggerhead sea turtle, alligators, dolphins, or perhaps an eagle. The drive from the Charleston Airport is about forty-five minutes. As you enter the main gates to Kiawah, you'll be given a car registration pass that reads "Please respect the wildlife that inhabits Kiawah Island. Alligators are potentially dangerous and extremely fast. They should never be fed or teased in any way." When you see alligators plying the lagoon waters, you'll understand the seriousness of this warning.

Accommodations: The Kiawah Island Inn, located in West Beach village, is the right choice for those who want to be pampered. The 150 rooms, distributed among four lodges, all have private balconies overlooking the ocean, pools, lagoons, or picturesque wooded areas; the services and conveniences are typical of a fine resort hotel.

The condominium villas, cedar-shingled or natural-wood frame structures, are dispersed throughout the island in different settings appealing to all different interests. You may choose one with an ocean view or one next door to the tennis courts, one alongside the lush green fairways of a golf course, one on a lake, or one nestled among oaks and hickories and sweet gum trees. These one- to four-bedroom units have well-equipped kitchens, and most of them have sundecks or screened porches—terrific spots for having breakfast or just taking in the views. One- to five-bedroom luxury homes are also available.

Rates vary depending on the season; the inn ranges from $95 to $260 and one-bedroom villas are $75–$250. Cribs are free at the inn, $15 per day in the villas; rollaways are $15 at the inn and $25 in the villas.

Dining: You'll never have a problem here; there are enough restaurants to meet varied moods and tastes. For South Carolina low-country specialties and continental fare, you might choose the Jasmine Porch (at the inn), which serves a buffet breakfast (mmm—French pastries and eggs Benedict) and dinner. Warm weather lures diners to the veranda to enjoy lovely views along with delightful meals.

The Sweetgrass Cafe is a casual dining spot in the Straw Market of West Beach Village; it's open for lunch and dinner and features tempting focaccia-crust pizzas and sandwiches to please any palate. Nearby is Scooper's, where the ice cream and pastries are hard to resist (who can pass up an ice cream flavor called Mississippi Mud?). Beside the inn's pool, Sundancer's serves salads, burgers, and other light fare for lunch and supper. At East Beach Village the restaurant is the Indigo House, an "island bistro" featuring Mediterranean, Caribbean, and the new Florida cuisine. In Night Heron Park (at East Beach Village), two elegant yet casual clubhouses, located at the golf courses, serve breakfast, lunch, and cocktails.

Photo courtesy of Kiawah Island

On Monday evenings families head to Mingo Point on the Kiawah River for an outdoor barbecue and oyster roast, followed by the down-home music of a bluegrass band. For evening cocktails and musical entertainment, try the Topsider Lounge at the Inn or Sundancer's, popular places to sip an old favorite or an exotic tropical drink. A casual food court is located in East Beach, offering a variety of quick meals.

Children's World: From early May through September and at Thanksgiving, Christmas, New Year's, and Easter, children and parents alike find Kiawah the perfect destination for a family vacation.

Energetic college students with training in sports and recreation supervise young visitors in four different age groups in activities designed to ensure happy, fun-filled days. In fact, there's much more to do than we have room to outline. In summer Kamp Kiawah is in swing from 9:00 A.M. to 4:30 P.M. Monday through Friday. The cost is $21.00 (half days are available); lunch is an extra $5.00. Divided into three groups—three to four years, five to seven years, and eight to twelve years—the kids enjoy swimming, treasure hunts, crabbing, storytime, and crafts. Kids Nature Club is a special program for eight- to fourteen-year-olds that is limited to twelve participants. Twice-weekly three-hour excursions with a staff naturalist allow them to have a hands-on, fun experience with nature ($14). More painless learning is provided by Kiawah Kollege, an award-winning program for all ages that allows exploration of Kiawah's ever-changing ecosystem. Ocean seining with a huge 40-foot net, canoe trips through the marshes, pond exploration, night walks on the beach, bird-watching—with more than 10,000 acres of marshland and five staff naturalists, the possibilities go on and on. Costs range from $3.00 to $15.00.

Discovery Series, a free weekly program, features speakers accompanied by live snakes or alligators, storytellers, and more. Kiawah has found a successful blend of activities that includes teenagers' favorite things: sports, music, food, and loose structure. Volleyball and basketball tournaments, "teen splash" (pool time only for them), T-shirt graffiti, and a Friday-night dance with DJ are just a sample of the options. There is also a River Cruise with teens from nearby islands, exploring the Kiawah River, maybe even sighting dolphins; limited to twenty kids, the cost is $25.

Children also enjoy the playgrounds filled with wooden climbing equipment, swings, and slides; the largest one at Night Heron Park is built in and among the trees, hardly disturbing the natural vegetation. The Heron Park Center features video games, live animals, and nature wear and gear, as well as a recreation concierge.

When you want to be together and join other families, afternoon and evening hours are filled with bingo, games, nature films, family movies, and cookouts; most of these activities are free. Particularly fun is the "dive-in movie"—movies shown at the pool, with swimming allowed. Baby-sitters are available when you want to indulge in a strictly grown-up evening.

Recreation: With four excellent eighteen-hole championship golf courses, golfers think they've discovered a little bit of paradise at Kiawah. Host site of the 1991 Ryder Cup and 1997 World Cup of Golf, The Ocean Course, designed by Pete Dyre, is known worldwide. The Cougar Point Golf Course was designed by Gary Player, the Turtle Point Golf Course by Jack Nicklaus, and the Osprey Point Golf Course by Tom Fazio; talent like this ensures challenge in a beautiful natural setting. You can enroll in group or private lessons or in a clinic, then practice newly acquired skills on the driving ranges and putting greens. The pro shops are well stocked with equipment, apparel, and accessories to enhance your game.

For tennis enthusiasts the West Beach Racquet Club offers sixteen courts, while the East Beach Tennis Club has twelve courts and a ball machine. Add a practice alley, resident pros, clinics, and group and private lessons and you have every opportunity to improve your game. Kiawah has been rated the sixth-best tennis resort in the nation by *Tennis* magazine. It offers free tennis clinics and one hour of free tennis daily to guests.

Swimmers take to the ocean from April through October or dip into one of the three pools at the Inn (one for adults only, one for the family, and one a children's pool). Two 25-meter pools are located in Night Heron Park and Turtle Point. You can sign up for swimming lessons for yourself or your child (even an infant). Other water sports, such as sailing, canoeing, and sailboarding, are also popular.

Bicyclists have more than 20 miles of hard-packed beach and paved trails to explore (rentals, many with baby seats, are available). Joggers find a good workout on the 1.1-mile parcourse fitness trail with twenty exercise stations. Try your luck fishing in the lake or creek and surf casting in the ocean, or introduce your child to the fun of crabbing, where an old chicken neck can net beautiful blue-legged crabs. Adult exercise classes (aerobics and water exercise) are offered weekdays during the summer. Nature lovers can participate in numerous expeditions into wilderness areas and river tours for a close look at the low-country wildlife and vegetation.

If shopping entices you, the Straw Market at West Beach Village and the Town Center at East Beach Village have stores offering clothing, books, stationery, games, toys, jewelry, and gifts. And nearby Charleston (only 21 miles away) can charm you with historic tours and antiques shopping. With all it places at your disposal, Kiawah may tempt you back for many return visits. ≈≈≈

Palmetto Dunes Resort

P.O. Box 5606
Hilton Head Island, South Carolina 29938
(843) 845–6130, (800) 845–6130
Web site: www.palmettodunesresort.com

Hilton Head Island, the second-largest barrier island on the East Coast, lies at the southern tip of South Carolina, in a semitropical setting. Trees, birds, and wildlife abound, and winters are generally mild. First settled in the mid-1500s, it is steeped in history and renowned now as a resort destination.

Hilton Head is also famous for fine golfing. Palmetto Dunes offers some of the finest golfing in the country (backed by names like Robert Trent Jones and George Fazio) along with an array of other sports and activities. Whether your interests lead you to poolside sunning, a rigorous game of tennis, leisurely strolls on the beach, boating, or fine dining, you'll enjoy the lively variety and relaxed setting, which are designed to please all members of your family.

Palmetto Dunes encompasses 2,000 acres of Hilton Head Island with 3 miles of white sandy beaches on the Atlantic Ocean. Give in to the warm sunshine and gentle sound of the waves and you'll soon forget your regular workday routine. Broad Creek is west of Palmetto Dunes, and 10 miles of man-made lagoons weave through the property; water sports abound. From April through October daytime temperatures are in the seventies and eighties; through the rest of the year, you'll need only sweaters and jackets. Winter and early spring are known as "value season," spring and fall are for golf, and summer is for everything.

Accommodations: Five hundred one- to four-bedroom villas are located on the ocean, along the fairways, overlooking peaceful lagoons, and at Shelter Cove on Broad Creek. With tasteful decor, fully equipped kitchen, and private balcony, patio, or deck, you're surrounded by comfort and convenience. In the low season (November through March), daily villa rates are $106–$331; during the fall (September and October), $126–$361; and in the high season (April through August), $126–$451; size and location determine the rental fee. A minimum stay of two nights is required; the rates drop for four nights or more. A wide variety of packages is offered, so be sure to check. Maid service and cribs are also available, for an extra charge. In addition to the villas, some private homes can be rented.

Dining: Cooking in your villa is quite convenient and economical, but the many restaurants at Palmetto Dunes will no doubt lure you for delightful meals. Sample the breakfast buffet at The Cafe (in the Hyatt) or the Palmetto Cafe (in the

Photo courtesy of Palmetto Dunes Resort

Hilton). Golfers on the go can get breakfast and sandwiches at the grill found at each of the three pro shops on the golf courses; Scott's is casual dining at the harbor for lunch or dinner, with popular croissant sandwiches. Patti Arbuckle's Restaurant and Bar has great food, live entertainment, and the island's largest selection of appetizers. Sit on the patio and watch a spectacular sunset on the marsh. Alexander's, with excellent seafood in a beautiful setting overlooking the lagoon and canals, is open for dinner only.

At Shelter Cove there are four restaurants: Little Venice (lunch and dinner) for Northern Italian dishes; Harbourmaster's (dinner), which combines great seafood and beautiful views of the harbor; Kingfisher, for informal seafood dinners; and San Miguel's, for a taste of Mexico. P.J.'s Incredible Edibles offers New York deli–style foods of gourmet quality. Eat in, take out, or have it delivered. And this is only at Palmetto Dunes. On Hilton Head Island itself, more than 200 restaurants vie for your gastronomic attention—indeed, deciding on a restaurant could become the evening's main activity! For nighttime entertainment you might try Club Indigo or Scarlett's.

Children's World: There's a playground at the Hilton where children can burn off energy; additional ones are being planned as more and more families vacation here. Palmetto Dunes Activities Center includes children in many activities, both free and with a small charge, with and without parents. Water balloon contests, sandcastles, canoeing, crabbing, and arts and crafts are scheduled throughout the day. From June through August, however, the real fun for ages four to twelve is at Vacation Station at the Hilton, which is open Monday through Friday from 9:00 A.M. to 3:30 P.M. and on weekends during the winter. Full days ($25 guest/$35 nonguest) or half days ($20 guest/$25 nonguest) provide children with a wealth of activities: swimming, crabbing, fishing, beach games, face painting, and dolphin watching, just to mention a few. Kids are enthusiastic about their adventures and new friends, and their stories will no doubt amuse you at day's end. From 6:30 to 11:00 P.M. on weekends, pizza, movies, games, and stories occupy their time while parents enjoy an evening out.

Awesome Adventures is a sports camp for nine- to sixteen-year-olds and provides an awesome amount of fun. Owner Jim Slagle is an experienced and highly motivated leader of youth sports and a parent himself. The program accommodates all skill levels and combines island history and ecology, learning a new sport (or perfecting an old one), and plain old outdoor, active fun. Activities featured include mountain biking, scuba diving, sailing, canoeing, sailboarding, sea kayaking, horseback riding, and much, much more. The $85 per day fee includes lunch, all extras, equipment, and instruction.

While there's nothing structured for teenagers, there are plenty of activities that they like; beach games and sports provide opportunities to meet other teens and socialize or maybe take a walk to Harbor Town.

For younger children and for evenings when you want a grown-up dinner, you may request a copy of a list of local baby-sitters. There are professional child-care centers on the island; the resort staff will be happy to share this information with you.

Recreation: Golfing at Palmetto Dunes is like a dream come true for most players. There are three eighteen-hole golf courses, one designed by Robert Trent Jones, one by George Fazio, and the newest by Arthur Hills. Filled with challenge, finesse, and beauty, the courses range over gently rolling grounds and often skirt lagoons; the views of the Atlantic are a real bonus. Two other championship courses are in Palmetto Hall Plantation, about 4 miles north of the resort. To hone your skills, sign up for some instructional classes or practice on the driving ranges and putting greens. The pro shops can meet all your needs in equipment, fashions, and accessories.

The Palmetto Dunes Tennis Center will snare the tennis buffs in your party. The nineteen clay courts and two hard-surface courts (six of which are lighted for evening play) provide more than sufficient opportunity to test your game. You may want to try one of the four Supergrasse courts; the play is quick and challenging on a combination of artificial grass and sand. Serious players join clinics or lessons, and less active enthusiasts enjoy weekly exhibition matches by the pros. For appropriate apparel and equipment, you'll find the pro shops can accommodate you. Villa guests enjoy free tennis.

There are twenty-seven swimming pools at Palmetto Dunes—yes, twenty-seven. The possibility of a quick swim always seems just steps away, as all the pools are nestled among the clusters of villas. Swimmers also enjoy a refreshing dip in the ocean after sunbathing or collecting seashells on the beach.

Bicycling (rentals available) is a fun and relaxing way to explore the beautiful grounds of the resort; the tree-lined paths are often used by joggers too. In-line skating is a popular mode of travel as well. Rental canoes, paddleboats, catamarans, and sailboats are on hand when you want to spend an afternoon on the water, but if you'd rather leave the work to someone else's hand, sign up for a narrated tour of Broad Creek or a dinner cruise in the moonlight. Sailing and fishing charters can be arranged. Palmetto Dunes is also home to the largest sailboarding school on the East Coast.

For those in your family (like teenage girls) who consider shopping as recreation, the Low Country Factory Outlet Village just at the gateway to Hilton Head Island offers good stores and better prices.

Shelter Cove is a fifteen-and-a-half-acre deep-water harbor and a Mediterranean-style seaside village. Besides restaurants and villas, Shelter Cove has a collection of shops and boutiques, where you'll find interesting gifts to take home.

Awesome Expeditions offers two-hour guided salt marsh tours by kayak for $30, where you'll encounter local wildlife, and perhaps even a dolphin. And Captain Jim on the "Crabber J" gives the kids a fun experience in crabbing—and good lessons in ecology as the crabs are returned to the water unharmed after some games. ≈≈≈

Seabrook Island Resort

1002 Landfall Way
Seabrook Island, South Carolina 29455
(843) 768–1000, (800) 845–2475
E-mail: resort@charleston.net
Web site: www.seabrookresort.com

Sunshine and sandy beaches; lazy strolls under moss-draped oaks, palmettos waving in the breeze; enough fresh crabs, shrimp, and oysters to make your mouth water; golf, tennis, horseback riding, marina, fitness center, and water sports—is this a little bit of paradise? Visitors to Seabrook believe so. All this is only about thirty minutes from beautiful historic Charleston; it almost

Photo courtesy of Seabrook Island Resort

seems like you can have your cake and eat it too. A vacation at Seabrook is not exclusively a golfing trip or just an opportunity to develop a spectacular tan. You can go crabbing, ride horses, or join an exercise class in the morning, then discover the history and charm of Charleston in the afternoon. Take a house tour, visit nearby plantations, or go shopping, then return to the resort for an evening of dining and entertainment. Activities and events for every member of the family support Seabrook's "something for everyone" philosophy. The resort is open year-round.

Accommodations: The one- to three-bedroom villas—all with fully equipped kitchens, many with sundecks or balconies—are distributed throughout the 2,200 acres of Seabrook Island property. Some are oceanside, with expansive views of the Atlantic and close to the Beach Club, some line the scenic fairways of the golf courses, and some overlook the racquet club, marshlands, and tidal creeks. Rates depend on size, location, and time of year. During low season, from November through early March, villa rates are $100–$215; early March to mid-August is high season, at $150–$500; and mid-August to early November, $130–$370. Rates are for villa accommodations only; most recreational activities have separate charges. Weekly rates (for five to seven nights) provide a savings, as do tennis, golf, equestrian, or getaway packages. A family recreation package during June, July, and August is a good value, as it gives 20 percent discounts on most things, including golf.

Dining: With three restaurants, you'll have no trouble finding the cuisine and atmosphere to satisfy your taste and whim. The Island House Restaurant is elegant and offers traditional Southern cuisine and tempting seafood specialties. Here you might choose a sweet-potato soufflé or prawns stuffed with crabmeat. Bohickets Restaurant is next door, with equally good food in a more casual atmosphere. For steak and seafood and an ocean view, head to the Seaview Restaurant, more informal than the Island House and more family oriented. At Cap'n Sam's you can pick up quick take-out orders (great for picnics or snacking by the pools or in your villa), or stop at the Village Market for groceries and a deli sandwich. A friendly atmosphere in which to sip a drink and discuss the day's events is provided at the poolside Pelicans Nest, Half Shell Lounge, and Bohickets Lounge. Island House and Bohickets are open year-round; the others are seasonal.

Children's World: From Memorial Day to Labor Day, kids and teens have their own Monday-to-Friday Kids Club recreation program. Children ages three to eleven meet from 9:00 A.M. to 4:00 P.M. in the Kids Club, where activities include golf and tennis clinics, pony rides, crabbing adventures, swimming, treasure hunts, nature hikes, puppet shows, storytelling, and arts and crafts. The cost is $31 for a full day, or $18 per half day. The full-day rate includes lunch.

Older children from twelve to nineteen are invited to the basketball and volleyball units by day and to the Recreation Pavilion every night from 8:00 to 11:00 P.M. This is their own time for video games, pool, Ping-Pong, Foosball, air hockey, and socializing. Special theme parties, teen casino night, and even teen cruises are planned. Game nights are also planned for the entire family at a small cost—Win, Lose, or Draw; Bingo; and Ice-Cream Socials.

The fun keeps on rolling at holiday times like Christmas and Easter. Added to the regular activities may be Christmas caroling and a visit from Santa or an Easter decorations crafts class and an Easter egg hunt. A day of adventures will give your child fond memories for years to come. With all of this, normal babysitters may seem a bit of a letdown, but they are available.

Recreation: Golfing's fine in the Carolinas, and Seabrook has two vastly different eighteen-hole courses. Crooked Oaks was designed by Robert Trent Jones; it struts past majestic oaks and dips along the sea marshes. Ocean Winds, designed by Willard Byrd, catches some of the tricky ocean breezes that make the play interesting. A fine teaching staff can help you smooth out the rough spots of your game, and the pro shop can fill in the gaps for clothing, equipment, and accessories.

Enjoy one of thirteen clay tennis courts at the Raquet Club. The Raquet Club offers a pro shop and a staff of pros who can do wonders for your backhand in individual or group lessons.

With 3½ miles of glorious ocean beach, you might suspect that water sports tempt many visitors here. There are sunbathing, swimming, ocean fishing, and shelling. Canter along the beach at the edge of the surf or take a leisurely ride through the forests—both are possible at Seabrook, one of the few resorts with an on-site Equestrian Center. The center offers trained instructors who can give you tips to improve your technique. Six swimming pools more than accommodate serious swimmers and sun lovers. With their palm trees, gardens, and lovely surroundings, they also charm serious loungers in for just a quick splash. Perhaps you don't want to sing for your supper, but if you want to *catch* your supper, try fishing (in the ocean or the creeks) or crabbing and shrimping in the tidal marshes. Bicycle along the island's 10 miles of roads—many rental bikes come equipped with baby seats—or join the current craze for in-line skating.

The Recreation Pavilion takes care of a lot of your needs (rental beach chairs, in-line skates, bikes, and fishing and crabbing equipment) and is the focus of the Family Fun Program—activities that all the family members can enjoy together, like nature walks, family games, cookouts, bingo, and water volleyball. You may even challenge your child to an evening of video games.

Within 1 mile of Seabrook's gate, enjoy the Bohicket Marina for chartered deep-sea fishing, creek fishing, and three family-style restaurants and shops. For the essentials and the fun of shopping, Seabrook has several stores: the Village Market for groceries, the Seabrook Shoppe for gifts, clothing, souvenirs, and sundries, and the golf and tennis shops for the latest fashions and equipment. ≋

The Tides

Irvington, Virginia 22480
(804) 438–5000, (800) 2–4–TIDES

In eastern Virginia, peninsulas of land reach out like fingers between the many rivers heading into the Chesapeake. It is a region steeped in history, from the early seventeenth-century settlements of Jamestown and Yorktown to the family homestead of Robert E. Lee. Its people have always had close ties to the water, originally for commerce and travel and today for recreation.

The northernmost of these peninsulas, bounded by the Potomac River and the Rappahannock River, is known as the Northern Neck. On its southern shore, on one of the Rappahannock's inlets, sits The Tides resort—two hotels, the Inn, and the Lodge. The hotels are surrounded by water, and yachts literally dock in the front yard. A sense of happiness and pride permeates the resort. The Tides is small and very much a family affair. It emphasizes uncrowded luxury and informal elegance in a leisurely atmosphere that supports its motto: "The place where nice people meet."

Accommodations: With 134 rooms at the inn, you might choose a room in the main building or a semisuite (some with balconies) in the Windsor House or the Lancaster House. Cribs are available, and room rates are per person, modified American plan. Inn rates range from $160, double occupancy (includes breakfast and dinner) in the main building to $915 for the Robert E. Lee Suite. Children under ten are free, while children ten to fifteen pay a $55 meal charge. A 10 percent surcharge is applied when staying only Friday and/or Saturday. The high season at The Tides is May to October; the Inn is closed from January to mid-March. Sixty rooms at the Lodge do not include meals in the rate of $125 daily.

Dining: Breakfast and dinner are served in the main dining room. Breakfast is from 7:30 to 10:00 A.M., with an "early bird" continental breakfast or a "sleepy-head" breakfast later in the morning. Lunch can be taken in the main dining room, at the poolside Commodore's, at Cap'n B's on the Golden Eagle Golf Course, and on many days aboard the yacht *Miss Ann*. Imagine your fun and pleasure as you cruise the coves and waterways while enjoying a gourmet meal. Cap'n B's is a popular spot even with nongolfers, as the 400 rolling acres with lovely lakes and unspoiled woodlands add an extra dimension of pleasure to your dining. Adjacent to the main dining room is the Chesapeake Club, where expansive views, music, and dancing can relax and entertain you. Dress is casual during the day, with coat required in public rooms during the evening.

Children's World: In addition to the beach and swimming pool, a grassy playground with slides, swings, climbing bars, and Chesapeake Bay Lighthouse attracts young guests. From Memorial Day to Labor Day, The Crab Net Kids, a complimentary youth program, is in session Monday through Sunday, from 10:00 A.M. to 4:00 P.M., with lunch ($10) at the pool and swimming twice a day. Crafts and games, scavenger hunts, sand sculpting, bicycling, boating, and crabbing keep youngsters from four to twelve years old busy. On Wednesday, Friday, and Saturday evenings from 6:00 to 9:00 P.M., children meet as a group for a "coketails and pizza party," followed by a movie. Baby-sitting is available at $7.50 an hour for one child; add $1.00 an hour for each additional child.

Recreation: With water on practically all sides of the inn, boating is a natural sport here. You can take off in a small craft like a sailboat, canoe, or paddleboat or check out the yacht program and cruise the creek, the river, and the bay. The weekly routine schedules varied yachts for luncheon cruises, cove cruises, and bayshore picnics. No additional fees are charged for use of the sailboats, paddleboats, and canoes, or for the yacht program. In fact, rates include almost all activities—tennis, nine-hole par three golf course, bicycles to explore scenic Irvington, evening music and dancing, the fitness and health facility, oyster roasts in season, and nightly parties.

The Tides Lodge, located just 200 yards across Carter's Creek, is connected to the inn by gondola service. The Lodge is used as another service and facility of The Tides. For example, the three tennis courts at the lodge, one of which is lighted, supplement the four at the inn. Three golf courses (forty-five holes) skirt the waterways and dip back into the trees. A nine-hole executive course is on the inn's property; the eighteen-hole Tartan Course is across the creek at the lodge; and the most challenging course with more hilly terrain is the championship Golden Eagle, 2½ miles from the inn.

Many of the ponds along the golf courses are well stocked for the fisherman who may also, in search of a saltwater catch, line up a trip with the dockmaster. A saltwater pool overlooks a small sandy beach, and Ping-Pong, pool table, video arcade, croquet, and shuffleboard are available in the activities cottage. For your evening entertainment enjoy dancing, movies, bingo, or a pleasant stroll.

Nearby sightseeing excursions lead to Stratford Hall Plantation (the birthplace of Robert E. Lee), Christ Church, and Epping Forest, where George Washington's mother lived. Colonial Williamsburg is just an hour and fifteen minutes away and makes a nice day excursion. ≈≈≈

Wild Dunes Resort

5757 Palm Boulevard
Isle of Palms, South Carolina 29451
(843) 886–6000, (800) 845–8880
E-mail: reservations@wilddunes.com
Web site: www.wilddunes.com

Have you ever seen a three-year-old scamper across a sandy beach to the ocean? A biker pedal down paths through the marshes? A fishing boat return to harbor after a successful day's mission? A sailboat catch the sun and the wind in one skillful motion? An ace serve zing across the net? Or a golf ball soar over the fairway and over grand oaks on its way to a perfectly manicured green? Wild Dunes can package all of these images into quite a family vacation for you.

Wild Dunes has garnered some of the best features of the Carolina coastal islands and wrapped them up into a fine year-round resort. It is recognized by *Better Homes and Gardens* as one of thirty "Favorite Family Resorts." This relaxed and gracious community occupies 1,600 acres of the northern part of the Isle of Palms, just thirty minutes from historic Charleston. Bounded by the Atlantic Ocean on the east and the Intracoastal Waterway on the west, Wild Dunes delights in mild temperatures, soft ocean breezes, and fresh salt air. Relax and rejuvenate your spirits here in South Carolina's low-country.

Accommodations: Wild Dunes offers AAA four-diamond accommodations with the new Boardwalk Inn. The ninety-three-room inn is located in the heart of the resort. These luxurious accommodations provide amenities of the finest full-service hotels and access to world-class recreational facilities. Until mid-June and after Labor Day, daily rates for the Boardwalk Inn are $139–$239. From mid-June until Labor Day, daily rates are $149–$239. Wintertime (November to mid-March) nightly rates are $109–$169. Rates are based on double occupancy. The one-, two-, and three-bedroom villas are grouped in two- to five-story buildings. Many are arranged along the beach, some border the tennis center, others look out on the fairways of the golf course, and still more enjoy the seclusion of the woods and marshland scenery. Inside decor ranges from dramatic, bold interiors to soft pastel furnishings that reflect nature's seaside colors; a fully equipped kitchen is standard in every unit. Cribs can be provided for infants and toddlers.

The high season at Wild Dunes is mid-March through mid-November. Spring and fall rates for a one-bedroom villa range from $165 to $212; three-bedroom villas range from $202 to $344. From mid-June to mid-August rentals are on a weekly basis only, ranging from $1,113 for a two-bedroom near the beach, to

$2,121 for a four-bedroom oceanfront. Wintertime nightly rates are $124–$179 for a one-bedroom and $173–$292 for a three-bedroom.

Private homes are also available. The location of a rental property will determine the price; an oceanfront location commands the highest rate. Included with all rentals are local phone calls, on-property transportation, and one hour of tennis court time per bedroom per day. Golf, Town and Country, and Winter Extended Stay packages are available.

Dining: It is not surprising that seafood is highlighted on the menus of Wild Dunes' restaurants; gumbo and she-crab soup are favorite low-country dishes. But beef eaters can find tasty, tender selections here too. With the opening of The Boardwalk Inn, Wild Dunes also gained a luxurious restaurant. The Grill, serving breakfast, lunch, and dinner, features a light interpretation of French bistro fare in an elegant atmosphere. Edgar's, located at the Links Clubhouse, features southern cuisine; a children's menu is available. The Grand Pavilion, open only in summer, has turn-of-the-century architecture, an old-fashioned boardwalk, Coney Island–style food, and an airy gazebo. If you have a hunger attack on either golf course, you're in luck. Hot dogs, sandwiches, and drinks are to be found at the Half-Way House, on the Links, and on the Harbor Courses year-round. The Dunes Deli & Pizzeria features light fare for breakfast and lunch, as well as grocery items. At least twelve restaurants offer a variety of dining on nearby Sullivan's Island and the Isle of Palms.

Children's World: Ranked number one by *Tennis* magazine for having the "Best Kids' Program," Wild Dunes knows just how to make your little ones' vacation special. Wild Dunes' summer program for kids runs from the end of May through Labor Day and is complimentary for guests. Toddler Time provides structured morning (9:00 A.M.–noon) and afternoon (1:00–4:00 P.M.) sessions with two full-time staff members. Parents are welcome to drop in, as kids enjoy tumbling, storytime, and arts and crafts. On Tuesday mornings they can have "Breakfast with Barney" (oh boy!) and make their own creations at the pancake and waffle bar. Baby-sitting is also available by the hour or day for a fee. Older children, from five to twelve years, are part of the Wild Adventure Club, held Monday through Friday from 9:00 A.M. to 4:00 P.M. Kids enjoy beach games, swimming, crabbing, scavenger hunts, putt-putt golf, and other "wild" adventures.

Li'l Dune Bug Club allows the kids (ages five to twelve) to leave the parents at home for a night out to play games, watch movies, and munch goodies. These sessions are held Monday through Saturday from 6:00 to 10:00 P.M., the cost is $12.00 for the first child (the second is only $8.00), and kids get a T-shirt to wear and keep. A special version of this program, Parents' Night Out, allows parents who dine at Edgar's Restaurant to leave their children ages two to twelve upon presentation of receipt. Space is limited, so reserve in advance.

Activities for teens include beach volleyball, psychedelic tie-dye, dances, pizza parties, and cookouts. There is generally a $7.00 to $10.00 fee for materials, food, and so on. Video movies and special pool games allow teens to socialize and "hang out."

Recreation: A day of golf can begin on one of the two eighteen-hole golf courses designed by Tom Fazio. The older course, the Wild Dunes Links, is on the resort's ocean side and provides interesting play, with its many water holes. Two holes edge by the sand dunes of the beach and are dramatically beautiful as well as challenging. The newer Harbor Course is across the island, surrounding the marina and harbor, and has its own fair share of demanding water holes. A practice range, professional instruction, and a pro shop can help you over the hurdles with improved style and equipment.

In addition to golf, Wild Dunes offers tennis facilities, which have been ranked in the "Top 10 Greatest U.S. Tennis Resorts" by *Tennis* magazine. With a total of seventeen Har-Tru courts, including seven lighted for night play, tennis players might not want to go home. Tennis instruction can take the form of private or group lessons, clinics, and camps for a week, a weekend, or an intensive one-day session. Along with its well-stocked pro shop, this tennis facility leaves you very few excuses for not improving your game.

The IOP Marina has 200 boat slips. Here you can dock your own vessel or rent a boat for fishing in the Gulf Stream. Join a charter if you need an experienced captain's guidance in snagging the big ones, or finish off a day with a cruise in Charleston's harbor. Besides taking deep-sea excursions, fishermen can cast their lines in the ocean's surf, the creek, and the lagoons.

Swimmers have pools at most of the villa complexes, the main pool at the Swim Center, two oceanfront pools on the Grand Pavilion, the pool at the Boardwalk Inn, and, of course, the beautiful Atlantic Ocean. Joggers and bikers share the nature trails, where pine, oak, and magnolia trees grow; the hard-packed sand beach is also suitable for running and biking. Along the 2-mile stretch of beach, you'll find sunbathers, strollers, and seashell collectors, and just offshore, sailors and sailboarders. At the beachfront picnic area, the kids' playground consists of natural-wood climbing equipment under the trees. For a close look at the egrets, herons, and pelicans of Wild Dunes, take the canoe trip through the creeks and marshes.

Many family events, such as a sailing class, bingo, and an afternoon ice-cream party, are planned each week. Be aware, however, that there are charges for most of the activities. And when you decide to take a break from the fun and recreation, don't forget how close Charleston is. In a day of sightseeing, you can enjoy a historic Charleston tour of antebellum houses, fine restaurants, and shopping for antiques or at more modern boutiques.

Nighttime comes alive at Wild Dunes. Featured entertainer Ronnie Johnson heats it up at Edgar's Bar five nights a week with his style mix of rock, country, and Jimmy Buffett. From mid-June to mid-August the resort features a Sunday welcome party, "Shaggin' at the Beach" on Tuesday and Friday, karaoke on Wednesday, and steel calypso music most afternoons. ≋

SOUTH

Alabama

Florida

Georgia

Amelia Island Plantation

P.O. Box 3000
Amelia Island, Florida 32035-3000
(904) 261–6161, (800) 874–6878
Web site: www.aipfl.com

Like many of its counterparts along the coasts of the Carolinas, Amelia Island Plantation is a well-planned and carefully executed development that combines resort living with an appreciation for natural beauty. Similarity to its sisters is no surprise, for this land was purchased in the late 1960s by Charles Fraser of Sea Pines in Hilton Head, one of the first resorts to blend nature's beauties with gracious amenities. In many ways Sea Pines set the standard for resort communities that followed.

Amelia Island Plantation, which opened in 1972, occupies 1,330 acres of the southernmost island in the Golden Isle chain along the Eastern Seaboard of the United States. Open year-round, it is just off the coast of northeast Florida, about a forty-five-minute drive from Jacksonville. Besides palmettos and oak trees, a 4-mile sandy beach, marshlands, and lagoons, this corner of paradise is blessed with mild temperatures year-round and balmy ocean breezes. Amelia Island Resort is a two-time winner of *Family Circle* magazine's "Best Family Beach Resort" award.

Accommodations: You can lodge in oceanfront hotel rooms—many with private decks or balconies—or in a villa overlooking the ocean or a lagoon, bordering the tennis complex or one of the fairways of the golf course. These one- to four-bedroom apartments have complete kitchens; many have private patios, balconies, or screened porches. Architecturally, the multilevel accommodation buildings arranged throughout the property are of various contemporary styles, with stucco or natural-wood facades.

Rates depend on the size and location of the unit and on the number of people occupying it. For four people in a two-bedroom ocean-view villa, rates vary between $273 in winter, $459 in spring, and $408 in summer and fall. The off-ocean price range is $219 (winter), $358 (spring), and $309 (summer/fall). Cribs are provided for little ones at $10 per night or $40 per week (four to seven days). Weekly rates are available, and package plans such as six-day/five-night family vacations are offered. All lodgings are connected to the recreational and dining facilities via a complimentary shuttle bus.

Dining: When cooking in your villa seems just too strenuous after a day of sunbathing, gather the family at the Verandah in Racquet Park. Located in a building tucked among old oak trees, the dining room has large windows overlooking

Photo courtesy of Amelia Island Plantation

the tennis courts. Sample such fresh seafood from the Atlantic as oysters, flounder, shrimp, and crab in the family-style atmosphere.

More elegant dining is available in the Amelia Inn. With expansive views of the ocean, this restaurant features escargots, quail, and roast duck, and desserts like Southern pecan pie. In addition to dinner, breakfast and a sumptuous brunch on Sundays are offered.

The Coop is a come-as-you-are breakfast and lunch spot where the menu includes salads and sandwiches, hamburgers and hot dogs. Also appropriate for breakfast and lunch is the Golf Shop Bar and Restaurant at Amelia Links, or the Longpoint Clubhouse. At the Beach Club Seaside Sports Bar, burgers, wings, and ribs are served; TVs and electronic games add action to a meal. Seaside Sweets, at poolside (seasonally), will satisfy your sweet tooth, while the Dunes Club Bar serves light lunches and tropical drinks poolside between Sea and Turtle Dunes.

Children's World: Kids cAMpELIA children's program entertains kids year-round. Activities include swimming, crabbing, and arts and crafts. Take nature walks and enjoy many activities with the resident naturalist. As additional activities are too numerous to mention, contact the resort directly for age, cost, and time specifications.

At Aury Island, a tree house and a dock for fishing and crabbing are reserved just for the twelve-and-under set. At the Beach Club little ones have their own wading pool and a playground filled with wooden climbing equipment. To find a baby-sitter, you can pick up a list of names and numbers at the main registration desk.

Recreation: The Amelia Links, twenty-seven holes of golf designed by Pete Dye, offer variety in play, as each of the nines has its own personality. One nine-hole course weaves through groves of oak and palmetto trees, another course challenges with play through the marshlands, and the third skirts the ocean, with three holes along the sand dunes and sea oats of the beach. Another nine holes were added in 1998, bringing the total of Amelia Island Plantation's golf holes to fifty-four. The eighteen-hole Long Point Golf Course was designed by Tom Fazio. Lessons can be arranged through the pro shop, where you will also find equipment and fashions.

Racquet Park is well situated among beautiful live oaks, a lovely setting for twenty-one courts. Some are lighted for evening play. The site of the Bausch and Lomb Women's International Tennis Association Championships, this tennis complex offers adult and junior clinics, ball machines for solo practice, and a pro shop for equipment and apparel.

Also part of Racquet Park is the Health and Fitness Center. Complete with racquetball, indoor heated lap pool, exercise equipment, steam room, sauna and whirlpool facilities, aerobics classes, and the soothing techniques of a masseuse, it fills the bill for a good workout or relaxing rejuvenation.

Swimmers can choose the ocean or pools for their hours of fun in the sun. In addition to the Olympic-size pool at the Beach Club, each of the groups of villas (except the Lagoon Villas) has a swimming pool—twenty-one pools in all.

Along the 4-mile beach, you can collect shells, sunbathe, play volleyball, ride horseback (the Seashore Stables are just 2 miles away), and fish in the surf for whiting, sea trout, and bluefish. Surrounding the island in bays and sounds and the Gulf Stream are tarpon, marlin, swordfish, flounder, trout, redfish, red snapper, and king mackerel. The waters in this area give up some beautiful prizes, and for advice, insider's hints, tackle, and information on charters, head to the Amelia Angler.

Bicycle along 7 miles of trails (rental bikes with baby seats and children's bikes are available), take a paddleboat out to explore the lagoons (maybe you'll spy an alligator or a white heron), jog along the wooded paths and down the beach, or maybe even challenge the kids to a half hour of video games at the Beach Club Game Room.

For an outing of a different sort, you may browse through the shops of Amelia Village or discover the Victorian district of Fernandina Beach at the north end of the island. The Amelia monthly calendar is worth checking upon your arrival; here you'll learn of classes, movies, hayrides, and cookouts. ≋

Bluewater Bay Resort

1950 Bluewater Boulevard
Niceville, Florida 32578
(904) 897–3613, (800) 874–2128
Web site: www.bwbresort.com

I magine the serenity of a safe harbor, a lush wooded landscape bordering clear blue waters, a sunset over the bay, and a blue glow that settles over still waters and docked boats at dusk. You feel light-years away from the office, staff meetings, and business lunches. In northwest Florida, Bluewater Bay is nestled on the northern shore of Choctawhatchee Bay and can certainly provide that get-away-from-it-all feeling. You'll relax in the peaceful surroundings of Bluewater Bay, but you'll never be bored. The resort is open year-round.

Accommodations: The hotel accommodations overlook the marina at Ward's Cove and include one- and two-bedroom suites as well as the more standard single and double rooms. At the other end of the spectrum are the Villas of St. Andrews, freestanding homes with two and three bedrooms, tucked in among oak and magnolia trees. The name itself alludes to the fine old golf course in Scotland, so it's no surprise that from these homesites you have lovely views of the golf course.

In between these extremes, you may choose a Mediterranean-style town house on the water or surrounded by gardens, a bayside villa featuring one- and two-bedroom apartments, one of the golf villas bordering the first and second fairways, or a two- to three-bedroom patio home near the swim and tennis center.

Cribs are available for a nominal charge, and the rooms have refrigerators for your toddler's milk and juice as well as your own refreshments. Rates range from $65 to $165 a night during the low season (November through February) and from $85 to $225 a night in the high season. Weekly and monthly rates are also available.

Dining: The Clubhouse Restaurant serves breakfast, lunch, and dinner. Seafood from the local waters is always a good choice from the varied menu. Children have a special menu.

Children's World: From Memorial Day to Labor Day, children ages three to twelve don their Bluewater Day Camp T-shirts and join the summer youth program. In this program, which operates Monday through Friday, 9:00 A.M. to 4:00 P.M., kids find adventure and fun under the direction of trained counselors. Junior golf, sailing and tennis clinics, arts-and-crafts classes, swimming instruction, nature hikes, and treasure hunts are typical elements of the program. Six- to twelve-year-olds can enroll for a full day for $16, while the three- to five-year-olds participate in the mornings for $10 a session. Teens are rounded up three days a week for excursions to an amusement park, a canoe ride, a bowling party, or a miniature golf tournament.

There's an occasional kids' dinner and movie night. Individual baby-sitters, drawn from among the resort staff and local people, are available for younger children and in the evenings; the hotel staff will make the arrangements for you.

Recreation: Although the atmosphere is relaxing and laid-back, you'll never be wanting for something to do. The thirty-six-hole championship golf course shows the imprint of its designers, Tom Fazio and Jerry Pate. Respecting the natural setting, they've brought nature and the golfer together in a congenial blend. At the tennis center twelve of the nineteen courts are lighted for nighttime play. Investigate the tennis and golf pro shops for your equipment and fashion needs.

And if water sports are your true love, there are oh so many to entice you. Swim in one of four Olympic-size pools, or splash in the waters of the bay. The 120-slip marina provides full services for your days on the water. Bring your own boat, or rent a catamaran, sailboard, or powerboat. Line up a sport-fishing charter to the nearby Gulf of Mexico, leisurely fish in the bay, join a canoe trip down the Blackwater River, or take in a round of shuffleboard. Whether you're active or relaxed, Bluewater Bay accommodates everyone from the young to the young at heart. ≈≈≈

The Breakers

One South County Road
Palm Beach, Florida 33480
(561) 655–6611, (888) BREAKERS
Web site: www.thebreakers.com

In the 1880s Henry Flagler, a railroad magnate and cofounder of Standard Oil, was advised to spend time in Florida for his health. From this happenstance evolved a world-class luxury resort. Flagler discovered the warm climate of the Atlantic Coast, was captivated by the scenery, expanded railroad lines down the Eastern seaboard, and set into motion the development of Palm Beach as a winter playground of the wealthy.

Photo courtesy of The Breakers

The original Palm Beach Inn, built in 1896, was destroyed by fire in 1903. A second hotel, The Breakers, also succumbed to fire in 1925. Efforts to rebuild were begun immediately, and the new facility was opened at the end of 1926. The project was inspired by buildings of the Italian Renaissance; the era's artistic influence is evident in the loggias, courtyards, and hand-painted vaulted ceilings that adorn The Breakers. Open year-round, the hotel has completed a $100 million renovation and maintains its status as a Mobil five-star and AAA five-diamond resort. The grand beauty of this sparkling structure is perhaps met only by its natural setting on 140 acres of lush semitropical landscape bordering the blue-green waters of the Atlantic Ocean.

Accommodations: The 572 well-appointed and recently renovated guest rooms, including 47 suites, have views of the ocean, the well-tended formal gardens, or the golf course. During the summer (low season), from June 1 to September 16, rates for a single/double room are $180–$395 per day; there is no charge for children under seventeen sharing a room with parents. Cribs and rollaways are provided at no charge. Rates are about 20 percent higher during the fall and spring; during the high season, from January to the end of April, rates range from $360 to $675 per day. Extraordinary holiday and vacation packages are also available.

For those who enjoy more privacy, there is the Flagler Club, The Breakers' concierge level located on the top two floors, with restricted access and additional guest services and amenities. Rates here are $295–$540 (varies by season).

Dining: Dining at The Breakers can be as formal or as casual as one desires. An array of hot and cold breakfast items, as well as an a la carte menu, is available in the Circle Dining Room. Lunch is available at The Reef Bar, Palm Beach's only bar on the beach, offering refreshing libations and light snacks, and at the new Beach Club Restaurant, the heart of The Breakers' new spa, featuring classic luncheon fare and selections of spa cuisine. Lunch and dinner are served in The Seafood Bar, an upscale oceanfront raw bar reminiscent of the plantation homes of old Florida; Flagler's Steakhouse and Terrace Grill, featuring oversize steaks and chops; and Henry's Place, a cozy English pub specializing in traditional English dishes. For dinner, The Pasta House offers traditional Italian fare in a warm, friendly atmosphere. At The Florentine, with its Continental and Mediterranean influences, jackets are required and reservations are recommended. To say The Florentine's wine list is exceptional is an understatement; it has earned *Wine Spectator's* "Grand Award" for the past seventeen years. More than 500 vintages are represented in the new display wine cellar.

At The Breakers restaurants, the under-elevens have their own menus. Children under three eat free, and everyone gets a special coloring book.

Children's World: With its broad spectrum of amenities, creative recreational programs and activities, and pervasive family-friendly mindset, The Breakers was deemed worthy of the "Premier Property Award" by the Resort and Commercial Recreation Association (RCRA). The resort has formed a Kids' Advisory Board, composed of eight young people, ages five to twelve, who meet quarterly to advise the resort on children's wants and needs. In response to this advice, there is a year-round children's program called Coconut Crew Camp.

Children ages three through twelve enjoy Coconut Crew Camp's year-round supervised activities, including active sports, contests, pool and beach games, arts and crafts, indoor games, seashell hunts, nature walks, lawn games, swimming, croquet, and more. Offered from 9:00 A.M. to 12:30 P.M. ($30 per child, lunch included); or 12:30 to 3:00 P.M. ($20 per child).

Coconut Crew Summer Camp for children ages six through twelve offers an exciting list of events. Summer Camp takes place June through August, 9:00 A.M. to 3:00 P.M. Monday through Friday. The camp focuses on a new theme each week, incorporating field trips, afternoon swimming, professional instruction in golf and tennis, and more. The cost of the camp is $45 per day for hotel guests and includes lunch (some field trips may require an additional charge).

The agenda for all programs is relaxed and flexible, so your child has the freedom to choose only specific events or to stay with the group for longer periods. Baby-sitting is available, even on a twenty-four-hour basis.

Recreation: Allow yourself to be pampered; a staff of 1,500 people is dedicated to making a stay here quite memorable. Stroll through the beautiful gardens or the half mile of private beach, linger under the palm trees, relax on a patio surrounding a fountain, or indulge at the new Oceanfront Spa and Beach Club.

There are two eighteen-hole golf courses: the Ocean Course, Florida's oldest eighteen-hole golf course, and the newer Breakers West Course, in West Palm Beach. With water hazards and stately coconut palms at many holes, play can be challenging as well as incredibly scenic. Complimentary golf clinics with the Todd Anderson instructional staff are offered at The Breakers, as well as one-, two-, and three-day programs in the Todd Anderson Gold academy (fees vary). The Golf Club houses two restaurants and a pro shop; a resident pro is available to assist you in your game.

With fourteen Har-Tru tennis courts, five of them lighted, you shouldn't have to wait to play. A pro shop and private lessons or clinics can provide inspiration to improve your game. A junior tennis program begins with peewees, ages three to seven, and continues on through junior academy/tournament training.

The new Beach Club offers four pools, including a lap pool and children's pool, a Jacuzzi, and ten new cabanas. The Spa at The Breakers features seventeen private treatment rooms, steam and sauna rooms, men's and ladies' lounges, a beauty salon, and an ocean-view fitness center.

Sunbathe beside the majestic Atlantic, or sip a tall, cool cocktail on the patio or at the Reef Bar. Bicycle or jog on the paths through the gardens, join a deep-sea fishing or fly-fishing excursion for an offshore adventure, go snorkeling, or sign up for scuba instruction. For periods when you are not feeling so energetic, play a game of shuffleboard, croquet, horseshoes, bocci ball, bridge, or backgammon. Other events throughout the week include exercise classes such as water aerobics, yoga, and tai chi, family movies, shopping at any of the resort's nine boutiques, and historical tours. Add lectures, crafts, garden tours, concerts, shopping on the famous Worth Avenue, and cooking demonstrations and you'll have to stretch your vacation to fit it all in. ≋

Callaway Gardens

Pine Mountain, Georgia 31822
(404) 663–2281, (800) 282–8181
E-mail: info@callawaygardens.com
Web site: www.callawaygardens.com

Cason Callaway was a textile industrialist in Georgia. In the 1930s he became so enamored of the countryside around Pine Mountain that his life began to change. He turned from industry first to farming and then to gardening. He learned that the plumleaf azalea was peculiar to this area of Georgia, and he was determined to nurture it and share its beauty with others. He established the Ida Cason Callaway Foundation, in honor of his mother, and opened his gardens to the public in 1952. While the gardens remain the focal point of the setting, the resort has grown to include gracious lodging, pleasant restaurants, and sports activities ranging from golf and tennis to swimming and fishing. This naturally wooded and carefully cultivated land—14,000 acres of lakes, woodlands, and gardens—is located 70 miles south of Atlanta, in the Appalachian Mountain foothills of west Georgia.

Accommodations: The Callaway Gardens Inn, near the entrance to the gardens, is a 350-room hotel, which also houses restaurants, lounges, and the Fitness Center. From mid-March through December a double room starts at $110 a night. During the winter months rates start at $96; suites are $200–$300 a night.

Next door to the inn is the Tennis and Racquetball Club; next to that are the Mountain Creek Villas: one- to four-bedroom units with fireplace, screened porch or patio, and fully equipped kitchen. Nightly rates for a two-bedroom villa are $280–$325, depending on the season. The weekly rate during the summer is approximately $2,500.

Many families opt for one of the Country Cottages, which are arranged in small clusters amid tall trees near Robin Lake. All have well-equipped kitchens; some have fireplace, screened porch, deck, or outdoor grill. Daily rates for a two-bedroom cottage range from $252 to $295. During the summer the weekly rate for a two-bedroom cottage is $2,078. The weekly rate includes admissions to the gardens and to the beach at Robin Lake and participation in the summer recreation program for families. Modified and full American meal plans are offered, and golf and tennis packages are featured. Cribs are provided at no charge; rollaway beds are charged at a $15 daily rate in the inn only.

Dining: In the inn are the Plantation Room, known for its buffets—particularly the Friday-night seafood buffet—and the Georgia Room, featuring fine South-

Photo courtesy of Callaway Gardens

ern cuisine enhanced by candlelight and flowers. While the former is open for breakfast, lunch, and dinner, the latter serves dinner only (dress code).

With red-checked tablecloths supporting the atmosphere that its name connotes, the Country Kitchen, located in the Country Store, serves breakfast, lunch, and dinner in a friendly, family-style setting. It's famous for its muscadine bread and country bacon. The Gardens Restaurant, where lunch and dinner are available, and the Veranda, for dinner only, are at the edge of Mountain Creek Lake; both are open seasonally. Sandwiches and snacks are available in the Champions Restaurant. The latest addition to Callaway dining is the Flower Mill Restaurant near the cottages.

The Vineyard Green Lounge is a great spot for an evening cocktail, with live entertainment nightly.

Children's World: For thirty-nine summers Florida State University's Flying High Circus has performed at Callaway Gardens. With the big top pitched at Robin Lake Beach, this area becomes the focus of the Summer Family Adventure Program, June through mid-August. If daily (except Wednesday) circus performances are not enough to charm youngsters, the performers also act as counselors, directing kids in games and sports and teaching them a few juggling tricks and circus acts too. In addition, kids go sailing, swimming, waterskiing, rollerskating, and biking. They take riverboat rides, attend golf and tennis instruction, and grow imaginative in crafts classes. Kids ages three to eighteen can participate. The Summer Discovery Program provides an informal look at the animals, plants, and ecology at Callaway Gardens. Family events, such as barbecues, square dances, and movies, are also planned.

These are one-week programs (Sunday to Sunday) with special introduction and orientation for which there is no charge when renting a cottage on a weekly basis. If, however, you cannot schedule a full week in a family cottage and are staying a couple of days at the inn, you can enroll your child on a daily basis, for $35 a day. Besides the program, there are children's playgrounds at the inn and at the cottage area.

Recreation: The gardens are a continuous source of beauty, pleasure, peace, and serenity. This is a place to enjoy, to reflect, and to learn. The colorful, changing displays of begonias, snapdragons, geraniums, zinnias, pansies, tulips, marigolds, chrysanthemums—the list seems endless—are presented in the outdoor garden of the Sibley Horticultural Center. Visitors who explore the walking trails are treated to mountain laurel, hydrangeas, narcissus, magnolias, dogwoods, crabapples, hollies, wildflowers, and 700 varieties of azaleas (the famous plumleaf blooms during the summer). At Mr. Cason's Vegetable Garden, you can wander through row after row of more than 400 different types of fruits and vegetables. Workshops on topics like flower arranging and bonsai techniques are available year-round. The John A. Sibley Horticultural Center is a five-acre, innovative greenhouse design that is an architectural as well as a horticultural feat. The Day Butterfly Center houses up to 1,000 butterflies (representing more than fifty species) in a lush tropical setting.

The newest addition to Callaway Gardens is the world's largest azalea garden. The Callaway Brothers Azalea Bowl features both hybrid and native azaleas in a forty-acre landscape.

Besides its magnificent gardens, the resort also offers more traditional diversions. Four golf courses (three eighteen-hole courses and one nine-hole course) unroll past forests and lakes. The names of the courses are descriptive of their surroundings—Mountain View (the most challenging), Gardens View, Lake View (the most picturesque), and Sky View. A driving range, two pro shops, and a year-round instructional program complete the golfing facilities.

The Pete Sampras in your party has ten lighted tennis courts from which to choose. Eight clay and two Plexipave courts are at the Tennis and Racquetball Club, which also houses two racquetball courts and the pro shop. The instructional program includes private or group lessons, or you can practice on your own with a ball machine.

Robin Lake is the center of lots of summer fun, from paddleboat rides and circus performances to swimming and sunbathing along the mile-long sandy beach. Besides the lake, overnight guests can enjoy the pools at the inn, at the Mountain Creek Villas, and at the cottage area.

On the shores of Mountain Creek Lake is a boathouse where you can rent a motorboat and fishing tackle—the lake is stocked with bass and bream—or a Sunfish sailboat, paddleboat, or canoe. You can discover the lakes from their shores as you bicycle along the trails and paths.

You may want to spend an afternoon at an organ concert (daily during the summer) in the chapel on Falls Creek Lake. For indoor exercise the Fitness Center offers equipment for unwinding. For an afternoon of history, you can take the 15-mile trip to Warm Springs and Franklin Roosevelt's Little White House. ≈≈≈

Cheeca Lodge
Islamorada, Florida 33036
(305) 664–4651, (800) 327–2888
E-mail: cheecalodge@aol.com
Web site: www.cheeca.com

S tretching more than 150 miles south from Miami, the Florida Keys enjoy a subtropical climate and a friendly, laid-back philosophy. Just getting there is an adventure. As you travel along U.S. Highway 1, you get the feeling that you're the string connecting a necklace of islands. And sometimes there are no islands—just a narrow ribbon of concrete in the middle of a very wide ocean—or two! The Atlantic Ocean and the Gulf of Mexico both border this strip of islands. Islamorada is just 75 miles from Miami, but really it is another world.

Accommodations: Cheeca Lodge is a twenty-seven-acre luxury oceanfront resort (AAA four diamond), with more than 1,000 feet of palm-lined beach, not often found in the Keys. A variety of accommodations—154 villa rooms or suites and forty-nine rooms in the main lodge—are spread throughout the landscaped grounds. Generous in size, all guest rooms are air-conditioned and also have ceiling fans, and most have a private balcony. Sixty-four villa suites feature kitchen, screened-in porch, living room, and one or two bedrooms. Mid-December to April rates are the highest, when standard rooms range from $295 to $650 and one-bedroom suites are $400 to $1,500. In summer the rates drop to $100–$250 for rooms, $315–$1,100 for one-bedroom suites. Children under sixteen stay free in their parents' room. Specials and packages are offered year-round.

Dining: Savor fine dinners at The Atlantic's Edge, a plantation-style restaurant with lovely panoramic views of the ocean. Dine inside or outside next to the free-form swimming pool at the Ocean Terrace Grill, sampling the local spe-

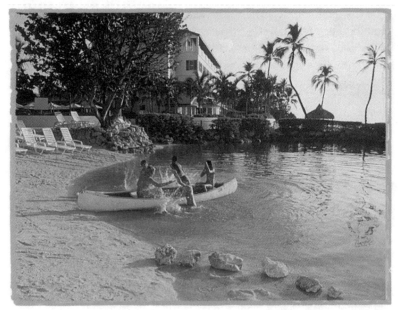

Photo courtesy of Cheeca Lodge

cialty, stone-crab claws, or soups and sandwiches; here there is a special children's menu. Another indoor/outdoor dining option is the Light Tackle Lounge, great for snacks, cocktails, and piano entertainment in the evenings.

Children's World: Award-winning Camp Cheeca has a purpose: learning about the environment while having fun. Children ages six to twelve are busy from 9:00 A.M. to 4:00 P.M., Tuesday through Saturday in the summer, weekends year-round, and for special holiday weeks. There is a morning session on Sunday. A full day costs $26; a half day is $15. Learning to snorkel and fish, doing nature art or sand sculpture, feeding the fish or exploring the beach—everything has an ecological approach that kids really respond to. There's a good mix of activities, with field trips, scavenger hunts, arts and crafts, and Saturday Sundae (everyone's favorite). "Kids Night Out," Saturday from 7:00 to 9:00 P.M., costs $6.00, which includes entertainment, snacks, and games. When three children or fewer are present, camp will be open only for the morning session. Families with three or more children receive a reduced rate of $24 full day, $14 half day. Box lunches are available for $5.75. Baby-sitting is $10 an hour, with a three-hour minimum.

Recreation: You can be on the go from dawn to dusk, or make the most strenuous activity of the day deciding between a hammock, chaise longue, or tiki hut on the beach. Consider renting a paddleboat, catamaran, kayak, or beach cruiser bicycle, or try parasailing. Maybe just a pool float is more your speed. The three pools are all very different; a free-form swimming pool, a lap pool, and a saltwater lagoon keep boredom at bay. Play tennis on one of the six courts, or try the executive golf course. Take a self-guided walk along Cheeca's Nature Trail, or watch the sunrise from the pier. Or maybe the sunset.

It's a fisherman's paradise here, with more than 600 species of marine life and a calendar of what's running each month that fills a page. No wonder Islamorada is known as the sportfishing capital of the world. A nice touch is that the chef will, on request, prepare your hard-won catch. Cheeca has its own Dive Center, with equipment and instruction. The *Cheeca View* doubles as a dive boat twice a day, then does sunset and moonlight cruises. The biggest problem is trying to fit all the options in.

Theater of the Sea, the world's second-oldest marine park, is a natural lagoon where humans and marine animals interact (kids love getting kissed by a sea lion!). They've gone beyond a glass-bottom boat—here they have a bottomless boat. Hmm, neat trick. If you want to range farther afield, the concierge can help arrange a swim with the dolphins, or a trip to either Key West, the southernmost U.S. city, or Pennekamp State Park, the first underwater state park. Combine a visit to Miccosukee Indian Reservation with an airboat ride through the Everglades. ≋

The Cloister

Sea Island, Georgia 31561
(912) 638–3611, (800) SEA–ISLAND
Web site: www.seaisland.com

C harming, gracious, and so civilized—The Cloister brings all this to mind. Family holidays at this fine old resort are fun-filled, but the elegance of a bygone era prevails. The Cloister boasts that here children learn manners as well as golf, tennis, and swimming. The dress-for-dinner standard and the children's weekly dances (seasonally) reinforce this philosophy.

Sea Island's rich history dates back to the antebellum days of the Old South, when a large cotton plantation was active on what is now the Sea Island Golf Club. The ruins of a slave hospital standing near the Clubhouse recall this period. Early in this century the property was acquired by Howard Coffin, an automobile engineer who had visions of creating a resort on this lovely 900-acre island, with its temperate climate and ocean breezes. His dreams were realized in the construction of The Cloister. Designed by Addison Mizner, who is known

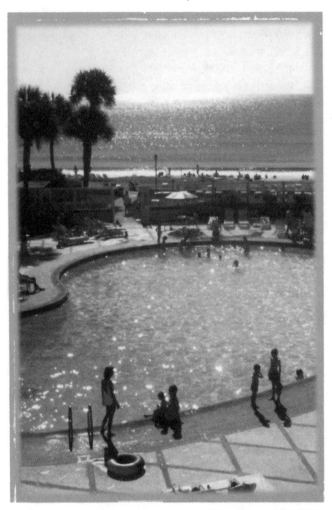

Photo courtesy of The Cloister

primarily for his work in Palm Beach, this "friendly little hotel" (as Coffin described it) opened its doors in October 1928. It successfully weathered the Depression and over the years has warmly greeted guests from the rich and famous to the mere plebeian of good taste. Ivy-covered walls, gently swaying palm trees, impeccable gardens, and wide verandas set the stage for a memorable vacation. The resort is open year-round.

Accommodations: Accommodations are provided in the main building (the original hotel) set back a couple of hundred yards from the beach, in the River House fronting on the Black Banks River, and in guest and beach houses. The original structure has a Mediterranean style with red-tiled roofs and courtyards. The architecture of the newer buildings and the gardens complement this style and maintain the flavor of a gracious island retreat. Rooms range from standard, tastefully decorated bedrooms and baths to superior rooms and oceanfront suites.

Based on a full American plan, daily rates per person (double occupancy) are $171–$433, depending on the type of room, from mid-March through November and at Christmastime. From December through February (with the exception of Christmastime), rates are slightly lower. In addition to three full meals a day, these rates include most recreational activities except golf, tennis, spa, shooting school, and horseback riding.

Children sharing a room with their parents are charged for meals only, $18–$72 a day, determined by the age of the child. For most of July and all of August, they're not even charged for meals. In addition, the eighteen-and-under group is exempt from golf and tennis fees (playing times may be restricted) when sharing a room with parents. Cribs are provided at no charge.

Dining: Dining is elegant as well as very appetizing and sumptuous. In the dining rooms of The Cloister (including the Patio, the Georgian, and the South Georgian), gentlemen wear coats and ties for evening dinners. On Wednesday and Saturday evenings, ladies frequently choose to wear cocktail dresses, while men wear dinner jackets. More casual attire is appropriate at the Beach Club (open for breakfast, lunch, and seafood dinner buffets) and at the golf clubhouses for luncheon and dinner.

American and continental cuisines are featured. Given the oceanside location of the resort, it's no surprise that fresh seafood specialties are prominent on the menus. Whether you choose the gracious setting of the dining rooms, with fresh flowers on the tables and lovely views of the gardens, or the casual atmosphere of the clubhouses, you'll find that the careful attention to preparation makes meals a visual delight as well as a culinary treat.

For light refreshments during spring and summer, there's a snack bar near the swimming pools at the Beach Club, and high tea is served afternoons during cooler months in the Spanish Lounge. Special evenings are frequently scheduled, such as a supper at Rainbow Island.

Children's World: The junior staff will charm your child with active days. During the summer, from June through Labor Day, and during Thanksgiving and Christmas holidays, energetic, friendly counselors provide daily supervised play for youngsters ages three (no pull-ups or diapers, please) through twelve, from 9:30 A.M. to 3:00 P.M. (9:00 A.M.–1:00 P.M. for the three- and four-year-olds) at no charge. Activities include swimming, fishing, crabbing, art sessions, games, and nature walks, just to mention a few.

During the summer months children ages four through eleven can even join their counselors for dinner from 6:00 to 9:00 P.M. (Sundays and Family Beach Supper nights excluded), allowing parents dinners at leisure. For younger children baby-sitters are available.

It's essential to check the weekly calendar for additional events, because the junior staff also plans various activities for different age groups. Teen dances and pool parties, Ping-Pong tournaments, swimming and hamburger parties, and crabbing parties frequently appear on the agenda.

Recreation: Whether you choose a leisurely stroll along the 5 miles of sandy beach, a rigorous game of tennis, a round of golf, or a refreshing dip in the pool, your vacation stay can be as relaxing or active as you wish.

The Racquet Club offers seventeen well-maintained clay courts, an automated practice court, and instruction by a professional teaching staff. Even a little criticism of your backhand is easy to take in a setting graced by oak trees and azaleas. At the pro shop you can pick up equipment and new tennis togs and sign up for a tournament.

The Sea Island Golf Club is located not on Sea Island but on neighboring St. Simons Island; it's just a short drive over the small bridge spanning the Black Banks River. Once you arrive you'll be charmed by the Avenue of Oaks—majestic moss-draped oak trees leading up to the clubhouse. There are thirty-six championship holes; each of the two eighteen-hole courses has a different personality, whether it's oceanside, along the marshes, or past beds of flowering azaleas and dogwoods. Also operated by The Cloister is the St. Simons Island Club, with another fine eighteen holes providing lots of variety for avid golfers. Each location has its own clubhouse with dining facilities, a well-stocked pro shop, and excellent teaching pros for private lessons and clinics. The Golf Learning Center, a joint venture of Sea Island and *Golf Digest,* offers state-of-the-art practice and learning facilities. There's a driving range at each club, and back on Sea Island you'll find a putting green and a chip 'n' putt area when you want to work in some extra practice time. And if you're a real devotee, rest assured that golfing interests do not fade with the setting sun; join the discussions with the pros at golf seminars two evenings a week.

The Beach Club overlooks the Atlantic, so you can choose an ocean swim or a few laps in one of the two pools. Besides a dining room and a snack bar, the Beach Club offers Ping-Pong, volleyball, shuffleboard, and a terrific soak-up-the-sun atmosphere. Other water sports include sailboarding and sailing in the ocean, snorkeling and scuba diving, and boating and fishing in the river. After excursions through the waterways, you might try exploring the grounds as you jog, bike, or ride horseback. Many folks enjoy a horseback ride along the beach, or you may contact the stables about moonlight supper rides. At the Shooting

School you'll find instruction in sporting clays, trap, and skeet shooting as well as all the equipment necessary to learn these sports. And after golf, tennis, swimming, sailing, and skeet-shooting lessons, if you're still dying to try something new or brush up on dusty skills, sign up for dance instruction. After a couple of sessions, you'll no doubt be a hit dancing nightly to the hotel's Sea Island Orchestra.

The Sea Island Spa offers a full range of services. You can join an exercise class, develop an individualized program, consult a nutritionist, have a massage, and relax with a facial.

Special programs are planned throughout the year; they may be just the thing to schedule a family vacation around. Food and wine seminars, bridge festivals, a garden series, and a personal financial-planning seminar are standard events at The Cloister.

At any time of the year, be sure to check the weekly calendar. You might want to see a movie, play bingo, listen to a classical piano concert, head to an exercise workout, join a nature walk, or take in a lecture on the local wildlife. But don't crowd your schedule too much, for one of the nicest pleasures at The Cloister is strolling through the gardens and discovering the camellias, gardenias, wisteria, geraniums, and petunias. ≋

Club Med/Sandpiper

3500 SE Morningside Boulevard
Port St. Lucie, Florida 34952
(561) 398–5100
Web site: www.clubmed.com

Club Med is practically synonymous with a carefree, fun-in-the-sun holiday, a tradition going back more than forty years. The only warm-weather village that Club Med operates in the United States is Sandpiper, and it's not only a mini club but a baby club as well. Located in Port St. Lucie, Florida, about an hour's drive north of Palm Beach, the Club Med village covers more than 400 beautifully landscaped acres along the St. Lucie River. The verdant green landscape and the clear blue waters make an attractive setting for a fun-filled, sun-filled vacation.

Accommodations: Sandpiper is one of the most luxurious Club Med properties, termed the "Finest." It seems more like a deluxe hotel, boasting brick-colored tile floors covered with kilim carpet, original artwork by local artists, and a separate dressing area, with large closets. Unlike most Club Med villages, the rooms here have telephone, TV, and mini fridge. Each room has a private balcony or terrace and is located in one of several 3-story buildings near the river.

Weekly rates for adults range from $1,000 (summer/fall) to $1,150 (winter/spring); Christmas, Presidents' Week, and Easter are higher. Children's rates are from $700 to $800. During many weeks a baby age four to twenty-three months or a child age two to five years is free with a full-paying adult; check with the Club for these dates. Sandpiper is one of the few Club Meds with daily rates; these range from $145 to $170 for adults and $100 to $115 for children ages four months to eleven years.

A Club Med membership is required; this is a one-time fee of $30 per family plus an annual membership fee of $50 per adult, $20 per child. The rates include accommodations, all meals, the children's program, and most of the activities, with instruction.

Dining: The main dining room is informal, serving breakfast, lunch, and dinner buffets. Dining at Club Med is a bountiful experience, with selections of American, French, and continental delicacies. (It's also a good chance to meet people and socialize.) The Club has its own baker and pastry maker—yum. No fewer than twelve different fresh-baked breads are served at every meal. But not to worry, there are enough activities daily to work off any calories from overindulging. A special kid-friendly menu is served to children early at lunch and dinner. Parents may join their children while they eat, and the G.O.s (*gentils organisateurs*—French for "gracious organizers") supervise as well. Highchairs and booster seats make life easier for the little ones. After their early dinner kids return to the mini club. Mom and Dad, meanwhile, savor a superb and blissfully quiet dinner, perhaps in one of the two specialty restaurants—beautifully decorated, smaller and more intimate, table service is the order of the day here. Choose La Fontana, with the freshest of fish, or The Riverside, which offers fine French dishes. Complimentary wine is served with lunch and dinner, thanks to the French heritage of the Club.

Children's World: Kids are thoroughly entertained at Club Med. In fact, you may almost have to make an appointment to see your little one. The Baby Club is available for infants ages four to twenty-three months. Strollers, baby phones, bassinets—all the necessary equipment can be borrowed; and a pediatrician is either in the village or on call, plus one registered nurse. Each baby gets her own crib, and there's even a special Baby Chef, who prepares the food using only natural ingredients. Lunch is handled by the G.O.s, but parents are on duty for dinner. Need juice or milk in the middle of the night? No problem; just go to the twenty-four-hour convenience room. Depending on their ages, babies are changed, fed, napped, and played with in the adjacent garden, with swings and toys. The more mobile go on walks or play on the beach. A new service available only at this Baby Crib is "Twilight Care." Babies are brought back to the

Baby Club at 7:00 P.M., in their pajamas, and can sleep there while parents take in a show or stroll along the river.

The Petit Club is for two- to three-year-olds, the Mini Club is for four- to seven-year-olds, and the Kids Club entertains eight- to eleven-year-olds. Each has its own area, its own G.O.s, and an unbelievable number of activities. In addition to all the usual activities of children's programs, Club Med also offers circus workshops, with real trampolines, trapeze and low-wire work, juggling, trick bikes, and clowns. At the end of the week, the entire group puts on a show under the Big Top for adoring parents. It's really terrific, and the kids are so proud of themselves. Children also rave about the scuba experience in the swimming pool, with kid-size masks, fins, and tanks. In one-on-one instruction, even four-year-olds get to breathe under water—what a thrill! There's intensive tennis for kids eight and older, and soccer, softball, in-line skating, sailing, waterskiing—and much more, all included in the one price.

Recreation: The sun is warm, the water inviting. You have five swimming pools to choose from and a little sandy beach where you can splash in the river. A shuttle leaves hourly for the twenty-minute ride to the Atlantic for ocean swimming. In the calm water of the river, you can glide along on a sailboat and later have a go at waterskiing. Tennis clinics are held daily on the nineteen courts; after intensive two-and-a-half-hour sessions, you will surely find improvement in your game. A normal program with one-hour daily lessons at all levels is another option. Aerobics classes, calisthenics, and volleyball games always pop up on the agenda. Perhaps you prefer a routine in the fitness center or biking and jogging along the paths through the property. Maybe you can sneak in a trial swing on the trapeze—it's scary, but very safe.

Speaking of swings, unique to Sandpiper is a concentrated golf program, including two eighteen-hole championship golf courses designed by Mark Mahannah, called Saints and Sinners; a driving range; a free nine-hole par three; an enclosed driving range, with free lessons at all levels; two putting greens; a chipping green; and a practice sand trap. For serious golfers the Golf Academy provides two and a half hours daily of instruction and course play at an additional cost.

The Mini Clubs run from 9:00 A.M. to 9:00 P.M. Afterward the whole family can enjoy the evening entertainment, usually a show or participatory fun. After the kids finally fall into bed, the nightclub continues into the night.

If you have time, which we doubt, Club Med offers a mind-boggling array of excursions. You may not want to mention it to the kids, but Disney World is only two hours away. Also nearby are the Kennedy Space Center, hot-air ballooning, and deep-sea fishing. Palm Beach shopping is also within close striking distance. ≋

Hawk's Cay Resort

Mile Marker 61
Duck Key, Florida 33050
(305) 743–7000, (800) 432–2242

Located in the heart of the Florida Keys is Hawk's Cay Resort, a tropical sixty-acre island. The resort was built in the late 1950s and has hosted numerous presidents and film stars. The rambling Caribbean-style hotel sets the tone for the relaxed, elegant atmosphere that you'll find here. Ceiling fans, indoor plants, wicker furniture, and French doors in the lobbies and lounges echo the easygoing pace. The temperatures are mild, averaging in the low eighties in the summer and the low seventies in the winter, and the water stays warm and comfortable year-round. Water sports, from deep-sea fishing, sailing, diving, and snorkeling to swimming, sunset sails, ecotours, and water-skiing, are, naturally, the main focus of this island resort. The only living coral reef in the continental United States is just offshore. There are a variety of diving programs, including a special program for the physically challenged.

Accommodations: This comfortable inn has the ambience and style of a Caribbean resort. Most of the 160 rooms and 16 suites have views of the Atlantic Ocean or the Gulf of Mexico. Each has a private balcony, separate dressing area, and a small refrigerator. During the high season, December through April, room rates range from $220 to $375; suite rates, including the presidential suite, range from $425 to $850. Low-season rates, May through mid-December, are $180–$250 and $235–$750, respectively. The resort has added 130 new two- and three-bedroom villas that offer water settings and a full kitchen with four different styles. They are the perfect home away from home for families.

Dining: If you like fresh seafood, you'll find dining here a treat. There are four tempting restaurants to choose from, each with its own distinctive style and menu selections.

Start the day with a fabulous breakfast buffet presented in the Palm Terrace. Breakfast hours begin as early as 7:00 A.M. and continue until 10:30 A.M. For casual lunches and dinners, the Cantina at poolside offers a variety of Mexican fare, as well as rum concoctions that recall the island's history as a stopover for Prohibition rumrunners.

The WatersEdge, dockside at the marina, is open for dinner, specializing in fresh-off-the-boat seafood and steak. Porto Cayo features Italian specialties, accompanied by the sounds of an internationally known pianist.

Photo courtesy of Hawk's Cay Resort and Marina

Children's World: Children's programs at the resort feature a variety of opportunities for children of all ages (baby-sitting services also can be arranged). Daily activities include tiki boat races, field trips, scavenger hunts, fishing, ecology tours, and a kids' night out.

New in July 1999, the clubhouse features a children's theme swimming pool and fitness center, an area designed especially for teens, and an additional location for indoor games and activities.

Located just off the main lobby, your child will find a room filled with the latest electronic games.

Recreation: The water tempts, entices, and captures the heart of visitors. It establishes the mood and is the setting for most of the recreation. Swim in one of the many pools or the saltwater lagoon, or stretch out beneath the tropical sun.

Discover the mysteries and wonder of undersea life. The coral reef offshore is home to a colorful array of tropical fish and is one of the best spots in the country for snorkeling and scuba diving.

Fishing here puts you in the big league, and it's exciting. Just offshore you'll find red snapper and mackerel, farther out in Gulf Stream waters are marlin, dolphin, and tuna, and in Florida Bay tarpon ply the waters. Charter a vessel at the marina for an excursion. The Marina at Hawk's Cay offers 110 slips and can dock yachts more than 100 feet long.

Explore the island by bicycle or take a self-guided walking tour to learn about the indigenous vegetation and tropical birds such as the brown pelican and the blue heron.

Unique to Hawk's Cay is the Chicago Zoological Society's Dolphin Connection, a program designed to study, protect, and increase public interest in dolphin biology and ecosystems. Training sessions at 10:00 A.M., 1:00 P.M., and 4:00 P.M. daily are complimentary and open to guests. Sign up for a once in a lifetime experience and swim with the dolphins. ≋

Indian River Plantation
Marriott Resort

555 Northeast Ocean Boulevard
Hutchinson Island
Stuart, Florida 34996
(561) 225–3700, (800) 444–3389
Web site: www.floridatreasures.com

Indian River Plantation Marriott Resort is tucked away on Hutchinson Island, a 16-mile lush barrier isle in a surprisingly subtle spot in the Atlantic. This natural island playground enchants guests with its serene nature and intimate island hospitality. Edged on one side by aquamarine ocean waves and complemented by the shimmering Indian River on the other, the resort stretches across 200 acres of plantation landscape and hosts a range of sun-splashed options,

Photo courtesy of Indian River Plantation Marriott Resort

from miles of shell-colored shores and a seventy-seven-slip marina to the Tree Top Jungle Bunch Kids Camp and a selection of aquatic adventures.

Accommodations: The retreat offers 298 riverside-to-oceanfront guest rooms and suites, with daily rates ranging from $59 from June through October, to $279 January 16 to April 17 and December 19–31 (depending on room type and days of stay). One- and two-bedroom villas overlook the water or the golf course; each has a fully equipped kitchen and private balcony. Rates range from $199 a night from June through October, to $399 January 16 to April 17 and December 19–31. Special rates apply for golf, honeymoon, holiday, and seasonal packages; complimentary cribs are provided.

Dining: Dining options tempt any appetite, offering enticing seafood delights and casual, bistro-style fare. Panoramic views from Scalawags, a seafood restaurant overlooking the Indian River, surround guests in perfect pastel sunsets while savory dishes are served. Combining a kaleidoscope of colors and a market-style ambience, Gratzi offers a selection of light Italian fare with sit-down service, an expansive deli, and gourmet take-out options. Bunkers, a newly remodeled restaurant catering to famished golfers seeking a quick bite, features a pub menu for post-play fare and cheer. The Emporium Cafe treats families to an all-American selection, from burgers and conch fritters to delectable ice-cream sundaes. Poolside tiki bars offer light bites and snacks for lunch and dinner.

Children's World: The Tree Top Bunch Jungle Kids Camp, an educational recreation activity program for children ages four to twelve, delights island tykes with activities such as bike rides, nature walks, swimming, arts and crafts, and a special Kids' Night Out. Closely supervised, kids experience the unique island atmosphere with children their own age from 9:00 A.M. to 2:00 P.M. Monday, Wednesday, Friday, and Saturday for $25 per child, including lunch. Additional children from the same family receive a $2.00 discount. Teens enjoy shared activities as well, with movie nights, teen shoreline fishing, and teen in-line skating parties scheduled monthly. The resort is transformed into a pirate's lair with "Pirate Island," a fun, family-oriented summer program.

Recreation: Stuart is the "Sailfish Capital of the World," where first-time mates to seasoned fishermen pursue the coveted game fish. Indian River Plantation's full-service seventy-seven-slip marina offers deep-sea and river charter fishing and backwater trolling excursions. If you prefer cruising to catching, relax aboard the *Island Princess*, the resort's own luxury vessel, and scout out the lifestyles of the rich and famous along the Indian River. Year-round guided eco-tours to explore the area's flourishing natural surroundings take guests through mangrove-woven waterways, seeking dolphins, manatees, sea turtles, and native birds. Aquatic adventures abound from the Atlantic Ocean to the Intracoastal Waterway, where seafarers frolic by sailboat, Wave Runner, windsurfer, and kayak. For more relaxing recreation take a dip in one of the resort's four pools.

Golfers of all skill levels enjoy the challenging fairways and greens of twelve courses in the area, as the resort is the gateway to an array of championship and executive courses, including Nicklaus, Fazio, and Player designs.

Guests preferring their backhand to the back nine can indulge in thirteen NovaGrass tennis courts at the heart of the island. With a quick-drying surface, the courts bounce back from a good soaking in about an hour. Health enthusiasts will find a newly installed fitness facility with a complete line of workout equipment and an all-glass wall providing a panoramic view of the tennis courts. ≋

Marco Island Marriott Resort and Golf Club

400 South Collier Boulevard
Marco Island, Florida 34145
(941) 394–2511, (800) 438–4373

An island oasis drifting off the southernmost tip of the Florida Gulf and nearly lost in the Ten Thousand Islands, Marco Island Marriott Resort and Golf Club blends a tempting twist of tropical passions and sun-

Photo courtesy of Marco Island Marriott Resort and Golf Club

splashed excitement into an enchanting, unforgettable island escape. The resort's privileged travelers get lost in the intriguing contrasts: Waves of sun-drenched beaches, always-warm Gulf waters, and passionate sunsets present a tame, pampered complement to the tangled wildness and sweeping sawgrass prairies of Florida's famous Everglades nearby.

Accommodations: All of Marco Island Marriott Resort and Golf Club's 735 guest rooms and suites have private balconies. Poolside or beachfront lanais—each with a private balcony entrance—and a secluded cluster of seaside villas complete the resort's accommodations. Daily rates, depending on size, are $110–$169 in the low season (May through November) and start at $265 in the high season (December through April). Packages are available.

Dining: Shimmering turquoise-flecked waters, sweeping pearlescent sands, and lush, cascading gardens create an enchanting tropical backdrop and alluring ambience for five distinct restaurants and four lounges at the resort. Here you'll find everything from a seabound beach hut and classic pizzeria to the finest Northern Italian cuisine. Quinn's on the Beach cooks up a treasure trove of savory seafaring delights from dawn until after dusk. The elegant charm and romance of Ristorante Tuscany, overlooking a poolside courtyard with 150 palms, enhance an array of tantalizing choices such as Portabella Trifolati. At the Voyager Restaurant, open for dinner and a superb Sunday champagne brunch, a range of tasty treasures begins with appetizers such as succulent escargots and Maryland-style crab cakes. For anytime eating, Café del Sol creates popular family fare. Aromas of just-baked bread and bubbling tomato sauce entice sun-seeking crowds to the Pizzeria for huge slices of homemade pizza, subs, barbecue, hot dogs, spaghetti, ice cream, and frozen yogurt. The resort also has a Tiki Bar and Grill, specializing in chilled concoctions.

Children's World: The Kids Klub at Marco Island Marriott Resort and Golf Club—the first resort in North America to be awarded The National Parenting Center Seal of Approval—is a pinnacle of pint-size fun, occupying youngsters ages five through twelve with cool pool dips, sandcastle creations, coconut bowling, arts and crafts, and zany relay races. Special Saturday evening programs allow parents a slice of solitude under the South Florida stars. The unique Rainy Day program offers hours of indoor entertainment for the whole family.

Recreation: Choreographed by a team of fun-in-the-sun experts, daily activities include aquaslimnastics, tennis aerobics, island bike and trolley tours, beach volleyball, Ping-Pong, and step aerobics. Sun worshippers and soul searchers relax under thatch-topped tiki huts, play beach volleyball, or scour the shore for seashells. Endless gulf activities include sailing, kayaking, windsurfing, waterskiing, bumper tubing, and parasailing. Three sparkling pools and a children's wading pool are available. Golfers can enjoy a 6,925-yard, eighteen-hole executive golf course. The extensive clubhouse facility includes an elaborate pro shop, complete locker room facilities, clubhouse grill for breakfast or lunch, and John Jacobs' School of Golf. For tennis enthusiasts there are thirteen Har-Tru and three hard-surface courts (four lighted for night play), a tennis shop, daily clinics, private lessons, round-robins, match mate services, and special instruction for young learners. Fabulous fishing is accessible, or you can work out with Florida-style aerobics and fitness programs. Be sure, though, to save time for island shelling adventures or some on-site shopping. ≈≈≈

Marriott's Grand Hotel Resort and Golf Club

1 Grand Boulevard
Point Clear, Alabama 36564
(334) 928–9201, (800) 544–9933
Web site: www.marriott.com/marriott/PTLAL

The charm and graciousness of the Old South has not faded in southern Alabama. Marriott's Grand Hotel has preserved its rich tradition of elegant service as a premier resort for more than 150 years. Known as the Queen of Southern Resorts, the hotel is set on 550 acres in Point Clear, on a peninsula in Mobile Bay. In this secluded location the quiet lagoons, majestic oak trees draped in hanging Spanish moss, and beautiful gardens can make you

Photo courtesy of Marriott's Grand Hotel Resort and Golf Club

forget the worries and concerns of the workaday world. Leave your troubles and anxieties on the doorstep and enter this vacation retreat, where your biggest dilemma will be whether to play a round of golf, ride horseback in the peaceful landscape, stroll along the sandy beach, or sip a mint julep while watching the sun set over the bay.

The fascinating legacy of the Grand Hotel captures the heart of many a history buff. First discovered as an ideal location for a resort retreat in 1847, the hotel was the site of lively antebellum social events in its early years. Then, during the days of the Civil War (or as some folks down here still call it, the War of Northern Aggression), it served as a hospital for Confederate soldiers. After the war the hotel resumed its original function and once again became the center for leisure activities. A fire in 1869 and a hurricane in 1893 destroyed some of the old facilities, but rebuilding efforts and expansion were frequently undertaken in order to maintain accommodations for guests. Today's main hotel building was constructed in 1941. In 1967 the Bay House was added, and 1983 witnessed a restoration of the existing rooms and the addition of two buildings—the North Bay House and the Marina House.

Accommodations: The main building has been described as rustic, but don't be deceived; this is rustic in a grand old manner. The lobby here is a charming octagonal structure that focuses on a massive fireplace. From its wide planks of pine flooring to its cypress-beamed ceiling, visitors immediately sense a warm, hospitable atmosphere. There are a total of 306 guest rooms in the different buildings and the cottages. Many rooms are decorated with white cypress paneling and ceiling fans (maintained primarily for ambience, but also to capture the bay breezes; air-conditioning relieves the sultriness of summer days). Open year-round, the hotel has several rate structures. In the winter season, daily room-only rates range from $94 to $124 midweek, $104 to $164 weekends. Special rates that include breakfast for two are just $10 more, and children under five can dine from the special children's buffet. Summer rates are higher: For example, the breakfast-for-two plan is $159 to $179 weekdays or $219 to $239 weekends. There is no charge for cribs and rollaways.

Dining: The Grand Dining Room offers an elegant atmosphere for breakfast, lunch, and dinner. An orchestra performs nightly here during dinner and afterward for dancing. Since the hotel is located on Mobile Bay and so close to the Gulf, many of the house specialties rely on the fresh local seafood. Oysters, red snapper stuffed with crabmeat, and seafood gumbo are a few of the selections. The hearty-meat-and-potatoes fan will find excellent prime rib of beef. The gourmet will be enticed by the elegant Bayview Room, for intimate and scenic dining.

For a sumptuous buffet breakfast, try the Grand Buffet in the Grand Dining Room, where you may sit in a gazebo area with beautiful bay views. Lunch is served not only in the Grand Dining Room, but also at the Lakewood Golf Club, which is set in a wooded landscape. While soaking up the sunshine, you may choose the Poolside Grill and Snack Bar for a light lunch (seasonal). The Birdcage Lounge also provides light snacks and delightful cocktails with spectacular views.

Children's World: The Grand Fun Camp is in operation from Memorial Day to Labor Day and on all major holidays. Every day but Sunday a group of friendly hostesses coordinates fun-filled activities. Five- to twelve-year-olds frolic from 10:00 A.M. to 4:00 P.M. and from 6:00 P.M. until 10:00 P.M. Swimming, shuffleboard, putt-putt golf, arts and crafts, video games, fishing, and sandcastle building entertain children, who will no doubt entertain their parents as they recount a day's adventures. Special events include movies and puppet shows. Individual baby-sitters are also available on an hourly basis ($5.50 and up per hour).

Recreation: In the old days of the resort, two favorite spots were the wharves—one for men and one for women, because sunbathing and swimming in mixed company were unacceptable. Having come a long way since then, the Grand now offers innumerable popular activities for its guests. Given this prime location and mild climate, water sports attract many visitors. After a little warm-up fishing in the bay, you might take on the challenges of deep-sea fishing. Your catch may be your evening's dinner, prepared especially for you by the hotel chefs. Reserve a sailboat or paddleboat for an afternoon's outing, or bring your own boat to the forty-slip marina. Splash in the waters of the bay along the sandy beach, or take a dip in the beautiful pool, the largest pool on the Gulf Coast.

If you're more of a landlubber, the championship thirty-six holes of golf are a suitable diversion. Regardless of their level of play, all golfers appreciate the rolling, wooded setting of oak and pine. The facilities of the club abound—instructors, carts, putting greens, and locker room. The eight rubico tennis courts lure many ace players, and novices can enroll for lessons with one of the pros. And no day of golf or tennis is complete without the requisite stop at the pro shops; there's always that extra bit of new equipment to pick up. Head to the stables for horseback riding around the picturesque lakes and lagoons, or jog or bicycle (rentals available) through the gardens and along the boardwalk.

Slower-paced activities include croquet, putting green, and video games, or you may want to wind up the day in the hot tub. In the 1930s The Grand Hotel advertised itself as the place of "Every Creature Comfort." Many visitors today feel that reputation has withstood the test of time. ≋

The Resort at Longboat Key Club

301 Gulf of Mexico Drive
P.O. Box 15000
Longboat Key, Florida 34228
(813) 383–8821, (800) 237–8821
Web site: www.longboatkeyclub.com

An island retreat, The Resort at Longboat Key Club specializes in relaxation and recreation for golfers and tennis players. Located on a barrier island in the Gulf of Mexico just west of Sarasota, it doesn't shortchange swimmers and sun worshippers either. The Resort enjoys a lush, tropical setting between the Gulf and Sarasota Bay that seems worlds away from your regular routine, yet it is only fifteen minutes away from the Sarasota Airport.

Accommodations: Seven modern buildings, 4 to 10 stories high, are arranged throughout the property to afford guests magnificent views of the gulf, the bay, and the golf course fairways. Of the 232 accommodations, each with its own balcony, the majority (220) are suites, each with a king-size bed, a sleeper sofa, and a fully equipped kitchen. Summer is the low season, when guest rooms range from $125 to $230 a night and suites start at $160 a night;

the deluxe two-bedroom suites command $295 to $460 a night. During the high season (Christmas and February through late April), a guest room is $265 to $335 a night, while suites cost $315 to $735 a night. During the rest of the year, prices fall between these parameters. Up to two children (seventeen and younger) can stay in a suite with their parents at no additional charge.

Dining: Dining can be as elegant or as casual as you choose. On the sophisticated side is Orchids. Tempting fresh seafood dishes are frequently featured on its menus. For more casual dining drop by Spike 'n' Tees, and for truly relaxed mealtimes, saunter over to Barefoots, at poolside.

Children's World: The Kids' Klub operates daily from Presidents' Day weekend through Labor Day and on holiday weekends throughout the year. Experienced counselors direct youngsters ages five to twelve in a full 9:00 A.M.–3:00 P.M. program. Swimming, beach fun, volleyball, basketball, field trips, and arts and crafts are all part of the schedule. The program is complimentary, though fees may be charged for special field trips. The average cost of individual baby-sitting is $6.00 an hour, with a four-hour minimum.

Recreation: The Islandside Golf Course has eighteen holes, and the Harborside Course has twenty-seven holes. With palm trees and quiet lagoons throughout these courses, who can have a bad game? Two complete pro shops, a golf school, and professionals to guide players in private lessons and tournaments round out the picture for golfers.

Thirty-eight Har-Tru tennis courts await your ace serves and graceful lobs. Six of these are lighted for night play. Tennis play is complimentary. Two tennis shops, ball machines, a videotaped game analysis, and a professional staff will urge you on to better play.

Swimming in the outdoor pool or the gentle waters of the Gulf may top off your day. Bicycle along the nature trails, stroll on the snow-white beach, or spend an afternoon snorkeling or sailing. You can even organize a deep-sea fishing expedition through the concierge.

The Resort's newest recreational amenity is a 4,000-square-foot Fitness Centre, which features weight-training and cardiovascular equipment as well as instructor-led aerobics classes. Fitness Centre equipment is available to guests on a complimentary basis. For soothing life's daily stress and the ultimate in personal pampering, neuromuscular, sports, and Swedish massage is also available.

≈≈≈

South Seas Resort

P.O. Box 194
Captiva Island, Florida 33924
(800) CAPTIVA
Web sites: www.southsearesort.com; www.ssrc.com

Located at the northern tip of Captiva Island on the Gulf of Mexico, 3 miles off Florida's southwest coast, Captiva Island is connected to the mainland via Sanibel Island and the Sanibel Causeway. South Seas Resort is approximately 30 miles from the Southwest Florida International Airport in Fort Myers.

Dubbed "Florida's Tahiti" for its subtropical climate and lush foliage indigenous to the Southern Hemisphere, Captiva Island—famous for its shell-covered beaches—was recently rated one of America's most romantic beaches. South Seas Resort is a 330-acre island resort with 2½ miles of beach, a full-service yacht harbor and marina, recreational options from golf and tennis to island excursion cruises and water sports, fine restaurants, shopping, children's programs, and a complimentary open-air trolley transportation system.

Accommodations: The South Seas Resort boasts more than 600 luxurious units, ranging from deluxe hotel rooms and villa suites to three-bedroom beach homes and cottages. Contact South Seas Resort for additional accommodation information and costs.

Dining: The resort's legendary King's Crown Restaurant features exquisite architecture and an award-winning culinary team. Discover fine dining in an elegant waterfront setting where New American cuisine is graciously served, traditions of yesterday are preserved, and new traditions are created. *Florida Living* magazine readers have honored King's Crown with the distinction of "Best Restaurant with a View." Chadwick's Restaurant features casual dining in a tropical setting. It is open for breakfast seasonally, and lunch and dinner menus feature daily breakfast and lunch buffet, a Sunday champagne brunch, and evening theme buffets, including Caribbean Celebration Buffet, Bourbon Street Bash, Key West Clambake, and Seafood Extravaganza.

Dine indoors or in the open air at Cap'n Al's Dockside Grille overlooking the Yacht Harbour. Cap'n Al's serves breakfast, lunch, and dinner daily. Enjoy Mama Rosa's Pizzeria, offering eat-in or take-out dining; the convenience of delivery is provided after 5:00 P.M. Choose from mouthwatering pizza, garden-fresh salads, and delicious subs. Fresh dough is made daily on the premises. Uncle Bob's Ice Cream Emporium serves delicious, old-fashioned soda fountain and ice-cream treats and tempting candies, and sells educational toys and kites. Pelican Pete's Pool Bar is a full-service bar specializing in tropical libations; poolside dining at the north end features grilled sandwiches, snacks, and more.

For dining entertainment the King's Crown Lounge, located in the King's Crown Restaurant, offers cocktails and live, easy-listening entertainment. Chadwick's Lounge has a full bar and live entertainment nightly. A steel drum band is featured Tuesday evenings and a jazz quartet during dinner on Thursday evenings.

Children's World: Activities for all ages are available. A professional staff organizes daily itineraries of recreational and educational activities. Explorer Kids' Club, for children ages three to eleven, includes activities such as Nature Camp, Pirate Mania, Circus at South Seas, and Dinner Theatre. Supervised social events for teens, such as parasailing, waterskiing, volleyball tournaments, pool parties, canoeing, kayaking, and golf are sure to provide hours of enjoyment.

Recreation: Dozens of recreational activities are available to guests of South Seas Plantation, including a par thirty-six, regulation nine-hole golf course; tennis on twenty-one courts; biking; and water sports, including game fishing, sailboarding, snorkeling, sailing, and excursion cruises to nearby islands.

Family activities and workshops also feature yoga, professional fitness training, aerobic exercise classes, canoe excursions, sailing clinics, guided shelling excursions, family fishing, shell art, and more. A variety of nature activities for the whole family include Dolphin and Manatee Awareness, Shells of Captiva, Wildlife Refuge Trips, and Birds of Captiva. *The Explorer Bulletin,* a current schedule of activities, is given to guests upon check-in. Preregistration is required for all activities.

Shopping at South Seas includes quality boutiques, gift shops, pro shops, grocery store and gourmet deli, ship's store, and full-service beauty salon. ≋

The Westin Innisbrook Resort

36750 U.S. Highway 19 North
Palm Harbor, Florida 34684
(727) 942–2000, (800) 456–2000
Web site: www.westin-innisbrook.com

Just 25 miles from Tampa International Airport on Florida's sparkling west coast lies the pride of the Florida resort market, The Westin Innisbrook Resort. This beautiful property includes more than 1,000 acres tucked away from the mainstream of city life and traffic, in a picturesque setting that is beautifully landscaped and heavily wooded with mature oaks and pines. The resort is open year-round, which is very good news for the golf enthusiast, as here you will find ninety holes of championship golf on five pristine courses. Innisbrook became a member of the honored Westin Hotel and Resort family in July 1997,

Photo courtesy of The Westin Innisbrook Resort

and has since enjoyed the addition of several new services and facilty enhancements that are sure to keep guests returning year after year. The resort has planned a $50 million renovation over the next few years to include refurbishment of their spacious guest suites, as well as the addition of several new recreation facilities and dining establishments. Convenient to all of central Florida's attractions including Walt Disney World, SeaWorld, and Busch Gardens, this is a setting that the whole family will adore.

Accommodations: Twenty-eight lodges containing 1,000 guest suites are located throughout the resort. Starting at 800 square feet for the popular Club Suite, to more than 2,000 square feet in a two-bedroom deluxe unit, a stay at Innisbrook affords all the comfort and conveniences of home. Each suite offers a fully stocked kitchen, daily newspaper and complimentary Starbucks coffee, a beautiful line of personal soaps and shampoos, complete in-suite bar, and private patio or balcony overlooking the golf courses and lush landscape.

Depending on the season, the rates for accommodations range from $115 to $485 per night. Children under eighteen stay free in the same room as their parents or guardians.

Dining: Dining at the resort offers a variety of cuisine, from a casual, family-style restaurant to the newly opened DY's Steak House. DY's was fashioned by the owners of the famous Shula's Steak House, offering the finest steak, seafood, and signature martinis in the state. Try Turnberry Pub for a casual, all-American menu that is sure to please the whole family, as well as light Mexican fare at the new Iguana Cantina. If dining poolside sounds enticing, you'll savor the aroma coming from the open-pit grill at The Grill at Loch Ness. Breakfast and lunch are also served at each golf clubhouse, and for those who seek the privacy and comfort of dining in their suite, Café Express offers gourmet food, promptly delivered. A spectacular Sunday brunch is also offered seasonally.

Children's World: At The Westin Innisbrook Resort there is plenty of fun in store for kids of all ages. Offered year-round, the resort's Camp Innisbrook children's program (a Westin Kids Club program) offers a fun-filled day for ages four through twelve. Every day of the week brings a different theme curriculum, which includes swimming, crafts, movies, games, playground time, miniature golf, and group sports, as well as golf and tennis clinics geared to each age. Evening programs are also offered seasonally, allowing mom and dad to enjoy a late round of golf or dinner for two, all the while knowing the children are having their own special fun. Be sure to check with the resort for various summer programs offered each year for toddlers, small children, and teens.

Recreation: Best known for outstanding golf, Innisbrook is considered a true golfer's paradise with ninety holes of championship golf on five well-groomed courses. The resort's Copperhead and Island courses have been ranked in *Golf Digest*'s Top 50 Resort Courses in America. And if you're looking to improve your game, look no farther than the Innisbrook Troon Golf Schools, operated at a private instruction facility at the resort. Three- to five-day programs are offered, as well as specialty schools focusing on a specific aspect of the game or for ladies only. There are daily clinic and instruction programs with the resort's award-winning instructional staff. Three complete practice facilities are also available for practice on any part of your game, day or night.

For the tennis enthusiast, eleven clay courts are available for open play, as well as a complete instructional program for all levels. There are also six swimming pools, basketball, miniature golf, jogging and nature trails, fishing, biking, and a complete fitness center. Of special interest is the new $3.4 million Loch Ness Pool and Spa. This unique recreation park offers a 15-foot cascading waterfall, two winding water slides, a plunge pool, two sand beach areas, and zero-based gradual entry—great for smaller children who are just learning to swim. Already a family favorite, Loch Ness also offers a monster-size spa that seats thirty-six! Fabulous white-sand beaches are also nearby, as well as a variety of water parks and specialty shopping.

A centrally located clubhouse was added in 1999, with guest registration, a lobby bar, a new restaurant, a golf shop, specialty shopping, and a grocery/deli. Upcoming plans at the resort include the addition of a new full-service spa with eighteen treatment rooms and the latest in massage and spa offerings. ≋

MIDWEST

Illinois

Indiana

Michigan

Minnesota

Missouri

Wisconsin

Eagle Ridge Inn and Resort

U.S. Route 20
Box 777
Galena, Illinois 61036
(815) 777–2444, (800) 892–2269

With 6,800 acres of rolling, wooded terrain and sixty-three challenging holes of golf, Eagle Ridge is a major Midwest resort. When you're not on the links, you'll find that 220-acre Lake Galena is a focus of resort activity. Located in northwest Illinois just minutes from historic Galena, with its well-preserved nineteenth-century architecture, Eagle Ridge is only 150 miles from Chicago.

Accommodations: The Eagle Ridge Inn, with its eighty rooms, sits at the edge of the lake. In addition, resort homes are scattered throughout the hills and consist of one- to five-bedroom accommodations. During the peak season, from May 14 to late October, inn rooms are $199–$279 a night (children sharing a room with parents are free); the resort homes are $199–$940 a night. The resort homes are also available for weekly rental, and many different packages are offered.

Dining: An elegant dining spot in the inn is the Woodlands Restaurant, where you'll enjoy steaks, pastas, and seafood along with beautiful views of the lake. Next door is the Woodlands Lounge, for cocktails and more casual dining. Each golf course has its own snack bar and nineteenth hole! The Clubhouse Bar and Grill offers great views of Eagle Ridge's newest golf course, The General, and a casual dining menu of appetizers, soups, salads, sandwiches, and wonderful entrees. When stocking up on provisions, stop by the General Store for delicious deli selections and freshly baked pastries.

Children's World: The Kids Klub is in operation from Memorial Day through Labor Day as well as weekends and holiday times throughout the year; it is designed for four- to twelve-year-olds. The 9:00 A.M.–4:00 P.M. day is filled with swimming, hiking, boating, games, and arts and crafts; the fee of $28 a day includes lunch. A half day with lunch is $23; a half day without lunch is $20. On three nights a week, dinner, movies, and games entertain children from 7:00 to 10:00 P.M. ($23 an evening). Teens enjoy a Saturday-evening excursion (to $25) that might include a volleyball game, bowling, Alpine slide, or movie outing—all with dinner at a local pizza parlor. Individual baby-sitting is available at $10 an hour.

Recreation: The North and South Golf courses provide eighteen holes of championship golf set in rolling hills and wooded countryside. The nine-hole

East Course, characterized by elevated tees, is an excellent test of accuracy. The latest addition, The General, is a challenging layout that opened in 1997. For serious instruction the professionals of the Troon Golf Institute at Eagle Ridge can guide you in everything from the basics to business golf. One-, two-, and three-day programs are offered.

On Lake Galena, fishermen go in search of bass, walleye, and crappie, and boaters head out in paddleboats, canoes, and pontoons. Swimmers can take a dip at the indoor pool adjacent to the fitness center in the inn. Horseback riding along 40 miles of trails begins at the Shenandoah Riding Center. Rent a mountain bike, or hike the trails to seek out native plants and wildlife. For a solitary excursion the fitness trail has twenty-one exercise stations, or round up the whole family for a volleyball game (two courts) or a tennis match (four courts). From the end of July to mid-August, you can combine an Eagle Ridge holiday with watching the Chicago Bears in summer practice at nearby Platteville.

In the winter, sports lovers turn to tobogganing, sledding, and ice skating. Forty miles of cross-country ski trails are carefully groomed. Nearby Chestnut Mountain offers downhill skiing on seventeen runs. ≋

French Lick Springs Resort
8670 West State Road 56
French Lick, Indiana 47432
(812) 936–9300, (800) 457–4042
Web site: www.frenchlick.com

French Lick Springs is a curious name with an interesting history behind it. This area of southwest Indiana was settled by French traders more than 200 years ago. Subsequently, mineral springs were discovered, and, because animals lapped the waters from the wet rocks, locals dubbed it "The Lick." The British moved in during the early nineteenth century, and by the 1830s the first hotel was built on this site because visitors were attracted to the healing powers of the mineral waters.

At the end of the century, fire destroyed the original buildings, but the property was purchased and the facilities reconstructed and expanded by Thomas Taggert, then mayor of Indianapolis. Under Taggert's guidance French Lick Springs developed into a first-class resort, with restaurants, golf courses, and a spa. The turn-of-the-century elegance and the devotion to health and recreation were maintained for the next thirty years. Popularity waxed and waned through the Depression, World War II, and the postwar years. For the last nearly

Photo courtesy of French Lick Springs Resort

four decades restoration has been emphasized; today French Lick Springs encompasses 2,600 acres of the rolling foothills of the Cumberland Mountain range and is dedicated to making the "Golden Days" of the Taggert era an ongoing reality. It is open year-round.

Accommodations: The rambling main building and its adjacent wings house almost 500 rooms and suites. The large and gracious front porch hints at the relaxed pace that prevails here. Rates for accommodations vary depending on the size, location, and view of a room; they range from $79 to $99 per day, based on double occupancy. Children under age seventeen are free; cribs are $10 a day. Package plans are available for golf, tennis, holiday weekends, and the Spa's health and fitness programs.

A modified American plan is available (breakfast and dinner). The cost is $30 per day per adult, $20 per day for ages six to twelve years, and free for children five and younger.

Dining: Dining possibilities are many and varied. Chez James is the right choice for an intimate, gourmet dinner, while Le Bistro is a casual steak-and-sandwich restaurant open for lunch and dinner. Combine pizza and bowling at the family-oriented Pizzeria in the Recreation Center, and don't forget to stop at Double Scoops for ice cream. The Country Club Restaurant overlooks the golf course, and the Hoosier Dining Room serves Sunday brunches and international buffet dinners. Sip cocktails in the Derby Bar, the Country Club Lounge, or Le Bistro Bar.

Children's World: The Pluto Club, for five- to twelve-year-olds, starts Memorial Day weekend and runs through Labor Day. Counselors guide kids in arts and crafts, swimming, hiking, and games. The fee is $1.00 an hour. Younger children (three to five years old) have a less rigorous program, for which the fee is $2.00 an hour. Lunch is available for $3.50.

From September to May children's activities are offered Saturday afternoons. At the Christmas and Easter holidays, more elaborate programs are planned.

The unsupervised outdoor playground, filled with swings, slides, monkey bars, teeter-totters, a merry-go-round, and a sandbox, is also a big hit with youngsters.

Children's Tennis Clinics and "Horse Sense" programs are also available for a fee. These supervised activities last about an hour and include instruction. Teen events such as mini-golf tournaments, horseback rides, and scavenger hunts are organized by the Social Staff but are not supervised.

Daily family and social activities are open to children accompanied by an adult; these include hayrides, cookouts, bingo, treasure hunts, lawn sports, and card games.

Recreation: You may not be able to shine in sports quite like Boston Celtic whiz Larry Bird, a native son of French Lick, but at least you have the facilities here where you can focus on improvement. On the gentle, wooded hills, through stands of butternut and oak trees, you can play golf from mid-March to mid-November on two eighteen-hole courses, one of which was designed by Donald Ross. The golf clinics offered April through September put you through the paces in improving your swing, grip, and stance and provide guidance in scrutinizing a course with a bit of strategy.

The tennis complex includes eight indoor courts and ten outdoor lighted courts. Tennis players, too, can have workouts in clinics that cover analyzing a stroke and planning a strategic performance in doubles.

Choose a mount from among thirty horses (lessons available) and head for the trails through the hills; take to the hilly terrain on foot, hiking along the many paths; or hop a surrey to see the scenery. Try out the skeet and trap range, or go for a warm lazy swim in the indoor or outdoor pool. Stroll through the gardens and challenge other guests to lawn games like shuffleboard, volleyball, croquet, badminton, and horseshoes. Rent a bicycle, go bowling (six lanes), play pool, or hit the video games in the Recreation Center. During the winter, cross-country skiing, horse-drawn sleigh rides, and ice skating draw attention.

Don't forget the tradition of the magical quality of the mineral waters. At the Spa you can have mineral baths and massages. Work out in the exercise room, soak in the whirlpool, and block out the rest of the world while sitting in the sauna; a total fitness program can be designed for you.

Nearby activities include the restored Pioneer Village at Spring Mill Park, Marengo Caves, skating at the Roller Dome, and a train ride at the Railway Museum. ≋

Grand Geneva Resort and Spa

Highway 50 East at Route 12
7036 Grand Geneva Way
Lake Geneva, Wisconsin 53147
(414) 248–8811, (800) 558–3417
Web site: www.grandgeneva.com

Tucked into the southeastern corner of Wisconsin, between Milwaukee and Chicago, are Lake Geneva and the Grand Geneva Resort & Spa. Less than a day's drive from nine states and sixty million people, the resort sits in the midst of 1,300 acres of pristine Wisconsin countryside and has as its stated goal "to be a destination for relaxation and pleasure." Built in the 1960s as a Playboy Club, it has undergone extensive renovations and reopened in 1994 with a brand-new image. The town of Lake Geneva has been called "the Newport of the Midwest," and that flavor is cultivated here.

Accommodations: A total of 355 guest rooms and suites overlook the rolling green hills and clear blue lake (some also overlook a courtyard parking area, so specify view desired when you book). Decor is that of an elegant and comfortable vacation home. In summer, rooms are $219–$259 and in winter $119–$159. Suites range from $189 to $259 in winter and from $279 to $389 in summer. One- to three-bedroom villas are available on-site; summer rates are $269–$419 and winter rates are $189–$309.

Dining: Almost everyone likes Italian food, so the bistro-style Ristorante Brissago is sure to please. Open for dinner only, the restaurant features homemade pastas, and the atmosphere is special without being stuffy. Another restaurant choice, The Newport Grill, puts the kitchen right on display, so you get the full effect of sight and aroma as well as the taste of typical Midwestern dishes such as grilled steak, chops, and fresh seafood. The Grill is open for lunch and dinner and serves a bountiful Sunday brunch. The Grand Cafe offers American cuisine, with a children's menu; it's open for breakfast, lunch, dinner, and a special Sunday buffet. Snacks and sandwiches are available in the Links clubhouse at the Golf Pro Shop. For evening cocktails or live entertainment, stop by the Newport Lounge or the Lobby Lounge.

Children's World: The Grand Adventure Kids Club operates year-round on weekends and holidays, daily from Memorial Day through Labor Day, for ages four to twelve years. The morning session is from 10:00 A.M. to noon ($15); the afternoon session is from 1:00 to 5:00 P.M. ($30); the full-day session from 10:00 A.M. to 5:00 P.M. includes lunch ($40). The evening session is from 6:00 to 9:30 P.M. ($20).

Activities include arts and crafts, pony rides, swimming, paddleboating, hiking, and evening movies.

Recreation: All the amenities for a resort vacation are here. Two PGA tour-quality golf courses lure golfers. The Highlands, one of the first Scottish-design courses in the United States, was designed by Jack Nicklaus and Pete Dye. The other course, The Brute, is one of the longest courses in the Midwest, measuring 6,997 yards. Putting greens, driving ranges, and scrupulous attention to grooming keep golfers coming back. Pick up a tennis game on one of the four indoor or five outdoor courts, or work out at the Sport Center, which features a variety of cardio and weight-resistance equipment. A private lake provides paddleboating or hydro-biking opportunities. Exercise your arms with a rowboat or your legs with a paddleboat, or just relax and cruise beautiful Lake Geneva on one of the excursion boats, like the *Lady of the Lake,* a modern reproduction of a Mississippi paddle-wheel steamer. More water opportunities present themselves at the indoor and outdoor pools or with some serious swimming in the lap pool. Jogging, biking, and fitness trails wind through the property, taking advantage of the natural beauty.

You may want to spend the entire day in the Spa. Day membership is $10 for guests and includes use of the whirlpool, sauna, steam, and robes. Fitness classes, therapeutic baths, herbal wraps, antistress facials and massages, and a variety of body masks are just a few of the treatments guaranteed to make you feel like a new person. Enjoy them a la carte or preplanned, for example, an antistress day ($114) or custom spa day ($133).

In the wintertime Grand Geneva has its own mountain for skiing. Even if there is no snow in Wisconsin, with snowmaking, there will be snow at the resort. Twelve slopes descend from the top elevation of 1,086 feet, with a 211-foot vertical drop. Night skiing, 10 kilometers of cross-country skiing, and a special area for snowboards ensure winter fun for everyone. The Ski School uses Station Teaching to allow individuals to progress at their own rate, mastering each "station," then moving on. ≋

Grand Traverse Resort

Acme, Michigan 49610
(800) 748–0303
E-mail: gtresort@traverse.com
Web site: www.gtresort.com

Long known as the Cherry Capital, this area of northwest lower Michigan has a lot more to offer visitors than just its beautiful orchards and fine fruit. Besides providing memories of Ernest Hemingway, who spent many summers here and used this area as the setting for several short stories, Grand Traverse Resort offers guests golf, swimming, sailing, cross-country skiing, and a complete sports complex and health club. Set on 1,400 acres of forests and orchards with ½ mile of shoreline on East Grand Traverse Bay, the year-round resort boasts fine golf courses designed by Jack Nicklaus and Gary Player.

Accommodations: The resort hotel, which houses 238 rooms, is adjacent to the Traverse Pavilion, the site of summertime barbecues and wintertime ice skating. The 310 condominium units are spread throughout eight clusters of buildings. Some overlook the bay, and some skirt the golf courses; many have a fireplace. A shuttle service connects the condominiums with the other resort facilities. Rates range from $109 a night (hotel room, low season) to $409 a night (three-bedroom condo, summer). The deluxe Tower encompasses 186 suites, two lounges, a restaurant, and twenty boutiques. This is consummate luxury, with a private two-person whirlpool in each bathroom. Children under eighteen sleep free when sharing a room with their parents. Be sure to inquire about the many package plans. Cribs are available at no charge; rollaway beds are provided at a daily charge of $15.

Dining: Sweetwater Cafe features an open kitchen in the center of the restaurant and serves American fare plus select pasta dishes; it is open seven days a week for breakfast, lunch, and dinner. The Trillium Restaurant, located in the Tower, serves regional American dishes. A children's menu is available in most restaurants. The Club Deli, in the Village Health Club, also provides an informal setting for dining and cocktails. Other choices include Jack's Lounge, the Trillium Nightclub for dancing and nightly entertainment, and the Shores Beach Club, on the bay.

Children's World: For seven- to twelve-year-olds, a day camp is scheduled half days and full days, Monday through Sunday in the summer, and weekends the rest of the year. Activities include arts and crafts, games, swimming, exercise classes, and hiking; fees may be charged for some events. For younger children day care is available in the Cub House, a 2,000-square-foot children's

Photo courtesy of Grand Traverse Resort

center. Each event through the day is geared to a specific age group; you must register in advance for each event. An adventure playground near the Village Health Club also keeps youngsters well entertained, and the electronic game room may keep them mesmerized. Individual nannies can be scheduled with the assistance of the health club staff.

Recreation: The pride of Grand Traverse Resort is The Bear. Designed by Jack Nicklaus, this golf course meanders through cherry and apple orchards, with plenty of hardwood forest areas for contrast; it is quite scenic as well as challenging. The older course, Spruce Run, also offers championship play. The resort's third course is a championship course designed by Gary Player, complete with a state-of-the-art clubhouse. Located within walking distance of the main resort, the clubhouse serves all three courses. Future plans are to also build a Lee Trevino–designed golf course. The Jim McLean Golf School program provides sessions from May through September.

The Village Health Club is a championship setup too. With four outdoor and five indoor tennis courts (instruction available), four racquetball courts, indoor and outdoor swimming pools, and an exercise/weight room, you'll get quite a workout. Afterward you'll probably head straight to the saunas. In the Tower, a full-service spa and salon provides all the pampering you need. Mountain bikes and in-line skates are available for rent.

If water sports capture your interest, try swimming, sailing, or sailboarding, or take an evening cruise or a charter fishing trip on the bay. Fishermen seek out the many lakes and streams for trout and salmon. Hike or jog through the hills and past the orchards; the scenery is so good for the soul that you may not notice you're also helping your body.

But don't be deceived; Grand Traverse is not just a summertime resort. In the fall trees burst into autumn colors and make a beautiful backdrop for horse-drawn hayrides and trips to nearby wineries for sampling and festivals. In the winter cross-country skiing takes over; Nordic trails weave through the forests and gently rolling hills. Private lessons and group clinics are offered at the Village Nordic Center. Take a sleigh ride through the woods, or go ice skating in the Traverse Pavilion. And remember, while working out at The Village Health Club, you'll never know how low the temperature dips outside. In the spring, when the weather is warm enough for you to want to pick up a golf club, the cherry orchards come to life. The white blossoms of the trees blanket the hillsides for more than half the month of May. ≋

Grand View Lodge

134 Nokomis
Nisswa, Minnesota 56468
(800) 432–3788
Web site: www.grandviewlodge.com

Nestled among the Norway pines on the north shore of Gull Lake is Grand View Lodge, the focal point of this 900-acre resort. Built in 1918 of native cedar logs and now a National Historic Site, the lodge welcomes guests during its April-to-October season. In addition to the lodge, sixty-five cottages border the lake. Located 142 miles northwest of Minneapolis, the Lodge is within a fifteen-minute drive of seven golf courses, Paul Bunyan Center, and animal parks.

Accommodations: The twelve rooms in the lodge are comfortable for couples, while a cottage is the right choice for a family. Since these range in size from one to eight bedrooms, owner Fred Boos explains that they "try to fit the cabin to the family." Some cabins feature a kitchenette and living room; all have decks as well as large picture windows and views of the lake. Suites and town houses overlooking The Pines golf course also are available. Daily maid service is provided for both the lodge and the cabins. Reservations are accepted on a

Photo courtesy of Grand View Lodge

daily as well as weekly basis. Rates from $95 to $140 per person per day include two meals a day, golf at the Garden Course, discounted golf rates at The Pines and The Preserve championship courses, tennis, and the children's program. For children the charge is $10–$55 a night, American plan, depending on the age of the child.

Dining: There are several dining rooms: the main dining room in the historic lodge, Freddy's in the Pines Clubhouse, The Preserve Steak House in the Preserve Clubhouse, Sherwood Forest (also a historic building), and Italian Gardens. Dress is casual. Barbecues on the beach are often planned. Children may dine with their parents or their counselors. A special menu for children features fresh fish, steaks, chicken, and ribs. Cocktails are served on the large, three-level redwood deck or in the North Woods Lounge, where you'll hear live music nightly. The smorgasbord is a traditional Sunday event—great fun and all you can eat.

Children's World: From Memorial Day weekend to Labor Day weekend, Grand View has three separate and very well-organized programs, for children ages three to six, six to ten, and ten to thirteen. There is a wonderful wooden playhouse in the woods with slides and climbing equipment, a well-stocked play area, and the beach along Gull Lake. The programs run from 9:00 A.M. to 3:00 P.M. and from 5:30 to 8:00 P.M., Monday through Saturday. The schedule includes arts, games, storytime, movement activities, exercise, swimming, peanut hunts, hayrides, and visits to a game farm. A talent show is held on Friday; Saturday is carnival night for everyone.

The staff is college age and generally has past experience with children. The program is free except for special tours and trips. For those under age three, the front desk can arrange baby-sitting ($3.00 to $5.00 per hour) with either an off-duty staff member or selected local persons.

Recreation: The lake attracts swimmers, fishermen, sailors, and sunbathers. Here you can also venture out in a pontoon or kayak or practice some water-skiing. A twenty-seven-hole championship golf course is aptly named, given its setting: The Pines. The nine-hole Garden Course depends more on floral configurations in the layout of the holes. The newest championship golf course, The Preserve, is located 10 miles north of The Pines.

A tennis complex with eleven Laykold courts is set among tall trees. Court time is free. The tennis pro teaches guests in private lessons, organizes tournaments, and conducts free group lessons for children eight to nineteen years old. Two hitting walls and an automatic ball machine allow for extra practice before a good match. The staff horticulturist conducts tours of the newly developed gardens, introducing guests to the extensive collection of flowers and shrubs. ≋

Harbour View Inn

P.O. Box 1207
Mackinac Island, Michigan 49757
(906) 847–0101
Web site: www.habourviewinn.com

For a truly unique vacation experience, take your family to Mackinac Island where the main modes of transportation are by bike or horse-drawn carriage. Mackinac Island is accessible by auto, plane, or boat. When arriving by automobile, you will find passenger ferry services to the Island conveniently located in the downtown areas of Mackinaw City and St. Ignace. Secure overnight parking and luggage handling services are available from both ports. If you choose to arrive by boat or yacht, complete marina services are available.

When you visit the Harbour View Inn you are visiting a great place for families who love history. This stately manor was built in 1820 by Madame La Framboise, a Great Lakes fur trader and granddaughter of Returning Cloud, Chief of the Ottawa Indian Nation. The Inn, featured in *Colonial Homes* and *Traverse,* has also been awarded three-diamond status by AAA.

Accommodations: Charming Victorian detail has been preserved for your stay at the Harbour View Inn. Elegant accommodations offer views of the historic harbor or the landscaped gardens. In-room whirlpools and balconies are also available and a complimentary deluxe continental breakfast is served each morning. Chateau LaFramboise rooms are decorated in a blend of French and Victorian styles, while a Mackinac Island Summer Cottage theme defines the Carriage House and Guest House rooms. Spacious studio-style suites are also available. Daily rates range from $125 to $325 depending on the type of room or suite and the season.

Dining: A variety of dining opportunities are within close proximity of the Harbour View and include Three Brothers Sarducci Pizza, Zach's Deli, the Pilot House, Martha's Ice Cream and Sweet Shop, Letterman's Astor Street Cafe, and many more. The contrast in offerings is sure to please the whole family.

Children's World: Mackinac Island will provide hours of adventure for your child. You can rent bicycles, in-line skates, boats, horses, or even carriages for family fun. Make sure you visit Fort Mackinac and the Butterfly House. Take a carriage tour or visit the Haunted House. If you get tired of what you can find to do on land, try one of the cruise or fishing charters, or you can always relax at the beach. Child care is available.

Recreation: For the golf enthusiast try the Grand Hotel Golf Course. For a rigorous workout, explore the parks and hiking trails that help make Mackinac so unique. If you decide to visit during the winter months, the island offers skiing and sleigh rides. ≈≈≈

The Homestead

Wood Ridge Road
Glen Arbor, Michigan 49636
(616) 334–5000

The Great Lakes are truly great—and not just in size. While Lake Michigan's 22,400-square-mile area is indeed impressive, imagine the possibilities it affords in recreation and relaxation: swimming, boating, and fishing in the water, and on land, hiking and biking the wooded trails beyond the lake's sandy beach. At The Homestead all this great potential is realized, combined with tennis facilities, variety in dining, and comfortable, attractive lodging. When the weather cools the swimmers give way to skiers, who discover nature's wintertime beauty.

Photo courtesy of The Homestead

The Homestead is located on the northwest shore of lower Michigan. Its 500 acres embrace gently rolling land covered with pine trees, aspens, and oaks; 1 mile of sandy beach on Lake Michigan; and 6 miles of shoreline along the banks of Crystal River. Surrounding the resort is the Sleeping Bear Dunes National Lakeshore; besides ensuring The Homestead's secluded position, this national preserve opens up additional opportunities for nature explorers. The resort is closed in April and November.

Accommodations: The Village is the center of most activities, as accommodations, restaurants, shops, and a heated swimming pool are located here. Fiddler's Pond and Little Belle in the Village offer guest rooms and suites overlooking the pond. One- to four-bedroom condominiums, each with a full kitchen, are located on the beach, along Crystal River, on a ridge overlooking the shoreline, and in the Village. Crystal River cuts through the hills and runs more or less parallel to the lakeshore a short way before emptying into the lake. Where the river and the lake merge is another center of activity, the Beach Club.

Fiddler's Pond rooms are $69–$159 a night and Little Belle $89–209 a night. A one-bedroom condominium unit ranges between $126 and $311 a night, depending on the location you choose; lakefront and lakeview units are the most expensive. The rates for larger units graduate to $633 a night for a four-bedroom home/condominium. These rates are applied during the summer and on weekends through the year; package plans are also available. Cribs are provided at no charge; children are free when staying in their parents' room.

Dining: At the Beach Club the Cafe Manitou draws diners to its ideal location on the beach; open daily in the summer only, its setting and attire are casual.

Around the bend in the Village, Nonna's boasts a bountiful breakfast and Northern Italian dinners, and Whiskers attracts pizza and burger fans. Also in the Village, at Cavanaugh's you can pick up groceries or deli sandwiches for lunch and snacks all day long. In the winter skiers gather in CQ's Cabin for its cozy atmosphere and friendly conversation.

Children's World: The children's summer program runs from late June through late August and entertains guests from toddlers to teenagers.

Daily, half and full days keep five- to twelve-year-olds busy with soccer and volleyball games, hiking, fishing, exercising to music, and arts and crafts. The Kids Kamp cost is $25 for half days and $40 for full days. Activities for this group and for teens are published in a weekly calendar. Kids can also join junior golf or tennis programs.

Teenagers enjoy a loose schedule that focuses on meeting other teens during canoe races, volleyball games, tennis matches, and pizza parties. Like the events for the younger group, some are free, while others require a fee. Private swimming lessons can be arranged, and tennis clinics are offered for young adults ages twelve to seventeen and juniors ages six to eleven.

In the winter the children's program teaches five- to twelve-year-olds fun-in-the-snow activities with ski lessons. It is offered for two and a half hours twice a day, Friday through Sunday and on holidays, from mid-December through March. The fee is $25 for a half day or $65 for a full day with lunch.

Any time of year, individual baby-sitters can be hired, at approximately $5.00 per hour. The resort staff assists in making the arrangements.

Recreation: The clear waters of Lake Michigan are fine for sailing, boating (rentals available), fishing, and swimming. Maybe still a little nippy in June, the lake's temperature averages sixty-five to seventy degrees by July and August, and its sandy bottom is particularly attractive to young swimmers. The river waters tend to be warmer, and both the Beach Club and the Village have a heated pool and a hot tub, so guests have their pick of swimming conditions. You can also enjoy the spa at the Beach Club. Fishing is good sport in the river as well as in the lake, and canoeing up the river allows you to investigate the local wildlife.

Hike, jog, and bicycle (children's bikes and bikes with children's seats are available for rent) on the 24 miles of wooded trails; a self-guided nature tour can introduce you to the area's flora and fauna.

Visit the nearby Sleeping Bear Dunes National Park, take a ferryboat ride to the islands in Lake Michigan, sample the wines of local vineyards, or just take a relaxing stroll along the beach at sunset.

For tennis players the Beach Club, with its five clay courts, is the site of many exciting matches. Here you can join a clinic, take private lessons, and watch real talent during professional exhibitions. If you're still looking for things to do, drop by the aerobics exercise class; work out on the fitness trail, with twenty exercise stations; head to the playground at River Park; or throw your hat into a volleyball tournament. Now here's ingenuity in utilizing space: In 1995 a nine-hole par three golf course opened—built in part on the downhill ski slopes!

In the winter 36 kilometers of trails attract cross-country skiers to The Homestead's wooded hills, and the frozen ponds are ideal for ice skating. Downhill skiing is modest, with thirteen runs and 350 vertical feet, but the view down a snowy slope to whitecaps on the lake is an uncommon juxtaposition you'll long remember. All runs benefit from artificial snowmaking, and those lighted for nighttime skiing add another dimension to a winter holiday. ≋

The Lodge of Four Seasons
Championship Golf Resort and Spa
State Road HH
Lake Ozark, Missouri 65049
(573) 365–3000, (800) THE–LAKE
Web site: www.4seasonresort.com

L ake of the Ozarks, a man-made lake developed in the 1930s, has provided scenic and recreational diversions for the residents of central Missouri for sixty years. Overlooking the lake, in the wooded gentle hills of the Ozarks, is The Lodge of Four Seasons. Opened in 1964, The Lodge has grown over the years into a major year-round resort with extensive recreational facilities and award-winning restaurants. Today it is a convenient escape from city cares for the residents of St. Louis and Kansas City and is sought as a vacation spot for visitors from farther afield as well.

Accommodations: Guests choose from 290 newly renovated guest rooms or 80 two- and three-bedroom condominiums—frequently more suitable for families. Charleston is The Lodge's newest condo development, built around a secluded cove with a breathtaking view of the lake. Some units have private boat slips. Condominium prices range from $249 to $395 a night, March to November; the rates are $95 to $225 in The Lodge. Rates are lower during the rest of the year. Children under eighteen share their parents' room and Fun Pass at no extra charge; complimentary cribs are available. The Fun Pass gives

Photo courtesy of The Lodge of Four Seasons Championship Golf Resort and Spa

access to the executive nine-hole golf course, movies, and scenic cruise. The cost is $10 per adult per day.

Dining: Toledo's offers a unique combination of great dining and live entertainment. Toledo's moderately priced menu features a variety of fresh selections incorporating specialties indigenous to the area. A children's menu is available, as well as an extensive wine selection, winner of the 1997 *Wine Spectator* award. Enjoy the finest cuts of certified Angus beef (or turkey steak if you prefer) at HK's Steak House, located on the golf course; it features a custom-designed, elevated charcoal grill. Have breakfast or lunch at Roseberry's Café, in a casual, family-style setting. The Atrium Café is the place for baked goods hot from the oven; for tasty deli sandwiches, stop at the Country Deli. In the evening relax with cocktails in the Lobby Bar and watch the world go by, or listen to live jazz in Toledo's. Studios Entertainment and Dance Club is the place for dancing and live entertainment.

Children's World: The Adventure Club provides a fun-filled day of activities for children age three to twelve. The Adventure Club is open every day (seasonally) from 9:00 A.M. to 4:00 P.M., and offers a weekend Kids Night Out from 6:00 to 9:00 P.M. Half- and full-day adventures are available; there is a daily charge for each child. Lunch is provided in the full-day program. Enjoy swimming, nature walks, fishing, games, movies, arts and crafts, theme days, and cookouts. The Adventure Club's staff is certified in Red Cross first aid and water safety training.

Recreation: The sports enthusiast will be well satisfied at The Lodge of Four Seasons, named one of the "Top 50 Golf Resorts" by *Condé Nast Traveler.* One championship eighteen-hole golf course was designed by Robert Trent Jones Sr., and interests players with its narrow, undulating fairways and glimpses of the lake's blue waters. A second eighteen-hole championship golf course, Seasons Ridge, is carved into the rolling Ozark terrain, where multiple tee boxes accommodate golfers of all skill levels. Golf instruction is offered at both of these courses. In addition, golfers can turn to the nine-hole course to sharpen their skills. Equipment and attire can be purchased at the pro shop, if you've forgotten anything. If water sports are your life's love, you certainly won't feel slighted with both indoor and outdoor pools to enjoy. Swimmers can also venture out into the lake or sunbathe on the private beach. The lake is a favorite of boaters; the full-service marina can handle more than 200 boats and is the base for lake activities, from boat rentals and waterskiing to fishing guide services and parasailing. The Lodge of Four Seasons also offers a scenic excursion boat that takes guests on a smooth journey around the lake.

Guests can unwind at Spa Eminence. Try a full body massage or a "salt glo"; whatever your pleasure, the spa offers many relaxing choices. Browse through on-site shops, catch a movie in the lodge's cinema, or simply take a stroll through beautifully landscaped Japanese gardens. If you have any energy left, bike or hike along wooded paths, and try your hand at trapshooting. Racquetball, volleyball, basketball, tennis, and Ping-Pong are even more options to fit into a busy schedule. At the end of a very full day, you may choose to stop and have a drink at the Lobby Bar, dance at Studios Entertainment and Dance Club, or retire early for a well-deserved repose. ≋

Ludlow's Island Lodge

P.O. Box 1146
Cook, Minnesota 55723
(218) 666–5407, (800) 537–5308
Web site: www.ludlowsresort.com

Minnesota has a reputation as the land of 10,000 lakes (ever wonder who counted them all?), and Ludlow's Island Lodge is well situated on one of these—picturesque Lake Vermilion. The resort facilities are located on Ludlow's Island and on the north and south shores of the lake. A boat shuttle connects the three areas. Water-related activities are the primary recre-

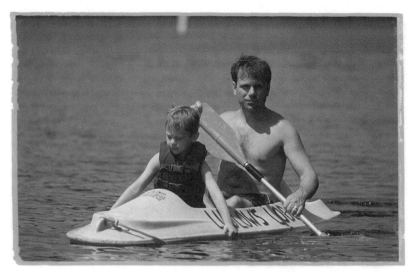

Photo © Jack Rendulich, courtesy of Ludlow's Island Lodge

ation at this wooded resort. Fishing, swimming, sailing, and exploring any of the 365 islands provide wonderful experiences. The seclusion among the pines and birches, with the lake practically at your front door, makes this retreat a real back-to-nature experience. The resort is open from May through September.

Accommodations: Eighteen cabins with enchanting names like Stardust, Evergreen, and Twilite are located on the island and the shores. Designed with knotty pine or cedar interiors, all have a fireplace and outdoor deck; most have a screened porch. They range from one to five bedrooms, with a fully equipped kitchen (yes, even a dishwasher and microwave). Daily rates start at $165 for two adults and $30 for each child. Summer weekly rates start at $1,350 for two people.

Dining: Ludlow's offers full menu choices for evening meals delivered to your cabin. Each cabin has a menu with items ranging from $9.50 to $17.50. Pizza and burgers are also available. The order is placed with the lodge by 5:00 P.M. and delivered to your cabin by 7:00 P.M., to be served on cabin dishes.

Children's World: Planned activities just for children are scheduled only an hour or two each day, Monday through Friday. Boat rides, nature hikes, and fishing derbies introduce kids to the surrounding woods and waters. Movies are shown in the afternoons. The two-story tree house and a small camping island for overnight trips are probably the biggest attractions for the younger set, but the swings, the lake (with a section roped off for children's safety), and the sandy beach are good play areas too. Kids also enjoy the video-game room,

Ping-Pong, and exploring the trails in the forest, just like Paul Bunyan of Minnesota lore. The recreation complex on the south shore has a children's play area. The management can help arrange baby-sitters ($5.00 an hour).

Recreation: Fishing buffs relish this bit of paradise on the south shores of Lake Vermilion. Walleye, bass, and crappie lure fishermen to these waters. Each cabin is provided with a 16-foot aluminum boat. And there's no excuse for not landing the big one; a fishing clinic is held every week, and a guide is available for private excursions. The staff at the lodge will fillet and freeze your catch. Besides fishing boats, the lodge has canoes, kayaks, paddleboats, and a sailboat for guests' use.

The recreation center houses an indoor racquetball court, two tru-flex tennis courts, and an exercise area. After a good workout there, you may enjoy a leisurely swim or a relaxing sauna. Along the north shore you can take a stroll down the 1½ mile hiking trail. There are also many miles of hiking and biking trails in the area. ≋

Marriott's Tan-Tar-A Resort and Golf Club
State Road KK
Osage Beach, Missouri 65065
(573) 348–3131
Web site: www.tan-tar-a.com

Located in central Missouri, Marriott's Tan-Tar-A Resort rests comfortably in the foothills of the Ozark Mountains. The resort complex covers 420 acres and sprawls along the shores of the scenic Lake of the Ozarks. The hilly terrain and lakeside exposure provide a lovely backdrop for the many recreational activities. Tan-Tar-A is only a three-hour drive from either St. Louis or Kansas City.

Accommodations: The 930 guest rooms and suites are in the main resort buildings and in smaller two-story accommodations bordering the lake and the golf course. Some have a fireplace and a deck or patio. The high season is mid-May to mid-September, when rates are $99–$165 a night. During the low season (November to mid-March) prices drop to $65–$110 a night. In the remaining months the rates are $89–$145 a night.

Dining: The casual family-style restaurant, the Cliff Room, has a large deck for outdoor dining. Here, between 5:00 and 7:00 P.M., children eight years old and younger eat free. For a fancier evening try Windrose on the Water, where you'll enjoy luscious steaks and fresh seafood. If all you want is a quick bite, there are fast-food facilities nearby. At the golf course The Oaks serves breakfast and lunch, overlooking the course.

For liquid refreshment The Landing is a daytime pub, The Jetty Bar is adjacent to the Arrowhead Pool, and Tradewinds is near the Tradewinds Pool. Mr. D's also serves cocktails, and The Nightwinds Lounge offers live music for dancing in the evening.

Children's World: Camp Tan-Tar-A, for children ages five to ten years, is in session Monday through Friday, from early June through mid-August and at holiday times the rest of the year. The fee for the 9:30 A.M.–4:00 P.M. schedule is $25 for the first day and $20 for each additional day. Activities include swimming, beach games, races, treasure hunts, and crafts. Also, kids ages seven to ten can join a guided fishing tour for two hours ($25 per child).

A less structured routine is found at the Children's Playhouse, which is open to four- to ten-year-olds, Saturday from 9:00 A.M. to 5:00 P.M. and Monday through Saturday evenings from 6:30 to 11:00 P.M. Here counselors supervise children as they play with the array of toys, board games, puzzles, and books. During the spring, fall, and winter, the schedule at the Playhouse is limited to all day Saturday and Friday and Saturday evenings. The fee is $4.00 an hour for the first child and only 50 cents an hour for each additional child. These same rates apply for individual baby-sitters.

Recreation: The lake is the venue for boating fun for everyone. You can rent ski boats (waterskiing instruction available), sailboats, paddleboats, kayaks, fishing boats, and Wave Runners. You can even try parasailing. Though there's a small sandy beach nice for sunbathing, the lake is primarily the domain of boaters and fishermen. Swimmers usually opt for time at one of the five pools (four outdoors, one indoors).

Golfers can take on the challenges of The Oaks (an eighteen-hole course) or Hidden Lakes (nine holes). The Racquet Club houses tennis and racquetball courts as well as billiards. Outdoors and adjacent to the club are basketball and volleyball courts. Tennis buffs can also try the indoor or outdoor tennis courts near the Racquet Club.

At the fitness center you can use the exercise room as well as the indoor pool, and you can indulge in the many programs at the Windjammer Spa. Facials, massages, aromatherapy, and detoxification treatments are just some of the pleasures from which to choose.

Back in the great outdoors, find a good horse at the stables for a nice trail ride, rent a mountain bike, jog along the paths around the property, test your skill at the trap range, or challenge the kids to a round of miniature golf. If you still have time and energy, try bowling, shuffleboard, horseshoes, and Ping-Pong. Even the shoppers in your family will have plenty of fun in the dozen shops, featuring jewelry, toys, fashions, and country crafts. And be sure to take an evening cruise on the lake; the *Ozark Princess* sails four nights a week during the summer season.

In the winter ice skating is available for both adults and children. ≋

Mission Point Resort

One Lakeshore Drive
Mackinac Island, Michigan 49757
(800) 833–7711
Web site: www.missionpoint.com

Mission Point Resort is privately-owned property encompassing eighteen acres of Mackinac Island lakefront. The resort is situated along the southeast coast of the island and is just minutes from downtown. The island's turn-of-the-century ambience is enhanced by the noticeable absence of cars, since the only access to the island is by ferry or plane. This all-American lake-shore retreat is complemented by the natural adventures and historic discoveries of Mackinac Island. The island boasts the nation's second oldest park, and pine forests are threaded with hiking and biking paths as well as unusual limestone foundations and caves.

Taking advantage of existing architecture, Mission Point has renovated The Observation Tower, offering island visitors extraordinary views of Lake Huron and the Straits of Mackinac. This all-glass structure on the resort's property serves as the perfect spot to watch sailboats approach the southeast coast during the island's annual yacht races.

Accommodations: Mission Point has 242 guest rooms and suites, including family suites. The resort has a health club, art gallery, and much more. All the resort's guest rooms and suites, including the new outdoor Hot Tub Suites, celebrate the beauty of Northern Michigan. The heated swimming pool, therapeutic massage, saunas, and hot tubs are great ways to relax. You may want to spend some of your time on The Greens on Mackinac on the water's edge or on The Courts enjoying tennis, lawn bowling, or croquet.

Dining: The resort has three restaurants. At The Great Straits Seafood Company, new to the culinary collection, world-renowned Chef Ernst Ackermann adds his flair to a culinary palette of fresh fish and steaks. For the casual side of island dining, try The Round Island Bar and Grill where guests can watch passing freighters while enjoying appetizers, sandwiches, and spirits in a warm setting. Freighters Deli and Outdoor Cafe offers sandwiches and salads for guests on the go as well as indoor and outdoor dining with spectacular views of Lake Huron and the Straits of Mackinac. It's worth noting that the resort has gourmet picnic baskets to go, a great addition to a day of island exploration. Children twelve and younger dine free of charge.

Children's World: Mission Point Resort's children's program Discovery Club is staffed with dedicated, trained counselors. Discovery Club offers island field trips and exciting activities, such as Wild Kingdom Day and Space Day, for children ages four through ten. The fee for the program is $12.00 for a full day or $7.00 for a half day. Families with more than one child receive a 50 percent discount for each additional child registered in the program.

With a 3,000-square-foot area in which kids spark their imagination with a variety of interesting activities, Discovery Club includes a Parent and Toddler Room, Gross Motor Skills Rooms, and a Kreative Korner Room, as well as some of the kids' traditional favorites like the 12-foot teepee. The active atmosphere of the Resort is complemented by Mackinac Island itself, a natural adventure park, offering outdoor explorations and historic sites.

While at Discovery Club kids enjoy a variety of supervised opportunities including arts and crafts, learning ancient Indian lore, plus field trips to the Island's Butterfly House, the 150-year-old British Fort, or along the Island's bluff for bald eagle spotting. Discovery Club is not only fun, it is a safe place to leave young guests while parents enjoy the Resort's art gallery, Island boutiques, or the nearby championship golf courses. Parents are encouraged to sign up children one day in advance, allowing the counselors to plan appropriate activities and guarantee its one-to-six counselor/child ratio. As an added convenience, pagers are available for parents of young guests.

Recreation: Experience the island by guided tours or independent exploration. Attractions include miles of forst trails for hiking, horseback riding, and carriage tours. Sites you won't want to miss are Fort Mackinac (circa 1780), the restored British and American military outpost where you can see colonial reenactments, period characters, and cannon firings; Mackinac Island State Park, which encompasses two-thirds of the entire island and preserves natural forests; Benjamin Blacksmith Shop, where you see, smell, and even feel the heat from the nineteenth-century forge as craftsmen still practice their skill; Astor Warehouse (circa 1820), where mink, muskrat, otter, and beaver pelts were graded for Indians and fur traders; Biddle House (circa 1820), a restored home of a prominent fur trader that brings to life the domestic side of island history; McGulpin House (circa 1780), the oldest structure on the island; and Skull Cave—to name just a few.

If you still want more to do, the Activities Desk can arrange for Mission Point guests to tee off at one of six championship golf courses. Sailing cruises are an invigorating experience and fishing charters yield catches of perch, whitefish, and Chinook. Whatever you choose to do, you can be sure that a brand new experience is waiting for you and your family at Mission Point Resort. ≈≈≈

Ruttger's Bay Lake Lodge

Box 400
Deerwood, Minnesota 56444
(218) 678–2885, (800) 450–4545
Web site: www.ruttgers.com

I f you have ever entertained thoughts of owning your own lakefront cottage in the land of 10,000 lakes, Ruttger's Bay Lake Lodge may satisfy your yearning. Set on 400 acres directly on Bay Lake, in north-central Minnesota, the Lodge emphasizes relaxed outdoor recreation in surroundings of clear lake waters, tall trees, and pine-scented air. Open from May 1 to October 31, it is family run and family oriented. With its tradition of old-fashioned hospitality, the lodge allows you a well-deserved escape to the peace and serenity of the North Woods.

Accommodations: For years the lakefront cottages and the Lodge rooms have been favorites among vacationers. To these have been added condominiums, villas, and town houses. Many have views of the lake, and all include a refrigerator. Rates are $82–$159 per person per day, modified American plan. Children under three are free, while the rate for four- to eight-year-olds is one-third the adult rate and for nine- to fifteen-year-olds, one-half the adult rate. Cribs are provided at no additional charge with a weekly package plan.

Dining: The modified American plan is mandatory for cottage guests, and the homemade pastries are practically a requirement. The main dining room is an inviting setting, with natural logs, an open-beamed ceiling, and a stone fireplace. Lunches are also served on the deck overlooking the lake at the Pro Shop Grill or Auntie M's Kafferhaus. You may cook lunch for yourself in the condos or town houses. The Terrace Cocktail Lounge has picture windows that are great for viewing the North Woods while sipping a cool drink.

Children's World: Kids' Kamp is a supervised and complimentary program for children, in operation from mid-June until Labor Day, every day except Sunday, on the modified American plan. Beginning at age four, kids join their counselors from 9:00 A.M. to 2:00 P.M. The counselors organize the day for fishing, swimming, crafts, treasure hunts, nature programs, and talent shows. A playground is equipped with swings, sandboxes, a merry-go-round, ropes, slides, and seesaws. Three times a week the children can join a dinner and movie evening from 5:30 to 8:30 P.M. Baby-sitting can be arranged by the staff for approximately $3.50 per hour.

Recreation: With such a beautiful lake, you might find yourself drawn to the water almost continuously through the day—for sunning, swimming, waterskiing, fishing, and boating, and for building sandcastles along the beach. Swimmers also enjoy the indoor and outdoor pools, and tennis fans turn to the two Omni-turf and three Laykold courts. Round up a game of volleyball, basketball, or horseshoes; play Ping-Pong and shuffleboard; or go walking through the woods. Practice on the putting green, and plan a round of golf on the eighteen-hole championship course or the Lodge Nine. And treat yourself to relaxation in the card room or TV room, the whirlpool, or the sauna. The staff naturalist directs programs introducing visitors to the loon, osprey, and bald eagle. Waterskiing, sailboats, motorboats, pontoon boats, and fishing boats are available. ≋

Shanty Creek

1 Shanty Creek Road
Bellaire, Michigan 49615
(800) 678–4111
E-mail: info@shantycreek.com
Web site: www.shantycreek.com

S hanty Creek, located in northern Michigan, is actually two resorts in one, which translates into a bit of variety for guests. Summit Village is elegant and contemporary, while Schuss Village is modeled on an Alpine village. Together they encompass 4,000 acres of rolling woodlands on the shores of Lake Bellaire. In the summertime golfing is the favorite activity; in winter skiing is the preferred sport.

The summer of 1999 witnessed the grand opening of The Lodge at Cedar River. This eighty-four-room, all-suite luxury hotel offers outstanding views of the new Tom Weiskopf–designed Cedar River Golf Club and the newest ski runs on the Schuss slopes.

Accommodations: Lodging choices are innumerable: guest rooms, studios, condominiums, and chalets. Some are equipped with a fireplace or whirlpool; others have a deck. You might have a view of the lake, the forests, a fairway, or the Alpine village. Rates start at $84 a night for a guest room and rise to $340 a night for a deluxe two-bedroom condominium. Children ages seventeen and under stay free when occupying a room with their parents. Cribs can be added to your accommodation for a fee of $5.00 a day. The many package plans offer good savings.

Dining: The Lakeview Dining Room is an elegant restaurant at Summit Village. At Schuss Village a down-home, fun, family atmosphere prevails at the more casual Ivan's Mountainside Grill. For light meals and easy dining, try La Bodega Deli and Arnie's at The Legend Pro Shop. The Beach Club, right on the shores of Lake Bellaire, also provides refreshments.

Children's World: When the weather warms up, just as the golf season begins, infants to ten-year-olds can be accommodated in a daily child-care program. From 9:00 A.M. to 5:00 P.M., children join together in storytime, movies, arts and crafts, and music. The fee is $22 full day, $15 half day. Lunch is $5.00 extra.

From early June through Labor Day, Kid's Korner explodes with summertime fun: nature hikes, basketball, volleyball, scavenger hunts, shuffleboard, and swimming. This program is designed for children ages six and older. The fees and hours are the same as above.

When the ski season starts in November, the daily child-care program applies to infants to six-year-olds. In addition to stories, movies, and indoor play, the older children discover the excitement of outdoor play in a winter wonderland. The same fees as above are charged for this program.

Young skiers, ages three to five, combine indoor play with sledding and ski instruction in their 9:30 A.M. to 3:30 P.M. schedule. The fee is $45 a day and includes ski rental and lunch.

Kid's Academy, for older children (ages five to eleven), runs from 10:00 A.M. to 4:00 P.M. daily. This is more serious instruction but still doesn't lose sight of the fun of skiing. The fee is $35 full day, $30 half day with lunch, and $25 half day without lunch. Ski rentals are not included in these fees.

At any time of the year, baby-sitting can be booked through the concierge for $5.00 an hour.

Recreation: Golfers experience a bit of a dream come true here. The resort's original golf course is the eighteen-hole Summit Golf Course. Another championship eighteen holes comprise the beautiful Schuss Mountain Course. And the crowning gem is The Legend, an exciting eighteen-hole course designed by Arnold Palmer. With the carefully maintained courses complemented by an experienced teaching staff, all golfers will surely improve their games here. The new Cedar River Golf Club, designed by Tom Weiskopf, is sure to win accolades from all players.

Other summertime activities include tennis, with eight courts; biking on the mountain trails; and boating. At the Fitness Center work out on the Nautilus equipment, head to the racquetball courts, hit the steam room or sauna, and wind up the day with a massage. With indoor swimming pools and a heated pool outdoors, swimmers are satisfied whatever the season.

The ski season starts in November and continues through late March or early April, depending on how generous Mother Nature has been. There are forty-three runs for downhill skiers, almost 20 miles of groomed trails for cross-country skiers, and two terrain parks for snowboarders. When you're not on skis, pile the whole family into a horse-drawn sleigh for an old-fashioned ride in the woods. ≈≈≈

SOUTHWEST

Arizona

New Mexico

Texas

Angel Fire Resort

Drawer B
Angel Fire, New Mexico 87710
(505) 377–2301, (800) 633–7463
Web site: www.angelfireresort.com

Impressed by the pink glow on the mountains, Indians named this area "the land of Angel Fire." This year-round resort in the ancient Sangre de Cristo Mountain range of northern New Mexico allows for escape, renewal, and rejuvenation. Angel Fire encompasses 20,000 acres of mountain scenery and beauty and extends its southwestern ambience with a warm, neighborly feeling in spite of its size.

Accommodations: Angel Fire can accommodate approximately 4,000 guests in a variety of lodges and condominiums scattered through the village area. At first glance so many guests conjures up images of crowds, but remember that this still leaves five acres of land per person! In addition, the Starfire Lodge and Angel Fire Resort Hotel offer rooms and suites, so you may take your choice of accommodation styles. Prices range from $75 to $160 for a room up to $125 to $345 for a three-bedroom unit. Cribs are provided at a nominal nightly fee. Prices vary depending on season.

Dining: Hungry? The village has eleven dining areas. Choose from a variety of foods including Italian, Mexican, or steak house specialties. Dress is casual, and selected restaurants cater to children, with special menus for them. For relaxing with drinks, most of the restaurants and clubs have lounges, many with inviting fireplaces. The Angel Fire Country Club matches up spectacular mountain views with tasty breakfasts, lunches, and dinners. Live entertainment enlivens weekends at Angel Fire.

Children's World: The Angel Fire Resort offers children's programs in both summer and winter.

During the winter, from Thanksgiving to the end of March, the focus is on skiing and snowboarding. Young skiers ages three to twelve can join the Children's Ski and Snowboard Center, which runs from 8:30 A.M. to 4:00 P.M.; a $65 to $75 daily fee covers lessons, lift tickets, rentals, and lunch. And in case you do not believe your eyes, indeed a Disneylike "Snow Bear" does ski with the children.

Very young or nonskiing children can participate in daily activities at the Angel Fire Resort Day Care. Children six weeks to twelve years old can join the fun on an hourly basis from 8:00 A.M. to 5:00 P.M. daily. These sessions are a combination of indoor play—such as games, treasure hunts, and crafts—and

Photo courtesy of Ben Blakenburg and Angel Fire Resort

outdoor play that emphasizes fun in the snow—such as "snowercise" and snow sculpture. The fee is $6.00 per hour, $45 for a full day, or $30 for a half day. Parents must supply diapers, bottles, formula, and other supplies.

Recreation: The primary diversion in winter is skiing or snowboarding. Angel Fire has hosted the World Cup Freestyle Competition, but don't be intimidated. More than two-thirds of the trails are for beginners and intermediates. The vertical drop is 2,077 feet, and the longest trail is a cruising 3½ miles long. Six chairlifts cover 30 miles of trails, two ski shops are ready to rent or sell equipment and accessories, and lessons are available. The Nordic skier can enjoy unlimited trails at the Angel Fire Resort Golf Course. In varying levels of difficulty, these trek through aspen, spruce, and ponderosa pine groves. Sleigh rides and snowmobiles round out the wintertime fun.

Once the snow melts, these same trails offer fantastic opportunities for mountain biking, hiking, backpacking, and horseback riding. Catching a trout from the annually stocked lake can be an exhilarating experience, but if fishing is not your sport, you can canoe and sail in these waters. Have a swim in the pool, play tennis, or bicycle on the paths around the village. At an elevation of 8,600 feet, the eighteen-hole golf course weaves through a wooded terrain. Practice on the driving range and putting green, or enlist the expert advice of the golf pro. Summer Adventures offers such things as white-water rafting or gold panning for a fee. Whatever your activity, the crisp mountain air enhances it. ≋

The Arizona Biltmore

Twenty-fourth Street and Missouri
Phoenix, Arizona 85016
(602) 955–6600, (800) 950–0086

The Arizona Biltmore is often referred to as the "jewel of the desert." At the entrance to the grounds, Main Drive is lined with lovely private homes and landscaped with citrus trees and flowering oleander, petunias, and pansies. The main structure at the end of this drive is an architectural masterpiece. Inspired by Frank Lloyd Wright and constructed of Biltmore block-tile, the buildings reflect the gracious charm and innovative spirit of the 1920s. Exploring the thirty-nine acres of this fine establishment is an adventure in architectural history and a delightful experience in imaginative landscaping. Stroll along the beautifully manicured lawns and gardens for visual delights in carefully tended beds of yellow pansies or pink petunias or multicolored snapdragons. In dining, shopping, and recreational activities, The Biltmore has consistently maintained its reputation as a world-class resort. It is open year-round.

Accommodations: There are 750 well-appointed rooms and suites, approximately 100 of which are located in the main building. The others are arranged in several buildings and cottages bordering flower beds. Many rooms have mountain or garden views, and all rooms have been recently remodeled. Standard rooms cost $165 in the summer, $350 September to December, and $370 January 1 to April 30. Resort rooms are more spacious, with extra-large bathrooms and private balcony or terrace. Those rates are $215, $435, and $475 for the above dates. Children under eighteen can stay free in the same room with their parents. Cribs are provided at no extra charge.

Dining: Enjoy regional and American cuisine for breakfast, lunch, and dinner in the casual atmosphere of the Biltmore Grill and Patio or The Café. A children's menu is available. Or you can experience the award-winning New American specialties at Wright's, where the striking architecture enhances the enjoyment of the food. Wright's serves lunch and dinner. Private wine tastings can be arranged—the Biltmore has one of the most extensive wine lists in the region. If you're near the water slide and new pool, try the Cabana Club Restaurant and Bar for sandwiches and cool drinks during the day and cocktails and entertainment in the evening. The grand atmosphere of the lobby also provides several grand options for the tummy. Traditional tea is served from 2:30 to 5:30 P.M. The Squaw Peak Lounge allows you to sit either indoors or outdoors, listen to music, and savor the view of the mountain along with your drinks and hors d'oeuvres. For the morning hours, The Café serves a bountiful breakfast buffet, including espresso, cappuccino, imported coffees, and delicious pastries served for your

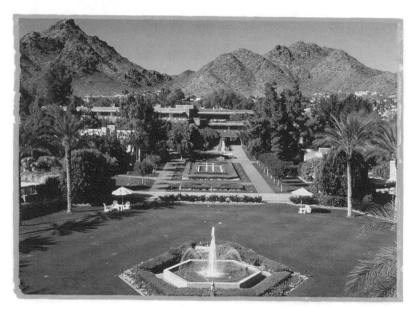

Photo courtesy of The Arizona Biltmore

satisfaction. The Gift Shop is a nostalgic soda fountain for small gifts, breakfast, lunch, snacks, and, of course, ice-cream sodas.

Children's World: "Kids Kabana—A Learning Center" is a well-planned activity center where children ages four to twelve can enjoy a variety of activities—crafts and computers as well as outdoor activities such as swimming, croquet, putting, or cycling. It is open daily year-round from 9:00 A.M. to 5:00 P.M.; the cost is $10 per hour (two-hour minimum), $30 for a half day, and $55 for a full day. Children under four may visit the center at the same rates if accompanied by a responsible adult.

Recreation: Merely the setting of The Biltmore could charm you for days on end, but once the inner spirit is renewed, try your hand at some of the many recreational activities. Eight lighted tennis courts attract tennis enthusiasts; schedule yourself for a tennis clinic or private lessons.

The avid golfer can take on one of the two eighteen-hole PGA courses or refine a technique on the putting greens and driving ranges. At the pro shop you can seek out the guidance of the teaching staff, pick up some vital accessories, or rent equipment.

The eight swimming pools can mean either invigorating laps or a relaxing dip. One of the twenty-three cabanas will protect you from the desert sun, and the 92-foot water slide is guaranteed to get a "wow!" To check out the scenery and still test your athletic abilities, rent a bicycle or jog along the trails flanking the Salt River Canal. Indulge at the Biltmore Spa, which offers more than eighty European body and skin treatments, fitness center, steam room, saunas, and whirlpool. Or perhaps you will alternate rigorous athletics with less demanding games of croquet, lawn chess, and volleyball.

If shopping is your interest, discover a varied and extensive line of merchandise in the hotel shops: jewelry, silver, regionally crafted products, both Southwest and Native American artists; and tennis, golf, and swimming clothes and accessories. Adjacent to the grounds is the Biltmore Fashion Park, filled with more shops and restaurants and reached by a shuttle bus. ≋

The Bishop's Lodge

P.O. Box 2367
Santa Fe, New Mexico 87504-2367
(505) 983–6377
Web site: www.bishopslodge.com

Just a five-minute drive north of Santa Fe, 1,000 acres of the foothills of the Sangre de Cristo Mountains comprise the range of The Bishop's Lodge. At an elevation of 7,200 feet, this area of north central New Mexico shares its warm sunny days with cool crisp nights. The clean mountain air, the setting, and the atmosphere of the lodge combine to emit the flavor and tradition of the old Southwest. The adobe architecture reminiscent of a Spanish and Native American heritage and the friendly spirit of the resident wranglers give The Bishop's Lodge its true Western flair.

In the nineteenth century, the ranch was the home of Archbishop Jean Baptiste l'Amy, a pioneering French cleric who became the Southwest's first Catholic bishop. His life was the inspiration for Willa Cather's novel *Death Comes for the Archbishop* (good background reading for an introduction to the history and topography of the region). The property was bought by the newspaper publisher Joseph Pulitzer and then acquired in 1918 by James Thorpe. The Thorpe family operated the lodge as a vacation resort until 1998, when it was bought by The Coastal Hotel Group, a management company that operates boutique family resorts and properties. The facilities have undergone expansion and renovation during the years, but the private chapel built by the archbishop still stands, a sentinel to the lodge's history. The lodge has been open year-round since 1994.

Accommodations: The lodge's eighty-eight rooms and suites are grouped in several adobe buildings nestled among fruit trees and flower beds. The North and South lodges are the oldest, both having been grand summer homes before

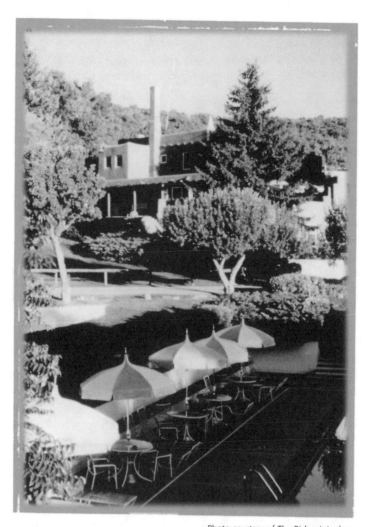

Photo courtesy of The Bishop's Lodge

World War I; the newest one, "Chamisa," contains fourteen deluxe accommodations above the banks of the Tesuque Creek. Many of the rooms are decorated in warm earth colors with a Southwestern flair; deluxe rooms include fireplaces and many have outdoor sitting areas. European plan is available year-round; based on two adults, daily historic rooms are $110 in winter, $195 spring and fall, and $230 to $271 from late May to early September. Deluxe room rates for the same periods are $185, $295, and $345 to $408. Children under four stay at no charge; others pay $15 per day. Cribs and rollaways are available on request. In summer, modified American plan rates are offered for $328 to $369 standard, and $443 to $469 deluxe; each additional person in the room is either $10 (under three) or $64. Besides lodging and two meals, these rates include the supervised children's program. Special packages are offered throughout the year.

Dining: New American and Southwestern cuisine are featured in the main dining room; jackets for gentlemen are suggested at the evening meal. The decor is classic Santa Fe: beamed ceilings, Navajo rugs, Spanish chandeliers, and four life-size murals done in the 1920s by W. E. Rollins. You can also have a box lunch prepared and enjoy your own picnic. For cocktails and snacks there's El Rincon, a delightful corner bar opening onto the Firelight Terrace, which offers sunsets, stars, and firelight as accompaniments to Mexican margaritas.

Children's World: During the summer months, kids four to twelve years old can participate in full-day programs (8:00 A.M.–4:00 P.M. and 6:00–9:00 P.M.) of supervised activities, such as swimming, tennis lessons, pony rides, picnics, games, and fishing. Children can even have meals with their counselors in their own dining room or at picnics, pool parties, and cookouts. In addition, a pond stocked with trout and an outdoor play area of swings, a slide, and a sandbox translate into active fun for kids. Included with the modified American plan, the program is also available to European plan guests in day ($40 per child, meals included) and evening ($30) sessions.

Recreation: Recreation at The Bishop's Lodge starts with horseback riding in the wide open country. Experienced cowboys match you and your ability with the appropriate steed from a stable of more than seventy horses and then guide you on trail rides throughout the lodge's 1,000 acres. The cost is $35, children must be over eight years and 4 feet tall, and the maximum weight is 225 pounds. Free pony rides are offered for the little ones at 11:30 A.M. daily. A memorable experience is the Sunrise Ride through the canyons and foothills of the Sangre de Cristo Mountains followed by a hearty "cooked on the range" breakfast of eggs, pancakes, and biscuits. The Santa Fe National Forest is adjacent to the grounds of the lodge and provides more opportunities to explore the scenery on horseback.

But if you're a little skittish about mounting a horse, you can fill your days with lots of other recreational fun: Hike on the trails through the foothills, fish the mountain streams for trout, swim in the pool, and bask in the sunshine. At the Tennis Center, you can play on one of four courts, have a lesson with the resident pro, and purchase some new accessories at the pro shop. On the skeet- and trapshooting ranges, experts offer instruction, and rental equipment is provided. Play a game of Ping-Pong or treat your sore muscles to a relaxing hour in the whirlpool and sauna. The nearby country clubs of Santa Fe, Cochiti Lake, and Los Alamos grant lodge guests golfing privileges on their eighteen-hole courses. Be sure to take at least a day to discover the narrow streets, interesting adobe architecture, quaint shops, and art galleries of old Santa Fe. Open-air performances of the Santa Fe Summer Opera Festival are a special attraction for summertime visitors. Pueblo Indians show their jewelry and pottery on blankets around the Palace of the Governors or the famous Indian Market, and visitors are welcome to the colorful ceremonies at nearby pueblos. ≈≈≈

Flying L Guest Ranch

P.O. Box 1959
Bandera, Texas 78003
(830) 460–3001, (800) 292–5134
E-mail: sales@flyingl.com
Web site: www.flyingl.com

Bandera, 40 miles northwest of San Antonio, claims to have invented dude ranching during the Depression when an enterprising rancher decided to take in "dudes" for extra money. So now, with true Texan style, they have laid claim to being the "Cowboy Capital of the World." Seven rodeo world champions have hailed from here, however, so there may be something to it. Set in the midst of the beautiful Texas Hill Country, this is not the Texas of the movies. Here there are verdant green hills, oak and maple trees, wildflowers and flowing rivers, not sagebrush and sand.

The Flying L Ranch was first settled in 1874. It became a dude ranch in 1946 when Jack Lapham, a retired Air Corps colonel, started to realize his dream of a place where "a modern person can go and find himself in the midst of yesterday." (OK, who can figure out the name of the ranch based on this story? You already did? Good!) The ranch became a favorite "watering hole" for celebrities, including John Wayne, Tex Ritter, Buck Owens, Chill Wills, Slim Pickens, and Willie Nelson, and the television program *The Cisco Kid* was filmed here.

Accommodations: You can bunk in style here—all forty-two suites have two rooms and a bath, real Texas-style lodging with room to spread out. The suites are in guest houses either with a Hill Country view or along the golf course and are geared toward comfort, with refrigerator, microwave, coffeepot, and color TV. Daily rates in low season are $80 to $99 per adult; high season (summer and holidays) rates are $95 to $115 per adult. Children twelve to seventeen are two-thirds of the adult rate, and ages three to eleven are half of the adult rate. Children under three stay free, but there are no special facilities for them. Discount rates are given for five nights or more.

Dining: Two full meals are included in the rate and are hearty samples of Texas barbecue, mesquite grill, and Mexican specialties. Seven days a week, at 7:00 A.M. sharp, start your day with a continental breakfast. Then, four days every week enjoy a breakfast buffet in the Main House dining room, and on the other three days, feel like a real cowpoke as you head down to the river on a haywagon for a creekside breakfast hot off the coals. Lunch is on your own, with burgers and fries at the pro shop or an afternoon picnic from your refrigerator. Dinner is from 5:30 to 7:30 P.M., either in the Main House dining room or creekside. Vegetarians beware—this is Texas, with meat every night! At 5:00 P.M. the Branding Iron Saloon opens, and there's family entertainment every night—cowboy music, dancing, gun slinging, or a rodeo, usually topped off with a marshmallow roast and s'more making. Do the kids love that!

Children's World: Children are divided into two groups, ages three to five and six to twelve. Programs run from 8:45 A.M. to noon and from 1:00 to 4:30 P.M. Activities include feeding animals, nature walks, scavenger hunts, sports, fishing, and crafts, such as making leather bracelets and vests. Golf and tennis clinics are included for the older children along with trail rides with the grownups, while the little ones can take pony rides at the Kids Korral every day. The program runs Monday through Saturday during summer, spring break (March–April), and holidays. And, as they say at the Flying L, "there ain't no nickel-and-dimin' here"; it's all included in the lodging rates.

Recreation: The only activity not included in your price is golf. When they say pack your shootin' irons, they mean golf clubs, pardner. Drive, chip, and putt on the par seventy-two, fully irrigated course. A driving range lets you perfect your skills if you don't get distracted by the beautiful view; private lessons are also available. Try the outdoor heated swimming pool or venture off the "Ranch" to the Medina River for a little inner tubing or canoeing. Tennis, hayrides, rodeo events, a playground, and a seasonal petting corral add to the fun. Riding lessons are available for the "young uns," as are instructions in horse grooming, saddling, and roping.

In the Bandera area, fish in the crystal waters of Medina Lake, tour a working Longhorn ranch, visit the Cowboy Artists Museum in Kerrville, tour the World War II Nimitz Museum, or enjoy antiquing in the German town of Fredericksburg. On Bandera's Main Street there's a working blacksmith shop. Nearby excursions include San Antonio (the Alamo, Market Square, and the River Walk) and various theme parks such as SeaWorld, Fiesta Texas, and Splashtown. Visit natural wonders such as the caverns or tour the Lone Star Brewing Company to see how beer is made. All in all, the ranch promises "a rootin', tootin' time." ≋

Hyatt Regency Hill Country Resort

9800 Resort Drive
San Antonio, Texas 78251
(210) 647–1234, (800) 233–1234

The Texas Hill Country is as much a state of mind as it is a region. It certainly doesn't look like Texas—its green rolling hills, abundance of water, and variety of trees surprise the first-time visitor. San Antonio calls itself "a big city with small town charm," and, as the #1 tourist destination in Texas, has a multitude of attractions for families to enjoy—including the famous Alamo, centerpiece of Texas history, and the River Walk, lined with shops and restaurants along the tree-shaded banks of the San Antonio River.

Twenty minutes from downtown, a scenic drive meanders through the landscape, culminating at the lobby entrance, reminiscent of a Texas ranch house and complete with fireplaces and overstuffed furniture—even a shady back porch. In fact, the resort's 200 acres are a part of the Rogers–Wiseman Ranch, honored for being in continuous agricultural production at the hands of one family for one hundred years or more. Hyatt has successfully adapted a full-scale destination resort into this casual, laid-back lifestyle; the results are downright pleasurable. Enjoy a championship golf course, nature trails, a health club, and

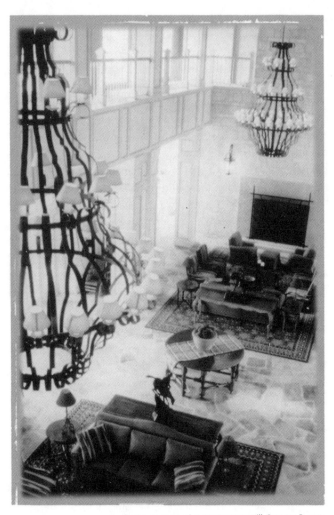

Photo courtesy of Hyatt Regency Hill Country Resort

a wonderful four-acre water park featuring the 950-foot-long Ramblin' River—the centerpiece of the property and the greatest place to get into an inner tube, kick back, and just relax.

Accommodations: Traditional German-style Hill Country architecture with native limestone and decorative wood exterior, the two- and four-story hotel has nine guest-room wings, housing 500 rooms. A stand-alone two-story luxurious guest house styled after a ranch house is in the courtyard—there's even an authentic windmill! As usual with Hyatt, the rooms are large and well decorated, ranging from standard to Regency Club level, with no-smoking rooms and suites available. Room rates are from $190 to $315; suites from $295 to $2,250. Children under eighteen are free in the same room as parents. Packages are a good value and may include golf, the children's program, or other family excursions. Be sure to ask.

Dining: The flavor is definitely Tex-Mex, so expect tortillas even for breakfast, but you have lots of options here. The Springhouse Cafe features regional specialties, a large buffet and salad bar, and Sunday brunch. A wood-burning oven makes great pizzas. In the clubhouse, The Antlers Lodge has the ambience of a country lodge and puts the accent on regional Southwestern cuisine of steak, chicken, and seafood. Many entrees are mesquite-grilled and accompanied by a spicy Tex-Mex sauce. Also here, golfers will find sandwiches and light snacks in the Cactus Oak Tavern at the halfway point on the golf course. The General Store offers hamburgers, deli sandwiches, and home-baked cookies as well as licorice sticks, wine, sodas, fresh coffee, and muffins. In the evening, relax at Aunt Mary's Porch, an open-air bar just off the lobby, or kick up your heels at Charlie's Long Bar, an old-fashioned Texas saloon complete with tin ceiling and a 56-foot copper-top bar. Yes, they have the tequila with the worm. Pool, shuffleboard, backgammon, and chess enhance the bar area.

Children's World: Camp Hyatt, developed in 1989, offers not only supervised programs but children's menus and an opportunity to buy a second room for the kids at half-price. Custom tailored for ages three to twelve, Camp Hyatt operates during holidays, weekends, and daily throughout the summer. The program runs from 9:00 A.M. to noon and from 1:00 to 4:00 P.M. and keeps the kids busy with games and activities. There is a special Camp Hyatt room with a different schedule for every day of the week. The cost is $18 for a half day; $30 for a full day (lunch included for $5.00 additional), or $26 for the Friday and Saturday evening sessions from 5:00 to 9:00 P.M.

Recreation: Golfers enjoy the Arthur Hills–designed course with its 170 acres of rolling, scenic terrain. It truly blends into the countryside and has been recognized as one of the premier courses in the United States. Tennis is available on three courts, with a pro on hand. Walking, jogging, and biking paths crisscross the property, and the health club features aerobics classes and all the latest equipment—and, of course, a massage to help you recover from your workout.

By far the most popular spot, though, is the Ramblin' River, modeled after all those Hill Country river experiences. Pick up an inner tube, drop your cares, and let the lazy current carry you away. The journey varies from brisk to slow and allows riders to swim, walk, or take detours into two swimming pools, a cascading waterfall, or even a little sand beach.

Day excursions to SeaWorld, Six Flags, Fiesta Texas, Splashtown water park, or many of the nearby Hill towns, each with its own personality and charm, can pleasurably fill your days or evenings. Visit the Natural Bridge Caverns, with active formations more than 140 million years old, or stroll through Bandera, the self-proclaimed "cowboy capital." The Alamo is a must, and the IMAX production, *Alamo—the Price of Freedom,* does help in understanding the role of the Alamo and in bringing it to life (although it's pretty violent at times). Missions, museums, and Market Square, which feels like shopping in Mexico, are all nearby. ≋

Hyatt Regency Scottsdale at Gainey Ranch

7500 East Doubletree Ranch Road
Scottsdale, Arizona 85258
(602) 991–3388, (800) 233–1234

Entering the private road that leads to this resort does not prepare you for the beauty of this lush and luxurious oasis in the midst of the Arizona desert. Water surrounds, cascades, falls, bubbles, flows, even sprays from the air; water and flowers are everywhere. You feel as though you are part of the landscape, not separated from it. Twenty-eight fountains, forty-seven waterfalls, and hundreds of palms, fir trees, and flowers create a twenty-seven-acre garden, part of the 560-acre Gainey Ranch, a planned residential complex that includes golf, parks and lakes, private homes, and businesses.

Accommodations: The double "H" shape of the 4-story resort provides five courtyards and four glass-enclosed atriums, with a movable 820-square-foot glass wall at the center of the lobby that allows a panoramic view of the McDowell Mountains and Sonoran Desert. The main building, inspired by the desert work of Frank Lloyd Wright, houses 493 rooms and suites; on either side are seven two- and four-bedroom freestanding casitas with fireplaces and terraced balconies overlooking the lake. The decor blends with the desert setting, using natural textures and artifacts. Children under eighteen stay free in existing bed space of parents' rooms, and every room has the Disney channel. Rates vary according to season: High season (February to May), rooms are $395; $505 in the Regency Club, which offers VIP service, complimentary breakfast, beverages, and evening hors d'oeuvres. January and fall season is approximately $20 lower, and June to early September is the lowest season, with rates from $175 to $215. Casitas range from $1,250 to $3,045 per night.

Photo courtesy of Hyatt Regency Scottsdale at Gainey Ranch

Dining: The Golden Swan is the hotel's specialty restaurant, named one of the best in the world by *Travel/Holiday* magazine and one of the top five in the Southwest by *Condé Nast Traveler*. One can dine indoors or out, in a charming gazebo nestled inside a lagoon. A special Sunday buffet, the "Chef's Brunch," is served right in the kitchen, where you can watch and talk with the chefs, making sure your food is hot and fresh. The Squash Blossom restaurant is open for breakfast, lunch, and dinner, with a warm Southwestern ambience and regional specialties (try the Arizona toast or a wide variety of salads and sandwiches or fajitas). Ristorante Sandolo is a casual Italian bistro, overlooking the pool, where the servers serenade you. After you dine, enjoy a Venice-style gondola ride on the resort's waterways. Again, a *sandolier* will sing to you. (You can enjoy the gondola ride for $5.00 even if you don't eat.) Both restaurants have indoor/outdoor seating with very clever "air-conditioning." A very fine, invisible mist cools and moisturizes the air above you, making it comfortable year-round. Poolside, you'll find two bars, the Waterfall Juice Bar, and the Water Garden Cafe, serving snacks, lunch, yogurt, and fruit drinks. The new Coffee Bar features gourmet blends complemented by homemade Italian biscotti. In the evening, watch the cascading fountains and listen to classical flamenco guitar or perhaps a marimba band as you relax in the Lobby Bar.

Children's World: Camp Hyatt Kachina, designed in 1989, is the prototype children's program for all Hyatt resorts. It operates daily year-round and offers three- to twelve-year-olds a well-balanced program of activities focusing on the flora, fauna, culture, and geography of the area. A specially appointed Camp room has all the crafts and games children like best, and the playground, Fort Kachina, has lots of climbing and "imagination areas." And don't forget the ten swimming pools, one complete with a white sand beach and a 3-story water slide. Each day has a different theme, such as Rootin' Tootin' Reptiles, It's a Pow Wow, South of the Border, or Feathered Friends. Age groups are three to five and six to twelve. The morning session, from 9:00 A.M. to noon, is $25, and the afternoon session, from 1:00 to 5:00 P.M., is $35. Lunch, from noon to 1:00 P.M., can be added to either session for $10. The full-day costs $60, including lunch, and $35 per evening session from 5:00 to 9:00 P.M., including dinner. If you have an active child who loves the program, the best deal is all day (9:00 A.M. to 9:00 P.M.) and all meals for $85. During holidays the resort offers family camp "destination specific" activities designed for the entire family, from cowboy roping, cowboy guitarists, and Native American storytelling to family fun sing-alongs round the campfire.

Recreation: Where do we start? With the twenty-seven-hole championship golf course at Gainey Ranch Golf Club? Actually, it's composed of three separate, individually designed courses—the Dunes; the Lakes, with five lakes and lots of water hazards; and the Arroyo, the most difficult. Or with the eight tennis courts or 3 miles of jogging and cycling trails? Or the Sonwai Spa, with state-of-the-art equipment, classes, sauna, and massage? Let's start with the 2½-acre water playground—most impressive in this dry, desert area. The design is a combination of Roman, Greek, and art deco and is truly spectacular. Zip down the 30-foot water slide, stroll over an aqueduct connecting six of the ten pools, swim around (or through!) the "Big Gun," a 5-foot-wide waterfall, or "thunderfall" as the hotel terms it, at the end of the aqueduct. Relax in the Grecian temple with 16-foot hot tub and four "cold plunges" in each corner. Water comes from all directions—from fountains, trailing down tall glass columns, and from waterspouts along the roof. Build sandcastles on the beach at one end or play volleyball at the other. Kids never want to leave this watery fantasyland.

Phoenix attractions include a zoo, a desert botanical garden, and stately old homes; in Scottsdale, find an IMAX theater, the world's highest fountain, and shopping on Fifth Avenue. View large cats in the wild at Out of Africa; experience a re-creation of the Old West at WestWorld or Rawhide, Arizona's largest Western-themed attraction. Pick up a copy of *GUEST* for lots more ideas. If you have time to venture farther, the concierge will help you plan excursions to the

Grand Canyon (five hours away) or Montezuma Castle, a 600-year-old Pueblo Indian cliff dwelling only ninety minutes away. Who knew the desert could be like this? ≈≈≈

Inn of the Mountain Gods

P.O. Box 269
Mescalero, New Mexico 88340
(505) 257–5141, (800) 545–9011

Not many families can boast a vacation on an Indian reservation. At the Inn of the Mountain Gods, your family can enjoy all the amenities of a full resort while learning some of the history and customs of the Mescalero Apache tribe. They are a proud people with infinite respect for the land and an eagerness to introduce you to the natural beauties of a setting believed to have been home to the Apache gods. Whether horseback riding or big-game hunting, Indian guides navigate excursions over the rugged terrain of this 460,000-acre reservation. The reservation, established over a hundred years ago, sprawls through the Sacramento Mountains of south-central New Mexico. Open year-round, the Inn sits on the shores of the 140-acre Lake Mescalero. The clear blue waters of the lake provide the setting for many water-sports enthusiasts (fishermen and boaters) and the picturesque backdrop for golfers and tennis players. Views of nearby Sierra Blanca (12,000 feet) complete the scenic ambience.

Accommodations: The 253 guest rooms (including twenty suites) are located in lakeside buildings adjacent to the main lodge. Each has a private balcony, which allows impressive views of the lake and the mountains. Prices range from $95 to $135 a night for a double room depending on the time of the year; May through September is the high season. Slightly higher rates are applied for suite accommodations. There is no charge for children twelve years and younger sharing a room with adults (each room has two double beds), but a rollaway carries a $14-per-night fee. Package plans are arranged for golf, skiing, and hunting.

Dining: The lobby of the main building greets guests with a massive, copper-sheathed fireplace; this is a popular gathering spot for afternoon and evening cocktails. The Gas Kan Lounge also serves refreshments in the piano bar, which provides evening entertainment, and on the sundeck, which affords views over the lake.

Photo by The Amador Studio, courtesy of Inn of the Mountain Gods

The Dan Li Ka in the main building serves a buffet breakfast, casual lunches, and more formal dinners. Specializing in American and continental cuisine, the menu offers steak, veal, seafood, and chicken dishes and many tempting desserts. The Apache Tee Bar and Cafe is adjacent to the golf pro shop; it is open year-round for breakfast, lunch, and dinner. Top O' The Inn Deli features sandwiches made fresh while you wait, salads, and desserts; it's open from 11:00 A.M. until late for the night owl. A snack bar is located at the swimming pool.

Children's World: Children's events are low-key. The Tee Pee Arcade is open for children eight years of age and older. There is no supervised play; for younger children an adult is a must. Children twelve and older can meet guides for horseback riding without parental supervision. For infants and toddlers, individual baby-sitters can be arranged.

In the wintertime kids six years and older can learn how to ski in the ski school of nearby Ski Apache Ski Area.

Recreation: The most unusual sport offered at the Inn is big-game hunting on the reservation. Because of a conscientious wildlife preservation program, elk, deer, antelope, bear, wild turkey, and quail are plentiful. Apache guides lead expeditions into the heavily wooded mountain terrain. Package plans are available for hunters during the season from mid-September through December; these include facilities for processing and packaging game. You can also enlist the services of a taxidermist for trophy preparation.

More traditional sports include golfing on an eighteen-hole championship course designed by Ted Robinson. This well-maintained course on rolling terrain skirts the lake and winds through tall pines and aspen. A resident pro is on hand for lessons, and there's a well-stocked pro shop. For tennis players, six outdoor courts are located on the lake. You can arrange private lessons or enroll in a clinic through the tennis pro shop.

On Lake Mescalero water sports are popular. Canoes, rowboats, and paddleboats can be rented at the boat dock. The lake's good stock of rainbow and cutthroat trout adds up to fine fishing. Swimmers and sunbathers are found at the heated outdoor pool and adjacent whirlpool overlooking the lake. There's a wading pool too.

The stables, a couple of miles from the Inn, maintain twenty to twenty-five horses. You can take half- or full-day trail rides with a guide. Combining exercise and solitary scenic enjoyment, some visitors take to the jogging and hiking trail around the lake or rent bicycles. Equipment is available for several lawn games such as horseshoes, badminton, volleyball, and soccer. Casino Apache provides lively indoor entertainment. After a full day of activities, you might enjoy wandering through the gift shop, where you'll find lovely Indian jewelry, weaving, and pottery.

Wintertime brings skiing at the nearby Ski Apache Resort. Snowmaking equipment aiding Mother Nature translates into a ski season from Thanksgiving to Easter. Owned and operated by the Mescalero Apache Indians, the ski area includes in its services lessons for all levels of skiers, restaurants, a lounge, and a ski rental and repair shop. Guests at the inn are shuttled daily to the mountain, where they find thirty-two designated groomed trails and a vertical drop of 1,700 feet.

At the Inn there are recreational fees for many of the activities (golf, tennis, and horseback riding). Package plans for golf, tennis, and skiing, for example, eliminate the need for additional assessment. ≋

Los Abrigados Resort and Spa

160 Portal Lane
Sedona, Arizona 86336
(602) 282–1777, (800) 521–3131

Close to the Grand Canyon and just two hours from Phoenix, Sedona is noted for its spectacular red rock formations and scenic canyons. For centuries, it has been a sacred place to The People, the earliest inhabitants, and legend holds that the Grandmother Spirit of the World still lives here.

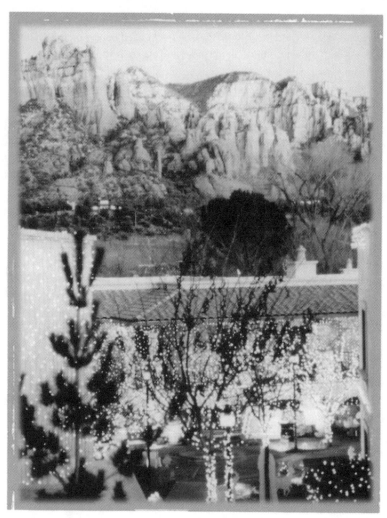

Photo courtesy of Los Abrigados Resort and Spa

There is a magic quality in the air that many attribute to the energy points that converge here. At the least, the light, color, and awe-inspiring rocks combine with the many artisans living here to create something special.

Accommodations: Los Abrigados, Portuguese for "the shelters," is in the heart of the small town of Sedona but stands in the midst of twenty-two acres of private ranchland/park and feels secluded. All of the 173 guest suites have oversize living rooms and separate bedrooms plus a balcony or private patio. Many feature a private whirlpool and fireplace. The plazas, walkways, and bridges connect the suites and main hotel area. Suites range from $225 to $395; $240 reserves one with spectacular views of the red rocks. Children under fifteen are free in the same room with parents.

Dining: Steak and Sticks, for casually elegant dining with a Southwestern flavor, is the domain of award-winning chef Scott Uehlein (serving breakfast and dinner). Imaginative dishes with an accent on indigenous ingredients make dining an adventure. Also available here is the "spa cuisine," healthful and lighter versions of many favorites. On-The-Rocks Bar & Grill serves lunch, snacks, and dinner in a casual atmosphere and features a large-screen television—the area's largest. Steak and Sticks and On-The-Rocks both feature children's menus. More restaurants are right next door at Tlaquepaque Village, a re-created Mexican village/plaza with tiled courtyards, fountains, and many craft shops.

Children's World: Children are always welcome at Los Abrigados and various activities are planned during the summer months from year to year. Available at the resort are a pool, playground, and basketball and tennis courts. More fun abounds in the surrounding area with jeep rides, horseback riding, and other events that can be arranged by the concierge.

Recreation: After a game of tennis or volleyball, relax at the heated outdoor pool and chat with other guests. Enjoy the jogging and walking trails or just sit by the creek and dream. The centerpiece of activities here is the Sedona Spa— 10,000 square feet of state-of-the-art equipment and professional services providing a combination of fitness and relaxation. Massage, full body treatments and masks, facials and fitness classes/personal training contribute to physical and mental well-being. Nearby are two championship golf courses, designed by Robert Trent Jones and Gary Panks. Hiking, fishing streams, horseback riding, and jeep tours can also be arranged. The Grand Canyon is a two-hour drive, and closer is Oak Creek Canyon, with Slide Rock State Park, aptly named for the stretch of slippery creek bottom that forms a natural slide. For Southwestern art at its best, Tlaquepaque demands a visit (see Dining).

Red Rock Fantasy is the West's largest holiday light display, with more than one million lights. From late November until mid-January it transforms Los Abrigados into a spectacular holiday light show. ≋

Sheraton El Conquistador Resort and Country Club

10000 North Oracle Road
Tucson, Arizona 85737
(520) 544–5000, (800) 325–7832
Web site: www.sheratonelconquistador.com

The Arizona desert climate is perfect sporting weather practically year-round. The sun shines warmly and the humidity is low, just the right combination for the world-famous saguaro cacti that seem to be everywhere. It's also the perfect combination for nudging that golf ball farther down the links or sending an ace across the tennis court. El Conquistador wraps up tennis, golf, horseback riding, and terrific sunshine together for a holiday present for you. It sits among imported palm trees and native cacti with stark mountains towering behind it. The golden tan stucco facades and the red-tiled roofs of the low-rise buildings blend well with the colors nature has given the surrounding landscape.

Accommodations: More than 400 rooms and suites are decorated with contemporary-style furnishings. The use of Mexican tiles and brick in ornamental designs adds to the Southwestern ambience. All the rooms have balconies or patios that open up to the mountains, the golf course, or a flower-filled courtyard, and each room has a mini bar. During the high season from January through April, a double room is $230–$310 a night and in the low season (June through Labor Day), $100–$125 a night; autumn and spring rates are $165–$240 a night. No charge is applied for children (seventeen and younger) staying in their parents' room. Golf, tennis, and equestrian packages are offered.

Dining: Innovative Southwestern cuisine is served in the informal, but elegant White Dove. For a fun evening of Western fare, head to the Last Territory for thick, juicy steaks broiled over a mesquite fire, barbecued ribs, and chicken. The Sundance Cafe is a casual restaurant for breakfast and lunch. Around the pool, sip a bit of cool refreshment from the Desert Spring, and indoors have your favorite cocktail at the Lobby Lounge. Dos Locos serves Mexican favorites and gourmet pizzas; the country club, La Vista, offers American cuisine with a classic French flair.

Children's World: Camp Conquistador offers daily summer activities for kids six to twelve years old. In an 8:00 A.M. to 3:00 P.M. schedule, youngsters take

Photo courtesy of Sheraton El Conquistador Resort and Country Club

nature walks; play tennis, volleyball, and basketball; show off artistic talents in crafts classes; and swim. Two sessions are offered, or an all-day session including lunch is available.

Children's movies are shown at the country club and individual baby-sitting arrangements can be made through the concierge.

Recreation: Tee up for the nine-hole or either of the two eighteen-hole golf courses, and watch your shot soar a bit farther in the clean desert air. Even taking lessons is no chore when the setting is so beautiful. Play tennis day or night on any of the thirty-one lighted courts. Lessons are available, too, for tennis and for racquetball (seven courts).

At the stables, choose a horse for a breakfast ride or a sunset champagne trail ride. Jog on one of the four designated trails ranging from $1\frac{1}{2}$ to 7 miles in length. Fitness centers are located at the main hotel and at the country club; join an exercise class, then wind down in the whirlpool or sauna and pamper yourself with a massage. Take a dip in one of the four swimming pools. Rent a bike or get the whole family into a game of horseshoes, badminton, or volleyball. Explore the exciting possibility of a balloon ride, or poke around the Arizona terrain during a desert jeep ride. ≈≈

Tanque Verde Guest Ranch

14301 East Speedway Boulevard
Tucson, Arizona 85748
(520) 296–6275, (800) 234–3833
Web site: www.tanqueverderanch.com

In the Arizona desert, 2,800 feet high in the foothills of three mountain ranges, Tanque Verde Guest Ranch has been serving travelers for more than one hundred years. Once merely a stagecoach stop, today it is a year-round resort. The area is rich in the history of Native Americans and Spanish settlers who dubbed the area Tanque Verde—immortalizing the deep pools of artesian water found here. Located 12 miles outside Tucson, it borders Saguaro National Park. The saguaro cacti are immediately recognizable to anyone who has seen a western movie or a picture of the desert. They stand quite tall, with "arms" curving up toward the sky. From here visitors can take side trips to Tucson, to old Spanish missions, and to Mexico, which is about a ninety-minute drive away.

Accommodations: The seventy-one guest rooms and suites are located in the main ranch house and in individual cottages called "casitas"; most of the casitas have patios and corner fireplaces. The decorative motif is Native American, and antiques and original art are carefully arranged to lend a warmth to the inn. Cribs are available, and there are refrigerators in the rooms. During the high season (mid-December through April) full American plan rates for a double room are $250–$340 per day; from May to mid-December, $175–$250 per day. Rates increase with the number of people; anyone age three or over is considered "people," and therefore pays the full rate. Triples range from $375 to $445 in winter, $310 to $345 in summer; quads are $450 to $530 and $375 to $410, respectively. These prices include not just meals and lodging, but also riding, ranch activities, tennis, and the children's program.

Dining: Everyone eats at long tables in the one main dining room, encouraging an informal, friendly atmosphere. Dress is casual and appetites are generally big due to the desert air and the exercise. American and continental dishes are standard fare and, as expected, Spanish and Mexican specialties also appear on the menu. A separate children's dining room is reserved for youngsters and their counselors, who can take all meals together. Children are also welcome to dine with their parents. Many guests look forward to outdoor dining, enjoying hearty Western meals either on the range or at poolside.

Children's World: The Ranch offers a year-round, seven-day-per-week, fully supervised program for four- to eleven-year-olds. Horseback riding forms the core of the program and is adjusted to fit the abilities and interests of the youngsters. Children under twelve must ride with the children's program; adults may join their children on these rides.

Besides riding, children are offered tennis lessons, nature programs, hikes, swimming, and some evening activities. The program is from 8:00 A.M. to 3:30 P.M., and 6:00 to 8:15 P.M. The cost is included in the daily rates. For infants and toddlers, baby-sitters can be hired for $5.00 to $6.00 per hour.

Recreation: Active relaxation is the byword at Tanque Verde. The clear desert air and low humidity, coupled with abundant sunshine, make all the activities pleasant. Horseback riding is the major part of the program. Whether you're interested in a slow-moving trail ride or a spirited sprint, the right mount can be found from a string of one hundred horses.

Early morning and late afternoon are perfect times for strenuous outdoor activities such as tennis (five courts). In the middle of the day, seek out one of the two swimming pools or perhaps the lake for a cool dip. Numerous guided nature walks introducing visitors to the Arizona desert ecology are conducted along trails throughout the 25,000 acres. Some 200 species of birds have been identified in the area, making the ranch very popular with avid bird-watchers. The final touch to the active relaxation concept is the El Sonora Spa, well equipped with its swimming pool, sauna, whirlpool, exercise room, and lounge. In nearby Tucson, six championship golf courses grant playing privileges to ranch guests. ≈≈≈

Taos Ski Valley

P.O. Box 90
Taos Ski Valley, New Mexico 87525
(505) 776–2291, (800) 776–1111

N ine hundred years ago the Pueblo Indians settled the area around Taos. They were followed in the sixteenth century by the Spanish and in the nineteenth century by fur traders. In the early 1950s, Ernie Blake searched carefully for just the right spot for a ski resort and rediscovered this bit of northern New Mexico. Since then, skiers have been coming to Taos Ski Valley for the incredible powder snow and the glorious sunshine. Several ski magazines are calling Taos one of the hottest places to ski, citing the steep, challenging terrain and trails for all abilities so all levels may ski together. Once again, Taos has the #1 ski school in North America, featuring the Ski-Better-Week. Grouped according to ability, each group remains with the same instructor, developing new, close friendships and improving skills.

Photo © Jeff Caven, courtesy of Taos Ski Valley

A three-hour drive from Albuquerque, Taos Ski Valley combines lodging, restaurants, shops, and a beautiful mountain. The town of Taos is only 18 miles away and, with its Indian and Spanish heritage, is an interesting alternative for dining, shopping, and entertainment. The Ski Valley operates during the ski season only, which generally runs from Thanksgiving through mid-April.

Accommodations: Although there are inns and hotels in the town of Taos, every skier's dream is to be on the mountain. The Taos Valley Resort Association (800 number above) represents more than 95 percent of all lodging in and around Taos. For lodges right near the slopes—such as Hotel St. Bernard and the Thunderbird Lodge—rates for a one-week package run $1,490 per person double occupancy; besides your room, this package includes meals, lifts, and morning lessons. Condominiums right at the slopes charge $758–$1,105 per person for a one-week package; based on four people in a two-bedroom unit, this fee covers lodging, lifts, and morning lessons. All facilities offer a nightly rate, but the week package, known as a Ski-Better-Week, is good value for your money.

Dining: Whatever your dining mood, you'll be satisfied in Taos with more than fifty restaurants to choose from. On the mountain there are quick and easy stops like the Phoenix Restaurant; the Whistlestop Cafe, serving hamburgers, sandwiches, and pizza; and the Bavarian. At the base, you can go really casual at the Snack Bar or delightfully international at the restaurant in the Thunderbird Lodge or very family-style at the nearby Amizette Inn. In the town of Taos, try Cajun and Creole at Carl's French Quarter, seafood at Casa Cordova, or Mexican at Casa De Valdez. And of course there's always your own fine cooking in your condominium!

Children's World: The Kinderkafig, Taos Ski Valley's 18,000-square-foot child-care facility, is designed for children between the ages of six weeks and twelve years. The Kinderkare (six weeks to two years old) full-day program includes two snacks, lunch, and nap time. The half-day program includes snack and either snow play or nap time. Reservations are required. Walk-ins are accepted on a space-available basis. The cost for this program is $68 for a full day, $32 for a half day, or $15 per hour. The Junior Elite program (three to twelve years old) includes all-day lesson, lift ticket, lunch, and rentals. Reservations are required for children kindergarten age and younger. Little ones must be potty-trained. Cost is $68 per day or $390 for six days.

Also for kids, there's ice skating or tubing on the bunny hill on Wednesday, Friday and Saturday nights between 4:00 and 7:00 P.M.

Recreation: Partially located in the Carson National Forest, the Taos ski area is in the Sangre de Cristo Mountains, the southernmost part of the Rockies. The base village sits at 9,207 feet, and the peak towers above at 11,819 feet, affording skiers more than 2,600 feet of vertical drop down seventy-two different slopes. This is a challenging mountain with just over 50 percent of its runs classified as expert; however, even the novice can feel that classic mountaintop high, since some beginners' runs descend directly from the peak. In a ski season that lasts from about Thanksgiving to Easter, the average annual snowfall is over 320 inches, plus snowmaking on more than 98 percent of beginner and intermediate terrain.

When you can pull yourself away from the open bowls, dramatic chutes, and lazy meandering-down trails lined with spruce and aspen, you might consider cross-country skiing, a sleigh ride, or an evening skier's seminar on such topics as avalanches and adjusting to the altitude. Skiers in January experience the added pleasures of Taos's jazz festival.

Late spring and summer bring great white-water rafting, trout fishing, mountain bikes and hikers, horseback riding, and golf. Six museums, art galleries, and music festivals entertain those less athletically inclined, and the Taos Chamber of Commerce (800–732–8267) even publishes a *Kid's Guide* with advice from local children. ≋

ROCKIES

Colorado

Montana

Utah

Aspen Chamber Resort Association

425 Rio Grande Place
Aspen, Colorado 81611
(970) 925–1940 for guest information
(970) 925–9000 and (800) 262–7736 for reservations
Web site: www.aspenchamber.org

Big Sky of Montana

P.O. Box 160001
Big Sky, Montana 59716
(406) 995–5000, (800) 548–4486
E-mail: groupsales@bigskyresort.com
Web site: www.bigskyresort.com

The sky isn't really bigger in Montana—not by scientific measurements, that is. But don't tell the folks around here that. These die-hard Westerners believe they've got the market cornered on the best, biggest, bluest sky ever; and if you don't watch out, by the end of a visit here, you'll be a believer too.

In the wintertime, skiing Lone Mountain (summit elevation 11,166 feet) can make you feel like it's almost possible to touch that beautiful, clear sky. Lone Mountain and adjacent Andesite Mountain are carved with seventy-eight runs that add up to fine skiing at Big Sky. During the summer, these mountains and their evergreens, the sunshine and clean mountain air make the perfect setting for hiking, horseback riding, mountain biking, scenic gondola rides, whitewater rafting, and fishing as well as golf and tennis.

Open year-round, Big Sky is located in southwestern Montana just north of Yellowstone and is surrounded by rivers and national forests.

Accommodations: Huntley Lodge is at the base of Lone Mountain; the Explorer chairlift is right out the back door. The lodge has more than 200 rooms, some with views straight up the mountain, and an outdoor heated swimming pool, sauna, and Jacuzzi. Huntley is the hub of Big Sky, since events are posted in the lobby. Its dining areas and lounges also draw visitors.

Regular season rates are in effect from the beginning of February through the end of March and range from $186 to $229 per night for a double room. During the rest of the ski season (except Christmas), rates are reduced 15 to 20 percent. Summer rates are $132–$152 a night for a double. The larger loft rooms are more expensive, and children ten and younger stay free in their parents' room. Cribs and rollaways are $15.

Photo courtesy of Big Sky of Montana

At the area's condominiums, the studios and one- to four-bedroom units have kitchens and fireplaces. While all the complexes (Stillwater, Skycrest, Lake Hill, Arrowhead, Beaverhead, Shoshone, Snowcrest) are at the base of the mountain, Snowcrest is closest to the lifts. During the regular winter ski season, rates are $138–$687 a night, depending on the unit's size. During the low ski season, rates are discounted 20 percent. In the summer, the condominium rates range from $102–$525. Some complexes feature heated swimming pools, saunas, and Jacuzzis.

Dining: If you are staying in Huntley Lodge or just cannot face cooking after a busy day, you can dine at the Huntley in the large dining room. In the winter take the sleigh ride up into the mountains for dinner in a log cabin, and in the summer join an outdoor Western barbecue. Next door to Huntley Lodge is a collection of shops, restaurants, and bars in the Mountain Village Mall. Here you'll find casual spots for pizzas, deli sandwiches, and delicious ice-cream sundaes. In the evening, Chet's Bar in Huntley Lodge is popular for its warm atmosphere, nightly entertainment, and regular game of poker.

Children's World: During the ski season, the Handprints on the Mountain Daycare Center in the Mountain Village Mall is open every day from 8:30 A.M. to 4:00 P.M. for children six months and older. Little ones enjoy a combination of indoor and outdoor play: sledding, stories, songs, and arts and crafts. The fee is

$55 a day for two years and older, and $65 for six- to twenty-three months old. The four- through six-year-olds at the center have ski lessons two hours a day in addition to their indoor activities. The daily rate for this group is $80. Older children six to fourteen years can enroll in the Ski Day Camp. The daily fee is $54 for an active 9:45 A.M. to 3:00 P.M. program. Kids ten and younger ski free.

The game room in Huntley Lodge, open from 10:00 A.M. to 10:00 P.M., offers video games and television. No special activities are organized for children during the summer, but any time of the year baby-sitting arrangements can be made through the activities desk at Huntley Lodge. The average rate is $8.00 per hour. There are free family activities organized daily throughout the winter.

Recreation: The 4,180-foot vertical drop takes you through open bowls and tree-lined trails. The average annual snowfall is an amazing 400-plus inches. Skiing starts mid-November (an opening guaranteed by snowmaking if Mother Nature is skimpy with her supply) and continues on into April. Whatever your level of skiing, you can join lessons at the ski school. Cross-country skiers enjoy treks over broad meadows and through stands of pine trees. Just 5 miles from Huntley Lodge, the Lone Mountain Guest Ranch maintains 45 miles of cross-country trails. When you're not on skis, swim in one of the heated pools or take a trip to Yellowstone for snowmobiling and sightseeing.

When the weather warms up, the mountains are terrific for hiking and backpacking. For horseback riding you can link up with Big Sky Stables through the activities desk in Huntley Lodge. You may prefer adventures in white-water rafting or the quiet solitude of fishing for prize-winning trout in the mountain streams.

The eighteen-hole golf course was designed by Arnold Palmer and is well situated in the mountain meadows. Play tennis (six courts, two of which are at the lodge) and volleyball, or relax with a Swedish massage or a leisurely guided nature walk, learning the wildflowers of Big Sky. ≈≈≈

Breckenridge Ski Resort

Box 1058
Breckenridge, Colorado 80424
(970) 453–5000, (800) 789–SNOW
Web site: www.snow.com

The town of Breckenridge is 139 years old, and skiing at Breckenridge is more than 35 years old. Quite a good combination! An old gold and silver mining camp proud of its history, Breckenridge is a charming town with carefully restored buildings that attest to its Victorian-era heyday. And the

Photo courtesy of Breckenridge Ski Resort

years of skiing have resulted in the development of 2,043 acres of skiing territory on four beautiful mountain peaks. All this skiing in a historic setting is a
one-and-a-half-hour drive west of Denver—not so close that it is inundated by
locals, yet close enough that once you land at Denver International Airport, your
ski holiday begins with a scenic tour through the Arapahoe National Forest on
your way to Breckenridge.

Like every Western mining town turned ski resort, Breckenridge has numerous hotels, vacation homes, and condominiums that can be investigated
through the Breckenridge Resort Chamber (800–221–1091). Best known as a
winter recreation area, Breckenridge is in fact open year-round. Beaver Run
Resort (800–525–2253) and the Village at Breckenridge (800–800–7829) warrant special attention because of their locations and amenities. With lifts just
steps away from either one, these self-contained resorts make life just a little bit
easier for families. Besides their own restaurants and shops, each resort houses
a child-care center.

Accommodations: Beaver Run is an attractive complex of granite and wood
buildings just skirted by the Country Boy trail and is home to the Beaver Run
Superchair. The hotel rooms are spacious, and condominiums vary from suites
with in-room spas to four-bedroom units. Fireplaces and private balconies are
features of all the condominium units; the condominiums have fully equipped

kitchens. Children are free when staying with their parents, and cribs for infants and toddlers are provided without charge.

During the high ski season, February 1 through the first week of April, a double hotel room is $210 and a one-bedroom/one-bath condominium that sleeps four is $280 a night. During the rest of the ski season, rates are lower, with the exception of the holiday period at the end of December when higher rates are in effect. In the summer season, from late April to mid-November, the rate for a double room is $90 a night and $125 a night for a one-bedroom/one-bath condominium.

The Village at Breckenridge is a Western-style resort with 332 units, ranging from hotel rooms to condos; the Liftside Inn building features studio apartments; and Plazas I, II, and III house one- to three-bedroom condominium units. Most of the accommodations have kitchens, fireplaces, and balconies with views of the mountains or Maggie Pond, the ice-skating center. Children twelve and younger sharing a room with their parents are free; crib rental is available upon request.

The Village defines the ski season as early November through late April; during this time a double hotel room is $120–$195, studios are $125–$210, and a one-bedroom/one-bath condominium is $160–$290. Rates are lower during early and late weeks of the season and higher at holiday time. During the summer a double room is $85–$120 a night, and a one-bedroom/one-bath condominium is $115–$160 a night.

Dining: Elegant dining at Beaver Run takes place at Spencer's Steaks and Spirits Restaurant in a warm setting enhanced by oak and cane furnishings. Menu offerings include a selection of USDA choice beef entrees, seafood favorites, and other specialties like the "all you can eat" prime rib. The Copper Top Cafeteria and Bar is open winters only for skiers, but the deli is good for snacks year-round, and two bars provide evening and nighttime amusement.

For elegant dining in The Village at Breckenridge, try the Breckenridge Cattle and Fish Company, which features steak, game, and prime rib. The Maggie Restaurant and Cafe Breckenridge are casual spots open for breakfast, lunch, and snacks. Enjoy Italian food at The Village Pasta Company and casual pub fare at The Village Pub. Jake T. Pounders is ready to quench your thirst after that last, long run of the day.

In town more than five dozen restaurants and saloons (out West bars are called saloons—don't forget that!) offer atmospheres from quiet to lively and cuisines that run all over the globe—Mexican, Italian, Greek, German. A popular spot for steak and seafood is the Whale's Tail on Main Street. The ice-cream shop, also on Main Street, makes for a nice break during an evening walk.

Children's World: Breckenridge's children's centers offer kids ages three to twelve a frolicking good time while they learn the joys of skiing in programs designed for specific age groups. Children's centers are located at both the Peak 8 and Village base areas. Parents must provide ski equipment, and lunch is provided for children enrolled in full-day programs. Reservations are recommended for children five and younger. Snowboarding instruction is also available. During the 1998–99 ski season, full-day lessons for three- to five-year-olds were $62, lessons for six- to twelve-year-olds were $62, and teen (thirteen to seventeen years old) classes were $46.

For children too young to ski or who don't ski, Breckenridge provides fun and nurturing environments. Children's centers are conveniently located at base areas: The Peak 8 Children's Center accepts children two months through five years and the Village Children's Center cares for children three to five years of age. Both centers include facilities that have everything kids need to enjoy their day: cribs, toys, art supplies, lunch facilities, and loving trained personnel. These popular programs fill up quickly, so make a reservation (required) by calling (800) 789-7669.

Recreation: If you said to some skiers that you'd found 139 trails, an average annual snowfall of 300 inches, a season from late October to early May, and a vertical drop of more than 3,398 feet, they might think you'd died and gone to heaven. Breckenridge gives you all this on its four interconnected mountains—Peak 7 is the latest addition in skiable terrain, while Peak 10 boasts the highest elevation, at nearly 13,000 feet. It also gives outstanding views over Summit County, 60 percent expert runs, 26 percent intermediate runs, 14 percent beginner runs, bowl skiing, above-the-timberline skiing, and lots of famous Rocky Mountain powder. You can line up a free guided tour of the mountains or plunge right away into group or private instruction.

Cross-country enthusiasts head to the Breckenridge Nordic Center, where more than 40 kilometers of groomed trails open up. Try snowmobiling at Tiger Run Tours; ice skating on Maggie Pond, at the base of Peak 9; and a horse-drawn sleigh ride to a steak-and-baked-potato supper in heated tents on the mountain.

At both the Village at Breckenridge and Beaver Run, you can jump into the indoor/outdoor pools, relax in one of the many outdoor hot tubs, or, if your muscles weren't tested enough on the slopes, finish up in the exercise rooms. An additional Beaver Run attraction is an indoor miniature golf course, where you can count on a fun family evening.

During warm-weather months venture out from the resorts and go biking through town, hiking in the woods, fishing in mountain streams, sailing on Lake

Dillon, horseback riding on trails bordered by wildflowers, and white-water rafting on the Arkansas and Blue Rivers. Breckenridge's eighteen-hole championship golf course was designed by Jack Nicklaus. And during July and August, the mountains ring with classical and jazz music from the Breckenridge Music Institute. ≋≋

The Broadmoor

P.O. Box 1439
Colorado Springs, Colorado 80901
(719) 634–7711, (800) 634–7711

As majestic as the neighboring Rocky Mountains, The Broadmoor reigns over Cheyenne Lake and 3,000 surrounding acres. The original hotel, known today as Broadmoor Main, was built in 1918 by Spencer Penrose, an enterprising man who made his fortune in gold mining in Cripple Creek (less than 20 miles from Colorado Springs) and copper mining in Utah. He dreamed of fashioning a Colorado resort along the lines of the grand European hotels that he had seen. The Mediterranean-style structure, with its pink-stucco facade, almost glimmers in the sunshine. Inside the Italian Renaissance trappings include wood-beamed ceilings, crystal chandeliers, gilt-framed mirrors, and hand-painted wall and ceiling decoration. Penrose's dream was realized— The Broadmoor fared well indeed when compared to its European counterparts. And the guests who followed were as impressive as the hotel, from royalty and presidents to movie stars and millionaires.

Over the years, facilities and buildings were added to the original complex. Broadmoor South stands next to Broadmoor Main and is architecturally compatible with the original, because its design utilizes light-colored stucco for the exterior walls. Across the lake is Broadmoor West. A modern structure, it nonetheless blends well within the context of the resort as a whole. In 1995, 150 new guest rooms were completed. The most luxurious accommodations on the property, the architecture of the new wing is reminiscent of Broadmoor Main. The newer structures reveal precise attention to architectural design, aesthetic decoration, and fine art. The resort is open year-round.

Accommodations: Some 700 rooms and suites are divided among the four Broadmoors. All are handsomely decorated and look out at either the clear blue Cheyenne Lake or the dramatic Colorado mountains; it's a tough task to find a view less than terrific. Broadmoor West features rooms with private balconies. During the high season, from the first of May to mid-October, the European plan is $280–$425 a night. Suites are higher. Cribs are provided at no additional charge. For an extra $15 a night, a rollaway bed can be added to your room. Rates are lower during the remaining six months of the year, and are based on one to four persons.

Dining: On the top floor of Broadmoor South, The Penrose Room is an elegantly formal restaurant, with traditional menu, superb views, dinner music, dancing, and an Edwardian decor, with emphasis on elaborate styling. Charles Court, in the west building, offers fine dining without the formalities, yet still with wonderful lake views. One of the world's most extensive wine lists (more than 600 choices, with prices ranging from $12 to $1,300 a bottle!) complement such entrees as Colorado elk with lingonberry compote, blue-veined goat cheese gnocci, and pine-nut-crusted rack of lamb.

Also at Broadmoor Main are the Tavern, exquisitely adorned with Toulouse-Lautrec lithographs, and the Lake Terrace Dining Room, opening onto the Sun Lounge, with palms, ficus trees, and a tiered Italian fountain. Sunday brunches here are an extravaganza featuring more than seventy items. Julie's, a sidewalk cafe along the west bank of Cheyenne Lake, offers a relaxed shirtsleeves-and-shorts atmosphere for sandwiches, salads, and burgers, while Espresso is a favorite stopping place for cappuccino, pastries, quiche, sandwiches, and eclairs. One of the merriest dining spots is the Golden Bee, an authentic English pub located behind and below the International Center; it is open for lunch and dinner and until the wee hours, with live ragtime and sing-alongs. Stratta's Italian Restaurant, in the spa complex, is open for breakfast, lunch, and dinner and boasts "cuisine vivant" along with classic Italian favorites. Relax and find entertainment in any of six different lounges including the Stars' Club and Cigar Bar. From piano music to full orchestra dancing to sports on the big-screen TV, it's all there for your enjoyment.

Children's World: Children ages three to twelve are revved up for active pursuits Monday through Saturday, mid-June to mid-August, Christmas and Easter, in the Bee Bunch Program. From 9:00 A.M. to 5:00 P.M., kids swim in one of the pools, explore the lake in a paddleboat, join games, and visit the zoo. And just wait until your child tells you about feeding the ducks! Golf, tennis, and cooking lessons or horseback riding provide more thrills, while games and crafts are quieter fun.

The youngsters meet again for dinner and games or a movie from 6:00 to 10:00 P.M. (summers only), granting their parents opportunities to sample the gourmet creations of the Broadmoor chefs. The children's meals are planned to ensure cleaned-up plates; the pizza, fried chicken, and hamburger dinners are favorites among the younger set and are included in the program cost of $40 daytime and $35 evening (for those four to twelve years old). The Toddler Bee Bunch Program is available 9:00 A.M.–2:00 P.M. for three-year-olds, at a cost of $25. Baby-sitting is available for $6.00 per hour, with a three-hour minimum.

Recreation: Golfing at The Broadmoor began when the original hotel opened in 1918. Donald Ross designed that first course and was followed by Robert Trent Jones, who added nine holes in 1950 and another nine in 1965. The Ed Seay/Arnold Palmer course was completed in 1976. Once avid golfers discover the challenging variety of these fifty-four holes, the incredibly scenic setting, the high-quality equipment and accessories of the golf shops, and instruction with the resident pro, they may never explore the rest of The Broadmoor—and that would be a pity.

Twelve Plexipave tennis courts are located at the Golf Club; two of these are bubble-enclosed, allowing tennis play to continue through the winter. Both golf clubs include tennis shops, where you can purchase new equipment and attire or investigate classes and clinics.

An afternoon can be spent swimming at any one of three heated swimming pools at Broadmoor Main, Broadmoor West, and the Golf Club. Rent a paddleboat for a spin on the lake or a bicycle for a tour around the lake. Stroll along One Lake Avenue to enjoy the twenty-plus shops.

The Broadmoor Spa, Golf and Tennis Club is more than 90,000 square feet of luxury: state-of-the-art fitness facility, full-service spa, full-service salon, and private locker rooms with all amenities, including fireplaces!

A nonstop itinerary of off-property activities includes white-water rafting, hot-air ballooning, skiing, fly-fishing, mountain biking, and hunting expeditions. Or perhaps you'll opt to take the famous cogwheel up to Pikes Peak. Check *The Broadmoor This Week* to stay abreast of the many resort activities. ≋≋

C Lazy U Ranch

P.O. Box 379
Granby, Colorado 80446
(970) 887–3344
E-mail: ranch@clazyu.com
Web site: www.clazyu.com

Ride 'em, cowboy! With a little time at C Lazy U Ranch, you could live up to this label. Experienced wranglers match you with just the right horse for you to call your own during a vacation stay, and they guide you through trail rides in the Colorado high country. Sitting at an elevation of 8,300 feet, less than a two-hour drive west of Denver, the ranch sprawls across more than 2,500 acres. A lot of territory to roam combines with warm sunny days that give way to cool nights—quite a setting for learning Western ways. For more than seventy years, C Lazy U has operated as a guest ranch. That adds up to a lot of experience, not only in riding and roping but also in welcoming and entertaining visitors. This working ranch is open for vacationers from mid-June to mid-October and mid-December through March.

Accommodations: About forty comfortable rooms and suites are in the Lodge and the guests' cottages that surround it. Seventy-five percent of these have a fireplace. During the summer and mid-December through New Year's, vacation stays are scheduled by the week, Sunday to Sunday. Guests can make reservations on a daily basis during the rest of the season.

Summer weekly rates per person are $1,200 to $1,650; Christmas weekly rates average $1,525 per person. Winter daily rates are $115 to $195 per person, and children receive a 20 to 40 percent discount. Children ages three to five are charged $200 a week less than the standard rate. These rates cover virtually everything you'll want or need during your visit: lodging, three meals a day, use of a horse, trail rides, use of the recreational facilities, and the supervised children's program.

Photo courtesy of C Lazy U Ranch

Dining: At C Lazy U you'll get the hearty meals that you need to maintain an energy level consistent with the fresh air and outdoor fun. The warm, rustic dining room is in the Lodge, the main building of the ranch. Here guests sit at tables set for ten—a good way to make friends—for relaxed family-style dining. But don't expect baked beans and coffee in a tin pot. More likely, you'll have Black Angus prime rib or jalapeño-stuffed mountain trout, for this five-star, five-diamond resort has outstanding menus. Children and teens eat earlier with their counselors, and after dinner families regroup for the evening activities. Buffet lunches are often served near the swimming pool, and evening cookouts are frequently planned. The Lodge also houses a comfortable living room and bar, where drinks and hors d'oeuvres are served nightly at 6:30 P.M. Another bar is located in the Patio House, the recreation center adjacent to the swimming pool; enjoy an evening cocktail and swap tall tales with other guests about the day's adventures.

Children's World: The way they take to things so easily, the kids may turn into wranglers before you do. And with C Lazy U's special attention to youngsters, they've got a good shot at calling themselves cowpokes by the time they head home.

Starting at age three (the ranch does not provide care for younger children), kids get a good introduction to life out West. They learn how to ride (at age six they can go out on trail rides) and a little of how to care for and feed horses, and they go swimming and fishing—all under the watchful eye of trained counselors. Everyone is assigned a horse for the entire week, based on individual ability, and children are divided into three groups: three- to five-year-olds, six- to twelve-year-olds, and teenagers. The Kids Corral is a comfortable indoor children's place for reading, art projects, and napping. A Game Room offers billiards, Ping-Pong, and Foosball. Teens, as they much prefer, have their own separate program of riding, hayrides, and cookouts. The children's program is available from early June to Labor Day and from mid-December through March. The last week of August is Baby Week, when children under three years are accepted.

Recreation: Naturally, the main attraction of a ranch is horseback riding. From a string of 165 horses, you'll be assigned a mount that suits your ability. With experienced wranglers you'll ride the high country across mountain meadows, through tall evergreens, along Willow Creek.

But there's a lot more to this ranch than just horses. Between trail rides sneak in a little fishing in the lake near the Lodge or at a secluded spot along Willow Creek, and have the trout for breakfast! Go hiking or spend an afternoon on the skeet range (the only activity not covered in the package rates), swim in the heated pool, or simply laze about nearby in the sunshine. Play tennis on two Laykold courts or try racquetball.

For less strenuous activities you may seek out The Patio House, the principal recreation center, which includes exercise equipment, locker rooms, complimentary laundry facilities, game room, bar, TV room (good news—there's no television or phone in the rooms!), and a large, all-purpose activity room with fireplace. And when you fear that saddle sores and tennis elbow may set in, retire to the whirlpool and saunas. In the evenings you'll join in on campfire sing-alongs, square dancing, and rodeos, just so you don't forget you're out West.

During the winter season guests take to skiing—cross-country on the 15 miles of trails maintained by the ranch and downhill at Winter Park and Silver Creek ski resorts, 25 miles away and accessible via the ranch's complimentary shuttle service.

But winter activities don't stop there. Enjoy horseback riding in the snow or in the 10,000-square-foot heated riding arena, or take a sleigh ride on an old-fashioned cutter and a world-class, $\frac{1}{2}$-mile sled run, or try dog-sledding. Ride an inner tube down the tubing hill or behind a speeding snowmobile, and ice skate or play hockey or broomball on the groomed skating pond. Then snuggle in for hot drinks, the fireplace, Western dancing, and cowboy songs. Yippee-yi-ay! ≋

Club Med/Copper Mountain

50 Beeler Place
Copper Mountain, Colorado 80443
(970) 968–7000, (800) CLUB MED
Web site: www.clubmed.com

C lub Med's Copper Mountain village is in Summit County, famous for terrific downhill skiing and its Rocky Mountain powder. Seventy-five miles west of Denver, the village is surrounded by the Arapahoe National Forest, sits at 9,600 feet, and looks up to a glorious mountain with a summit elevation of 12,360 feet. Copper Mountain is open from early December to mid-April.

You might be thinking "Club Med and kids? It has a nice ring, but is this for real?" Yes, at certain Club Med destinations, the swinging singles image has been shed and whole families can partake in the attentive yet carefree spirit of a Club Med vacation. Mini-Clubs cater to the younger set and support the Club Med policy of "The children, don't leave home without them."

Accommodations: In four interconnecting buildings, five to seven stories high, lodging is provided in cozy rooms with twin beds. The views of the mountains and the valleys are truly beautiful. Club Med's "pay one price" philosophy relieves you of many hassles, including repeated searches for your wallet. A one-week stay runs $970–$1,280 per person, depending on the season; for children three to twelve, there's a 25 to 40 percent discount. This price covers accommodations, meals, the children's program, ski lessons, and lift tickets. There is no extra charge for cribs or rollaway beds. It's necessary to have a Club Med membership to vacation here. Annual dues are $50 per adult, $20 per child, and a one-time family fee of $30.

Dining: The main dining room, with its floor-to-ceiling windows (you don't want to miss those mountain views), is the setting for breakfast and lunch buffets and multicourse, table-service dinners. There's a more intimate restaurant on the lower level. The cuisine is French and is as elegantly presented as it is carefully prepared. Wine is served at lunch and dinner (free of charge). Located near the dining room is a large bar as well as a cozy fireplace where après-ski begins. For evening entertainment see the nightly show, drop by the disco, or perhaps find a good bridge game in the card room.

Children's World: The Mini-Club, directed by an experienced staff, offers organized activities for three- to twelve-year-olds. This optional, free program is available 9:00 A.M. to 9:00 P.M., Monday through Saturday during the ski season. Children can join the group or their parents at any time, depending on family plans.

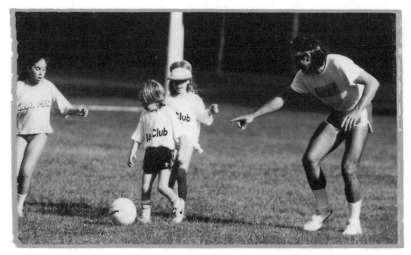

Photo courtesy of Club Med

Besides two hours of ski classes in the morning and the afternoon, kids go ice skating and sledding and have snow sculpture contests and arts-and-crafts classes. Don't worry about lunch and dinner; your child can enjoy the company of the counselors and other children at early mealtimes.

Recreation: Skiing at Copper Mountain just may lead to Rocky Mountain fever; with a 2,760-foot vertical drop, an average annual snowfall between 250 and 300 inches, and a season from early December to mid-April, it's not difficult to hit a skier's high. Fourteen chairlifts and seventy-six trails mean that long lift lines and crowded slopes are virtually unknown. The terrain offers beginner, intermediate, and expert runs, and Club Med's own ski school (two-hour classes mornings and afternoons) will guide you to improved downhill techniques whatever your level of ability. Classes are frequently videotaped, so be prepared for review and analysis with your instructor in the evening. For cross-country skiers, there are 16 miles of marked trails; however, no instruction or equipment is provided. Ice skating nearby on an outdoor pond is another favorite wintertime sport, as is snowboarding, with lessons for beginners.

Other activities include aerobics and stretch classes, jogging, and hiking. When the body grows weary, it may be time for pure relaxation in one of the Jacuzzis or saunas. The Copper Mountain organization has developed an athletic facility outside the Club Med property; for a small daily fee, Club Med guests have access to the tennis and racquetball courts, exercise equipment, swimming pool, saunas, and steam rooms there. ≈≈≈

Deer Valley Resort

P.O. Box 1525
Park City, Utah 84060
(435) 649–1000, (800) 424–3337
Web site: www.deervalley.com

Skiing for most folks means a little bit of the rugged outdoors—windburned cheeks, the raw natural beauty of mountain vistas, fresh tracks through pristine powder. Deer Valley has redefined skiing somewhat. It's all of the above but with an added twist. Instead of the Western flair you'd expect in Utah, there's a more sophisticated European atmosphere at Deer Valley. This is warm hospitality with a heavy dose of pampering—from the guest service attendants who help you unload your skis to the quite comfortable chairlifts to the signature food items in Snow Park Lodge.

Deer Valley, less than an hour's drive east of Salt Lake City, is actually three mountains: Bald Eagle Mountain, whose summit is 8,500 feet, Bald Mountain, which rises to 9,400 feet, and Flagstaff Mountain, with the summit at 9,100 feet. The hubs of activity are Snow Park Lodge at the base of Bald Eagle Mountain and Silver Lake Lodge at midmountain. Silver Lake Village is in effect the midmountain point, for it is from here that lifts ascend to Bald Mountain's summit. Snow Park Lodge houses a restaurant and lounge, the ski school, the ski rental shop, the children's center, and a well-stocked ski shop. Silver Lake Lodge has three restaurants and a smaller ski shop.

Both lodges are very tastefully designed; inside the columns are natural tree trunks at least 2 feet in diameter, and wood accoutrements abound—from the handrails to the ceiling beams, from the facial tissue dispensers to the trash cans. You'll find no plastic chairs and Formica-topped tables in the dining areas here—no indeed! Understated elegance and tasteful attention to detail are hallmarks of Deer Valley, the first country club for skiers.

Accommodations: The Stein Eriksen Lodge, located at midmountain, is a Norwegian-style hotel built of stone and wood. There are 130 luxurious rooms and suites, starting at $450 a night in the winter and $175 in the summer. Shops, restaurants, a swimming pool, and a health club complement this lodge.

In addition, there are more than 500 units at the base of the mountain, along the trails, and near Silver Lake Lodge. The condominiums range from one- to five-bedroom units with fully equipped kitchens and living areas with fireplaces. Most have private Jacuzzis and individual decks or balconies; some include saunas and some feature ski-in/ski-out access. Daily maid service is available. There are substantial savings during value seasons, typically early

December and early January, while rates increase during holiday periods. During the summer months rates range from $150 a night for a one-bedroom unit to $525 a night for a four-bedroom unit, with a minimum two-night stay. Contact Deer Valley Central Reservations for complete customized vacation planning.

Dining: Dining at Deer Valley is a gourmet experience. The Glitretind at the Stein Eriksen Lodge heads the list in elegance. The Snow Park Lodge and the Silver Lake Restaurant in the Silver Lake Lodge are "cafeterias." What misnomers! Though they're self-service, the lavish lunchtime displays (homemade breads and pastries, salads, quiches, deli sandwiches) are hardly typical of the standard quick bite between ski runs. In the evening The Seafood Buffet is offered at the Snow Park Lodge (mmm—iced shrimp and raw oysters on the half shell). The Mariposa at Silver Lake Lodge features table service for an elegant candlelight dinner. All these provide interesting alternatives to gourmet cooking in your condo.

Children's World: Deer Valley's Children's Center is a state-licensed facility providing indoor supervision and activities for nonskiing children. Located on the main level of the Snow Park Lodge, the center is open daily 8:30 A.M.–4:30 P.M. during the ski season and can accommodate infants as young as two months of age. Prices for enrollment are as follows: two- to twenty-four-month-olds, $70 for a full day (with lunch) and $55 for a half day; two- to twelve-year-olds, $58 for a full day (with lunch) and $45 for a half day.

Recreation: There are eighty-four downhill runs, eighteen chairlifts, and a vertical drop of 3,000 feet. Combine these with well-groomed trails and a restricted number of skiers on a daily basis—what more could a skier ask for? The mountains are beautiful, and the attention to them and to the skiers is high quality. Full- and half-day private and group lessons are available. Cross-country ski lessons are also offered nearby; trails roll over broad, open expanses and through aspens and evergreens.

If you don't have a sufficient workout on the slopes, maybe the exercise rooms will test your limits. Then relax your weary muscles in one of the saunas or Jacuzzis. Though primarily a winter wonderland, Deer Valley operates year-round. In warmer weather guests enjoy 45 miles of lift-served mountain biking, scenic chairlift rides, the Utah Symphony Series, and the Deer Valley Summer Adventure Camp. ≋

Flathead Lake Lodge

Box 248
Bigfork, Montana 59911
(406) 837–4391
E-mail: fll@digisys.net

Mix some city slickers with a few expert wranglers out in Montana horse country, toss in beautiful scenery and clear blue skies, and come up with quite a different vacation experience at Flathead Lake Lodge. On 2,000 acres in northwest Montana, just south of Glacier National Park, this dude ranch specializes in water sports and just about anything that has to do with horses, from riding them to shoeing them. The lodge is situated on the shores of Flathead Lake (15 miles wide by 30 miles long), and the surrounding timberland stretches up into the Rocky Mountains. The ranch is open from May 1 to October 1, and one- or two-week visits are standard.

Accommodations: The main lodge is the focus of activities and dining; in a warm and rustic setting, the old stone fireplace lures many guests to gather for cozy chats. There are guest rooms here and in the south lodge; some families find the two- and three-bedroom cottages particularly attractive. Many of the lodge rooms and the guest cottages have views of the lake. The weekly rate for an adult is $1,893; for a teenager, $1,448; for six- to twelve-year-olds, $1,254; for three- to five-year-olds, $938; and for infants and toddlers, $101. These fees include lodging, three meals a day, horseback riding, tennis, and use of the boats and sports equipment. Cribs are available at no additional charge.

Photo courtesy of Flathead Lake Lodge

Dining: Dining is a family affair, with good home cooking. Guests gather at the long tables in the lodge dining room or at the picnic tables out on the patio overlooking the lake. Everyone may sample buffalo or roast pig at an outdoor barbecue, along with homemade breads and pies. Children eat together before their parents, allowing grown-ups time to get acquainted and plan the next day's events. Sometimes adults meet in the Saddle Sore Saloon.

Children's World: The friendly staff—mostly energetic college students who can keep up with excited youngsters—guide children through the day's activities. They can swim, lend a hand with the daily chores, and learn to ride horses. Arts-and-crafts classes are offered from 10:00 A.M. to noon most weekdays. Children six years and older can join cowboys on the horseback-riding trails in the mountains. You might want to bring along a sleeping bag for your child; there's a campout in tepees near the ranch. Baby-sitting is also available.

Recreation: The great outdoors awaits you. Horses are a way of life here; ride 'em, rope 'em, or test your nerve and verve in competition. Take an early-morning breakfast ride to work up a good appetite, then enjoy a breakfast cookout amid the tall pines. Old-fashioned Western rodeos are part of the evening activities.

Take a dip in the large swimming pool or the crystal clear waters of the lake. Sailing, canoe races, and waterskiing may fill your afternoons. Cruises on the lake are organized several times a week. Fish in the lake or the nearby streams, and add a trout to a cookout dinner or spin a good story about the one that got away.

It's easy to find partners for a game of tennis (four courts) and to organize Ping-Pong or volleyball. You might take a stroll along the wooded trails and pick berries. You can schedule full- or half-day excursions for white-water rafting, river tubing, and wilderness fishing. The National Bison Range, only an hour away, attracts many visitors; seeing real live buffalo is a highlight for kids—and parents too. ≋

Keystone Resort

Box 38
Keystone, Colorado 80435
(970) 468–2316, (800) 468–5004
Web site: www.ski-keystone.com

L ike many fine Western ski resorts, Keystone first attracted settlers in search of the rich minerals in its mountains. Today visitors flock here seeking light powdery snow and the mountain high for which the Rockies are known. At the base of Loveland Pass, 70 miles west of Denver, Keystone has ninety-one runs on three interconnecting ski mountains and a vertical drop of more than 2,300 feet. The resort remains open year-round, so many folks, when summer rolls around, hang up their skis and head for Keystone's golf course (designed by Robert Trent Jones Jr.), the Keystone Tennis Center, and the Keystone Music Festival.

Accommodations: River Run Village at Keystone Resort is the largest ski area development project in North America. When finished, Keystone will have an estimated 4,560 residential units and lodge rooms. To date, two buildings have been constructed in River Run: Jackpine Lodge and Black Bear. Both buildings have ground-floor shops and restaurants, with three upper levels of mountain condominium homes. Upper-floor residential units total sixty-one. A third building, Arapahoe Lodge, includes thirty-six upper-floor condominium homes. Rentals are available. Prices are yet to be determined.

The Keystone Lodge is an elegant resort hotel with more than 150 rooms offering mountain views, most with a private balcony. Facilities here include an indoor/outdoor swimming pool, sauna, Jacuzzi, and three restaurants. Nightly rates during the summer are $190–$230 for two people; during the ski season rates are $170–$236 a night.

The Inn at Keystone is a six-story hotel with 160 rooms, just 200 yards from the lift. Rooms here are $130–$170 during summer, $135–$215 during ski season (from the end of November to the beginning of April). Children twelve and under stay free in the same room with their parents. Cribs are available.

In addition to River Run, 850 condominium units are arranged near the slopes, in the village, and bordering the lake; these studios to four-bedroom units have a fully equipped kitchen, and most have a fireplace. All complexes have a heated swimming pool, a sauna, or a Jacuzzi. In the summer one-bedroom units are $135–$195 a night, and a four-bedroom unit for eight people is $265–$360 a night. Winter rates are $140–$360 for a one-bedroom and $370–$960 for a four-bedroom unit. Package plans are offered for skiing, golf, tennis, and music festival vacations. A shuttle-bus service winds through the village and connects the mountain bases.

Dining: From romantic gourmet dinners in a mountaintop restaurant more than 2 miles high to family picnic lunches carried by llamas, unique and award-winning dining choices set Keystone Resort apart from other mountain resorts. The resort features more than a dozen dining options that range from gourmet six-course meals to a Western family-style cookout and include Summit County's only AAA four-diamond-rated restaurants—The Alpenglow Stube and Keystone Ranch.

At the Keystone Lodge, the Garden Room features continental cuisine and a Sunday brunch; the Edgewater is a casual restaurant open for breakfast and lunch. Among the numerous restaurants in the village, you'll find Pizza on the Plaza; Idabelle's, for Mexican fare; and Out of Bounds, for a sports bar/nightclub atmosphere. Lunch and dinner are served at both the Keystone Ranch and Alpenglow Stube. In summer you can hop a hayride to Soda Creek Homestead—in winter a sleigh ride takes you there—for a juicy steak dinner.

Children's World: At Keystone youngsters start skiing at age three. The Mini-Minor's Camp is a program of introductory skiing and sledding and indoor activities for four- and five-year-olds. Graduating from this, a child joins the Minor's Camp for six- to eight-year-olds; more ski instruction is integrated into the fully supervised day. The fee for all day, 8:30 A.M. to 4:00 P.M., is $72, including lunch.

The Children's Center is located at the Mountain House base area of the mountain and provides nursery care for little ones as young as two months. The fee for the day-care center is $46 a day.

During the summer Keystone's Children's Center provides attention for children two months to twelve years, 8:00 A.M.–5:00 P.M., in age-appropriate activities. Little ones are amused with a stock of toys; preschoolers enjoy nature walks, picnics, pony rides, and arts and crafts; and older children go swimming, boating, hiking, horseback riding, fishing, and take rides in the gondola. The daily charge for the program is $54; lunch is included except when baby food and formula are required. Baby-sitting services are also available, at an hourly rate of $8.00.

Recreation: With three interconnected mountains—Keystone Mountain, North Peak, and The Outback—Keystone offers terrain for skiers and snowboarders of all levels. Keystone Mountain offers mainly beginner and intermediate terrain, with night-skiing operations that keep the mountain open until 9:00 P.M. North Peak challenges guests with more intermediate slopes and runs that plunge down mogul-filled terrain. The Outback features only intermediate and expert runs. Some of Summit County's best tree skiing is found on The Outback. Skiers can find deep powder in open bowls adjacent to The Outback. And the twenty-acre snowboard terrain park features two half-pipes. Nighttime lighting makes Keystone's terrain garden the largest night-snowboarding operation in Colorado.

The ski season opens at Keystone in mid-October (Colorado's earliest opening date) and continues into early May. Whether you're trying to figure out what a snowplow is or you're looking for perfection in powder skiing, the more than 350 ski and snowboarding instructors can guide you through the 1,749 acres of skiable terrain.

Other winter sports at Keystone are ice skating at the Skating Center in the village, cross-country skiing from the Keystone Cross-Country Center into Arapahoe National Forest (cross-country and telemark lessons are offered), snowmobile tours into the backcountry, sleigh rides, and indoor tennis.

Summertime at Keystone means golfing on the masterfully designed Robert Trent Jones Jr. course; eighteen holes with a Scottish flair respect the woodlands, meadows, and a nine-acre lake. The course is open from June to mid-October; golf pros offer private lessons and clinics.

Keystone is a haven for mountain-bike enthusiasts. The resort offers a special program called Dirt Camp, a series of instructional mountain-bike camps that provides intense riding retreats for "mud studs" and "wannabes." Even if you're a beginner and conquering single-track, Dirt Camp helps you hone your mountain biking skills.

Another important summertime attraction here is the Music Festival. Ranging from classical to pop, the National Repertory Orchestra and the Summit Brass carry the season from June through Labor Day.

At the Keystone Tennis Center, two indoor courts permit year-round play, and an additional twelve outdoor courts expand summertime possibilities. Ball machines, video analysis, and group and private lessons aid the tennis player in his game.

Fishermen take to the local haunts for rainbow trout; boaters sail on Lake Dillon (5 miles west of Keystone) or skim across Keystone Lake in a paddleboat or kayak. Bicyclists ride the paths along Snake River, and hikers plod along the trails through wildflowers and aspens into the national forest. Horseback ride from the Keystone Stables through the Snake River Valley (breakfast rides are specialties), tour the high country of the Arapahoe National Forest by jeep, go white-water rafting down the Colorado and Arkansas Rivers, be treated to a lunch of rattlesnake meat and buffalo, or enjoy the great outdoors and mountain scenery on a gondola ride to Keystone Mountain's summit.

Reservations and more information on these activities (including dining at Keystone's award-winning restaurants) can be arranged by the Keystone Activities and Dining Center well before a guest arrives, so that everything is already in place at vacation's start. The number to call is (800) 354–4FUN. ≋

Mountain Sky Guest Ranch

P.O. Box 1128
Bozeman, Montana 59715
(406) 587–1244, (800) 548–3392
Web site: www.mtnsky.com

"Just turn me loose, let me straddle my own saddle underneath the Western sky." At Mountain Sky all guests (age seven and older) are assigned their own special horse. Careful matching of horse and rider according to the latter's age and skills ensures a compatible duo during a vacation stay. Under the guidance of experienced wranglers, you'll be swaggering like a Montana cowboy before the week is out.

Mountain Sky Guest Ranch has a rich history dating back to the mid-nineteenth century. This is no modern mock-up of Old West ranching. It was an active operation during the days of cattle empires and witnessed the excitement of the gold mining era. With its genuine Western flavor, Mountain Sky offers visitors a combination of "wide open spaces" and modern conveniences and comforts. Located just 30 miles north of Yellowstone National Park, Mountain Sky sits in Paradise Valley, in southwestern Montana. Surrounded by national forest and wilderness areas, the wooded mountainous landscape of Montana's high country is a beautiful vacation setting.

Accommodations: Guests are lodged in rustic but modern cabins; each one has a refrigerator. Rates are $1,925–$2,345 a week for an adult, $1,680–$1,890 for a child seven to twelve years old, and $1,330–$1,505 for a younger child. These prices include accommodations, all meals, use of all recreational facilities, and a horse for each guest (except those six and younger). Cribs are available at no charge. During the summer the vacation week runs from Sunday to Sunday; within a couple of days, you'll make friends not only with your horse but also with the other guests.

Dining: Meals are served in the dining room of the main lodge and at barbecue cookouts. Understanding that the atmosphere of the great outdoors can generate healthy appetites, the chefs often prepare hearty as well as gourmet meals. Rugged attire (jeans, boots) is standard most of the time; Tuesday- and Saturday-night dinners are a bit more formal. For good conversation and evening cocktails, drop by the Mountain View Lounge.

Children's World: In summer trained counselors guide children of all ages in a program of activities. The youth schedule includes arts and crafts, nature

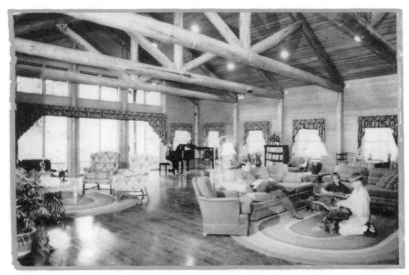

Photo courtesy of Mountain Sky Guest Ranch

walks, and swimming. There's even a small fishing pond reserved for children. Children ages seven and older learn horseback-riding skills with the Children's Wrangler. With the exception of family cookouts, children can stay with their friends and counselors for evening meals. The game room for teens features Ping-Pong, a jukebox, and a pool table. There is no additional charge for these activities; the supervised children's program is part of the weekly rate. For children not old enough to participate, baby-sitting arrangements can be made.

Recreation: Horseback riding is the primary sport at the ranch. Mounting your own horse and exploring hundreds of miles of trails can be as invigorating or relaxing as you want to make it. Besides morning and afternoon excursions, guests enjoy evening dinner rides.

In between take a dip in the heated swimming pool, play a game of tennis (two courts), or hike in the woods. Ping-Pong, volleyball, softball, and horseshoes are also popular games at the ranch. Anglers head to the mountain streams, where rainbow and brown trout are in plentiful supply. After active adventures, unwind in the hot tub or sauna. Capping off a fun-filled day, evening Western dances and campfire sing-alongs are frequently planned. ≋

Park City Mountain Resort

P.O. Box 39
Park City, Utah 84060
(801) 649–8111; (800) 222–7275 for lodging information
Web site: www.parkcitymountain.com

Park City was originally a mining camp in the nineteenth century. From the late 1860s to the 1930s, the wealth of silver in the mountains attracted miners with dreams of great fortunes. Today people flock to Park City not for the silver but for the incredible Utah snow.

As one local said, "Skiing is almost a religion here. People talk about when it snowed, how much it snowed, and what kind of snow it snowed when it snowed!" In the 1940s the potential of this snow was realized and the first runs were opened. By the 1960s the development known today as the Park City Mountain Resort had begun.

The town is at 6,400 feet, and summits rise to 10,000 feet. Just thirty-five minutes from Salt Lake City's airport and surrounded by the Wasatch Range of the Rocky Mountains, Park City is more than a mountain and luxury condominiums. The historic Main Street is lined with Victorian architecture containing shops, restaurants, and galleries and gives you a sense of what the Old West was all about. With a little imagination, you can just picture an old miner swaggering into a Main Street restaurant (it would have been a saloon in the old days), ready to make friends with some pretty dance-hall girl. The resort area is open year-round. A summertime calendar of events and activities can be obtained from the Park City Chamber of Commerce.

Accommodations: There are approximately 3,000 hotel rooms and condominium units in Park City at the mountain base, a couple of blocks from the runs, and throughout town. Prices vary depending on the proximity to the slopes and the amenities offered. The Park City Chamber of Commerce garners complete listings of accommodations in the area; call (801) 649–6100. A free bus connects all points in the town.

The Lodge at Mountain Village is at the base of the ski area and features ski-in/ski-out convenience. Surrounding the ice-skating rink and above the many shops and restaurants of the resort center, the accommodations range from studios at $239 a night to four-bedroom units up to $999 a night during the regular season (late January to early April). Package plans that include lift tickets are offered.

The Silvertown Lodge offers one- to four-bedroom condominiums, each with a fireplace and kitchen. It is a couple of blocks from the slopes, and prices

Photo by Hughes Martin, courtesy of Park City Ski Area

range from $134 to $215 a night for a one-bedroom to $240 to $399 a night for a four-bedroom unit, depending on the season.

Dining: With a well-developed resort village at the mountain base and a historic Main Street, the dining facilities are numerous, to say the least. Though most people lodging in condominiums find cooking at home convenient, the many eating establishments will probably entice you for a few meals out.

At the resort center are several refreshment spots, from the Olympic Spirit Store to the Rocky Mountain Chocolate Factory, with luscious bonbons and fudge, to Baja Cantina, with its generous portions of Mexican dishes. Moose's serves burgers, and Food for Thought has deli sandwiches and pastries.

Three restaurants are on the mountain, one of which, the Mid Mountain Lodge, was built about 1898 and is one of the top twelve mountain restaurants in North America (as rated by *Ski* magazine). Enjoy a variety of entrees and sandwiches, either inside or out on the 10,000-square-foot deck. Summit House, at the top of the gondola, has lighter fare. Steeps, in the gondola building, is the largest. The private club on the second floor offers table-service lunch and live entertainment for après-ski along with full bar service. Enjoy the grill on the outside deck or homemade soups from the first-floor cafeteria.

Main Street opens up another realm of dining establishments: the Claimjumper, for steaks and prime rib; Cisero's, for chicken, seafood, and pasta dishes; and Texas Red's Pit Barbecue, for spareribs and beef brisket. At Prospector's Square the Grub Steak Restaurant features prime rib, steak, and seafood.

Children's World: Park City Mountain Camp is provided for five- to twelve-year-olds throughout the summertime. The day camp focuses on outdoor activities of all types, including hiking, mountain biking, swimming, tennis, and golf, plus additional activities involving arts and crafts.

The Kinderschule at the resort center entertains youngsters three to six years old in a variety of indoor and outdoor supervised play. The friendly bears painted on the walls of the entrance to the school greet children in the morning at 8:30 A.M. and hint at the fun that lies within. The friendly staff guides them in arts and crafts and games in between their ninety-minute morning and afternoon ski lessons. The fee for a full day of activities (until 4:30 P.M.), including snacks and a hot lunch, is $79. You receive daily reports on your child so that you can track his progress as a skier. Morning and afternoon ski lessons only (one and a half hours each) are $43. The all-day mountain adventure, for older skiers, includes two hours of morning and afternoon lessons, plus lift ticket, for $89.

Children seven years and older can join group ski lessons; a five-day package plan that includes lessons and lunch is $355.

For younger children (eighteen months through kindergarten), Miss Billie's Kid's Kampus, a licensed child-care facility in Park City, is the logical alternative. Open year-round, Monday through Friday from 7:45 A.M. to 6:00 P.M., it also provides a "latch key" program for children up to nine years. Drop-ins are welcome. The cost is $55 for children up to three years, $50 for ages three and older, and includes lunch and a program of age- and season-appropriate activities. Call (801) 649–5437.

Recreation: With an annual average snowfall of 350 inches, a ski season from mid-November to the end of April, and 2,200 acres of skiable terrain, including ninety-three runs and bowls, fourteen chairlifts, and 3,100 vertical feet, Park City is one of the largest Rocky Mountain ski resorts. Whether you ride the six-passenger high-speed chair, Silverlode, or the chairs up to Jupiter Bowl, you'll find runs to meet your whim and your expertise. Whether you ramble down gentle slopes past old mining buildings, take on the moguls between groves of aspen, or get knee-deep in powder, plenty of variety will keep you happy. Park City allows snowboarding too, and there's even night skiing and riding, if you just can't bear to leave the slopes. Wolf Mountain is another whole mountain just down the road, and Deer Valley (see separate entry) is Park City's newest development. The ski school accommodates all ages and abilities in group and private lessons. Lessons are also available for cross-country skiers on a private basis.

Ice skating is another fun wintertime sport, and with the rink, rentals, and lessons available in the resort village, it's a convenient diversion. The resort village, which includes several restaurants, is also the center for many shops: ski rental and repair, fashions and ski accessories, gifts, T-shirts, toys, and hand-crafted items.

Though primarily a wintertime resort area, Park City is a destination for summertime vacations as well. The clean mountain air, the plentiful wildflowers, and the great outdoors beckon you. Hiking, horseback riding, tennis and racquetball (at specific condominium properties, the Athletic Club, and the Racquet Club), golf, and bicycling are favorite warm-weather activities. ≈≈≈

Snowbird Ski and Summer Resort

P.O. Box 929000
Snowbird, Utah 84092
(801) 742–2222; (800) 453–3000 for lodging and air reservations
Web site: www.snowbird.com

Snowbird's diverse terrain includes some of the most challenging skiing in the world. Yet surprisingly, the size of its intermediate, novice, and beginner areas is greater than the total terrain of many notable resorts. Every night more than half the slopes and trails are groomed, paving the way for beginner and intermediate skiers, while leaving the rest for those who seek the light, dry Utah powder. Whatever your proficiency and desire, Snowbird accommodates you with more than 2,500 acres of wide-open bowls, gladed tree runs, steep chutes, nightly groomed trails, and cruising boulevards. From the "snowcat skiing" in Mineral Basin to the terrific novice and intermediate terrain off the Thunder Chair, you'll be amazed by the sheer excitement of skiing the "Bird."

Here are a few facts about Snowbird: vertical rise of 3,240 continuously skiable feet; 2,500-plus skiable acres; average annual snowfall of 500 inches; many lifts, including one aerial tramway, seven double chairlifts, one high-speed detachable quad, and snowcats; a ski season extending from mid-November through late May; the longest descent, Gad Valley, at 3½ miles; the longest designated run, Chip's Run, at 2½ miles.

Snowbird enjoys one of the finest ski seasons in the world. Beginning in mid-November, the ski season regularly extends 200 days. In fact, skiers have even been known to celebrate the Fourth of July on the slopes.

Photo courtesy of Snowbird Ski and Summer Resort

Accommodations: A cozy slopeside pedestrian village, Snowbird harmonizes fittingly with the rugged, natural beauty of Little Cottonwood Canyon. Yet here you'll find all the services necessary to complete the perfect vacation. And everything at the resort—accommodations, restaurants, shops, skiing, and activities—is within easy walking distance.

Snowbird has three distinctive condominium properties: The Inn, The Lodge at Snowbird, and the Iron Blosam Lodge. Each offers homelike features, such as fireplaces and kitchens, with several different floor plans to suit your family's needs. Pools, saunas, exercise facilities, and other services are included or easily accessible. Snowbird's flagship accommodation, the Cliff Lodge, offers easy ski-in/ski-out access, full-service child care, shops, and a business center. It is adorned with the decorative luxury of North America's foremost Persian and Oriental rug collection. Three restaurants, two lounges, and the world-class Cliff Spa and Salon make it the perfect place to retire after an exhilarating day on the slopes.

Snowbird's 57,000-square-foot conference center includes fourteen meeting rooms and a 7,800-square-foot ballroom. These facilities, uncompromising services, and a professional staff are the reasons Snowbird has been awarded one of the industry's highest honors, *Meetings & Conventions* magazine's Gold Key Award.

Dining: The dining at Snowbird is diverse. With many restaurants and lounges to please a variety of tastes and styles, Snowbird dining offers everything from Niçoise-style striped sea bass to mountain-grilled burgers to coconut beer-

battered shrimp. Live entertainment and other après-ski activities also complement Snowbird's winter season.

Children's World: Snowbird offers ideal family vacations. According to *Skiing*
magazine, "Snowbird has come up with what might be the best family ski value
at a major ski area." The resort has been awarded the Family Channel's Seal of
Quality. From family ski zones to the Kids Park Mining Town replica, Snowbird is
certain to please young skiers. So don't bring the kids just because they ski for
free; bring them because Snowbird is one vacation they'll always remember.

Camp Snowbird, located in the Cliff Lodge, provides state-licensed infant
and toddler care. Available services at Camp Snowbird include daytime supervision, meals, ski lessons, and, most of all, a good time. In-room baby-sitting is
also available to lodging guests. Make reservations two weeks in advance.

Recreation: Snowbird's Mountain Host program offers free guided skiing
tours every day to acquaint guests with the runs and lifts best suited to their skiing abilities. All you need is a lift ticket and a smile to join the group and get
better acquainted with the incredible mountain.

Almost as famous as the snow, and every bit as great, is the ski school. More
than 200 professional instructors offer all-day or by-the-hour private and group
lessons. Or, if you want to take your vacation to new heights, try one of Snowbird's specialized seminars that address the specific interests and needs of
women, seniors, snowboarders, and experts.

The Cliff Lodge and the Snowbird Center house shops and boutiques specializing in products unique to Snowbird. From children's clothing to jewelry,
from a general store to a pharmacy, and from ski rentals to Snowbird's own signature clothing line, you're certain to find what you're looking for. ≋

Snowmass Village Resort Association

Box 5566
Snowmass Village, Colorado 81615
(800) 598–2006 for guest information,
(800) 598–2004 for reservations
E-mail: info@snowmassvillage.com
Web site: www.snowmassvillage.com

Aspen is one heck of a fine mountain. With more than 3,300 feet of vertical drop and exciting, challenging runs, it attracts very skillful skiers.
But when talking Aspen skiing, you've actually got four mountains to
consider: Aspen Mountain (sometimes called Ajax); Snowmass, 10 miles away;
and Aspen Highlands and Buttermilk in between. A combined skiable terrain

that totals more than 3,500 acres provides more runs and variety than you could possibly test in a two-week ski vacation. Lift passes are valid for all four mountains. Aspen is chic and supports an active night life; Snowmass is devoted to its motto "A Mountain of Family Fun." But who splits hairs when the best of both worlds is all within 10 miles? Though best known for skiing, both resort areas are open year-round.

Aspen's origins are rooted in the silver boom of the early 1880s. Many of the charming Victorian structures have been preserved and renovated; today they house boutiques, art galleries, hotels, and restaurants. Skiing in Aspen started in the 1930s and really took hold after World War II during conscientious development of the area as a winter resort. Aspen is just waiting to tempt you. Folks here boast that 70 percent of their visitors return every year and more than 90 percent come back sooner or later. So if you give it a shot, you may just have to plan on being hooked.

Accommodations: Whatever your preference in lodging, you should have no problem finding the perfect place to hang your hat in the Aspen and Snowmass area. From moderate to expensive, from quaint to modern, all the possibilities seem to be here. For the most part, lodgings in Aspen are in the village; at Snowmass they're slopeside with immediate access to trails. This is not, however, a hard-and-fast rule, and because shuttle buses always cruise the roads, there's no problem getting to the lifts and from one mountain to another.

The Aspen Club Lodge is at the base of Aspen Mountain and includes a swimming pool, Jacuzzi, saunas, and restaurant ($170–$425 a night, higher for suites). Just across from the Little Nell Lift is Aspen Square, a complex of about one hundred condominium units that features a swimming pool and saunas; nightly rates range from $139 to $429, with a seven-night minimum for most of the season. The Hotel Jerome on Main Street is a Victorian building more than one hundred years old; room rates are $255–$725 a night.

The Snowmass Lodge and Club in Snowmass Village combines hotel and condominium accommodations on 120 acres at the base of the mountain. The amenities include a restaurant and bar, indoor tennis courts (two), exercise equipment, swimming pools, and, for summer and fall holidays, eleven outdoor tennis courts and an eighteen-hole golf course. Double rooms start at $145 a night, going to $848 for a three-bedroom unit (depending on the date). There is a three-night minimum. Other hotels in Snowmass are the Wildwood Lodge, the Stonebridge Inn, the Pokolodi Lodge, the Mountain Chalet, and the Silvertree; among the more than twenty condominium complexes are Aspenwood, Shadowbrook, Crestwood, and Timberline. With close to one hundred hotels, lodges, inns, and condominiums in the Aspen area, it is indeed fortunate that the resort associations publish descriptive lists to help you sort through the possibilities. Inquire carefully about various pricing packages: five- or seven-day packages that include lifts and lessons, low-season rates, and family plans.

Dining: As with lodging arrangements, the possibilities in dining seem almost limitless. Whether you've got a hankering for pizza, quiche, fresh veggies and salads, a juicy steak, spicy Szechuan or Northern Italian cuisine, you'll find the right spot among the more than one hundred restaurants in and around Aspen. La Cocina Su Casa and the Cantina serve Mexican dishes; steaks and prime rib are typical fare at the Steak Pit. And, of course, restaurants and refreshment stops are at the mountain bases and on the mountains. For sweets, you can stop by the Paradise Bakery or Cafe Ink.

Among the twenty restaurants in Snowmass are The Stew Pot, featuring wholesome family fare; the Mountain Dragon, featuring Chinese food; and the premier restaurants La Bohème and Cowboys.

Children's World: Even the youngest traveling companion will not keep you from days on the slopes. From 8:30 A.M. to 4:00 P.M., Snow Cubs entertains eighteen-month to three-year-old children in a play program filled with puppet shows, stories, arts and crafts, snowman building, some skiing, and sledding; four- to six-year-olds participate in ski lessons as well as indoor and other outdoor activities in the Big Burn Bears program. The program is $78 daily or $360 for five full days and includes lunch and lift tickets. Late-afternoon and evening baby-sitters are also available through Snowmass Ski School. Family activities are scheduled all season long.

Powder Pandas is Buttermilk Mountain's ski school for three- to six-year-olds, 8:30 A.M.–4:00 P.M. Snowpuppies Ski School is Aspen Highlands' version of ski lessons and fun for ages three and a half to six, 9:30 A.M.–3:30 P.M. The daytime programs include lunch and snacks at each of these locations and cost $72 at the Highlands and $78 at Buttermilk.

The children's classes at the Snowmass Ski School organize seven- to twelve-year-old skiers from 9:30 A.M. to 3:15 P.M.; the cost is $65 per day. Also at the Snowmass Ski School, a special teen program is designed to bring together by age and ability skiers thirteen to nineteen years old; besides skiing, picnics, races, and sled parties are planned. The cost is $60 per day.

Operating a summer program (June through August) for five- to twelve-year-olds, Camp Snowmass emphasizes a healthy, active outdoor schedule of fishing, hiking, swimming, nature walks, horseback riding, visits to the nature preserve, and picnics. Overnights are planned during the season. For a day's events from 7:45 A.M. to 4:00 P.M., Monday through Friday, the fee is $50 (lunch is provided for an additional $5.00). Five- and ten-day packages are available for additional savings. Snowmass also offers free daily activities for kids and adults all summer long.

Recreation: From the end of November to mid-April, skiing is on everyone's mind, and regardless of your skiing ability you'll have plenty of runs to schuss down. Aspen's reputation as a mecca for advanced skiers is well earned, with 30 percent of the runs down Ajax ranked as expert, 35 percent advanced, and the remaining 35 percent intermediate. But beginners and intermediates should not grow faint in the face of overwhelming ventures, for the other mountains accommodate the not quite so adept. Aspen Highlands is 50 percent intermediate and 25 percent each in expert and beginner categories; the total vertical drop is 3,635 feet. The vertical rise at Snowmass is almost 4,400 feet, and more than 60 percent of the runs are intermediate. Buttermilk with 2,000 vertical feet caters more to novices, with almost half of its runs designated for beginners. A teaching staff that totals more than 1,000 ski professionals can introduce a beginner to the slopes (except at Aspen Mountain) as well as help an expert perfect techniques in mogul skiing, snowboarding, and telemarking. At Buttermilk and Snowmass, look for special three-day, first-time-on-skis or -snowboard packages.

Wintertime fun continues with ice skating at the Aspen Ice Gardens and the Silver Circle, dogsled rides at Krabloonik Kennels, snowshoe tours, cross-country skiing, sleigh rides at Snowmass Stables and T Lazy 7 Ranch, snowmobiling, and hot-air ballooning (yes, even in winter!). Many of the lodging complexes have swimming pools and exercise equipment. The tennis and athletic clubs also provide opportunities for indoor workouts. Evening entertainment includes films, concerts, plays at the Wheeler Opera House, and classical music at Harris Hall.

Though skiing is practically synonymous with Aspen, this place does not turn into a ghost town when the snow melts. During the summer, the hills are alive with cultural events. The Aspen Music Festival, nearly fifty years old, runs from the end of June to the end of August and is complemented by the Aspen Community Theater and the Jazz Aspen Snowmass Music Festivals. The Anderson Ranch Arts Center in Snowmass has a summer program of classes in photography, ceramics, painting, and printmaking.

You can just about have your pick of outdoor activities: horseback riding, hiking, jogging, rafting, kayaking, fishing, hot-air ballooning, and jeep tours. There is also lift-served mountain biking at Snowmass Ski Area. An eighteen-hole golf course is located on the west perimeter of Aspen; another is in Snowmass. Tennis courts at condominiums and racquet clubs dot the valley. But even in summer you have to take at least one gondola ride—to the top of Aspen Mountain for a spectacular view of this bit of the Rockies. ≋≋

Vail Valley Tourism and Convention Bureau

100 East Meadow Drive
Vail, Colorado 81657
(970) 476–1000, (800) 525–3875 (outside Colorado)
E-mail: reservations@visitvailvalley.com
Web site: www.visitvailvalley.com

Vail/Beaver Creek Central Reservations

P.O. Box 7
Vail, Colorado 81658
(800) 525–2257

L ots of folks talk of Vail and Aspen in practically the same breath. Usually these are people who have never visited either one. Granted, several similarities between the two come to mind: Both rank right at the top in excellent skiing, both are high in the Rockies west of Denver, both are chic and sophisticated, and to both have been appended newer developments that are more upscale and remote—Beaver Creek at Vail and Snowmass at Aspen.

Unlike Aspen's history as an old mining town, Vail grew up in the 1960s. The modern-day careful planning and systematic development give Vail its atmosphere; it is a well-laid-out, Alpine-style village designed with the pedestrian in mind (it's so nice that so few cars spoil the scenery). Actually, there are three village areas at the base of Vail Mountain—Vail Village, Golden Peak, and Lionshead—each with its own lodging, restaurants, and facilities, and each within walking distance of base lifts. In practical terms, though, since each abuts the next, most folks think of the tripartite as one friendly town. While Vail is 100 miles west of Denver, Beaver Creek is just 10 miles farther down the road. Opened in 1980, Beaver Creek, too, has been planned around a pedestrian village; in addition to the accommodations in the village, some lodges and condominiums are tucked among the grand spruce trees on the mountain. Shuttle-bus lines service the Vail Valley, within each village and between mountain bases. A year-round resort area, the Vail Valley also boasts of its summer beauty and offers art and music festivals, hiking, mountain biking, and more from April through October.

Accommodations: Lodging at Vail can be right at the mountain base a couple of skips from the chairlift and dripping with amenities, or back a couple of paces and not so overloaded with extras. Of course, the options are reflected in the rates. The Lodge at Vail, just steps from two chairlifts, has a heated swimming pool and a sauna, and some of its rooms feature a fireplace, balcony, and

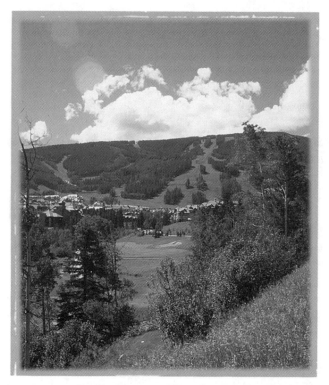

Photo courtesy of Vail Valley Tourism and Convention Bureau

kitchen; daily rates for a one-bedroom condominium during the regular season, early February to early April, are $730–$775 per night. At the Lion Square Lodge, located at the lower terminus of the gondola, a one-bedroom condominium (regular season) is $395 to $445 a night; this complex has a heated swimming pool, sauna, and whirlpool and some accommodations include a kitchen, fireplace, and balcony. The Landmark faces the pedestrian area at Lionshead and rents a two-bedroom condo for $375 to $695 a night; the facilities include two outdoor hot tubs and a heated outdoor pool, and the rooms have a balcony, fireplace, and kitchen.

Within walking distance of Beaver Creek Village is the Charter at Beaver Creek, a ski-in/ski-out lodge and condominium property with balconies and indoor pool; daily rates range from $195 to $340. Beaver Creek Lodge is slopeside and the only all-suite property in Vail Valley; its rates are $285–$365. The Hyatt Regency at Beaver Creek is also ski-in/ski-out; in addition, it offers the Camp Hyatt children's program for ages three to thirteen. Rates are $380 to $470 ($290 to $355 in the summer). The cost of the children's program is $7.00

an hour; winter hours are Monday to Sunday, 9:00 A.M.–10:00 P.M.; summer hours are 9:00 A.M.–4:00 P.M. Sunday through Wednesday and 9:00 A.M.–10:00 P.M. Thursday though Saturday.

The rates quoted are in effect during the regular season (early February to early April); Christmastime rates are higher. Summer rates can be as much as 50 percent lower than the winter rates. The January value season represents approximately a 20 percent savings over regular rates; during late November to the third week of December and in April, further savings can be realized. Discounts for children are just about universal. Some package plans include lodging, lift tickets, and group lessons. The options are numerous, and fortunately, the resort associations at Vail and Beaver Creek publish detailed, descriptive accounts of their accommodations and packages. Cribs are available at most facilities upon request.

Dining: Hungry for a hamburger? Eager to savor a juicy steak? Or is Mexican fare your idea of the perfect après-ski dinner? In the Vail Valley all this is possible, plus Italian, Chinese, French, and German food. With more than 110 restaurants and bars, there is lots of variety. Many restaurants are right in the lodges, such as the Lodge at Vail, Lion Square Lodge, the Landmark, and the Charter at Beaver Creek. Others, like McCoy's and the Coyote Cafe, are in the villages at the base of the lifts or in the pedestrian areas.

More are on the mountains: Cook Shack at Vail and Spruce Saddle and Rafters at Beaver Creek. These are not just quick, cafeteria-style mountainside rest stops; some hit gourmet standards. Whenever weather permits, outdoor barbecues are planned at the midmountain points. Many of the restaurants have children's menus—just ask.

Children's World: Even a two-month-old can comfortably visit Vail Valley. At Beaver Creek and at Golden Peak in Vail, the Small World Play School entertains little ones two months to six years old from 8:00 A.M. to 4:30 P.M. daily. The toddlers and preschoolers enjoy games, songs, crafts, and indoor and outdoor play in a schoolhouse atmosphere. Separate playrooms for ages two to eighteen months, nineteen to thirty months, and preschoolers offer closer supervision. The cost is $57 a day.

The Children's Skiing Center operates out of three locations—Lionshead, Golden Peak, and the Village Hall at Beaver Creek (so convenient no matter where you're staying!)—and divides children into two groups (three- to six-year-olds and six- to twelve-year-olds) for daily lessons from 8:00 A.M. to 4:30 P.M. Both groups have some indoor activities as well as skiing; the older children's schedule concentrates more on skiing. These programs average $75 a day, including lunch.

Photo by Jack Affleck, courtesy of Vail Associates, Inc.

In summer from early June to late August, five- to ten-year-olds can join Camp Vail, sponsored by the Town of Vail Recreation Department. On weekdays from 8:00 A.M. to 5:00 P.M., kids gather for mountain hiking, gymnastics, swimming, arts and crafts, films, and nature studies. The daily fee is $38 a child. More information is available by calling (970) 479–2292.

Recreation: The name of the game is skiing, and the Vail Valley has all the ingredients for an excellent ski holiday. In the middle of the White River National Forest, Vail Mountain rises to 11,250 feet; at Beaver Creek the summit is 11,440 feet. The vertical drop is more than 3,150 feet at Vail and close to 3,350 feet at Beaver Creek. An average annual snowfall between 300 and 350 inches (and an artificial snowmaking system) accounts for a season lasting from late November to mid-April.

Vail and Beaver Creek skiable terrain totaling 5,641 acres (lift tickets for the two mountains are interchangeable) provides variety for all levels of skiers, from gentle beginner slopes to challenging intermediates to exciting mogul and bowl skiing. At Vail the runs are ranked 32 percent beginner, 36 percent intermediate, and 32 percent advanced; at Beaver Creek the breakdown is 19 percent beginner, 43 percent intermediate, and 38 percent advanced.

So that you can cut tracks through the Rocky Mountain powder in style, a very large ski school (1,200 instructors!) can assist you. In addition to the typical group and private lessons for all ability levels, the Vail/Beaver Creek Ski

School offers free Meet the Mountain introductory tours: a morning of skiing with guest services staff who acquaint you with the area's history and topography, classes with videotaped analysis, and high-powered workshops in mogul and powder skiing. Or enroll in lessons in cross-country skiing, which is so refined here that distinctions are made between backcountry skiing, telemark skiing, and track skiing.

Other wintertime sports include ice skating at Dobson Ice Arena or Nottingham Lake, snowmobiling at Piney Lake, and ice fishing. An evening outing in a horse-drawn sleigh may be the right way to finish off a perfect day. Indoor evening entertainment includes nightclubs and movie theaters; favorite haunts for kids are the video arcades and the Vail Youth Center.

Even after the last skier comes down the mountain in late spring, fun in the Vail Valley continues. As in the winter, summertime activities focus on the beautiful outdoors. Hiking through stands of aspens along the trail systems up Vail Mountain and Beaver Creek Mountain, biking on paths through wildflowers, and fishing in mountain streams get you back to nature. Ride horseback at Eagle Ranch, Beaver Creek Stables, and Piney River Ranch, or muster up your courage for river rafting with Timberline Tours or Nova Guides.

Of the five eighteen-hole championship golf courses in the valley, one was designed by Jack Nicklaus and one (the Beaver Creek Course) by Robert Trent Jones Jr.; the clear mountain air and spectacular scenery lead to invigorating play. In Vail the twenty tennis courts, where clinics and lessons are scheduled, are located near Lionshead and Gold Peak; another twenty courts are scattered throughout the valley. And for purely taking in the scenery, ride the gondola or a chairlift. ≋

WEST

California

Idaho

Nevada

Oregon

Washington

The Alisal Guest Ranch

1054 Alisal Road
Solvang, California 93463
(805) 688–6411, (800) 4–ALISAL

I n the Santa Ynez Valley of southern California is a real working cattle ranch—The Alisal (from the Spanish word meaning "grove of sycamores"). Some things just don't change—cattle have been grazing here for almost 200 years. Fifty-two years ago the current owner's father, a cattleman himself, decided to open the ranch to guests. Today visitors enjoy the atmosphere of an active ranch and the facilities of a great resort on this 10,000-acre spread. Only forty minutes from Santa Barbara and two hours from Los Angeles, The Alisal is a welcome haven to harried city-dwellers. It is open year-round.

Accommodations: Decorated in classic California ranch design, seventy-three cottages accommodating up to 200 guests are clustered near the swimming pool and tennis courts or overlooking the golf course. All have a wood-burning fireplace, and front porch or garden areas. Based on a modified American plan, rates range from $335 to $455 a night, double occupancy; children three through five years are $40, and those ages six and older are $65 a night. Connecting suites are available for larger families.

Dining: The Ranch Room serves breakfast (a lavish buffet or a la carte) and gourmet dinners from a five-item menu that changes every evening. Jackets are required for gentlemen (ties optional) and ladies and children dress appropriately for fine dining. Parents with small children are encouraged to have dinner at 6:30 P.M., before the peak hours of 7:15 to 8:15 P.M. Lunch (not included in the room rate) can also be ordered from the Chuckwagon Grill (poolside snack bar) and at the Ranch Course Grill (open from 8:00 A.M. to 3:00 P.M.) on the golf course. The River Grill is open daily from 7:00 A.M. to 8:00 P.M. for all meals. Once in a while you can saddle up early for a breakfast ride or join a poolside steak fry. The Oak Room Lounge, an inviting room with a large fireplace, is decorated with warm colors, rustic Western artifacts, and Native American–style rugs. Cocktails and complimentary appetizers are served and stories of the day's activities or tall tales are shared. It's adults-only after 8:00 P.M., with live entertainment and dancing that begins at 6:30 P.M. During the summer and holidays, The Waggin' Tongue Lounge by the pool is open daily from 11:30 A.M. to 5:00 P.M.

Children's World: All summer long and at holiday times, counselors conduct an active schedule of arts and crafts, scavenger hunts, volleyball, hikes, croquet, and other outdoor games.

From age seven and up, children can participate in horseback riding on the trail rides or in private lessons. Younger children get corral rides and equestrian-care lessons. Everyone learns more about ranch animals at the on-site petting zoo. Children also love the private lake, where they can participate in fishing, boating, or canoeing. Summer evenings may include campfires with sing-alongs and stories, which are always better at the lake setting. Kid's Mini Rodeo is staged weekly in the summer—this is every kid's dream of being a cowboy come true. After watching wranglers perform, they get to participate in branding (on leather or wood), roping, and rodeo-style games; a Western barbecue completes the evening. In the summer the children's program (no charge) runs seven days a week, all day. Evening events may include a movie, storytelling, or a talent show. During the winter, supervised arts and activities go from 10:00 A.M. to 2:00 P.M., with golf, tennis, and horseback riding lessons filling in the other times. Although the program is free, some things such as lessons and horseback riding do have a charge. Check the daily program.

The summertime activities for teens involve their favorite things: eating, music, and sports.

Recreation: Be sure to saunter over to the barn to be matched with the perfect mount for the twice-daily trail rides ($50 per ride). A breakfast ride is offered three times a week in summer, twice a week during the rest of the year. More than 50 miles of trails meander through oak and sycamore groves in the rolling hills and along the lake. Wranglers are happy to share a bit of advice about riding, information about the ranch, or maybe even some tall tales along the way.

But the fun doesn't stop at the end of a ride. The gently rambling fairways of two eighteen-hole golf courses are graced with eucalyptus as well as oak and sycamore trees and occasionally a deer or two. Each of the two championship golf courses, The River Course and The Ranch Course, has distinct characteristics shaped by its unique terrain. The driving range, putting green, and practice trap can keep you so busy you'll ride off into the sunset on a golf cart rather than a horse! The resident pro and the pro shop can help with anything from lessons to new equipment. On the tennis courts (seven in all, located in one of the most scenic areas of the ranch) you're likely to find a good game from 8:00 A.M. to 5:30 P.M., or the resident pro conducting lessons (private and groups).

If your interests are more wet-and-wild, you might swim in the large outdoor heated pool or head to the lake and hop aboard a sailboat, rowboat, paddleboat, canoe, or kayak. Even beginners find lots of enjoyment in the sailing and fishing lessons offered. The lake—man-made, but mature and encompassing more than ninety-five acres—is stocked with bass, bluegill, and catfish, much to the delight of every fisherman.

After riding, golfing, playing tennis, swimming, sailing, and fishing, you can always jog, join a guided nature walk, play volleyball, badminton, horseshoes, shuffleboard, croquet, or archery, or take on the new challenge course. Tired yet? Indoors you might play pool or Ping-Pong in the recreation room or relax in the library with a good book or board game by the fireplace. Be sure to save energy for the evenings, filled with square dancing, cookouts, and movies as well. ≋

Coffee Creek Ranch

HC 2, Box 4940
Trinity Center, California 96091
(530) 266–3343, (800) 624–4480
Web site: www.coffeecreekranch.com

Coffee Creek Ranch is located in northern California, approximately 300 miles north of San Francisco. Surrounded by the Trinity Alps Wilderness Area, the ranch covers 127 acres along Coffee Creek and is home to wranglers and dudes alike. Whether you are an old pro at horseback riding or a greenhorn mounting up for the first time, the ranch hands will ensure that your horse and your excursion match your abilities. You can roam this territory all day long or ease into your new cowboy lifestyle more slowly with a half-hour lesson or a two-hour trail ride.

Accommodations: The fifteen cozy, secluded cottages (one or two bedrooms) are scattered among the trees. Weekly rates during the summer are $840–$860 for an adult, $820–$840 for a teenager, $720–$740 for a three- to twelve-year-old child, and $250 for little ones under three. Rates are approximately $95 less per person the rest of the year. Cribs, playpens, and high chairs are provided at no extra charge. Besides lodging, these prices include three meals a day and all recreational activities. Horseback riding is priced separately for the summer but is included in the lower rates for spring and fall.

Dining: Recognizing the healthy appetites that fresh air and exercise can generate, the main dining room serves up hearty, nutritious meals with fresh fruit and vegetables, Black Angus beef, and homemade bread. Outdoor barbecues and poolside cookouts are friendly evening events. Beer and wine are served in the Pony Room.

Children's World: In the summer months the youth program, a complimentary service operating 9:00 A.M. to 5:00 P.M., Sunday through Thursday, attracts children ages three to seventeen. On its fun-filled schedule are pony rides, archery, nature walks, pedal boating, gold panning, games, and crafts. For children under three the weekly rate includes baby-sitting while you're out on the trail. If additional baby-sitting is required, you can make arrangements for $5.00 an hour.

Recreation: Saddle up and head into the wilderness for an all-day ride or a two-hour ride. You'll venture up into the mountains and go through the wooded landscape along a clear fresh stream; maybe you'll spot a deer or a bear. Even novice cowpokes with a few lessons soon experience the friendly spirit of a trail ride.

When taking a break from riding, you might swim in the pool or in the creek; play volleyball, Ping-Pong, badminton, shuffleboard, and horseshoes; or hop aboard a hayride. Locals say that Coffee Creek yields up some mighty fine trout, so an afternoon with rod and reel may turn into a fresh fish supper. Perhaps you'll test your keen eye at the archery range, the rifle range, and the trap-shoot, or save your energy for evening square or line dancing. ≋

Forever Resorts

Lake Mead National Recreation Area
Callville Bay Marina
Lake Mead, Nevada
(800) 255–5561
Web site: www.foreverresorts.com

If you are looking for a unique vacation experience, houseboat rentals from Forever Resorts near Callville Bay on Lake Mead may be just what you are looking for. Created by the completion of Hoover Dam in 1935, Lake Mead is one of the largest man-made lakes in the world. The lake's contours vary from the expansive Boulder and Virgin Basins to countless small coves along the shoreline. The desert terrain surrounding it ranges from wide sandy beaches to dramatic canyon walls towering high above the water.

Everyone—novice or expert—renting a houseboat from Forever Resorts is given a "shakedown cruise" to learn how to easily operate a houseboat. Comforts uncommon to houseboating are included, even a complete kitchen. The finest equipment and friendly, professional service are what make a few days or a week at one of the Forever Resorts marinas a vacation to remember . . . forever.

Accommodations: Houseboats vary in size but standard features include a stove and oven, two built-in ice chests, two refrigerators (electric and gas), an electrical generator, a gas grill, five queen beds, one and a half baths, a captain's flying bridge, central air conditioning and heat, a microwave, linens/pillows, and even a waterslide. The 65-foot VIP Houseboat boasts a larger living area in the front salon, a hot tub on the upper deck, two full baths, an ice maker/trash compactor, a wet bar with refrigerator on the upper deck, a canopy on the upper deck, a dishwasher, and an intercom from the lower to upper helm. Rates range from $895 to $4,500 per package depending on the type of houseboat engaged, the season, and the number of days.

Dining: Culinary feasts are limited only by your imagination as each kitchen is fully equipped to make mealtime preparation a breeze.

Children's World: The lake behind Hoover Dam provides recreation for millions of people annually. Your child is sure to enjoy swimming, powerboating, houseboating, scuba diving, beach camping, sailing, windsurfing, fishing, rock climbing, hiking, and photography. If outdoor activities wear you out, you can always use the TV and VCR for movies or hooking up video games.

Recreation: The complete houseboat experience includes a tag-a-long powerboat, so termed because the boat is tied to the back of the houseboat while cruising. The tag-a-long is used for exploring, tubing, fishing, and just plain enjoying the lake, thus making the houseboat home base—a moveable floating resort. ≋

The Inn of the Seventh Mountain

18575 Southwest Century Drive
Bend, Oregon 97702
(541) 382–8711, (800) 452–6810
E-mail: reservations@7thmtn.com
Web site: www.7thmtn.com

A vacation in the woods and mountains of the great Pacific Northwest, the serenity of hiking in the forest, and the excitement of exploring the Deschutes River whisk you away from city life and everyday routines. The Inn of the Seventh Mountain, located in the Cascade Mountains of central Oregon, is a year-round family resort that boasts a cool forest setting and warm hospitality. The recreation department at the Inn plans activities for every member of the family, concentrating on water sports, swimming, tennis, and raft trips on the river in the summer and ice skating, cross-country skiing, and sleigh rides in the winter. Wintertime also means the thrill of downhill skiing at nearby Mount Bachelor (only 14 miles from the Inn).

Accommodations: You can choose from a variety of accommodations, from a lodge room to a full condominium apartment, depending on the size of your group. Most of the lodge rooms have a private balcony; the condominium units have one to three bedrooms, fireplace, kitchen, and balcony. Some of these units can sleep up to ten people. The architecture is modern and rustic, the natural-wood facades blending well with the wooded landscape. Prices range from $59 to $299 a night, depending on the size of the accommodation and the season (summer and fall are slightly higher than winter and spring). Cribs are available at no extra charge.

Dining: The Poppy Seed Cafe serves homestyle breakfast and lunch. Josiah's, open for dinner only, features seafood specialties and Northwest cuisine. For a light lunch or dinner, pick up a sandwich or salad at the Mountain Market. The lounge is open every night.

Children's World: In addition to individual baby-sitting, which the staff can help you arrange, events are scheduled all day long for your child's enjoyment. In summer and winter the recreation office publishes a flyer, *This Week at the Inn,* to help you keep track of all the activities. At Camp 7, a supervised play program for children ages four to eleven, a daily charge of $25 buys lunch, arts-and-crafts classes, movies, and more from 9:00 A.M. to 4:00 P.M. each day. Your child might also participate in a tennis clinic, take a hayride or a sleigh ride, search out treasures on a scavenger hunt, or hop aboard the children's storybook train. For some events, no fees are charged; others are priced individually

Photo courtesy of The Inn of the Seventh Mountain

(for example, $6.00 for a half-hour swimming lesson). There are also two playgrounds and a wading pool.

In season the Mount Bachelor Ski School (541–382–2607) offers lessons for youngsters. The Children's Ski School, called Mountain Masters, is for ages four to twelve. Divided by age (four to six and seven to twelve) and also by level of ability, several options are available. A full day, including lunch, is $45 for the younger children, $55 for the older group. Rentals are $5.00 extra. Morning or afternoon sessions (two and a half hours each) cost $32 for ages four to six years and $42 to $47 for ages seven to twelve. Teens join the adult lessons for $30 to $40. Reservations are recommended.

The West Village Main Lodge, at the base of the mountain, has a day-care center for little ones six weeks to six years old; activities are planned from 8:30 A.M. to 4:30 P.M. The fee is $31.00 a day or $7.50 an hour. Lunch is an additional $5.00. Sunrise Lodge has child care available. Rates and hours are the same.

Recreation: In summer you just have to discover the beauty of the Deschutes River. Take a relaxing canoe ride and get back to nature, or join a moonlight raft trip. For the more daring souls, there are guided white-water raft trips through the rapids. If you prefer to take in the scenic river from land, horseback riding is a great alternative; group trail rides run along the river and into the Deschutes National Forest. The National Forest is also a picturesque haven for hikers and joggers. For the fisherman the recreation office arranges trips to the favorite spots with a naturalist guide. Spend an afternoon in sail-boarding or waterskiing classes.

Back at the inn take a dip in one of the two pools, rent a bicycle, play a good game of tennis on one of the four Plexipave courts (group clinics and private lessons are offered), work out in an aerobic exercise class, try your talents in an arts-and-crafts class, go rollerskating, or get lucky in a bingo game. The rec office organizes all sorts of ball games—softball, volleyball, football, lacrosse, and soccer. Join a hayride, complete with a stop for a marshmallow roast, play Ping-Pong, take in a poolside movie, or head to the video-game room. Then relax in the sauna or one of the hot whirlpool baths.

The Oregon High Desert Museum, just 6 miles south of Bend, discloses the natural and cultural history of this region. The museum makes for a fun as well as educational afternoon.

This part of Oregon experiences beautiful Indian summers, so activities continue well into the fall. During the winter months the Inn's special events include ice skating, sleigh rides, cross-country skiing (with lessons for novices), and horseback riding in the snow-covered landscape.

The Inn is the closest lodging facility to the Mount Bachelor ski resort and provides daily transportation to the mountain base. With 3,100 vertical feet, 40 runs, double and triple chairlifts, and plenty of dry powder, Mount Bachelor means excellent downhill skiing for all levels of ability. The five lodges at the mountain have restaurants for breakfast, lunch, snacks, and cocktails; ski shops; and the ski school, which offers group lessons for all ranges of expertise as well as private lessons. The season lasts long here, attracting many visitors late into spring. The summit season even extends into the summer. ≋

Konocti Harbor Resort and Spa

8727 Soda Bay Road
Kelseyville, California 95451
(707) 279–4281, (800) 660–LAKE
Web site: www.konoctiharbor.com

Konocti Harbor Resort and Spa is a lakeside resort in northern California, approximately two and a half hours from San Francisco. If you're driving from the city or other points south, your vacation begins with a tour of the Napa Valley wine country on your way to Konocti. Open year-round, the inn sits beneath the 4,300-foot peak of Mount Konocti (an extinct volcano) on the southern shore of Clear Lake, which stretches 25 miles by 8 miles. All this clear blue water of California's largest lake provides the setting for much of Konocti's recreation: swimming, boating, and fishing. Although today you'll find just happy, active visitors heading to the water, a romantic Indian legend tells of a saddened princess whose many tears formed the lake.

Accommodations: Hotel rooms, apartments, and beach cottages comprise the 266 guest units at the Konocti. All have different features, but families like the beach cottages for their convenient location and kitchen, open-air porch, and space. Some rooms include a private balcony, and most afford views of the lake. The locations of some make the marina easily accessible, while others are near the tennis courts. Sixteen deluxe apartments are situated near the spa. The apartments and cottages have complete kitchens and living rooms, and many have been recently renovated.

During the high season (May through October), a double room is $49–$85 a night, and the apartments and cottages for four are $135–$175 a night. Lower rates are in effect the rest of the year. Children eighteen years and younger staying in their parents' room are accommodated free of charge. Roll-away beds and cribs are available for $10 a night. Tennis, fishing, spa, and golf package plans are offered.

Dining: For a relaxing evening meal, try the Classic Rock Cafe, which is open for breakfast, lunch, and dinner. Adjacent to the two pool areas are snack bars so that you don't have to interrupt a lazy day of sunning for refreshments. For evening entertainment The Full Moon Saloon beckons.

Children's World: Kids at Konocti practically live in the water, with hours spent on the lake swimming, boating, and fishing. They also take hikes and nature walks, play horseshoes, and putt around the eighteen holes of peewee golf. The events start at 10:00 A.M. Monday through Friday, break at 4:00 P.M., and pick up again from 5:00 to 10:00 P.M. for a night camp. The children's pro-grams are open only in the summer and the fee is $15 for each session. Little ones particularly like the two wading pools and the playground equipped with a slide, swings, and monkey bars, while those a bit older head to the recreation center for Ping-Pong, pool, and video games. Baby-sitting in the evening runs about $5.00 an hour.

Recreation: With Konocti's full-service marina, you can take your pick of water sports. Dock your own boat here or rent a paddleboat, Wave Runner, motorboat, or sailboat for an adventure on the lake. Go fishing in these waters where the rewards are many: largemouth bass, trout, crappie, and catfish. There's even a bass-fishing pro to advise you. Water-ski across the lake, or board the *Konocti Princess,* a nostalgic paddle wheeler, for an afternoon excursion. Swim in the lake waters from the small sandy beach, or do laps in one of the two Olympic-size pools overlooking the lake.

The Dancing Springs Health Spa is designed to pamper you a bit. This facility features an indoor pool and capable personnel who will help you relax with a massage, facial, or herbal body wrap. Take a fitness class or work out with free weights or cardiovascular equipment if you're feeling more energetic.

The eight tennis courts are lighted for evening play, and lessons with the tennis pro are available. After a good practice session with a ball machine, reward yourself with a new accessory from the tennis shop.

Five area golf courses, all within 20 miles, honor Konocti's golf packages. Round up a fast-paced game of softball, basketball, volleyball, or Ping-Pong, or slow down to a more relaxing tempo with horseshoes and shuffleboard. While jogging and hiking, explore the scenic, hilly terrain that borders the lake. ≋

La Costa Resort and Spa

2100 Costa del Mar Road
Carlsbad, California 92009
(619) 438–9111, (800) 854–5000
Web site: www.lacosta.com

L a Costa is a luxurious resort and a serious spa. In fact, it was the first establishment to revive the spa regimen as Americans became more health-conscious in the 1960s. Today you can pursue a program of exercise and sound nutrition, redefining your lifestyle after years of sedentary executive matters; or you can indulge in a program of sheer pampering, relieving the stress and tensions of the business world.

Located in Carlsbad, just thirty minutes north of San Diego and ninety minutes south of Los Angeles, La Costa enjoys lovely southern California weather and a picturesque setting of rolling hills.

Accommodations: Rooms, suites, and private homes number 478. They are situated around courtyards, near the tennis facilities, adjacent to the spa, and along the golf courses. Room rates are $250–$440 a night; one- and two-bedroom suites are $500–$2,200 a night, and the commodious two- to five-bedroom executive homes are $1,150–$1,650 a night. Children under eighteen staying in their parents' room are free; cribs are provided without charge. Be sure to inquire about the spa, golf, and tennis package plans.

Dining: La Costa's four restaurants offer variety in cuisine and ambience. For a casual atmosphere Brasserie La Costa is open for breakfast, lunch, and dinner. Besides tempting fare such as eggs Benedict and grilled veal chops, the Brasserie has a selection of spa-menu items, just as tasty but low in calories and fat. The Center Court Restaurant at the Racquet Club serves light meals for breakfast and lunch. For more elegant dining, Pisces specializes in fresh seafood, and Ristorante Figaro is devoted to Northern Italian cuisine. Both are open for dinner only.

Children's World: Camp La Costa is active year-round and operates from 10:00 A.M. to 5:00 P.M. daily. For five- to thirteen-year-olds, the fun includes golf and tennis lessons, swimming, kite flying, and arts and crafts. The fee is $40 a day and includes lunch. In the evenings Camp La Costa Nightclub takes over with dinner and entertainment from 6:30 to 9:30 P.M.; the fee is $30 a night. Individual baby-sitting can be requested through the concierge; the fee is $28.00 for the first three hours and $8.00 an hour thereafter.

Recreation: The spa programs and facilities are extensive. Facials from deep cleansing to mud packs, massages of the shiatsu and reiki variety, herbal wraps, body scrubs, exfoliation, and hydrotherapy baths are just some of the methods utilized to revive weary guests. Exercise facilities include swimming pools, a weight room, a cardiovascular room, and a jogging track. You can join one of the many exercise classes offered throughout the day or, with an exercise phys-iologist, you can devise a personalized fitness program. Individualized analysis also extends to dietary counseling and menu planning. Classes with psycholo-gists cover topics such as stress reduction and relaxation.

Golf enthusiasts find their exercise on the two eighteen-hole championship courses. At the Golf School the latest technology is used to scrutinize and improve your game. Tennis players have twenty-one courts at their disposal and can choose grass, clay, or hard-court surface. Clinics are held daily, and private instruction is easily arranged. The golf and tennis pro shops offer a wide range of equipment and apparel. Five heated swimming pools complete the picture of exercise potential at La Costa. ≋

MGM Grand Hotel/Casino

3799 Las Vegas Boulevard South
Las Vegas, Nevada 89109
(702) 891–7777, (800) 929–1111

Take the children to Las Vegas?! Are they out of their minds? Well, no. Surprisingly enough, about one in every twelve visitors is accompanied by a minor, and the number of children is increasing rapidly as Las Vegas consciously markets itself as a family destination, a unique entertainment capital. Where else can you see so many lights; watch a circus; experience Camelot with King Arthur and Merlin; have a taste of ancient Egypt, with a canal "Nile River" boat ride around a 30-story-high pyramid and a visit to King Tut's Tomb; or watch while pirates attack and sink a tall sailing ship (six times a day!)? The only problem is that you may need a vacation to recover from your Las Vegas vacation!

Accommodations: The MGM Grand opened in 1993, at a cost of $1 billion. Whatever words you use to describe it, you just keep coming back to "grand." With 5,005 rooms (751 suites), it is the self-proclaimed "City of Entertainment." Rooms are set in the four emerald-green hotel towers and are decorated in "Oz," "Hollywood," "Southern," and "Casablanca" motifs.

Typical guest rooms are 446 square feet in size, with Italian marble bathrooms and sunken tub. Las Vegas is a gambling town, and this seems to apply to the rate structure as well. Rates change daily, based on number of rooms available. The range for double occupancy is $69–$399; up to three children under age twelve can stay free, with $25 per extra person per day.

Dining: With seven restaurants and a Food Court to choose from, you don't ever have to dine in the same place twice. MGM Grand serves brunch and dinner, while the Studio Cafe is a twenty-four-hour coffee shop. The fare at The Brown Derby, Tre Visi and La Scala, Emeril Lagasse's New Orleans Fish House, and Gatsby's is pretty obvious, but the Dragon Court and Wolfgang Puck Cafe need exploring. Coyote Cafe serves up Southwestern specialties a la acclaimed chef Mark Miller, and twenty-six types of tequila at the "Tequila Bar." For evening entertainment select from two show rooms and five lounges/bars.

Children's World: Many hotels in Las Vegas have fun things or themes for children, but the MGM is the only one with a full children's program. The Youth Activity Center consists of four rooms of pretty much nonstop supervised activities. The preschool room, for three- to six-year-olds, has playhouse, tumbling mats, puppets, puzzles, and more. Seven- to twelve-year-olds have Foosball,

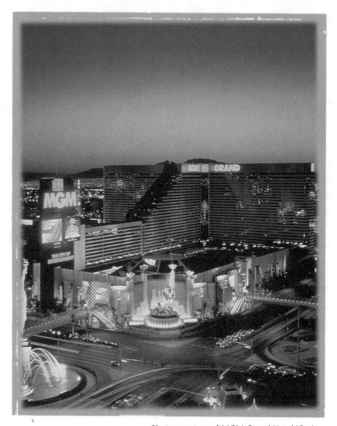

Photo courtesy of MGM Grand Hotel/Casino

Ping-Pong, board games, and mini-pool. An arts-and-crafts room is shared by all ages, and materials are plentiful, so there's no limit to what the kids dream up. The lounge area has beanbag chairs, large-screen TV/VCR, and—what else—SuperNintendo.

Excursions to the Grand Adventures Theme Park (with behind-the-scenes learning), the MGM Grand pool complex (nearly seven acres), and other unique hotel areas are planned for children ages six to sixteen years. The center is equipped with its own snack bar for meals and snacks.

For hotel guests the center is open seven days a week, year-round, with varying hours. Children can stay for a maximum of five hours at a time, with a two-hour break required. The cost is $6.00 per hour during the day and $7.00 per hour after 5:00 P.M. (Although the center is available to nonguests of the hotel from 8:00 A.M. until predetermined times, the rules and costs are different.) Always subject to availability.

Recreation: MGM Grand swimming complex has a huge pool and luxury cabanas. If all this gets to be too much, relax and rejuvenate at the Grand Spa, where you can be pampered with facials, body wraps, seaweed treatments, massage, even eyelash tinting. Rates are reasonable, and the 30,000-square-foot spa is open from 6:30 A.M. to 7:30 P.M.

In the same grand scale as everything else, there's not just one casino area here, but four. The gaming area, larger than four football fields, spans more than 170,000 square feet.

MGM Grand Adventures, a theme park adjacent to the hotel, has rides, theater, entertainment, food, and retail shops to provide hours of fun. The newest attraction, SkyScreamer, is the world's largest skycoaster. This dual-design skycoaster lifts one to three flyers to heights of approximately 220 feet. Flyers are instructed to pull their own ripcord to set into motion a free fall at speeds of up to 70 miles per hour.

Stroll along "The Strip" and marvel, but don't think that glitz and neon are all there is to Las Vegas. When you tire of all this concrete and fantasy, take a trek into nature and visit some of the scenic wonders nearby. Hoover Dam, more than 70 feet high, is considered one of the seven man-made wonders of the world; tours explain the dam and the generation of the electricity for all those Las Vegas lights. Lake Mead, next to the dam, offers boating activities; and about 50 miles north is the Valley of Fire State Park, named for the red and orange rock formations. Only about 20 miles west of Las Vegas is Red Rock Canyon, with scenic drives; and Old Nevada, a re-creation of a nineteenth-century town, with saloon, cowboys, and Wild West action. ≈≈≈

Northstar-at-Tahoe

P.O. Box 129
Truckee, California 96160
(530) 562–1010, (800) GO–NORTH (466–6784)

Tahoe has long been known for the clear deep waters of a 200-square-mile lake, the majestic mountain peaks of the Sierra Nevada range, and its proximity to the entertainment and nightlife of Nevada casinos. Northstar-at-Tahoe enables vacationers to partake of all of these. Open year-round, it is a 2,500-acre mountain resort just 6 miles from Lake Tahoe that offers winter and summer family sports activities. With the Nevada state line only 7 miles away, side trips to gambling casinos are manageable excursions for grown-ups.

Accommodations: The lodging facilities include hotel-type rooms, condominiums ranging in size from studios to four-bedroom units, and three- and four-bedroom homes. With the exception of the lodge rooms, all have a fully equipped kitchen and fireplace; many units have a private balcony overlooking the wooded landscape and the mountains. The wooden facades and rustic designs of the buildings blend well with the natural setting.

Prices range from $99 a night in the summer and $159 a night in the winter for a hotel room to $329 a night, summer, and $459 a night, winter, for a four-bedroom, two-bath condominium. Package plans are available throughout the year. The on-site transportation system is complimentary for Northstar guests. Cribs are provided at no additional charge.

Dining: The six restaurants at Northstar mean time off for the family cook. Timbercreek Restaurant serves dinner in the winter and summer. The Martis Valley Grille specializes in family-style dining, while Pedro's Pizza Parlor is a casual spot for lunch and dinner; the Basque and Pedro's are open only in winter. The two restaurants on the mountain are the Big Springs Day Lodge, open for breakfast and lunch, and the Summit Deck and Grill, open for lunch. Each offers an informal atmosphere and allows skiers to get back on the slopes quickly. The Clubhouse offers breakfast and lunch, indoors or outdoors, in summer only. The Village Food Company, in the Village Mall, is open year-round; with a deli, gourmet groceries, espresso bar, and video rentals, it also provides the supplies for a picnic or snacking in your condo.

Children's World: The Minors' Camp Child-Care Center is fully licensed and accepts children as young as two years old (must be toilet trained). In the winter it is open daily from 8:30 A.M. to 4:30 P.M. Under the guidance of an experienced staff, two- to six-year-olds paint, learn songs, listen to stories, play in the snow, and take walks; with snacks and a hot lunch, the full-day fee is $48.

At three years little ones can join the Ski Cubs Program; in addition to the nonskiing activities, these children receive one and a half hours of ski instruction during the day. The fee for child care plus skiing (equipment included) is $61 a day. Four- to six-year-old Super Cubs receive two and a half hours of ski instruction in addition to indoor activities at a daily rate of $71. When not with the other Cubs, a child under five years skis free with a ticketed adult.

The Star Kids Program is designed for five- to twelve-year-olds. The $69 daily fee covers three hours of lessons, lifts, and lunch.

The highlights of the summer program (mid-June to Labor Day) for children ages two (must be toilet trained) to ten are swimming lessons, nature walks, tennis, arts and crafts, and horseback riding. Day camp is in session Monday through Saturday, 9:00 A.M.–5:00 P.M. You can reserve a slot for your child for $26 per half day or $43 all day (includes lunch). A free half-day is provided with more than two nights' lodging.

Recreation: For downhill skiing at Tahoe, you can look forward to 2,200 vertical feet. The Northstar Village is at the base of Mount Pluto, which rises to a summit of 8,600 feet. There are sixty-three runs and nine lifts, and locals boast of sunshine 80 percent of the season. The ski school, with its 180 instructors, offers lessons for beginners through experts to help all visitors meet the variety of this mountain. Forty miles of groomed trails attract cross-country skiers; lessons, guided tours, and snowshoe rentals are available at the Cross-Country Center.

Après-ski activities may mean taking a sleigh ride or a trip to the Swim and Raquet Club, where you'll find saunas, spas, an adult lap pool, a fitness center, and a teen center, or enjoying a stroll through the Village Mall, which houses shops, restaurants, and bars.

During the summer other activities lure visitors outdoors to the sunshine and clean mountain air. Enjoy golf on an eighteen-hole course that wanders over meadows, past mountain streams, and through groves of tall pines and aspens. The Golf Course Clubhouse includes a pro shop and a restaurant. To work on improving your game, check with the resident pro for tips, or practice solo on the driving range and putting green.

Play tennis on one of the ten courts, take a swim in the adult lap pool or junior Olympic-size pool, or just soak up the sunshine on the poolside deck. The

Northstar stables provide well-groomed horses for riding the mountain trails and offer lessons and guided trail rides. Hiking and biking are also favorite sports in High Sierra country. For adventures in boating and fishing, the clear blue waters of Lake Tahoe await you. And music fills the air every summer Sunday afternoon with free outdoor concerts. ≈≈≈

The Rancho Bernardo Inn

17550 Bernardo Oaks Drive
San Diego, California 92128
(619) 487–1611, (800) 542–6096
Web site: www.jcresorts.com

L isten up, weary travelers. It is still possible to vacation in the classic style and relaxed atmosphere of an old California ranch. Set in the San Pasqual Mountains of Southern California, The Rancho Bernardo Inn is just thirty minutes north of San Diego. Here, on 265 acres, the Inn revives the elegance and charm of the early rancheros' way of life, capitalizes on the California sunshine and balmy weather, and adds fine sporting facilities as well—all to provide the perfect holiday for you. The Inn is open year-round.

Accommodations: As you might expect of an old Southwestern ranch, the architecture reveals a Spanish influence reminiscent of the area's heritage. The eight red-tiled haciendas house 287 rooms and suites. These are decorated in warm earth tones, highly polished wood, and local art. The high season is January through March and October through December, when a double room is $185–$215 a night. From April through September double rooms are $135–$180 Sunday through Thursday, $185–$215 on weekends. Children under twelve stay free; those over twelve pay $15. Ask about family packages that include some meals and admission to attractions. Cribs are provided at no charge.

Dining: El Bizcocho is the elegant French restaurant of the Inn. This mission-style dining room is open for evening dinner and Sunday brunch, for which gentlemen should wear jackets. Of the many tempting menu selections here, you might try the roast duckling in Calvados. More casual and open for breakfast, lunch, and dinner, the Veranda Room will lure you with its fresh seafood dishes, such as tiger shrimp provençale. The Sports Grill serves sandwiches and snacks on its patio, near the ninth hole. Tea, tasty sandwiches, and pastries in the Music Room make a perfect afternoon interlude to tide you over between a lovely lunch and a delicious dinner. For evening entertainment La Taberna features a piano soloist, and La Bodega offers dancing.

Children's World: An active, fun-filled Children's Camp is on the docket for some holidays and the month of August. Daily from 9:00 A.M. to 9:00 P.M., children ages five to eleven play tennis and miniature golf, swim, bake cookies, make kites, and go on scavenger hunts. Arts-and-crafts classes, croquet, movies, track meets, and cookouts are also on the schedule. A child can join the group for one or two activities a day or stay at camp all day long if he's got the energy. Older children, to age seventeen, have tennis, golf, basketball, swimming, and biking activities. An evening event for this group might be a luau or a carnival. The cost is $15 per half day; $20 for a full day. Second and third children in the family have reduced rates.

Recreation: Golf and tennis players are well cared for at Rancho Bernardo. Three nine-hole executive courses will whet your appetite for the eighteen-hole championship golf course. Planted with sycamore, eucalyptus, pine, and olive trees, the lush green fairways roll down the foothills to the valley. With five resident pros, individual and group lessons, clinics, tournaments, a driving range, and a well-stocked pro shop, you've got every chance in the world of polishing your game.

Tennis players are found on the twelve outdoor courts, four of which are lighted for nighttime play. The Tennis College has a twenty-plus-year history of providing programs to players of all skill levels. Stroke development, teamwork, and strategy are just some of the topics covered in the two- to five-day sessions. Private instruction is also available.

With some energy still left, you can head to the workout room in the Fitness Center, then unwind with a massage or a few minutes in the steam or sauna room. Have a pleasant dip in one of the two swimming pools, or bicycle and jog around the carefully tended grounds. Because of the sunny southern California weather, these sports continue year-round.

All of San Diego's attractions are twenty to thirty minutes away. The famous San Diego Zoo, SeaWorld, the Aerospace Museum, and a Wild Animal Park beckon. Enjoy a picnic in Balboa Park, or shop at Horton Plaza, a fabulous "mall" like no other. You can even take a quick trip to Mexico—it's an easy forty-five-minute train ride from downtown San Diego to Tijuana—for great bargains. ≋

Port Ludlow Resort and Conference Center

200 Olympic Place
Port Ludlow, Washington 98365
(360) 437–2222, (800) 732–1239
E-mail: portludlow@olympus.net
Web site: www.portludlowresort.com

S almon fishing and timber from the hardwood forests first drew settlers to this area of the Northwest. Today visitors are lured by the clear deep waters of Puget Sound and the spectacular scenery presided over by the majestic mountains of the Cascade and Olympic ranges. Open year-round, the Resort at Port Ludlow is situated on a bit of land jutting out into Puget Sound, and with this prime location it's no wonder that water sports are favored here. The Olympic National Park and National Forest are practically in Port Ludlow's backyard (less than 15 miles away), which makes this a good spot for those who want the peace and serenity of a back-to-nature vacation. The weather here is mild, so many outdoor activities (such as golf) continue through the winter.

Accommodations: For lodging you may choose a traditional bedroom/bath combination (many with lovely views) or a one- to four-bedroom condominium, depending on the size of your party. The condominiums have living room, kitchen, fireplace, private deck, and water views. Sit on your balcony at night to catch a whiff of the clean, pine-scented air. There are 185 units in all, arranged in nineteen wooden town house structures; surrounded by beautifully land-scaped grounds and bordering on wooded areas, these accommodations afford a sense of being close to nature.

Rates for a room alone start at $95 a night. A condominium starts at about $145 a night. Children twelve and under staying in their parents' room are free; cribs are available at no charge. Rates are lower in fall, winter, and spring.

Dining: The Harbormaster Restaurant, which serves breakfast, lunch, and din-ner, overlooks Puget Sound and grants visitors views of sun-sparkling waters and sailboats tacking in the breeze. The house specialties are steak and fresh seafood; maybe you'll have the Ludlow clam chowder, followed by a tasty crab or shrimp entree. The children's menu features fried chicken and fish and chips. A snack bar provides quick, light meals like hamburgers, sandwiches, and sal-ads. The Wreckroom Lounge offers thirst quenchers, nightly entertainment, and views of the marina.

Children's World: While no specific children's activities are planned at Port Ludlow, there are many facilities available for leisure-time fun, including a game room with Ping-Pong and pool tables, year-round swimming, tennis courts, and water activities of many kinds. The Recreation Department can also set up games of softball, volleyball, basketball, or horseshoes. Children are welcome and will enjoy the playground area, with jungle gym equipment, located near the main building.

Recreation: The twenty-seven-hole championship golf course, designed by Robert Muir Graves, dips past ponds and edges around tall fir trees; during a challenging game you're rewarded with beautiful views of the water. For practice sessions head to the driving range and the putting greens. The pro shop can meet your needs for equipment, accessories, and clothing. If you don't want to bring along your own clubs, rentals are available and the golf pro is on hand to give you pointers on your swing.

For tennis enthusiasts, two Plexipave courts are located near the Beach Club. The Beach Club also houses the squash court, year-round swimming pool, sauna, and game room with Ping-Pong and pool tables.

Beautiful Puget Sound is the focal point of many activities. The 300-slip marina handles both power- and sailboats. If you sail your own boat up the coast, this is the perfect place to dock. If not, you might want to rent a kayak or Lido sailboat and go exploring. Clamming, crabbing, and beachcombing along the shore are favorite pastimes here. With bicycling (rentals available) and hiking, you can get your exercise and see the scenery too.

Nearby Port Townsend, a fine example of a Victorian seacoast town, is a great diversion for a day. You can join a guided tour, which includes entrance into a few of the old homes, or you can discover the restaurants, shops, and interesting architecture on your own. ≋

San Ysidro Ranch

900 San Ysidro Lane
Montecito, California 93108
(805) 969–5046, (800) 368–6788

Elegant yet rustic is the best way to describe San Ysidro. A quiet charm pervades the property. From the many lovely gardens—the Citrus Garden, the Herb and Vegetable Garden, the Hacienda Garden, the Wedding Garden—to the trails into the Los Padres National Forest, a respect and appreciation for nature are apparent. One comes here to relax, to rejuvenate the soul as well as the body.

Once a waystation for Franciscan monks as they conducted their missionary work in the late 1700s, San Ysidro Ranch opened as a resort more than one hundred years ago. Today guests discover 550 acres of wooded countryside in the foothills of Montecito. Views extend into the Santa Ynez Mountains and down to the Pacific Ocean. San Ysidro Ranch is 3 miles south of Santa Barbara and just a ninety-minute drive north of Los Angeles.

Accommodations: Thirty-eight rooms and suites are arranged in twenty cottages. Each has a wood-burning fireplace and a private terrace; some have an outdoor whirlpool. The cottages have been christened delightful names, such as Creek, Outlook, Eucalyptus, and Acacia, each evoking the special milieu of its position. Room and suite rates range from $350 to $3,000 a night.

Dining: The Stonehouse Restaurant is developing a reputation as one of the finest in the Santa Barbara area. With culinary creations such as tortilla soup, lobster mushrooms in huckleberry vinaigrette, and salmon in chive sauce, it's easy to understand the appeal. Even the low-calorie spa dishes are hard to resist. Casual dinners and live jazz are the offerings of the Plow and Angel Pub, which dates from the time of the original resort (it was built in 1893). Outdoor dining at poolside is yet another option.

Children's World: Summertime at San Ysidro has much to offer the vacationing family. Along with their own facilities, which include tennis, swimming, bocci, and hiking trails, the resort can also recommend several local parks and attractions.

Recreation: Hiking on this terrain is a favorite among guests. The tennis courts (two) are situated on the highest plateau of the grounds; enjoy a rousing match along with panoramic views of the mountains and the ocean. Private instruction is available with the tennis pro. Work out at the health facility, with its weights and cardiovascular equipment; you might even schedule an appointment with a personal fitness trainer in order to devise a personal regimen. Or take your exercise in the outdoor heated pool.

The full spa and beauty treatments may be the highlights of your visit here. Aromatherapy facials, massages, herbal body wraps, reflexology, and stress-relieving treatments will add up to a new you. Some programs are combined with yoga lessons to maximize your revitalization at the Ranch. ≋

Schweitzer Mountain Resort

10,000 Schweitzer Mountain Road
Sandpoint, Idaho 83864
(208) 263–9555, (800) 831–8810
E-mail: ski@schweitzer.com
Web site: www.schweitzer.com

Way up in the northern part of Idaho's panhandle, just 60 miles from the Canadian border, is Schweitzer Mountain Resort. Set high in the rugged Selkirk Mountains, the skiing terrain sprawls over 2,400 acres. As it is a one-and-a-half-hour drive from Spokane and seven hours from Seattle, Schweitzer may not be the easiest resort to get to, but you rarely have to worry about the crowds. It is open year-round.

Accommodations: The Green Gables Lodge is at the base, and numerous condominiums supply ski-in/ski-out access. Rates range from $95 to $165 a night for hotel rooms; one- to three-bedroom condo units are $180 to $300; summer rates are lower. Additional condominiums are a bit of a walk to the lifts, and still other lodging facilities are in Sandpoint, 10 miles from Schweitzer. Many properties offer a "children ski and stay free" program, which applies to children twelve years and younger. Cribs are available at no charge.

Dining: Jean's Northwest Grill and Jimmies Bar serve Northwest cuisine for relaxing meals. But if you can't bear to take out much time from skiing, stop in the Outback or the Cafe for a quick lunch. Or you can rustle up meals in your condo.

Children's World: The Mogul Mice program delights young skiers from five to eleven years. Skiing and lunching with new friends and an instructor fill the hours from 10:00 A.M. to 3:00 P.M. The fee is $45 a day. Kinderkamp, a day-care center, is a suitable alternative for nonskiers (infants to six-year-olds). In the summer months children and their parents can rent mountain bikes, take chairlift rides, and enjoy Western-style barbecues and picnics, too.

Recreation: Schweitzer has a lot of skiing terrain and a lot of variety, from the open bowls, demanding good performance of advanced skiers, to gentle beginner runs. Two expansive bowls and fifty-eight runs with 2,350 skiable acres ensure that you won't get bored. Add to this 2,400 feet of vertical drop and more than 300 inches of snowfall annually and you've got the full picture. The season starts up at the end of November and continues to early April. After skiing you might take a sleigh ride through the woods.

During the summer months visitors to Schweitzer turn to hiking along the mountain trails, getting a real feeling for Idaho's backcountry. You may even be able to take a llama to carry your pack. ≋

Squaw Valley USA

P.O. Box 2007
Olympic Valley, California 96146
(916) 583–6985, (800) 545–4350

Squaw Valley—the name itself is synonymous with skiing. From the earliest days (would you believe 1949?), the sunny California weather combined with six high alpine peaks and 4,000 acres of lift-served terrain have made this a world-class ski area. Mother Nature deposits an average of 450 inches of snow between mid-November and April. The Sierra Mountains and Lake Tahoe provide a spectacular backdrop, and the vastness of the area contributes to a wide variety of skiing. Open year-round, Squaw Valley is located near the north end of Lake Tahoe.

Accommodations: A central reservation office (888–SNOW–321) will work with you to find the most appropriate lodging for your family and your needs. Hotels, motels, lodges, and condominiums all have various rates and package plans. Among the closest to the slopes are Squaw Valley Lodge, a ski-in/ski-out condominium ($160–$310), and the PlumpJack Squaw Valley Inn ($180–$495), located next to the tram, with sixty rooms. The Resort at Squaw Creek is a full service resort and hotel with a deluxe conference center and its own lift ($179–$475), plus a Robert Trent Jones Jr. golf course.

The Olympic Village Inn is a European-style condominium complex about 2 blocks from the lift ($165–$225). Each property welcomes children to stay free.

Dining: You will find many fast-food locations offering pastry, ice cream, cookies, pizza—even tacos. Some of these, such as Dave's Deli, Mother Barkleys, Salsa Bar and Grill, Le Chamois, and The Sundeck, are found at the base facility, the Olympic Plaza.

Up on the mountain head to Alexander's for panoramic views and light lunches of soups and salads. In the evening the vistas take on a different glow and the dining becomes more sophisticated. At the Resort at Squaw Creek, Glissandi is an elegant restaurant featuring French cuisine, while the Cascades Restaurant offers regional American fare. The Poolside Cafe is a casual, friendly dining spot.

The casinos and showrooms of Nevada are readily accessible for dining and evening pleasures. If you want to stay in the neighborhood, however, try the après-ski at Bar One, Le Chamois, or the Plaza Bar, where you'll find entertainment even after a strenuous day of skiing.

Children's World: Toddler Care is a program for children ages two to three years. Registration begins at 8:30 A.M. weekdays, 8:00 A.M. weekends and holidays. The center offers a full day of care and activity for $65 and a half day for $45. Four- to twelve-year-olds take to the joys of skiing in the Children's World. Hours and prices vary with the program selected. Lessons as well as other fun-in-the-snow activities keep this group well occupied.

The Resort at Squaw Creek runs its own summer activities for children. Mountain Buddies, designed for three- to thirteen-year-olds, concentrates on sports, nature hikes, and arts and crafts. Teens join forces in the Mountain Adventure program.

Recreation: The definite wintertime focus of Squaw Valley is skiing. Imagine yourself on an uncrowded run. The sun is shining and you kick up some powder as you stop to check out the scenery. Take off your goggles and look out over glistening white snow to the blue waters of Lake Tahoe. More than 70 percent of the runs are for beginner/intermediate skiers. Moreover, Squaw Valley is one of those rare places where this group is not confined to the lower elevations but can ski all day above 8,000 feet in the sunny, sheltered bowls. The vertical drop is 2,850 feet, and challenging slopes for expert skiers are not lacking. In fact, the 1960 Winter Olympics were held here. Squaw's six peaks are interconnected by thirty lifts that include a new 115-passenger cable car, a new twenty-eight-passenger Funitel (the first of its kind in North America), and four high-speed detachable quads. The ski school organizes classes and clinics for all levels, from beginners to racing competition. A coin-operated race course allows skiers to perfect their racing styles (and keeps them off the regular slopes!). Cross-country skiing, offered at the Resort at Squaw Creek, augments the snow diversions of Squaw Valley.

In the summertime the cable car operates for scenic tours, and the surrounding hotels focus on tennis, fishing, biking, horseback riding, and nature trails. Golf is top-notch here, with an eighteen-hole Robert Trent Jones Jr. course that weaves its way through mountains and meadows. Swimming pools, exercise spas, and racquetball/squash courts round out the pleasures. ≋

Sunriver Resort

Sunriver, Oregon 97707
(541) 593–1000, (800) 547–3922
E-mail: reservations@sunriver-resort.com
Web site: www.sunriver-resort.com

Nestled in the pines between the towering Cascade Mountains and the high desert, Sunriver Resort encompasses 3,300 acres and enjoys nearly 300 days of sunshine each year. Sunriver offers three championship golf courses—including Crosswater, chosen by *Golf Digest* as "America's Best New Resort Course"—and one of the most complete lists of recreational activities to be found. Experience more than 30 miles of bike paths, white-water rafting, canoeing, tennis, and organized children's, teen, and family programs. In the winter enjoy cross-country skiing, sleigh rides, a covered ice skating rink, an assortment of shops and restaurants, and world-class skiing at nearby Mount Bachelor. Sunriver Resort has its own shuttle to the mountain that will have you on the slopes within minutes.

Accommodations: Accommodations at Sunriver Resort include deluxe rooms and suites, featuring stone fireplaces and private decks; the suites accommodate two to six people and have a kitchen and dining/living room. Rates are $115–$225 per night, depending on the size and the season. Cribs are provided for a one-time charge of $7.00.

Approximately 260 private homes and condominiums can be rented on a short-term basis. With one to five bedrooms, these can easily sleep up to ten people comfortably. All include a well-equipped kitchen, living and dining areas, charming fireplace, and private deck. They are strategically located along the golf course, tucked in among the pines, facing the Cascade Mountains, or overlooking the Deschutes River. Prices range from $154 to $495 per night, size and season being the determining factors; summer and Christmas are the high seasons. The architecture is warm and rustic, modern yet compatible with the surroundings.

Dining: The Meadows at the Lodge specializes in Northwest cuisine and is open for breakfast, lunch, and dinner daily. The Merchant Trader Café, located on the lower level of the Lodge, features snacks and lighter fare for breakfast and lunch, and is open daily. The Grille at Crosswater Club is open during the summer months for lunch and dinner, and in the winter for lunch on Saturdays and dinner Thursday through Saturday evenings. Open daily during the summer months are The Turn at Crosswater and McDivot's Café at the Woodlands golf course, both offering lighter fare and refreshments for golfers.

In addition, Sunriver's Village Mall has a number of restaurants and a grocery store. Whether you cook in or dine out, the variety from quick sandwiches to gourmet fare satisfies almost any mood. For late-night fun, the Owl's Nest Pub in the Lodge offers cocktails nightly and live entertainment every Friday and Saturday night.

Children's World: Kid Klub gives children ages three through six and seven through ten a chance to develop new skills, interests, and friendships, as they create, discover, and experiment in Sunriver's unique environment. Each session revolves around a theme, including nature study, adventure, crafts, and games. Both day and evening sessions are offered daily from mid-June through Labor Day and over the Christmas holidays, and on weekends only the rest of the year.

Guided Adventures is designed for preteens and teens (ages eleven through fifteen) and is held during the summer months. Teen Time, offered year-round, gives young adults (ages thirteen to nineteen) the opportunity to meet other teens. Reservations are required for all youth programs, and costs vary by session.

In addition, youth summer activities include bicycle riding, swimming lessons, canoe or white-water raft rides, games, and tennis. The resident naturalists at the Sunriver Nature Center introduce children to the magic and mystery of the local environment and animals; the Nature Center is open year-round. In the winter, the rink at the Sunriver Village Mall makes a great spot for ice skating. Wintertime also means that all the services of Mount Bachelor are available.

Recreation: Sunriver Resort is proud to offer fifty-four holes of outstanding championship golf. Set amid rivers, meadows, wetlands, pine forests, and spectacular Cascade Mountain views, the Sunriver golfing experience offers incredible variety. Crosswater was designed by Robert Cupp and John Fought, and offers play exclusively for resort guests and Crosswater Club members. The Woodlands was designed by renowned architect Robert Trent Jones Jr. and consistently ranks among the top twenty-five resort courses nationwide. The Woodlands' tree-lined fairways, seven lakes, and strategically placed sand traps have earned Sunriver Resort the distinction of a *Golf* magazine Silver Medal Award. The Meadows, newly redesigned by Crosswater codesigner John Fought, opened in the summer of 1999. Playing to more than 7,000 yards, it has four sets of tees, meticulously prepared bent grass greens, and spectacular Cascade Mountain views. The Meadows is also home to the Sunriver Resort Golf Learning Center.

With twenty-eight Plexipave tennis courts, rimmed by tall pines and with blue skies overhead, who could possibly have a bad game of tennis? But if your swing needs some polishing, you can always sign up for lessons. Sunriver Resort is proud to offer Reed Anderson Tennis Schools, with classes ranging from one to five days, plus Tennis Express (one-hour programs) and Junior Tennis for ages four through eighteen.

Two swimming centers each have a heated Olympic-size pool, a diving pool, and a wading pool providing plenty of variety. The south pool also has a water slide and hot tubs. Also available are the Lodge Village pool and three outdoor spas.

The Deschutes River provides hours of enjoyment for fishermen, who snag brookies, rainbows, and German browns. The Sunriver Marina offers canoe, raft, and kayak float trips down the scenic and calm Deschutes. Marina staff will pick you up downriver and bring you back to the marina; the trips are offered mid-April to mid-October, weather permitting. For the more adventurous, local outfitters offer half-day and full-day white-water rafting trips down more turbulent portions of the Deschutes, leaving from the resort daily during the summer months.

For landlubbers in your party, rental bikes are available for excursions on the 35 miles of paved paths; guides at the Sunriver stables are ready to show off the scenery in rides along the river; the wilderness beckons interested backpackers. Trails past meadows and through the woods await joggers and nature lovers. Surrounding Sunriver Resort is the Deschutes National Forest, offering additional opportunity for back-to-nature serenity and elbow room. The Sunriver Nature Center has been offering extremely comprehensive, very reasonably priced programs for more than twenty-five years. Many nature walks, lectures, and programs are free; there are also archaeology tours, combined biking/bird-watching excursions, spelunking in Lava River Cave, and much more.

The Sunriver Racquet Club is a nearby sports facility with five racquetball courts, three indoor tennis courts, a swimming pool, an exercise room, a spa, and saunas. Use of these facilities is free for guests staying in Lodge Village rooms and suites; some private homes and condos have guest privileges at the Racquet Club as well, so check when you make reservations.

Sunriver Village has restaurants and interesting shops and boutiques. The Sunriver Music Festival takes place in August; orchestral programs are presented in the Great Hall, originally constructed as an officers' club when what is now Sunriver Resort was Camp Abbot, a U.S. Army Engineer Replacement Training Center for the Corps of Engineers during World War II. The Great Hall is composed of 511 logs, totaling 150,000 board feet of lumber. Completely restored to its original beauty, it serves as Sunriver's most popular ballroom and can accommodate approximately 350 people for dinner or meetings.

The High Desert Museum (8 miles from the Lodge) is a terrific educational introduction to the cultural and natural history of the Northwest, and it is a big attraction for kids and adults alike. The otter pond, where you can watch playful otters preparing their food, is a favorite highlight, as is watching the birds of prey in action.

At Sunriver you'll find a dozen ways to enjoy winter. Mount Bachelor is one of the West's top-rated ski areas. You'll find breathtaking views, plenty of deep powder, and slopes to challenge skiers and snowboarders of all abilities—from beginners to Olympic champions. You can head cross-country on miles of groomed forest trails or break your own path through snowy meadows. Trek the mountain outback by snowshoe, snowmobile, or dogsled, or take a leisurely tour in a horse-drawn sleigh. And at day's end back at the resort, slip into a steaming outdoor spa for a relaxing soak. ≋

Sun Valley

Sun Valley, Idaho 83353
(208) 622–4111, (800) 786–8259

Just the name Sun Valley calls to mind fantastic downhill skiing, beautiful powder, and gorgeous sunshine. Located in south-central Idaho, Sun Valley is a Tyrolean-style village perched on 2,054 acres of skiable terrain high in the Sawtooth Mountains. With a ski season that runs from late November to early May, spectacular scenery, and mountain air, Sun Valley is indeed a skier's paradise. Founded as a ski resort in 1936 by W. Averell Harriman, then chairman of the board of Union Pacific Railroad, to draw rail travel west, Sun Valley immediately became the playground of Hollywood stars, introduced the world's first chairlift, and began the long-running affair between Americans and skiing.

Winter activities include downhill and cross-country skiing, ice skating, and sleigh rides. In summer tennis, golf, hiking, and fishing move to center stage. The village, whose hub is the Sun Valley Lodge, supplements these activities with restaurants, lounges, shops, movies, a game room, saunas, and a playschool for children.

Accommodations: The Sun Valley Lodge is a full-service hotel with accommodations from standard and deluxe rooms to suites. The lodge also houses restaurants, a glass-enclosed swimming pool, a game room, massage facilities, and a sauna. Nearby is the Sun Valley Inn, another hotel, with its own restaurants and glass-enclosed swimming pool. In addition, there are 575 condominium units scattered in clusters about the village. They are studios and one- to four-bedroom units with kitchen; many have a wood-burning fireplace and private balcony. They may be near the tennis courts, the lake, the riding center, or the golf course.

Nightly rates at the lodge and the inn start at $110 and run to $285 for a deluxe suite. In the condominiums studio rates are $110 a night, and four-bedroom units (sleeping up to eight people) are $280 a night (graduated prices in between for one-, two-, and three-bedroom apartments). Package plans are available except from just before Christmas through January 1. Summertime rates are $75–$175 a night in the lodge and the inn, $100 a night for a studio, and up to $220 a night for a four-bedroom condominium. Children under fifteen ski and stay free, except during certain weeks of the year. There is no additional charge for cribs.

Dining: Twelve restaurants in the village please almost any mood from fancy to family style. Though many families cook meals in their condominium units,

Photo courtesy of Sun Valley Resort

occasional nights dining out mean a real vacation for the family chef too!

Open for breakfast, lunch, and dinner, Gretchen's, in the lodge, is a family restaurant featuring an American menu; the Konditorei, in the village, specializes in sandwiches, pastries, and ice cream; and the Continental Cafe, in the inn, is a cafeteria. Also at the inn, the Ram Dining Room (open evenings only) serves steak, seafood, and cheese and chocolate fondues.

For an unusual adventure in dining, take a horse-drawn sleigh ride to a rustic cabin nestled in the woods; at the Trail Creek Cabin, enjoy prime rib or Idaho trout near a warm fire. Or you can spend an elegant evening at the Lodge Dining Room sampling French cuisine. On Sunday the dining room also serves a sumptuous buffet brunch of omelettes, crepes, fresh fruit, and pastries. For après-ski refreshment or a nightcap, try the Boiler Room or the Duchin Room, where you'll find evening entertainment.

Skiers intent on not losing time on the slopes can stop in for meals and snacks at one of the four mountainside restaurants. They serve soup, salads, and sandwiches cafeteria style.

Children's World: While Mom and Dad are schussing down Bald and Dollar Mountains, children are not left out of the fun in this winter wonderland. The Sun Valley Ski School starts three- and four-year-olds in introductory classes at $32 an hour. Four- to twelve-year-olds enjoy a full day of activity (8:30 A.M.–4:00 P.M.), which includes four hours of lessons. The fee is $69 a day.

The Sun Valley Playschool entertains nonskiing little ones six years old and younger (even infants). The school is equipped with games and toys and a nap room for tots who grow weary of all the excitement. There are opportunities for ice skating and an outdoor playground for romping in the snow. The basic fee for the school is $55 a day per child; $65 a day for toddlers; and $85 a day for infants six months to one year.

In summertime, school activities for the six-and-under group turn to swimming, hiking, arts and crafts, boating, and hayrides; the same fees are charged in summer as in winter. The Sun Valley Day Camp is designed for six- to fourteen-year-olds. Horseback riding, tennis, golf, fishing, and backpacking are scheduled for these age groups. The fee is $50 a day, excluding lunch.

Recreation: Suitable terrain for all levels of skiers is provided at Sun Valley. With its wide open spaces and gentle trails, Dollar Mountain is favored by beginners and those who want a few warm-up runs. Bald Mountain is a challenge and caters to intermediate and expert skiers. Combined, these mountains offer seventy-eight runs, seventeen chairlifts, and 3,400 vertical feet. Sun Valley prides itself on lots of good skiing from well-groomed terrain to unpacked powder and short lift lines—the combination every downhill skier seeks. A complimentary bus service (operating continuously throughout the day) shuttles guests to the base of both mountains.

The Nordic and Snowshoe Center grooms 40 kilometers of well-marked trails for cross-country skiers through aspen trees, along the creek, and over sloping meadows. There are also 6 kilometers of designated snowshoe trails. Sun Valley was a pioneer in providing Nordic skiing specifically for children. Machine-set tracks designed for a child's stride cover 3 miles of the Nordic Ski Center and in some places parallel adult tracks, allowing an easy family cross-country-skiing experience. Backcountry skiers can tour the mountain from yurt to yurt (Siberian-style huts), finding a warm, welcoming meal and bed at each.

Private and group lessons are available in both downhill and cross-country skiing at beginner, intermediate, and advanced levels. At the ski shops you can rent equipment or purchase all the accessories necessary for either undertaking. Another favorite wintertime sport has become a year-round one here. Ice skates can be rented, and just behind the lodge is an Olympic-size skating rink where such greats as Sonja Henie, Peggy Fleming, and Dorothy Hamill have practiced. Saturday night ice shows are presented throughtout the summer.

Another year-round activity is swimming; there are two indoor heated pools (one at the lodge and one at the inn) and one outdoor Olympic-size pool. Relax in the sauna or the Jacuzzi, or make an appointment with the masseur in the lodge to ease your overworked muscles. The game room in the lodge offers pool tables, video games, and bowling alleys; or perhaps you'd like to take in a movie at the Opera House. The shops in the village might tempt you with their selections of books, gifts, fashions, jewelry, pottery, and toys.

Summer brings music festivals, parades, antiques and crafts fairs, bicycle races, and much more. Tennis and golf enthusiasts are in their heyday, for there are eighteen outdoor tennis courts, as well as clinics and private lessons with videotaped analysis. An eighteen-hole championship golf course, redesigned by Robert Trent Jones Jr., rolls over gently sloping terrain. Two nine-hole courses provide another option. At the pro shop, you can arrange for lessons and pick up extras in equipment and clothing.

Fishing in Silver Creek makes a pleasant afternoon for novice fishermen as well as experienced anglers; Sun Valley Lake is stocked with trout. The mountain trails are open to you for horseback riding and hiking in the wooded wilderness. Archery and trap and skeet shooting (instruction available) are also popular with summer visitors. Take a rowboat or paddleboat out on the lake, line up rentals at the bike shop, or plan a white-water raft trip. Whether winter or summer sports beckon you, you'll be captivated by the majestic mountains and the warm, friendly atmosphere of Sun Valley. ≈≈≈

The Westin Mission Hills Resort

71333 Dinah Shore Drive
Rancho Mirage, California 92270
(760) 328–5955, (800) WESTIN–1
E-mail: ranch@westin.com
Web site: www.westin.com

The 360-acre Westin Mission Hills Resort, located near elegant Palm Springs, is also adjacent to the Mission Hills Country Club, the site of world-class golf. The lush landscaping, verdant golf courses, and abundance of water belie its desert location, but the surrounding mountains and canyons, which reflect the sun and shadow and the clear starry nights, are stark and wonderous reminders of what lies beyond the resort's boundaries.

Accommodations: Southwestern adobe mixed with classic Moroccan design provides a distinctive architectural achievement. Blue domes reflect the cloudless skies; warm brown arches repeat themselves down a long pathway, framing the desert palms and mountains. The 512 guest rooms are scattered in sixteen low-rise pavilions interspersed with meandering walks, gardens, lagoons, and waterfalls. Guest rooms are of generous size, and most feature a private patio. January to April is the high season, when rooms range from $410 to $450; from June through mid-September, the rates drop to $169 to $189. The remaining months are a midrange of $320 to $340. Children under eighteen stay free in their parents' room.

Dining: Bella Vista features California cuisine for breakfast, lunch, dinner, and Sunday brunch. Typically Californian, it blends a sunlit atrium with palm trees. Indoor/outdoor dining is available. Another interesting juxtaposition is La Concha, which specializes in contemporary American dishes including seafood and Black Angus beef. La Concha is open for dinner in season, with entertainment nightly. Each of the three swimming pools has a cabana serving breakfast, lunch, snacks, and cool beverages; you need never leave the sun. For evening cocktails the elegantly casual Lobby Lounge offers drinks and hors d'oeuvres, or relax and imbibe poolside at Las Brisas if you can't tear yourself or the kids out of the water. Westin has prepared a nice list of family restaurants in the area for those who want to venture out.

Children's World: Westin Kids Club is a basic program at all Westin resort properties, designed to make family travel safe, convenient, and enjoyable. Children get special age-appropriate gifts upon check-in; parents get a safety kit, if desired (electric-outlet covers, adhesive strips, ID bracelets, and local emergency

Photo courtesy of The Westin Mission Hills Resort

numbers); and the room is ready with cribs, potty seats, or bed rails if needed. Jogging strollers, highchairs, and bottle warmers are complimentary, meals can be ordered in advance from a children's menu so that they are ready upon arrival at the restaurant, and a lot of information about local things of interest to families is available. It's a really comprehensive approach, and during the summer special rates and "Kids Eat Free" promotions are generally available.

The Cactus Kids program at Mission Hills bills itself as "the coolest thing in the desert." Operating daily year-round from 8:00 A.M. to 5:00 P.M., it costs $35 per four-hour session or $10 per hour. Lunch is additional. Reservations are requested at least one day in advance, and the program will be run for even one or two children. Activities include arts and crafts, volleyball, lawn games, movies, nature walks, and bicycle riding.

Recreation: Two championship golf courses, two practice ranges, and six greens and sand traps keep golfers happy. The Pete Dye Resort Course has his trademark deep bunkers and undulating fairways, while the Gary Player Signature Course is a mosaic of waterfalls, ravines, and lakes. Take lessons from the resident pros, or sign up at the Troon Golf Institute. Play tennis in the cool of the evening on the seven lighted tennis courts, or join the Reed Anderson Tennis School. Forget something? The pro shops have everything you need. Las Brisas is the largest of the three swimming pools; it was made to resemble the surrounding canyons and has a 60-foot water slide, two whirlpools, and spacious sundecks. Treat yourself to massage, herbal wraps, and facials at the Aida Grey Salon; work out at the fitness club; or follow a more leisurely pace with traditional lawn games such as croquet and shuffleboard.

If you need more action, Oasis Waterpark is nearby as well as Camelot Park, where you can enjoy miniature golf, bumper boats, go-carts, or batting cages. Take the Palm Springs Aerial Tramway 8,516 feet to the Mountain Station for a bird's-eye view, and hike through Mt. San Jacinto Wilderness State Park. Weather permitting (meaning when there is snow), Nordic skiing operates from November to April. At the opposite end of the environmental spectrum, explore the desert by jeep with experienced guides who can show you the secret life of the desert, or have a real Old West experience in a two-hour covered-wagon tour. As a contrast to all this nature, any teenagers in your party might gravitate toward the Palm Desert Town Center, the area's largest indoor shopping mall. ≋

CANADA

Alberta

British Columbia

Ontario

Quebec

Château Montebello

392 rue Notre-Dame
Montebello
Quebec, Canada J0V 1L0
(819) 423–6341, (800) 441–1414
Web site: www.cphotels.ca

You don't have to travel all the way to Europe for a vacation in a French château. Château Montebello is a luxury resort in a peaceful woodland setting located on the shores of the Ottawa River between Montreal and Ottawa.

Built of massive cedar logs by a team of craftsmen in 1930, Château Montebello served as an exclusive private club for forty years. In 1970 it became a resort open to the public year-round. Today the Château's old-world charm and contemporary elegance come together as a lovely holiday destination, with the distinction of being the world's largest log structure.

Accommodations: The Château has four wings radiating from the center, affording the guest rooms outlooks to the river and the forests. For the 210 well-appointed rooms, rates begin at $121 (U.S. dollars) a night, including breakfast. The summertime family package starts at $104 per adult per night, based on double occupancy; it includes breakfast and dinner, pontoon riverboat cruise (one hour), bicycle rental (three hours), canoeing (half day), and various other sports. With this package, two children age twelve and younger stay and eat free when occupying a room with their parents. Each additional child age thirteen to seventeen is $45.

Dining: Aux Chantignoles is the elegant gourmet dining room of the resort. This is also the venue for Sunday brunch. The Golf Club House is popular for lunch; the Igloo is an outdoor barbecue restaurant, ideal for lunch or dinner. Light snacks and refreshments are served at the Golf Terrace and the Excalibur Bar.

Children's World: The Kid's Centre, presided over by Monte the Beaver, is open from 10:00 A.M. to 5:00 P.M. daily from July to September, and weekends year-round. For children ages three and up, the cost ranges from $12 to $18 per day, depending on the hours and activities. Toys, games, and arts and crafts are mixed with outdoor activities such as swimming, hiking, and group games based on the ages and number of children in the program. While the Centre is open all day, activities are not necessarily nonstop for the entire time. The hotel often arranges special things such as treasure hunts. Special events for children and families are usually planned for holiday periods and weekends throughout the year.

Photo courtesy of Château Montebello

Recreation: The Château offers something for everyone. Originally built in 1929, the eighteen-hole golf course has been totally renovated, resulting in a more challenging and more scenic course. The golf school provides lessons and organizes clinics. The course is rated "Platinum" by *Canada's Golf Course Ranking Magazine.*

Dale Power, a former member of the Canadian Davis Cup Team, runs the tennis operation.

At the Health Club and Sports Complex, you can work out in the exercise room, play squash or tennis, swim laps in the indoor pool, or relax at the Spa in the saunas or whirlpools. The outdoor pool is a beautiful setting for relaxing, sunning, and swimming. Referee the kids in volleyball and badminton games, then round up the whole crew for bike riding or mini-putt.

The Spa offers professional services, including full-body massage, facials, body wraps of mud or algae, body exfoliation and polishing, and therapeutic baths using either relaxing pine and rosemary milk or stimulating mineral salts. What a treat after a full day of activity! Other activities include water sports, cruises, jet skiing, and horseback riding.

The whole family can discover the beauties of Kenauk, a 100-square-mile plant and wildlife preserve within 6 miles of the Château, with scores of activities—bird-watching, picnics, hikes with or without a naturalist, mountain biking, or fishing. Explore White Fish Lake by rowboat or canoe, float down the Kinonge River, or rent a motorboat at the Marina. It's a great place to laze away summer days enjoying nature. Omega Park provides a slightly different approach to nature. Drive along a 10-kilometer road through 1,500 acres of a woodland corral where native animals small (raccoons, wild boar, and deer) and large (bison, black bears, and wild sheep) roam free.

Snow brings enchantment to the woods and hills and is the focus of wintertime fun. The familiar activities of ice skating, ice fishing, sleigh rides, and snowmobiling vie with the more exotic: dogsledding, curling, snowshoeing, broomball, and deck hockey. More than 100 kilometers of cross-country ski trails beckon, or you may prefer just a walk in the snow and curling up with a good book in front of the huge six-sided fireplace in the Château. ≋

Deerhurst Resort

1235 Deerhurst Drive
Huntsville
Ontario, Canada P1H 2E8
(705) 789–6411, (800) 461–4393; fax (705) 789–5204
Web site: www.deerhurst.on.ca

The Muskoka region is Ontario's most popular holiday area. With its clear lakes and beautiful woodlands, it attracts visitors in summer and winter. Deerhurst Resort encompasses 800 acres on the shores of Peninsula Lake and allows guests to experience all the beauty of the area.

The original lodge at Deerhurst was opened in 1896 by Charles Waterhouse, with just eighteen guest rooms. Three generations of Waterhouses oversaw the expansion of the property and today it is one of the largest resort complexes in Canada.

Deerhurt is two and a half hours by car north of Toronto, or only forty minutes by air from Toronto to the resort's private airstrip.

Accommodations: Today's accommodations are a far cry from the lodge rooms (without baths) of the early days. The thirty-five guest rooms and suites are well appointed and comfortable and are grouped in condominium-style buildings with views of the lake, woods, pools, and golf course. Rates range from $66 (U.S. dollars) a night for a standard room to $494 a night for a premier three-bedroom suite. Children under eighteen stay free when occupying their parents' room. For an extra $43 per person per night, you can add a modified American plan meal package.

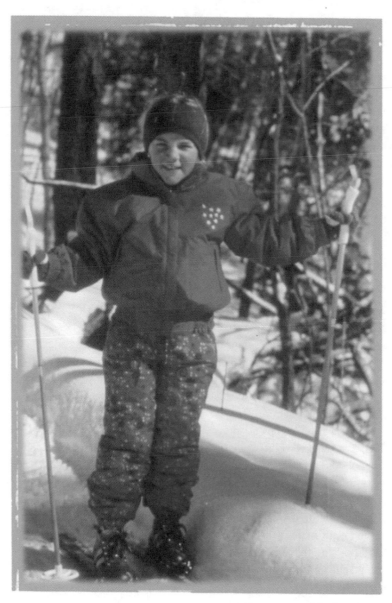

Photo courtesy of Deerhurst Resort

Dining: In the Lodge Dining Room, the chef displays his talents with regional bounty; venison, fresh fish, wild mushrooms, and wild berries are often featured in his creative dishes. The Lodge Dining Room is open for breakfast as well as dinner. The Pub in the Pavilion is casual and well suited for families; soups, sandwiches, pastas, and salads are typical fare here. Steamers Restaurant has a hearty menu and is open seasonally. The Poolside Deck, with views of the lake, serves barbecue favorites in the summer. Evening entertainment at the resort is lively, with a critically acclaimed musical stage show as well as dancing in the Cypress Lounge.

Children's World: Daily through the summer season, during school holiday periods, and on weekends throughout the year, Deer Club operates from 9:00 A.M. to 5:00 P.M. Children ages four to twelve swim, hike, make crafts, and enjoy the playground. The fee for a full day, including lunch, is $28 and $14 for a half day. Younger children, ages six months to three years, join the Bambi Club, which has its own premises especially suited to little ones. The cost is $40 full-days and $20 half-days.

Recreation: The eighteen-hole Deerhurst Lakeside Golf Course was built in 1966 and redesigned in 1988 with many enhancements. Built in 1991, the top-rated Deerhurst Highlands is a magnificent eighteen-hole course winding atop a ridge above the lake, resulting in a combination of challenging play and beautiful scenery. A driving range, practice tees, and target greens comprise the seven-and-a-half-acre instructional facility. A team of professionals direct private lessons and group clinics.

The Pavilion, a complete sports complex, consists of two indoor tennis courts, a racquetball court, three squash courts, a fitness room, a pool, and a whirlpool. Also available here is an Aveda Concept Spa, where you can relax in the steam and sauna rooms or schedule a massage, facial, body wrap, or hair-styling service.

If you prefer to exercise in the open air, three more swimming pools await you, and eight more tennis courts are outdoors (tennis lessons are available). Water sports on the lake abound: sailing, water-skiing, kayaking, fishing, and sailboarding. And don't forget to hike and jog along the nature trails in the beautiful Muskoka woods. Or try one of the resort's unique 4-by-4 off-road driving adventures.

In the winter guests turn their energies to cross-country skiing, ice skating, snowmobiling, and dogsledding (quite an unusual sport!). ≈≈≈

Gray Rocks Resort

Mont-Tremblant
Quebec, Canada J0T 1Z0
(800) 567–6767, Fax (819) 425–3474
E-mail: info@grayrocks.com
Web site: www.grayrocks.com

J ust 75 miles northwest of Montreal, in the Laurentian Mountains, you will find a charming four-season lakeside family resort with a French flavor. Although it's right in the middle of French-speaking Canada, Gray Rocks welcomes American visitors and English is spoken here routinely. You might choose to take the opportunity to brush up on your French, but rest assured that your interests uttered in English in the dining room, on the tennis courts, or during a ski lesson will be well received with warm French-Canadian hospitality.

Since its beginning in 1906, Gray Rocks has developed into a renowned ski, golf, and tennis resort with hotel and condominium accommodations for all tastes. The hotel, with dining room, fitness center, convention center, and bar, sits on the shores of Lac Ouimet. Gray Rocks' own ski mountain, Sugar Peak, rises right behind the hotel; beautiful views of Mont-Tremblant are also impossible to miss. Golf was the first sport in this area, followed by skiing. Today recreational pastimes also include tennis, water sports, horseback riding, mountain biking, or nature hikes.

Accommodations: Lakeside rooms with a private balcony are available in the hotel's Pavilion and Chalet Suisse. Fifty-six one- to three-bedroom condominiums are tucked in among the trees ¾ mile from the hotel. In summer, hotel packages include accommodation, buffet breakfast, table d'hôte dinner, access to the fitness center with indoor pool, use of the private beach and marina, daily activities, nightly entertainment, Kids Club supervised morning activities, and gratuities. Twice a week, guests can choose to eat a sunset barbecue dinner on the lakeside terrace by the beach; dinner is followed by a family party, games, music, and a bonfire. Rates vary from $67 (U.S. dollars) for a regular room during value season (May 21–June 23 and August 29–October 10)—with a bonus of two hours of tennis per person, per night's stay—to $101 for a Pavilion room with private balcony in summer season (June 24–August 28). A full American plan is available. One-bedroom, fully equipped, four-person condominium rates start at $108 per night. A meal plan is also offered to condominium guests.

In winter, guests enjoy a getaway similar to the summer hotel package, with free skiing at Gray Rocks or nearby sister resort Mont Blanc. The most popular winter package is the all-inclusive ski or snowboard week. For approximately

$764 per person (U.S. dollars), double occupancy, you will enjoy six nights of lodging; nineteen full-course meals; twenty-two hours of ski instruction or ten hours of snowboard instruction with the renowned Snow Eagle Ski School; video critique; seven-day lift ticket; races and awards; complete social program for adults, teens, and children; access to the fitness center with indoor pool; and gratuities. Gray Rocks' ski week is considered one of the best ski vacation values in North America. Other options: the ski or snowboard week with condominium accommodation (no meals), at approximately $393 per adult; the ski week with a Snow Eagle instructor at nearby Mont-Tremblant ski area; and the American Thanksgiving package. A children-stay-for-less plan (seventeen and under; kids five and under eat and stay free) makes Gray Rocks family friendly in summer as well as in winter.

Dining: The main dining room located at the hotel, with its fireplace and picture windows overlooking the scenic landscape, provides a pleasant ambience during meals. Continental and French-Canadian cuisines are featured. Cozy lounges with fireplaces and lake views are perfect to relax and mix with old and new friends. There's also a cafeteria at the ski chalet, located midmountain and accessible by car, shuttle bus, or skis. Both golf courses have a Club House with restaurant and lounge area.

Children's World: In summer, from June 27 to August 28, the children's activity program is in high gear. Youngsters join other children their own ages for supervised morning and afternoon events. Preschoolers ages three to five head to the playground, go on treasure hunts and hayrides, or frolic on the private beach. Kids ages six to nine go swimming and horseback riding, try their talents in arts and crafts, and join hayrides. Preteens (ten to twelve) and teens (thirteen and older) enjoy volleyball, tennis, hiking, canoeing, sailboarding, fishing, and various excursions.

For the aspiring tennis or golf pro, there's a famous junior camp. Gray Rocks' Matchpoint Junior Tennis Camp or Eagle Junior Golf Camp offer a great program for eleven- to sixteen-year-olds. Two-week sessions include lakeside accommodations, all meals and snacks, five hours of instruction per day, round-the-clock supervision, and a complete social program for approximately $1,098 (U.S. dollars) per child (one week session: $549 per child).

In the winter Gray Rocks' philosophy is to put children on skis as much as possible. Given that the resort's own gentle mountain is just out the back door, this philosophy is easily practiced. The children's ski classes are divided along age lines as well as ability; heaven forbid your first-time thirteen-year-old skier should be in a class with four-year-olds! Camaraderie in a peer group is important in the learning experience. Children and teens can also meet their friends in a variety of après-ski activities, such as cookie baking, face painting, treasure hunts, arts and crafts, Ping-Pong tournaments, parties, movies, water polo, and sleigh rides or bingo with Mom and Dad. You want to have some fun with your kids too!

Day-care service is available for ages six months to two years as well as private baby-sitting. In winter, a Ski 'n' Play program combines day care and one hour of ski instruction per day for three- to five-year-olds. The rate is $179 (U.S. dollars) per child, with the hotel/meals package free.

Recreation: Think of Gray Rocks as a university for sports. Its qualified ski, golf, and tennis instructors combine expertise with a sincere enthusiasm for teaching. Improvement of skills and self-confidence go hand in hand, and both are better achieved with ample doses of encouragement and humor. Since 1951, more than 200,000 ski weekers have enjoyed Gray Rocks' unique teaching methods in a safe, uncrowded ski environment.

The Snow Eagle Ski School has a fine reputation and more than fifty years of experience. Skiing is a major wintertime activity. The resort boasts of third-generation families who have learned to ski on these slopes and continue to return for their winter holidays. Though Gray Rocks has a modest 620-foot vertical drop, there's variety and, if not long, then challenging runs. Snowmaking facilities cover 95 percent of the slopes, ensuring a ski season from Thanksgiving through early April. Mont-Tremblant ski resort is less than 5 miles from Gray Rocks, so intermediate and advanced skiers can seek out additional challenges there. The ski boutique can meet your needs for rentals, repairs, fashions, and accessories. Cross-country skiing is a growing favorite at Gray Rocks. Nearby Domaine St. Bernard offers well-maintained trails through the woods, next to the river. A tour around the area is a lovely way to spend a winter morning, and a sleigh ride with the kids caps off a perfect day.

Summertime opens up another whole realm of outdoor sports and activities. There's a private sandy beach along a section of the lake. This is Canada, but summers are hot, so swimmers will be happy. The complete marina near the beach offers opportunity for canoeing, sailboarding, sailing, taking out a paddleboat, or enjoying an afternoon of fishing.

A championship eighteen-hole golf course will take you through lush fairways over diverse terrain framed by the rugged beauty of the Laurentians. Three learning holes are reserved for Eagle Golf Academy players. The combination of time-proven teaching strategies and small class ratios helps players take strokes off their game and turns newcomers on to the joys of the sport. Gray Rocks recently opened an eighteen-hole course designed by renowned golf architect Graham Cooke. The course winds its way along the Devil's River, offering superb views of the surrounding mountains. With bent grass tees, greens, and fairways, four sets of tees to choose from, and eighteen distinct and challenging holes, you will leave knowing you have played one of Canada's best courses.

Tennis buffs enjoy the twenty-two Har-Tru courts (ten near the hotel and twelve at the golf club). Tennis lessons with videotaping can help you isolate the improvements necessary for a good game. Gray Rocks' golf and tennis academies offer acclaimed two- and five-day clinics.

Jogging along the lake or hiking and horseback riding in the hills are excellent ways to explore the countryside and revel in the clean mountain air. You can enjoy a nice afternoon next to the beach playing lawn games, or get in shape at Le Spa fitness center. Le Spa features an indoor swimming pool, an exercise room, hot tubs, a sauna, and a professional massage service. Many activities are offered free of charge; some, such as golf, tennis, and horseback riding, carry additional fees.

Gray Rocks provides the area's only resort-based pet kennel. You can now travel with the entire family! ≋

Inn on the Park

1100 Eglinton Avenue East
Toronto
Ontario, Canada M3C 1H8
(416) 444–2561, (800) 332–3442 (United States),
(800) 268–6282 (Canada)

If you're in the mood for a slightly different vacation experience from that offered by most of the resorts we've listed, this is the place. Inn on the Park has the distinction of being a city hotel in a resort setting: Situated on 500 acres of parkland, it's right in the middle of Toronto, one of Canada's liveliest cities. It's the best of both worlds, with shopping, art galleries, and museums offset by the green grandeur of the surrounding park.

Accommodations: A twenty-two-story high-rise with 268 rooms in one tower allows views of the city, the park, or the inner courtyard. Nonsmoking floors, twice-daily maid service, complimentary parking, shoe polishing, and terry cloth robes are some of the amenities offered, and the hotel prides itself on excellent service. Guest rooms are classified deluxe ($110–$155, U.S. dollars per night); differences in size, location, and view determine the rating. Some superior rooms have a patio leading directly to the pool area. Deluxe rooms overlook the city and park. If you like more space, one-bedroom suites are $200–$220. Children under nineteen stay free in their parents' room.

Dining: The Harvest Restaurant is casual, with a children's menu of those all-time favorites—grilled cheese sandwiches, hamburgers, and spaghetti. During the summer months the Cabana serves light snacks by the pool. The Terrace Lounge has buffet or a la carte lunches and late-night snacks, when you can also enjoy a piano bar. What child doesn't adore room service? Here it's available daily. And, all the wonderful restaurants of Toronto are at your doorstep, waiting to be discovered.

Children's World: Innkidz is a very popular and highly organized program that is complimentary for hotel guests. Geared to children ages five to twelve, the program is available from 9:30 A.M. to 4:00 P.M. daily during the summer. Children gather at the Innkidz Centre on the first floor of the Tower for such activities as puppet making, outdoor games and swimming, and making sundaes or clay art. Special treats are a picnic on the helicopter pad and making cookies with the chef in the hotel kitchen. Counselors are art students and teachers, so the experience is very creative. At the end of every afternoon is Snak 'n' Yak, which provides a nice closure for the "kidz." Children under five are welcome if parents remain with them. Lunch can be ordered from the Harvest Room menu and charged to the room. Cribs, strollers, and high chairs are available, and the hotel will even provide diapers, powders, or thermometers if needed.

Recreation: At the hotel you can play a game of tennis, squash, or racquetball; work out in the fully equipped health club and then relax those muscles in the sauna or whirlpool; or try your hand at badminton, volleyball, or shuffleboard. Decide between the indoor and outdoor pools, then decide between swimming and lounging. Window-shop the boutiques and gift shop, get your hair fixed, or stop by the games room.

Toronto holds many treats for families. Kids like to wander through Ontario Place, by the harbor. Shops, eateries, an IMAX theater, and changing exhibits of dinosaurs or gemstones intrigue everyone. Go to the top of the C.N. Tower, the largest freestanding tower in the world; or check out the planetarium at the Royal Ontario Museum. Let the kids pick out a postcard in the gift shop, then try to find the original in the museum. The Ontario Science Museum has a lot of hands-on exhibits, and the Toronto Zoo is a nice excursion on a pretty day. ≋

Severn Lodge

Box 250
Port Severn
Ontario, Canada L0K 1S0
(705) 756–2722, (800) 461–5817
E-mail: severn@csolve.net
Web site: www.severnlodge.on.ca

Severn Lodge is beautifully located in the midst of the Georgian Lakelands of Ontario, only 90 miles from Toronto. Georgia Bay forms the northeastern part of Lake Huron and is named in honor of England's George IV. The area's piney woods, fine fishing, and clear waters attract many vacationers. And the Severn Lodge, on the shores of Gloucester Pool, adds to the natural features with its warm pride of being "owned and operated by the same family for families since 1937." The Lodge is open from mid-May to mid-October only.

Accommodations: Severn Lodge dates back to the late 1800s. Its turn-of-the-century ambience remains preserved in the many white clapboard buildings, log crisscross railings, and cobblestone sidewalks. All accommodations and facilities, however, are very modern.

Photo courtesy of Severn Lodge

Grouped in about a dozen individual buildings set among the trees and along the lake, the accommodations feature small living rooms, large windows for enjoying the lake views, and ample space for a crib or rollaway bed (for which there is no charge). Rates range from $69 to $88 (U.S. dollars) a day per person, double occupancy, and include three meals a day and all the planned activities and recreational facilities (except motorboats) of the lodge. Two-bedroom suites and some rooms with Jacuzzis also are available. When sharing a room with their parents, children under two years are free; two to five years are charged $37; six to twelve, $42; and thirteen to eighteen, $47. Two- to seven-day package plans are offered. During special family weeks in the summer season, rates for children twelve and younger are reduced 50 percent or more. Several housekeeping cottages are available nearby, and they share some of the facilities of the Lodge.

Dining: The charming, elegantly rustic dining room has a woodbeamed ceiling and many large windows that capture the views. The Canadian cuisine is accompanied by freshly baked breads and pastries. Picnic lunches can be prepared for guests who are off hiking or canoeing during the midday meal.

Children's World: The activities program for children, which runs from mid-June to Labor Day, includes hikes, crafts, volleyball and baseball games, swimming, diving and boating lessons, picnics, and movies. Add waterskiing, Indian Night, Talent Night, a Fish Derby, corn roasts, and bonfire sing-alongs and you know you have happy kids. No additional charges are applied for these events, and children of all ages are welcome to participate.

Every effort is made to include even very young guests, but when your little one is just not able to keep up with the group, a supervised toddler activity program will provide pint-size fun. Specially designed indoor and outdoor play areas for two- to five-year-olds are open daily from 10:00 A.M. to noon and from 4:00 to 8:00 P.M. The program is complimentary and includes arts and crafts, sandcastle building, and other beach and playground activities. The lodge staff can also arrange an individual baby-sitter for an extra cost. Favorites among the younger set are the sandy beach; the playground, with its swings, slide, sandbox, and climbing equipment; and the dock, for "just fishin'."

Recreation: Water sports are an important part of Severn Lodge. Wonderful swimming can be had either in the lake or in the heated swimming pool; perhaps you'd like to try the whirlpool spa at the deep-water dock. Maybe you would prefer to stay on top of the water in a fishing boat reeling in walleye, bass, muskie, and northern pike. Also on top of the water (with any luck, you *will* stay on top) is the complimentary waterskiing instruction offered several times a week. Free use of the Lodge's sailboats, sailboards, paddleboats, kayaks, and canoes can make an afternoon lazy or exciting, depending upon your skill. The resort has a unique collection of antique runabouts and motor launches. Rental fees are charged on a daily or weekly basis for outboard boats, motors, and Jet Skis; the Lodge offers free cruises and live evening entertainment during summer months.

On land you can jog or hike on the trails around the Lodge's one hundred acres or play a game of tennis. The recreation building, with its library and large stone fireplace, is quite inviting if relaxing is a favorite pastime; here you will find Ping-Pong, a wide-screen TV, card and board games, and a pool table. Nearby sightseeing (15 to 20 miles) takes you back in history; Sainte-Marie among the Hurons, a Jesuit Mission, and the Huron Indian Village are reconstructions of seventeenth-century settlements. You will also find horseback riding, golf, live theater, museums, casino gambling, and fabulous shopping in nearby lakeside villages. ≈≈≈

Sunshine Village

Box 1510
Banff
Alberta, Canada T0L 0C0
(403) 762–6500, (800) 661–1676
Web site: www.skibanff.com

High in the Canadian Rockies in Banff National Park is Sunshine Village, one of the best ski destinations in Canada. Perched along the Continental Divide, the peak elevation at Sunshine is 9,200 feet. Located only 85 miles west of Calgary and just 10 miles from the town of Banff, Sunshine is a three-mountain ski resort. More than $9 million in improvements await you at Sunshine, Banff's most visited ski resort.

Accommodations: The only accommodation on the mountain is the Sunshine Inn. A three-story complex consisting of eighty-five rooms and suites, the inn affords its guests ski-in/ski-out access. Rates start at $65 (U.S. dollars) per person per night. A five-night package, including lodging, lift ticket, and daily ski lessons, costs $350 per person, based on double occupancy during the value season (November to mid-December, from the second week of January to mid-February, and from late April to closing). The powder season is defined as the week before Christmas, the week after New Year's, and mid-February to late April, when the package costs $450. During Christmas week this package is $500.

Dining: The Inn's dining room, the Eagle's Nest, offers fine dining, from rack of lamb to fantastic sirloin steak. The Chimney Corner is a lounge offering cocktails and entertainment in the evenings. In the Daylodge, the Deli and the Cafeteria offer soup and sandwiches; the new Mad Trappers Saloon, located in the original 1928 Sunshine Lodge, is the place to go for drinks and burgers.

Children's World: For young skiers and snowboarders, Wee Angels (ages three to six) and Young Devils (ages six to twelve) provide a great time, with snow games, skiing, and other fun activities. Divided not only by age but also by ability, the kids set the pace for the day—how much they want to ski, and where. The 10:00 A.M.–3:00 P.M. program costs $26 and includes lift ticket, lunch, and lessons. A day-care center, Sunshine Kids Kampus, is open from 8:00 A.M. to 5:00 P.M. for children nineteen months to six years. Full-day cost is $23, and half-day is only $15.

Recreation: Sunshine Village is located on the Continental Divide, where you can ski the provinces of both British Columbia and Alberta off the same run. The top elevation at Sunshine is more than 9,000 feet and the base elevation is

5,440 feet, yielding skiers more than 3,500 vertical feet. Mother Nature drops more than 360 inches of snow here each year, which results in good skiing from mid-November through the end of May. Of the eighty-nine runs currently open, 50 percent are intermediate; the remainder are split evenly between beginner and expert, with Goat's Eye Mountain (elevation 9,200 feet) offering extreme-expert-only (Double Black Diamond) chutes and glades. Many of the runs are above the treeline, giving skiers that top-of-the-world feeling. Sunshine Village boasts North America's largest new ski terrain, Goat's Eye Mountain.

When not skiing, you may want to pursue less rigorous activities in the family games room or relax your weary muscles in the sauna or the Sunshine Inn's giant outdoor hot pool, rated Canada's best by *Ski Canada* magazine. ≋

Whistler/Blackcomb

Whistler Resort Association
4010 Whistler Way
Whistler
British Columbia, Canada V0N 1B4
(604) 932–4222, (800) 944–7853

If you're lucky enough to hear the whistling call of the indigenous marmots, you'll easily recognize how Whistler Mountain got its current name. Originally known as London Mountain, on the old Caribou Gold Rush Trail, this area saw its first settlers in 1914, an adventurous couple who built a fishing lodge on the shores of Alta Lake. Though still attracting fishermen in the summer, Whistler is famous today as an outstanding ski destination.

Skiers first schussed these slopes in the mid-1960s, and the early 1980s witnessed considerable expansion and development, primarily the opening of Blackcomb Mountain. The two mountains, Whistler and Blackcomb, are serviced by three base facilities. In the Coastal Mountains, Whistler/Blackcomb is just 75 miles north of Vancouver.

Accommodations: Hotels and condominiums are found throughout Whistler Resort. The larger facilities are the Canadian Pacific Château Whistler at the base of Blackcomb, with 543 units, indoor and outdoor swimming pools, a health club, and indoor tennis courts; the Delta Mountain Inn in Whistler Village, with 300 units, an outdoor pool, and indoor tennis courts; and the Crystal Lodge, also in the Village, with 137 units and an outdoor pool. But a smaller complex, such as the Hearthstone Lodge, Powderview, Whistler Resort and Club, or Whiski Jack Condos, might also be the perfect choice for your family.

There's also Marriott Residence Inn, with 186 units, slopeside on Blackcomb Mountain. Contacting Central Reservations at (800) 944–7853 is the first step in sorting out all these choices. A seven-night package, which includes lodging, lift tickets, and transportation to and from Vancouver Airport, starts at $722 (U.S. dollars) per person during the regular season (late January to late March). The value season is late November to mid-December and late March onward, when a seven-night package starts at $494 per person. Christmastime commands higher rates than the regular season, and stays during the month of January cost slightly less than the regular season.

Dining: With more than sixty restaurants and cafes, you'll never have trouble indulging your palate's whim, whether you crave French, Italian, Japanese, Mexican, or Greek cuisine. Three restaurants on Whistler and six on Blackcomb serve hearty soups and stews, burgers, pizza, and pasta to skiers reluctant to leave the slopes for very long. Some of the restaurants favored by families are Black's Restaurant, The Old Spaghetti Factory, and Hard Rock Cafe in the Village; Monk's at Blackcomb; and Hoz's Cafe, Boston Pizza, and Dusty's at Whistler Creek.

Children's World: Skiing starts young here. Wee Scamps on Whistler and Wee Wizards on Blackcomb take two- and three-year-olds from 8:30 A.M. to 3:30 P.M. for a combination of morning skiing and afternoon crafts, indoor activities, and storytime. More serious skiing carries on for four- to twelve-year-olds with Ski Scamps on Whistler and Super Kids on Blackcomb. Young skiers who are particularly proficient can join Red Star Scamps (six- to twelve-year-olds) on Whistler, and Mini Masters (seven- to ten-year-olds) and Superstars (ten- to thirteen-year-olds) on Blackcomb. For hot-shot teenagers, Whistler offers Club Free, and Blackcomb has Team Devo. The cost for these programs ranges from $37 to $41 for a full day including lunch, and groups are divided by ability as well as age. Special prices are available for half-day, three-day, and five-day programs. For nonskiing wee ones (ages eighteen months to three years), Blackcomb offers a program of indoor and outdoor play. Called Childminding, it runs from 9:00 A.M. to 3:00 P.M. and costs $34 for a full day, including lunch; $25 for a half day. Individual baby-sitting rates are $6.00 to $8.00 an hour.

While neither Whistler nor Blackcomb has a formal summertime program, there's lots going on. Blackcomb Mountain can also provide contacts for privately run ski and snowboarding camps offered in June and July. The Community Recreation Center has an indoor swimming pool as well as an ice rink for those who miss winter. And with glacier skiing, winter sports last through August, side by side with hiking, biking, and swimming.

Recreation: Two amazing mountains—get introduced to them in a morning or afternoon guided tour (free) and you'll begin to appreciate their 6,900 acres of skiable terrain and 5,200 feet of vertical drop. More than 200 trails, 10 bowls, and 3 glaciers provide all the variety any skier could hope for. Choose chutes filled with powder, steep runs through trees, broad trails perfectly groomed, or mogul monsters. The average annual snowfall of 360 inches is complemented by sophisticated snow-making capabilities. Both mountains open in late November, and skiing continues to late April on Whistler and late May on Blackcomb. Blackcomb opens again in mid-June for glacier skiing through August. You can book private and group lessons or join a camp specializing in skiing bumps or powder.

When taking a break from skiing, try ice skating and snowmobiling, or organize a sleigh ride. Cross-country skiers take to the 14 miles of track set trails through the forest and valley. For less strenuous exercise stroll through the village to discover its eighty shops or hit Whistler Wonderland for air hockey and mini golf.

In the summer golf is the premier sport, with three eighteen-hole courses, each with fine credentials. The Whistler Golf Course was designed by Arnold Palmer, and the Château Whistler Course was designed by Robert Trent Jones Jr. Jack Nicklaus was responsible for the newest course, Nicklaus North, which opened in 1994.

Hiking and biking across the Alpine terrain are favorites with summertime visitors. The five lakes provide fishermen, swimmers, and boaters with ample fun. Summer is also the season of music; the Country and Blues Festival takes place in July, whereas classical music is on the agenda in August. And if you can stretch your summer into September, stick around for the Jazz Festival. ≈≈≈

Indexes

Alphabetical Index to Resorts

Classic Resorts

The Greenbrier, White Sulphur Springs, West Virginia, 68
The Grove Park Inn Resort, Asheville, North Carollina, 71
The Homestead, Hot Springs, Virginia, 76
Marco Island Marriott Resort and Golf Club, Marco Island, Florida, 122
Marriott's Grand Hotel Resort and Golf Club, Point Clear, Alabama, 124
Mohonk Mountain House, New Paltz, New York, 56
The Mount Washington Hotel and Resort, Bretton Woods, New Hampshire, 32
The Sagamore, Lake George at Bolton Landing, New York, 61

Country Inn Resorts

High Hampton Inn and Country Club, Cashiers, North Carolina, 73
Highland Lodge, Greensboro, Vermont, 21
The Lighthouse Inn, West Dennis, Massachusetts, 27
Skytop Lodge, Skytop, Pennsylvania, 63
The Tyler Place on Lake Champlain, Highgate Springs, Vermont, 48
Whitney's Inn, Jackson, New Hampshire, 50

Resorts with Golf

The Arizona Biltmore, Phoenix, Arizona, 162
Bluewater Bay Resort, Niceville, Florida, 101
The Broadmoor, Colorado Springs, Colorado, 194
Callaway Gardens, Pine Mountain, Georgia, 106
The Cloister, Sea Island, Georgia, 111
Club Med/Sandpiper, Port St. Lucie, Florida, 115
Deerhurst Resort, Huntsville, Ontario, Canada, 266
Eagle Ridge Inn and Resort, Galena, Illinois, 134
Grand Geneva Resort and Spa, Lake Geneva, Wisconsin, 138
The Greenbrier, White Sulphur Springs, West Virginia, 68
Kiawah Island, Kiawah Island, South Carolina, 79
La Costa Resort and Spa, Carlsbad, California, 237
The Lodge of Four Seasons Championship Golf Resort and Spa, Lake Ozark,
    Missouri, 148
Marco Island Marriott Resort and Golf Club, Marco Island, Florida, 122
Marriott's Grand Hotel Resort and Golf Club, Point Clear, Alabama, 124
Palmetto Dunes Resort, Hilton Head Island, South Carolina, 83
The Rancho Bernardo Inn, San Diego, California, 244
The Resort at Longboat Key Club, Longboat Key, Florida, 127
The Sagamore, Lake George at Bolton Landing, New York, 61

Seabrook Island Resort, Seabrook Island, South Carolina, 86

Shanty Creek, Bellaire, Michigan, 157

Sheraton El Conquistador Resort and Country Club, Tucson, Arizona, 180

Skytop Lodge, Skytop, Pennsylvania, 63

Stratton Mountain Resort, Stratton Mountain, Vermont, 40

Sun Valley, Sun Valley, Idaho, 255

Sunriver Resort, Sunriver, Oregon, 252

The Westin Innisbrook Resort, Palm Harbor, Florida, 130

The Westin Mission Hills Resort, Rancho Mirage, California, 259

Whistler/Blackcomb, Whistler, British Columbia, Canada, 278

Wild Dunes, Isle of Palms, South Carolina, 92

Resorts with Horseback Riding

The Bishop's Lodge, Sante Fe, New Mexico, 164

C Lazy U Ranch, Granby, Colorado, 197

Coffee Creek Ranch, Trinity Center, California, 230

Flathead Lake Lodge, Bigfork, Montana, 204

Flying L Guest Ranch, Bandera, Texas, 167

Golden Acres Farm and Ranch, Gilboa, New York, 54

Mountain Sky Guest Ranch, Bozeman, Montana, 210

Rocking Horse Ranch, Highland, New York, 58

Tanque Verde Guest Ranch, Tucson, Arizona, 182

Lakeside Resorts

The Balsams Grand Resort Hotel, Dixville Notch, New Hampshire, 18

Bluewater Bay Resort, Niceville, Florida, 101

Deerhurst Resort, Huntsville, Ontario, Canada, 266

Eagle Ridge Inn and Resort, Galena, Illinois, 134

Flathead Lake Lodge, Bigfork, Montana, 204

Grand Geneva Resort and Spa, Lake Geneva, Wisconsin, 138

Grand View Lodge, Nisswa, Minnesota, 142

Gray Rocks Resort, Mont-Tremblant, Quebec, Canada, 269

Highland Lodge, Greensboro, Vermont, 21

The Homestead, Glen Arbor, Michigan, 145

Inn of the Mountain Gods, Mescalero, New Mexico, 175

Konocti Harbor Resort and Spa, Kelseyville, California, 235

The Lodge of the Four Seasons Championship Golf Resort and Spa, Lake Ozark, Missouri, 148

Seaside Resorts

Spa Resorts

Resorts with Skiing

Angel Fire Resort, Angel Fire, New Mexico, 160
Aspen Chamber Resort Association, Aspen, Colorado, 188
Big Sky of Montana, Big Sky, Montana, 188
Breckenridge Ski Resort, Breckenridge, Colorado, 190
Club Med/Copper Mountain, Copper Mountain, Colorado, 200
Deer Valley Resort, Park City, Utah, 202
Gray Rocks Resort, Mont-Tremblant, Quebec, Canada, 269
The Inn of the Seventh Mountain, Bend, Oregon, 233
Jay Peak Ski Resort, Jay, Vermont, 23
Keystone Resort, Keystone, Colorado, 206
Killington Ski and Summer Resort, Killington, Vermont, 25
Mount Snow, Mount Snow, Vermont, 29
Northstar-at-Tahoe, Truckee, California, 241
Park City Mountain Resort, Park City, Utah, 212
Schweitzer Mountain Resort, Sandpoint, Idaho, 249
Shanty Creek, Bellaire, Michigan, 157
Smugglers' Notch Resort, Smugglers' Notch, Vermont, 36
Snowbird Ski and Summer Resort, Snowbird, Utah, 215
Snowmass Village Resort Association, Snowmass Village, Colorado, 217
Squaw Valley USA, Olympic Valley, California, 250
Stratton Mountain Resort, Stratton Mountain, Vermont, 40
Sugarloaf/USA, Kingfield, Maine, 43
Sun Valley, Sun Valley, Idaho, 255
Sunriver Resort, Sunriver, Oregon, 252
Sunshine Village, Banff, Alberta, Canada, 277
Taos Ski Valley, Taos Ski Valley, New Mexico, 183
Vail/Beaver Creek Central Reservations, Vail, Colorado, 221
Whistler/Blackcomb, Whistler, British Columbia, Canada, 278

Resorts with Tennis

Amelia Island Plantation, Amelia Island, Florida, 98
Callaway Gardens, Pine Mountain, Georgia, 106
Club Med/Sandpiper, Port St. Lucie, Florida, 115
Gray Rocks Resort, Mont-Tremblant, Quebec, Canada, 269
Kiawah Island, Kiawah Island, South Carolina, 79
La Costa Resort and Spa, Carlsbad, California, 237
The Lodge of Four Seasons Championship Golf Resort and Spa, Lake Ozark, Missouri, 148

About the Authors

JANET TICE grew up in Oklahoma City and lived for twenty years in New York City. She earned an M.S. in Psychiatry from New York University, owned a travel agency for many years, and, in 1986, founded Families Welcome! a tour company specializing in family travel. She currently resides in Chapel Hill, North Carolina, with her daughter, Fabiana, and travels extensively, "but never enough!"

JANE WILFORD was born and reared in New Orleans, Louisiana. She earned a B.A. in Art History and History from Duke University and an M.S. in Library Service from Columbia University. In 1986 she moved to London, where she currently resides with her husband, D. Sykes Wilford, and sons, Sykes and Paul, and daughter, Sarah. The Wilford family has traveled extensively throughout the United States and Europe.

Your Best Vacation Memories are Made Right Here!

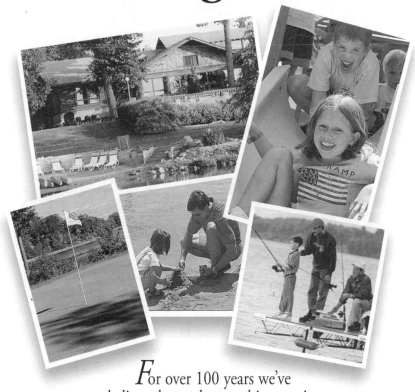

*F*or over 100 years we've
dedicated ourselves to this promise.

Ruttger's

A FAMILY TRADITION SINCE 1898

Bay Lake Lodge

Call 1-800-450-4545 for our vacation, golf, and conference planners.